Political Judgement

From Plato to Max Weber, the attempt to understand political judgement took the form of a struggle to define the relationship between politics and morals. This book by leading international scholars in the fields
of history, philosophy and politics restores the subject to a place at the
very centre of political theory and practice. Whilst it provides a range of
perspectives on the theme of practical reason, it also explores a series of
related problems in philosophy and political thought, raising fundamental questions about democracy, trust, the nature of statesmanship, and
the relations between historical and political judgement. In the process,
the volume reconsiders some classic debates in political theory – about
equality, authority, responsibility and ideology – and offers new and original treatments of key figures in the history of political thought, including Thucydides, Montaigne, Locke, Smith, Burke and Marx.

RICHARD BOURKE is Senior Lecturer in the Department of History at
Queen Mary, University of London.

RAYMOND GEUSS is Professor in the Faculty of Philosophy at the University
of Cambridge.

Political Judgement

Essays for John Dunn

Edited by

RICHARD BOURKE

AND

RAYMOND GEUSS

CAMBRIDGE UNIVERSITY PRESS
Cambridge, New York, Melbourne, Madrid, Cape Town, Singapore,
São Paulo, Delhi

Cambridge University Press
The Edinburgh Building, Cambridge CB2 8RU, UK

Published in the United States of America by Cambridge University Press, New York

www.cambridge.org
Information on this title: www.cambridge.org/9780521764988

First published 2009

Printed in the United Kingdom at the University Press, Cambridge

A catalogue record for this publication is available from the British Library

Library of Congress Cataloguing in Publication data
Bourke, Richard.
   Political judgement: essays for John Dunn / Richard Bourke, Raymond Geuss.
      p.   cm.
   Includes bibliographical references and index.
   ISBN 978-0-521-76498-8 (hardback)   1. Political science–Philosophy.
   I. Geuss, Raymond.   II. Dunn, John, 1940–   III. Title.
   JA71.B597 2009
   320.01–dc22   2009017299

ISBN 978-0-521-76498-8 hardback

Contents

Contributors

Richard Bourke, Senior Lecturer in History, Queen Mary, University of London

Biancamaria Fontana, Professor of the History of Political Ideas, Institut d'Etudes Politiques et Internationales, Université de Lausanne

Raymond Geuss, Professor of Philosophy, University of Cambridge

Geoffrey Hawthorn, Emeritus Professor of International Politics, University of Cambridge

Istvan Hont, Reader in the History of Political Thought and Fellow of King's College, University of Cambridge

Sudipta Kaviraj, Professor of Indian Politics and Intellectual History, Columbia University

Sunil Khilnani, Starr Foundation Professor and Director, South Asia Studies, School of Advanced International Studies, Johns Hopkins University

Victoria McGeer, Associate Research Scholar, Centre for Human Values, Princeton University

Philip Pettit, Laurance S. Rockefeller University Professor of Politics and Human Values, Princeton University

Adam Przeworski, Carroll and Milton Petrie Professor of Politics, New York University

Quentin Skinner, Barber Beaumont Professor of the Humanities, Queen Mary, University of London

Richard Tuck, Frank G. Thomson Professor of Government, Harvard University

Acknowledgements

The editors would like to thank John Haslam, Carrie Cheek, Karen Matthews, Thomas O'Reilly and Frances Brown at Cambridge University Press for their patience and skill in seeing this book through the editorial and production processes, and Dr Niall O'Flaherty of King's College London for assistance in preparing the original manuscript. Richard Bourke would in addition like to express his gratitude to the Alexander von Humboldt Foundation for the award of a Fellowship which enabled him to undertake and complete his contribution to this volume. In this context he would also like to thank Professor Eckhart Hellmuth for hosting him during the tenure of his Fellowship in the Historical Institute at the University of Munich.

Introduction

RICHARD BOURKE AND RAYMOND GEUSS

I

Something happened in the West when Socrates began to confront
the politicians of his day, the men who spoke in the assemblies and
led the armies and navies of Athens, stopping them in the market-
place and asking them to give an account of what they were doing
and why they were doing it. It was not exactly a new form of inquiry
that was being invented, but a new style of investigation. It is not as if
this were a complete and radical break with the past or the absolute
initiation of an inconceivably new practice, because as long as there
have been human societies there have been problems of coordinating
action, resolving disputes, and planning for the future; and planning
for the future in any detail means envisaging in words alternative
eventualities and courses of action. Once one specific possible future
has been put into words, it is open to others to describe a different
one. And how is discussion then ever to end? The oldest document of
Western civilisation, the *Iliad*, begins with a group of men engaged
in a common pursuit – the war against Troy – deliberating about how
they should act in the face of an unexpected event, a plague. The real
plot begins when Achilles refrains from putting an end to the public
discussion by killing the reptilian king, Agamemnon, out of hand,
and instead insults him.

Individuals and groups; envisaging the future whilst acting in
the present; merit as opposed to status; speaking as against doing;
cooperation versus conflict; intentions and their results; success and
failure: these and other related contrasts mark out a terrain which
humans learn to negotiate with as much dexterousness as they can
muster. Three centuries after Homer, immediately before the advent
of Socrates, during the generation of Thucydides and Protagoras,
human beings had not merely accumulated a certain amount of
rough-and-ready skill in this area, but had also begun to reflect

carefully about politics – about its nature, and its demands. Still, for better or for worse, Socrates' mode of questioning, systematically eschewing any reference to traditional practices, received authorities or institutional contexts, and devaluing the cognitive, practical or aesthetic ability of those who are unable to give a sufficiently explicit, abstract and consistent definition of the basic terms they use, does represent the first faltering step down a path which European thought has pursued ever since. Socrates opens what many have thought represented yet another contrast in the domain of collective human action, a contrast between practical skill and a theoretical grasp of 'politics'.

The sequence of transformations which the concept of politics and of what it means to have an understanding of politics has undergone from late fifth-century BC Athens to the early twenty-first-century international *oikoumene* is too complex to trace here in detail, but in the most recent past, say during the last fifty years or so, there has been a significant institutionalisation of the study of politics in universities and related research institutions. This development had two important consequences for the cognitive structure of the enterprise of understanding politics. First, it was associated with a shift from looking at politics from the viewpoint of participants – that is, of political agents – to that of studying political processes from the point of view of notionally impartial observers. Thucydides, the author of the first great work of politics in the West, was, as he tells us himself, a failed and consequently exiled Athenian general who knew of what he spoke from first-hand experience; something similar was true of Cicero, Grotius and Machiavelli. But by the end of the twentieth century studies of politics were being conducted by purportedly neutral, politically detached experts in area studies, psephology, international relations and rational choice theory. The second consequence was that the study of politics came under pressure to conform to certain pre-given conceptions of what a proper academic discipline must be like. Ideally, a respectable academic subject had to have an ontologically distinctive subject-matter ('living things' for biology, specifically designated rules of social coercion for law, texts for philology) or use one of the recognised methods (observation, some form of deductive reasoning, experiment, interpretation, and so on) or, best of all, both. A reputable academic discipline had to have a distinctive theoretical vocabulary of agreed-on, well-defined, universally applicable concepts, and some recognised core body of systematically established doctrine. Beyond this, a distinction was recognised between empirical and normative disciplines.

The empirical study of political institutions and processes ideally comprised an interconnected system of facts, generalisations, and universally applicable theories that could be used for explanation and prediction. The practical relevance for politics of the ability to predict, if such an ability actually existed, is obvious; if it is an established 'law' that 'democratic states do not go to war with one another', then this would be of great importance in helping decide what kind of military preparations a democratic state should make, and against whom.[1] This supposed law, of course, is useful only if it is possible to identify which states are democratic and which are not, and this requires the exercise of at least a rudimentary kind of judgement, the ability to discern under which concept a given actual state falls. There is not much question about the fact that it is possible to study politics in *some* sense as a low-level empirical or descriptive subject; and although this does not preclude great theoretical unclarity about exactly what it is that one knows when one asserts that Angela Merkel is the Chancellor of the Federal Republic of Germany or that the United Kingdom uses a 'first-past-the-post' electoral system based on geographically defined constituencies for the House of Commons, there is not really any genuine, or non-philosophical, disagreement that in both these cases one *knows something.*

It is less clear that this is the case when one considers what can be thought of as purely normative approaches to politics, except perhaps where norms are embodied in doctrines and backed by commands. Directives about how social and political life ought to be organised, and how individuals ought to act, have in the past been derived from Scripture or the teachings of Churches, but also from philosophical disciplines like ethics, for example in its utilitarian or Kantian variants, and most recently they have been derived from kinds of economic prescription, including forms of decision theory. That such

[1] For prominent examples of the diverse academic literature on 'democratic peace', see Dean V. Babst, 'A Force for Peace', *Industrial Research* 14 (April 1972), pp. 55–8; Michael Doyle, 'Kant, Liberal Legacies, and Foreign Affairs', *Philosophy and Public Affairs* 12 (Summer/Fall 1983), pp. 205–35; Samuel P. Huntington, *The Third Wave: Democratization in the Late Twentieth Century* (Norman: University of Oklahoma Press, 1991), p. 29.

directives can offer a kind of orientation and guide for action is not in doubt: 'Always do what the Pope says (when he is speaking *ex cathedra* on a matter of faith or morals!)' is a clear enough way to structure one's life, although adopting this norm will require the exercise of some judgement to determine when the Pope has been speaking *ex cathedra,* and when not, and, of course, also judgement about how to apply to particular cases papal injunctions that have been enunciated in a general form. Whether, however, any of these purely doctrinaire approaches can satisfy the expectations they themselves raise as guides to a satisfactory, much less a good, life, is, to say the very least, unproven, and for many of them the suspicion that they are masks for interests other than those they acknowledge is hard to resist.

II

Is this, then, what politics is about at its best – the exercise of judgement to subsume individual cases under explanatory and predictive general laws, or under universal principles of reason and morality? Over the course of a long and productive career John Dunn has made important contributions to a wide variety of areas of politics, and to the history of thinking about politics as well. Not, perhaps, the least of these contributions has been his break with some of the main constitutive features of the tradition of thinking about politics that has just been described. His work stands orthogonal to this tradition in a number of significant ways. Among these, two of his attempts to undo the impact of what can be seen as a Socratic paradigm of political understanding stand out. The first is his attempt to rehabilitate the standpoint and the cognitive and practical skills of the political actor, and this means recognising the importance of understanding the judgement of real political actors – where 'judgement' most definitely does *not* mean simply the subsumption of individual cases under pre-given concepts or rules.[2] Dunn's second and related innovation is his emphasis on the historical variability and context-specificity of political concepts, once again in opposition to the tacit Socratic and Platonic assumption that key political terms – 'justice', 'happiness',

---

[2] This of course is one of the core ambitions of John Dunn's *The Cunning of Unreason: Making Sense of Politics* (London: HarperCollins, 2000).

'freedom' and the like – designate in each case something that is definably the same *hic et ubique*. Both of these moves on Dunn's part have been intended as a challenge to traditional normative and cognitive approaches to the understanding of politics. Together they prompt us to reconsider how political action is standardly conceptualised, and how the judgement of political value is ordinarily understood.

'Property' did not mean 'the same thing' for Locke as it did for Hayek,[3] and 'democracy' very definitely did not 'mean', or even designate, 'the same thing' for fifth-century Athenians as it does for any of the European societies of the early twenty-first century.[4] In order to resolve the resulting semantic confusion, the strategy that comes most naturally to much contemporary analytic philosophy is that of distinguishing conceptually between the 'direct democracy' of the ancients and the 'representative democracy' associated with much modern political practice. Each of these might be supplied with some kind of 'Socratic' definition, but neither has anything inherently to do with the other. From this perspective, the fact that both phrases contain the same component ('democracy') is no more relevant than the fact that 'cat' and 'catapult' share their first three letters. Recognition of this fact has some signal cognitive advantages, but it also in some sense misses the point, because part of what it is to understand the *political* meaning of representative democracy is to see in what way it derives its motivational attractiveness and persuasive power from a historical transformation of the semantic potential of the Athenian original. Understanding 'representative democracy' politically in the contemporary world means, in part, seeing why it can present itself as the appropriate modern version of the project of collective self-rule which expressed itself more vividly and emphatically under the ancient system of direct democracy. The form such understanding takes will have to be one of a complex history of words and concepts, and of

[3] See John Dunn, *The Politics of Socialism: An Essay in Political Theory* (Cambridge: Cambridge University Press, 1984), pp. 9–10; John Dunn, 'Capitalism, Socialism, and Democracy: Compatibilities and Contradictions' in John Dunn, ed., *The Economic Limits to Modern Politics* (Cambridge: Cambridge University Press, 1990); and John Dunn, 'Property, Justice and the Common Good after Socialism' in John Dunn, *The History of Political Theory and Other Essays* (Cambridge: Cambridge University Press, 1996).
[4] See John Dunn, *Setting the People Free: The Story of Democracy* (London: Atlantic Books, 2005).

the human actions these seek to capture – and, more particularly, of the human use of such words and concepts under conditions of potentially large-scale social and economic change. The provision of such complex historical perspectives was never part of the Socratic programme, or of any of its direct or indirect successors. But adopting it as the appropriate prerequisite for understanding politics promises to transform our sense of what political judgement involves.

Politics will always happen where human societies interact and struggle, and social life will always require the activity of judgement. A historical understanding of political action, and the judgements of value that accompany it, is forced to proceed in the absence of guiding norms or determinate concepts. Political judgement may not be a constant mayhem of disorientation and confusion, but neither is it an activity of applying rules or ascertaining norms. Diagnosing an error or thoughtfully avoiding a clearly discerned cul-de-sac is not tantamount to having a firm grasp on 'the truth' or a comprehensive map of the terrain that we inhabit. John Dunn has consistently pressed the question of how such practical judgements relate to wider theoretical claims about politics. The papers collected in this volume were written by historians, philosophers and political scientists who have been in one way or another inspired by the perspectives Dunn's work has opened up. They are all centred in various ways on the question of what political judgement is, and what the prospects are for our coming to an understanding of it that might enable us to enlighten our own political practice.

The first section of the volume, comprising chapters by Raymond Geuss, by Victoria McGeer and Philip Pettit, and by Richard Bourke, deals with general issues about the nature of political judgement. Geuss begins by discussing what it might mean to construe 'judgement' not on the model of a human individual who entertains and then affirms or denies a proposition, but rather as a kind of action which is always located in a social, usually an institutional, context. His aim is to show how attempts to construe political judgement in the traditional terms of epistemology are bound to miscarry. The peculiar nature of the kinds of practical imagination involved in the formation of even the most straightforward political judgements ought to encourage us to consider political reasoning on its own terms, rather than as some sort of beleaguered extension of human reasoning as such. McGeer and Pettit, in chapter 2, examine how a focused analysis of the ways in which judgements are actually produced might help to improve its flexibility and reduce its pathological results. They underline the psychological vulnerability of human cognitive powers, and indicate how some of the perils of perception, particularly its in-built dogmatism and tendency towards inertia, are paralleled by problems associated with judgement. Judgement is in this sense resistant to change. How, McGeer and Pettit ask, can it be rendered comparatively open to innovation? They explore the idea that the techniques of rhetoric may have a useful cognitive role to play in freeing up the dogmatism of judgement, enabling people to entertain alternative perspectives.

Political innovation must aim at practical improvement. It is not some kind of inspired inventiveness, an idle search for a new style. It requires a sense of the stakes involved in seeking progressive change, an appreciation of the gravity of affairs. The flexibility needed in judging possible change requires a grasp of the significance of change. It depends on imagination and the cultivation of historical sense. It depends on a capacity to imagine the motivational force driving one's opponent's political values, an ability to conceive what is not present in one's own experience. Political judgement is therefore dedicated to imagining the world as it might be, but it must also be adept at assessing practical consequences as they would obtain in that hypothetical situation. In this sense it is a form of historical judgement. Richard Bourke addresses some of the issues that arise from taking seriously the claim that judgement is a *historically* located phenomenon, and the relation between the explanatory and justificatory ambitions of theories of judgement. The distinction between explaining and justifying political action has traditionally been rendered in terms of the difference between historical and philosophical approaches to politics. Taken together, the first three chapters in this collection illustrate how these distinct senses of what practical affairs involves affect how the role of judgement in politics is evaluated and analysed.

III

The second section of the volume explores the confrontation between philosophical and historical modes of understanding politics through the history of political thought itself. The chapters by Skinner, Hont and Kaviraj examine the fraught relationship between causal and normative judgements about political life. Together they illustrate the historical tensions that have existed between the demands of political theory and political practice. The formulation of the tension in these terms extends back as far as the Socratic monologue with which Plato concludes the *Crito*. But the recurrence of this ancient philosophical vocabulary has a tendency to obscure the emergence of new problems in modern contexts still depicted in traditional idioms of thought.

We began this Introduction by recalling that a dominant strain of Western thinking about politics in some sense originated with Socrates. But despite the powerful influence of Socratic argument on philosophy, his importance to the history of political philosophy in particular has always been susceptible to distortion: his vital presence has been mistaken for a central position in the field. This commitment to the centrality of Socratic political theory is itself as old as Plato. But the assumptions underlying Plato's characterisation of the Socratic project are controversial. Can an ethical and epistemological vocation, of the kind that Plato ascribed to Socrates, be properly described as political in its orientation? In the *Gorgias* Plato has Socrates utter the remark that he saw himself as rare, perhaps unique, among the Athenians insofar as he was a practitioner of the only true political craft (*politikê technê*). Socrates' profession of political expertise is based on his claim to aim in life exclusively at what is 'best' instead of fitting in with the common sense of popular opinion.[5] Political judgement is identified with philosophical discrimination, and philosophy with the criticism of prevailing norms. The Socratic legacy to the early political thought of Plato thus assimilates the art of statesmanship to the pursuit of moral theory.

One cumulative effect of the attempts pursued in this volume to deepen our understanding of political judgement is to cast doubt on the tenability of Socrates' claim to statesmanship. But doubt should not be mistaken for sceptical complacency. Scepticism about Socratic and Platonic political pretensions must always be on its guard because its target is so resourceful. When Plato has Socrates describe himself as a politician in the *Gorgias*, there is a sense in which the remark is supposed to be taken as ironic. The irony is not intended as a mere decorative display of wit; it is deployed instead as a provocation and

[5] *Gorgias*, 521d6–e1.

a challenge. Socratic irony has long been recognised as an instrument of fundamental criticism.[6] In presenting Socrates' mission as *political* in nature, Plato wanted to expose the degraded values driving current affairs – to attack the prevailing norms of Athenian political culture. Since the reigning justifications for political arrangements at Athens were based in Plato's view on the emptiest of claims to justice, the principled rejection of such hollow pretences could be characterised as an exercise in true politics.

In the *Republic*, the Socratic claim to statesmanship is restated, but further complicated. In Book VI of the dialogue Adeimantus responds to Socrates' definition of political justice in terms of the coincidence between philosophy and practical skill by subjecting the ambition of philosophical politics to ridicule: in practice philosophers are known to be either vicious or plain useless, Adeimantus protests. However, the appearance of vice among the pretenders to philosophy cannot be blamed on the love of wisdom itself, Socrates responds; the uselessness of philosophers is the fault of the failure to make good use of them. The blame here must be understood to lie with popular prejudice, not upright philosophers.[7] Philosophical judgement should in principle be seen as an expression of genuine political judgement, we are obliged to conclude, but under current circumstances it is disabled by the corruption of morals and the debasement of wisdom. What code of behaviour ought then to govern the conduct of philosophy towards practical affairs under conditions of moral and political corruption? The variety of possible responses to this question has given rise to an assortment of opposing schools of thought, but none of them has convincingly engaged the pressing demands of politics. This lack of theoretical purchase on the distinct characteristics of political struggle poses a challenge to the adequacy of our inherited notions of political judgement.

---

[6] On the historical and philosophical import of Socratic irony, see, variously, G. W. F. Hegel, *Geschichte der Philosophie* in *Georg Wilhelm Friedrich Hegels Werke: Vollständige Ausgabe*, ed. Phillipp Marheineke *et al.* (Berlin: Duncker and Humblot, 1832–45), XIV, pp. 59–67; Søren Kierkegaard, *The Concept of Irony*, ed. Howard V. Hong and Edna H. Hong (Princeton, NJ: Princeton University Press, 1989), pp. 259–71; and Gregory Vlastos, *Socrates: Ironist and Moral Philosopher* (Cambridge: Cambridge University Press, 1991), pp. 21–44.

[7] *Republic*, 487b1–491b1.

In Book IX of the *Republic* Socrates lays out for Glaucon what the implications of developing a philosophical paradigm of justice might be for the morally responsible citizen forced to act in a city pervaded by injustice. Should enlightened citizens neglect political affairs, Glaucon pointedly wonders? They should orientate themselves in terms of the best city they can imagine, Socrates answers, not the country in which they happen to have been born. The philosophical citizen will therefore focus on the care of his own soul – unless 'chance' presents the opportunity for radical reform.[8] John Dunn has argued that the various strands of Platonic political argument arising out of the confrontation between philosophical enlightenment and political injustice have developed into three theoretical options since the original composition of the *Republic*.[9] Each of these is distinctly anti-political in its orientation, while the third in addition entails the corruption of its underlying principles. This intricate set of statements formulated in connection with the responsibilities that confront the critical moralist in Plato's thinking can be interpreted as enjoining three different programmes of action.

The duty to care for one's soul or develop inner ethical harmony could be interpreted, on the one hand, as promoting an attitude of disengagement from practical affairs. Moreover, disengagement can in reality amount to unacknowledged complicity in the political arrangements which disengagement was designed to reject. But since the Platonic programme of ethical self-development is geared towards the formation of true principles of justice, it is prone on the other hand to promote a critical posture towards prevailing values. While straightforward complicity might be avoided here, the precise import of social criticism remains problematically inchoate. As a result, both of these options can be seen as at bottom anti-political in nature – the first, insofar as it is definitively removed from 'the practical dynamics of political conflict', in Dunn's words; the second, insofar as it is aimlessly dissenting, a directionless form of ironising complaint.[10] Neither approach offers a secure basis for the exercise of political judgement since politics is evidently absent in each case.

---

[8] *Republic*, 592a1–592b5.
[9] John Dunn, 'The History of Political Theory' (1992), repr. in *The History of Political Theory and Other Essays*, p. 31.
[10] *Ibid.*

But what of the third theoretical possibility, of the case where criticism might actually prove effective – where chance, as Plato put it, brings about the 'opportunity' for decisive action? There is an old charge frequently levelled against the moralising programme of Platonic political philosophy to the effect that any inkling of an opportunity for change would be sufficient to tempt the philosopher to grasp at immoderate power. Temptation of this kind is prone to trigger a style of politics bearing an anti-political character of its own. The captivating hope of realising a scheme of justice predisposes its possessor to sacrifice all realistic sense of practical possibility to the enthusiastic desire for comprehensive change. The seductive image of the philosopher-politician is at this point unmasked to reveal the reality of the hapless adventurer in political affairs. For a utopian political adventurer of this kind, the attraction of an irresistible political objective thwarts judgement of the causal means to achieve it.

The relentless pursuit of an ethical ideal of justice is standardly unravelled by developments on the ground. This bleak fact of human history testifies to the frailty of individual judgement forced to navigate a course between ideals and their realisation. The projected scheme of improvement is betrayed by the necessary means to its fulfilment. In practice, as Dunn analyses the situation, the purity of the project itself acts as a stimulus to the development of a form of politics subversive of the goal originally advertised. In place of radical reform in the name of justice, a revolutionary overhaul of political relations delivers all hope of reform into the hands of violent reaction.[11] This pattern of relationships offers a grim illustration of the cunning of unreason whereby the unintended consequences of a moral course of action lead to an unambiguous political deficit. Viewed in this light, the search for an easy correspondence between moral enterprise and

[11] *Ibid.* On this theme see also John Dunn, *Modern Revolutions: An Introduction to the Analysis of a Political Phenomenon* (Cambridge: Cambridge University Press, 1972; 2nd edn, 1989), pp. xv–xxix; John Dunn, 'The Success and Failure of Modern Revolutions' (1977), repr. in John Dunn, *Political Obligation in Its Historical Context: Essays in Political Theory* (Cambridge: Cambridge University Press, 1980); John Dunn, 'Understanding Revolutions' (1982), repr. in John Dunn, *Rethinking Modern Political Theory: Essays 1979–83* (Cambridge: Cambridge University Press, 1985); Dunn, *The Politics of Socialism*, pp. 12–14; John Dunn, 'Revolution' (1989), repr. in John Dunn, *Interpreting Political Responsibility: Essays 1981–1989* (Cambridge: Polity Press, 1990).

political process begins to look both misplaced and naïve. Platonising accounts of political judgement have always felt themselves vulnerable to this charge. They depend on somehow happening upon a practical vehicle for ethical insight: on chancing to find, as Plato expressed it, a sufficiently powerful political agent disposed to put moral knowledge into practice.

The story of Plato's luckless adventure in being induced by his companion, Dion, into assuming responsibility for the political education of the Syracusan Tyrant Dionysus II illustrates the precariousness of any such undertaking.[12] The philosophical expert is at the mercy of the bearer of political power. Virtue depends on favour, and favour requires trust. The clear message arising from the tale of Plato's effort to train Dionysus points at once to the treacherousness of relations of trust and to the extent to which the moral expert depends upon its offices. Despite this, there is a long tradition of political thought of basically Platonic provenance, extending at least from Erasmus to John Stuart Mill, which managed to trade on the prospect of educated expertise delivering up dependable political judgement. In each case trust formed the bond of union linking expertise with political power. However, it is in the nature of trust that its terms of exchange can be negotiated with various biases in view.

The dilemma is a general one: the exercise of political judgement often involves an assessment of the circumstances in which it is prudent to entrust the security of political rights to the guardianship of executive power. The trust implicated in this transaction is both an epistemological and a social relationship, conducted between individual agents and institutions. Most simply it involves an assessment of the likely intentions of other people, but it is often the case that the assessor is somehow obliged to the individuals under scrutiny. Under these circumstances, perception itself will be structured by social deference or dependence. Quentin Skinner's chapter in this

---

[12] The story has been handed down to us in the form of the Seventh Letter. This document is obviously Platonic in character, although it is doubtful that Plato actually wrote it. For recent responses to the place of the Seventh Letter in the Platonic corpus, compare Malcolm Schofield, 'Plato and Practical Politics' in Christopher Rowe and Malcolm Schofield, eds., *The Cambridge History of Greek and Roman Political Thought* (Cambridge: Cambridge University Press, 2005) with Rainer Knab, 'Einleitung' in Rainer Knab, ed., *Platons Siebter Brief* (Zurich: Georg Olms Verlag, 2006).

volume dramatises the dangers that accompany any act of political credulity. The most primitive form of political trust involves crediting the judgement of a ruler without security against the abuse of the resulting authority relation. It involves licensing the arbitrary initiative of a superior, releasing political prerogative from all dependence on consent.

The idea that consent imposes restraints upon the exercise of authority has always been a sufficiently indeterminate concept as to be capable of a variety of doctrinal applications.[13] John Locke has often been identified with a potent version of the doctrine, at least in part because of his association with the founding ideas of American constitutionalism. But, as John Dunn originally began to argue in the late 1960s, that association is largely a result of belated historical construction. Moreover, the theory of consent as actually formulated by Locke placed fewer limits on political action than has commonly been supposed.[14] Skinner's contribution underlines the relative weakness of the Lockean thesis in comparison with the more stringent criteria for consent publicised by republican and parliamentarian activists in the decades before Locke began to draft his *Two Treatises of Government*. By these criteria, consent ought to be construed as implying ongoing, active and explicit agreement to legislative measures in addition to evincing a basic acceptance of the terms of government.

Set alongside the principles adumbrated by John Milton in his *Tenure of Kings and Magistrates* for the legitimate exercise of authority, Locke's doctrine of popular consent appears to offer a means of justifying rather than disciplining the systematic alienation of individual judgement required by the division of political labour in civil society. Locke's theory of the state does still seek to

---

[13] For a sceptical analysis of the operation of popular consent extending as far as the 'face to face' societies of Ghanaian village life, see John Dunn and A. F. Robertson, *Dependence and Opportunity: Political Change in Ahafo* (Cambridge: Cambridge University Press, 1973), pp. 326–7, 384n44.

[14] On Locke's impact on political argument in the American colonies in the eighteenth century, see John Dunn, 'The Politics of Locke in England and America in the Eighteenth Century' (1969), repr. in Dunn, *Political Obligation in Its Historical Context*; on Locke's theory of consent, see John Dunn, 'Consent in the Political Theory of John Locke' (1967), repr. in Dunn, *Political Obligation in Its Historical Context*; and John Dunn, *The Political Thought of John Locke* (Cambridge: Cambridge University Press, 1969), Part III.

ground legitimate sovereignty on normative principles, but the rights
to which the norm of legitimacy gives rise are only exercised at the
point of violent rebellion. Short of this drastic option, popular consent lacks any means of practical expression.[15] The abstract formal-
ity characteristic of Locke's doctrine of political right is a product
of the hiatus separating his historical argument in Book VIII of the
second *Treatise* from the analysis of political principles presented
in Book VII. As a result of this separation, Locke's account of the
acquisition of popular rights in the *Two Treatises* drives a wedge
between the theoretical duties of authority and the limits imposed
by institutional accountability. As David Hume was to argue, by
casting the obligations of rulers in the form of a promise of responsibility to the ruled, political power on Locke's model was in practice
freed from restraint.[16]

Hume's objection to the core conception of Locke's thesis was
to form the basis of Adam Smith's attempts to advance a historical theory of government. Hume had pointed out that the Lockean
effort to found the obligations of authority on a contractual promise implied a historically insupportable account of the origins of
European governments whilst at the same time entailing a practically ineffective theory of government more generally. Istvan Hont's
chapter examines the impact of Hume's critique on the design of
Smith's history of jurisprudence. He shows how the historical argument painstakingly elaborated in Smith's Glasgow lectures on the
science of government pointed to a rejection of Locke's assumption
that constitutional government was a product of revolutionary resistance. It also challenged the notion that the possibility of resistance

[15] The precise political implications of Locke's moral principles have been inten-
sively debated since Dunn's 1969 study. For the range of subsequent interpret-
ations, see John Dunn, ' "Trust" in the Politics of John Locke' (1984), repr. in
Dunn, *Rethinking Modern Political Theory*; Richard Ashcraft, *Revolutionary
Politics and Locke's Two Treatises of Government* (Princeton, NJ: Princeton
University Press, 1986), *passim*; James Tully, *An Approach to Political
Philosophy: Locke in Contexts* (Cambridge: Cambridge University Press,
1993), pp. 9–68; and John Marshall, *John Locke: Resistance, Religion and
Responsibility* (Cambridge: Cambridge University Press, 1994), pp. 205–91.
[16] David Hume, 'Of the Original Contract' in *Essays Moral, Political and
Literary*, ed. Eugene F. Miller (Indianapolis: Liberty Press, 1985). On Hume's
response to Locke, see John Dunn, 'From Applied Theology to Social Analysis:
The Break between Locke and the Scottish Enlightenment' (1983), repr. in
Dunn, *Rethinking Modern Political Theory*.

was a guarantor of legitimacy. In place of both these suggestions, Smith proposed an account of the historically variable forms of trust which determine the submission of individuals to distinct systems of political rule.

Smith's account of the emergence of modern European systems of government was designed to provide a historical explanation for the compatibility between political specialisation and practical limits on the exercise of power. This in turn was intended to show how the concentration of sovereign political judgement in modern states coexisted with constitutional restraints upon power. From this perspective, the modern advent of absolute sovereignty did not have to entail a form of arbitrary rule. Modern political organisation enabled the most ferocious concentration of the power of decision. But it also separated this power of decision from deliberation and arbitration. In this way, political judgement under constitutional government could be rendered coherent and effective, while the processes by which that judgement was formed checked monopolistic control. Political decisions within constitutional governments were not therefore exposed to the arbitrary whims of individual judgement. They could be disciplined by processes of institutional regulation. Modern prudence ought to be seen not as an attribute of the wise statesman, but as a happy yet contingent by-product of constitutional organisation.

Smith's critical intervention is an example of a more widespread Enlightenment ambition to develop a historical political theory in lieu of resuscitating the ancient ideal of the philosophical statesman. But however much the reflective historian might be able to demonstrate the deficiency inherent in the idea of a sage lawgiver, however much such a figure might illustrate the comparative wisdom involved in trusting in the unintended consequences of social process, the need for an exercise of individual judgement on the part of rulers in the midst of affairs could never be dispensed with altogether. Reflecting late in life on the complex demands imposed on the conscientious legislator, Smith recalled the salutary case of Solon, whose judiciousness had been notoriously celebrated in Plutarch's *Life*, as exemplifying the virtue of political prudence. Questioned at the end of his career as to whether he had conferred the best system of laws on the Athenians, Plutarch reports how Solon responded that he had provided them with 'The best laws they would receive'.[17] Solonic reform was modified with reference to the expectations of its recipients. For political improvement to succeed, Solon's argument suggests, it has to be translated into a framework of acceptable change.

But what of the constant risk of mistranslation in political affairs? Sudipta Kaviraj's chapter focuses on the permanent threat of systematic mistranslation that is bound to afflict attempts to apply political judgements in today's world. The languages deployed to describe, evaluate and analyse the vast complex of social experience distributed across the globe are derived from a limited stock of modes of understanding about how politics actually is, or how it ought to be, organised. The unavailing character of Western political theory, and in particular its inadequacy as a guide to action in the face of the future, has been a persistent theme of John Dunn's work since the 1970s.[18] Kaviraj captures the misalliance between synoptic theory and actual practice by exploring attempts to put Western political ideas to work in India. His primary interest lies in an assortment of failed attempts to apply Marxist schemes of class analysis to the unlikely terrain of caste society on the Indian subcontinent. The comparatively successful fate of Nehruvian politics in India points to an important lesson. Practical politics stands in need of organising schemes of interpretation, but still judgement is required if theoretical schemes are to be meaningfully translated into practice.

IV

It would be easy to enumerate a succession of failed historical attempts to make reality out of implausible programmes of political improvement, and to show how judgement, in Solon's phrase, too often disregarded how laws might be 'received'. But the question then arises of the qualities of political intelligence that are necessary to preclude catastrophic failures of this kind. The third section of this volume examines what might be expected of successful political judgement, and of the characteristics of leadership required to put it into effect.

---

[17] Plutarch, 'Life of Solon', XV. Smith's reference to Solon appears in Adam Smith, *The Theory of Moral Sentiments*, ed. D. D. Raphael and A. L. Macfie (Indianapolis: Liberty Press, 1982), p. 233.

[18] See, in particular, John Dunn, *Western Political Theory in the Face of the Future* (Cambridge: Cambridge University Press, 1979).

The chapters by Geoffrey Hawthorn, Biancamaria Fontana and Sunil Khilnani range across a broad historical canvas, extending from Periclean Athens through early modern France down to modern India. In the process, they broach the topics of democracy in the ancient and modern worlds, the politics of empire in fifth-century BC Greece and twentieth-century India, and the problem posed by popular sentiment for the leadership of states. Their emphasis is on the fragility of human psychology under stress, and on the dexterity and ingenuity required to manage the impact of public opinion.

If Montaigne was the supreme analyst of the pathologies of public opinion, Pericles was the great master of its successful manipulation. This at any rate, as Geoffrey Hawthorn shows, was the assessment of his leadership intimated by Thucydides in his *History of the Peloponnesian War*. Pericles, as Thucydides pictured him, was 'first' among the Athenians, both partisan and manager of democracy during the city's greatest period of prestige – a representative of the *dêmos* in all senses, and so a champion of its imperial pride. The perfect embodiment of judgement in affairs, an exemplar of the practical virtues, he nonetheless ended his career as the chief architect of a war that undid the world he had done so much to produce. How can one explain such a phenomenal fall coming so fast upon the heels of a glorious rise to power? In the *Menexenus*, and again in the *Gorgias*, Plato strongly implies that the seeds of Athens' tragedy long pre-dated the 420s, and more particularly that decline pre-dated the untimely death of Pericles. Much like Cimon, Miltiades and Themistocles, Pericles was a victim of the populism he helped to foster.[19]

Athens is now 'bloated and festering' because of celebrated figures from the past like Pericles, Socrates complained to Callicles in the *Gorgias*.[20] Instead of the consummate artisan of practical wisdom, as Thucydides painted him, Pericles is presented as an exemplification of the systemic problems that only a philosophical statesman was fit to resolve. The loss of the Peloponnesian war, the descent into civil strife, and the slow decline of Athens in the fourth century stood in need of explanation, and Plato pointed to the democratic constitution of the Athenians as bearing the primary responsibility. Periclean prudence was still democratic prudence, leading to the corruption of responsible rule. The shortcomings of judgement characteristic

[19] *Gorgias*, 515d.   [20] *Gorgias*, 518e5–519a1. See also *Menexenus*, 234c–d.

of Athenian demagoguery were attributable to structural causes rather than to individual failures of nerve. However, Plato could have extracted precisely this conclusion, although not his own distinctive set of proposals for staging a recovery, from the text of Thucydides' *History* itself.

Hawthorn remarks how Thucydides seems to have cast Pericles as the prisoner of a situation that he was nonetheless able to exploit more skilfully than any of his competitors – as a source of encouragement for the very patriotism that limited his room for manoeuvre. Patriotism is at the mercy of its own intemperate passions, and so also in the end are those representatives who seek to exploit it. Politics is naturally an affair of passion – democratic politics above all others, especially democracies infatuated by the pride of empire. But while public life is moved by a combination of passion and interest, their alliance is neither harmonious nor controllable. Political judgement can strive to anticipate the probable consequences of this combination, but it is never in a position to alter the materials which compose it. In her contribution to this volume, Biancamaria Fontana emphasises the extent to which Montaigne remains the unsurpassed student of the whimsical life of the passions. But since passion for Montaigne disturbed all sense of common interest, judgement in public affairs had to place its trust in customary authority.

It is Socrates rather than Pericles who stands as the most consistent inspiration behind the *Essais*. Throughout the work, Montaigne brings together an engaging mix of cosmopolitanism and stoical apathy, both of which have their sources in the transmission of Socratic values. But at the same time he displays a fascination with the extremes of passion capable of deranging national politics. Montaigne was a close observer of the role of interests in social life, and of the formative significance of habituation to their constant presence. To that extent, he was an advocate of the utility of custom in sustaining conventions, an exponent of the 'stickiness' of judgement. But Montaigne was also strongly aware of the malleability of interests, of their government by the transient world of opinion. Passion and imagination hold sway over opinion, and so conventional beliefs are never truly secure.

One consequence of Montaigne's Pyrrhonian attitude to beliefs in society was recourse to a separation between the exercise of private judgement and the obligations of public allegiance. As a precedent for this commitment he cited the example of the 'bon et grand Socrate' as presented at the close of Plato's *Crito*. Refusing to save his life by disobeying the magistrate, Socrates chose outward conformity over the satisfaction of public protest.[21] But his choice at the same time pointed to the benefits of contemplation, which could only be enjoyed under conditions of civil harmony and obedience to authority. Such benefits included the rewards of philosophical self-mastery, sceptical detachment from the turbulence of the world, and the refinement of taste and judgement amid the commerce of private life. But Montaigne's emphasis on the availability of consolations of this kind was a product of reflection on a basic existential predicament. Since imprudence begins with the self, politics must begin with the care of the self, first in the form of a philosophical assault on vanity, and second in the form of psychological preparation for the slings of fortune. As he put it in his important essay 'De la præsumption': 'not being able to control events, I control myself'.[22]

However, in the face of such an attempt at self-control, the obvious fact asserts itself that events will happen anyway and others will seek to capitalise on how they chance to progress. The renunciation of affairs as serving self-regard and glory may have its compensations in terms of personal edification, but politics in the meantime still demands a response, and since worldly actors will continue to rise to try to meet its challenges the question of how these challenges can best be met must occupy a central place in human concerns. This, in other words, is the question of leadership, which is the subject of Sunil Khilnani's chapter. The virtues and vices of leadership that Khilnani itemises in connection with the exercise of judgement on Nehru's part bear some striking resemblances to the old Stoical repertoire resuscitated by humanist philosophers like Montaigne – the dangers of pride and presumption, the integrity of conviction, and the need to place passion under the control of calculation. But the nature of the relationship to the world is completely different in each case.

In a suggestive essay 'De la solitude', Montaigne sought to overhaul the old antithesis between the virtues of solitary self-cultivation and the virtues of public commitment. Withdrawal from affairs was

---

[21] *Crito*, 51e5–54d5. For Montaigne's comment on this section of the dialogue, see Michel de Montaigne, 'De la coustume et de ne changer aisément une loy receüe' in *Les Essais*, ed. Pierre Villey (Paris: Presses Universitaires de France, 1924, 1992), 3 vols., I, p. 118.

[22] Montaigne, 'De la præsumption' in *ibid.*, II, p. 644.

simply not enough, Montaigne protested against the advocates of philosophical *otium*: 'it is not enough to withdraw from the populace ... one must withdraw from the democratical constituents within oneself'.[23] The *topos* of the statesman's retreat from the bustle of the world, either to reflect on accumulated experience or to prepare for future engagements, is as old as that of the meditative philosopher immersed in solitude – Solon on his travels, Cyrus in his garden and Cicero in retirement are examples of the genre. Momentary distance from the pressure of events seemed a positive preparation for a rude encounter with them. It helped to nurture that indispensable characteristic of the capable politician, the sense of responsibility. But responsibility of this kind is precisely what the contemplative philosopher lacks, and what the Platonising tradition inevitably dissipates by succumbing to the desire – in John Dunn's phrase – of 'thinking politics away'.[24]

Khilnani's chapter recovers the aspiration to 'distance' in Nehru's stance, how he strove to find detachment from the cause that might have consumed him. But this distance was never equivalent to a rejection of affairs; he never spurned the passions of politics as distasteful, nor longed for the kind of spiritual guide that Gandhi found through his 'inner voice'. Together with distance, Nehru possessed conviction, and awareness that others were driven by conviction too. This awareness also fed his sense of responsibility. It imposed upon him a feeling for the gravity of judgement, an appreciation of the stakes involved in calculation and decision. The weight of responsibility is most keenly felt at moments of crisis, and Khilnani's analysis accordingly begins with the critical encounter between Jinnah and Nehru in the late summer of 1946, a year before the partition of India and Pakistan. The meeting was a failure; the next day brought the violence of the Calcutta killings; the path towards partition was now probably unstoppable. How should one anatomise the conflict of expectations that brought things to such an unfortunate pass?

In mid-August 1946 Jinnah pushed for the creation of separate self-governing territories for the protection of the subcontinent's Muslims. The demand was tantamount to a declaration of Pakistani secession from a prospectively independent India. The proposal was an

---

[23] Montaigne, 'De la solitude' in *ibid.*, I, p. 239.
[24] Dunn *The Cunning of Unreason*, p. 194.

affront not only to Nehru's immediate plans, but to his political and intellectual formation as well. Jinnah was driven at once by communal pride and popular fear. Security for the Muslim minority could only be provided by the (notionally) intimate bond of trust between mutually identifying rulers and ruled collected into a self-governing political unit. Nehru on the other hand expected the minority to find security in the scale of his preferred model of a Hindu–Muslim conglomeration. Jinnah's fears in this light seemed both unreasonable and a betrayal of principle – the principle of moderation through diversity.

Judging the fears of others to be unreasonable raises the problem of how one's opponents could consider this verdict to be itself reasonable. In trying to capture the various attributes of Nehruvian prudence, Khilnani cites Weber's lecture of January 1919 on the requirements of the successful politician. Passion (*Leidenschaft*), Weber contended, is first of all essential. But the sense of responsibility (*Verantwortungsgefühl*) is also vital. By the first of these we are moved to reason about politics, and by the second we are moved to reason politically. But to reason politically requires moderation, or the achievement of distance from the cause in which one is passionately involved. Distance therefore includes a kind of distance from oneself, without which judgement would be a mere vehicle for passion. Such distance must be informed by a sense of proportion (*Augenmass*).[25] In its absence the politician will be mastered by daily passions and become incapable of calculating the most propitious options or of taking the measure of the passions of one's opponents.

The great topics of twentieth-century politics – productivity and social justice; constitutionalism and nationalism; democracy and empire – crowded in upon Nehru's political judgement. In addressing these matters at large, the figure of the modern statesman has been condemned to bear the same burdens that Nehru bore in an exemplary fashion. Responsible modern legislators have had to struggle to balance passion with political feasibility, and to anchor the judgement of feasibility with an adequate sense of proportion. However, modern statesmanship has not been conspicuous for its successes in this

---

[25] Max Weber, 'Politik als Beruf' in Wolfgang J. Mommsen and Wolfgang Schluchter (with Birgitt Morgenbrod), eds., *Wissenschaft als Beruf 1917/1919 – Politik als Beruf 1919, Max Weber-Gesamtausgabe* (Tubingen: J. C. B. Mohr, 1981–), p. 17, pp. 73–4.

ongoing venture. Political judgement has in fact left a trail of sizeable disappointments. But academic reflection on these disappointments has been equally dissatisfying. We still lack a political theory of practical reasoning and judgement. Dunn's project has been to remind us of the seriousness of this lack and to warn against complacency in anticipating its continuance.

V

The pressing issues of democracy, equality and the best available forms of authority, first recognisably debated in the period between Thucydides and Plato, persist as challenges facing contemporary political prudence. The final section of this volume is devoted to showing that it is precisely these issues that demand to be explored in any serious treatment of the way in which political judgement is exercised in the contemporary world. Much of contemporary politics has been driven by the collision between ideals of popular justice and institutional limitations on public affairs. Indeed, a highly striking feature of current political discussion is its insistent concern with distributive justice and with the relation between economic inequality and the (postulated) political equality that is an integral part of the ideological carapace of Western democracies. Political judgement here must, arguably, strike a balance between contemporary aspirations and the realistic chances for attaining any significant amount of real equality in existing societies. Adam Przeworski's essay is a sober, and sobering, investigation of the limits within which that balance might be found. The struggle for democratic equality has been a potent force shaping both social and political expectations for two centuries and more. But the tantalising suggestion that those expectations stand in conflict with the structural realities of social and political organisation has haunted the landscape of politics at least since Tocqueville. This conflict has provided modern political judgement with its most persistent problems. Przeworski highlights the tension between the promise of equality and the demands of economic responsibility, between passion on the one hand and practical reason on the other – the very dilemma articulated by Weber.

At the beginning of this volume Raymond Geuss emphasises how even the realm of human passion – the realm of *wertrational* action, the politics of pure conviction – is itself subject to the demands of practical reason. The commitment to values is never completely divorced from an assessment of viability and a weighing up of consequences. But the results hoped for from dedication to values and the actual consequences which follow from the commitment to them are never very easy to match up. Indeed, they frequently collide with or contradict one another, as is so often the case with the contest between democratic ideology and democratic politics. Przeworski examines this contradiction as it afflicts the integrity of democratic ideals at the intersection of modern economics and politics. Democratic ideals have long been fed by a range of protean aspirations to equality, not least among these aspirations having been the struggle for equality of rule. Hobbes was perhaps the first modern political thinker to observe this connection between the struggle for popular power and the idea of an equality of rule. The legitimacy of modern democracy has been largely grounded on this notion. But while Hobbes appreciated the seductions of this alluring promise before the advent of modern forms of democratic government, he also pointed to the implausibility of the underlying idea. Przeworski's chapter stands in this same tradition of political scepticism. However, for him the implausibility of radical equality stems less from the instability inherent in the value than from its remoteness from the world of practical politics.

While the ideas informing democratic politics are in this sense remote from the practical functioning of public life, they are also in important ways alarmingly close. Richard Tuck's chapter is a timely reminder of how they have been brought close to the centre of Western political preoccupations since 9/11. Earlier in this Introduction, we cited the purported 'law' that democracies do not wage war on each other, sometimes claimed as the only true universal law in political science. But the existence of this 'law' would have been news to the ancients, who tended rather to think that democracies were inherently predatory and oligarchies more inclined to a peaceful enjoyment of what they had.[26] Under the impact of international terrorism politics today has been forced to consider anew the vintage association between popular political responsibility and predatory ambition. Tuck discusses some of the issues that arise when contemporary states are brutally confronted by the legacy that ancient democracy has left to modern ideas of legitimacy. The most dramatic confrontation of this kind was recently staged by the charge allegedly brought by Osama bin Laden to the effect that

---

[26] See Thucydides, *History of the Peloponnesian War*, I, xix.

the citizens of the United States should be held responsible for their governments since in terms of their own national ideology they ought to be recognised as the sovereign arbiters of its actions. If this charge is taken seriously, the underlying claims of democratic legitimacy must be seen as exposed to unprecedented provocation, coming from an antagonist that Western democracies had been accustomed to view as posing a military threat but certainly no kind of moral challenge.

Tuck's method is to explore the implications that follow from 'bin Laden's' announcement. If a people does indeed share in the democratic voice of its state, does it not also share in what the state's opponents might construe as its democratic guilt? Bin Laden's alleged intervention, together with Tuck's meditation on some of the consequences that follow from it, are both made possible by the equation of allegiance with responsibility in democracies. We might choose to consider this equation as spurious, or just overly neat. But the fact remains that the roots of this identification lie deep in the historical self-conception of Western democracy. Particularly since the advent of mass enfranchisement, mass canvassing and mass organisation in the mid to late nineteenth century, the identification has been as pervasive as its implications have been controversial.

Modern democracy is based on the idea of a correspondence between rulers and ruled. At a bare minimum this implies that the rulers are charged with addressing themselves to the interests of the ruled. But to discharge the duty of serving the popular interest, rulers must to some extent bear the people's passions. Democratic leadership must somehow represent the *ira et studium* of the population it leads. But in leading, leadership must at the same time strive for impartiality; it must therefore proceed *sine ira et studio*. In striving towards this ideal, statesmen implicitly absorb one of the goals of Western scientific procedure as one of their own principles of action. In his 'Wissenschaft als Beruf' of 1917, Max Weber pointed to key elements of a process of intellectualisation already present in Plato as marking a vital step in Western progress along the path of science. The core commitment arising out of Book VII of the *Republic*, Weber contended, was the commitment to theory, which insisted that standards of conceptualisation independent of the influence of power and status were at least possible.[27] However,

---

[27] Max Weber, 'Wissenschaft als Beruf' in Mommsen and Schluchter (with Morgenbrod), eds., *Wissenschaft als Beruf 1917/1919*, p. 17, pp. 10–11.

by comparison with mathematical reasoning, political reasoning is susceptible to conflicts of value. For that reason, it may not be very useful to think of the ingredients of practical reason as behaving like rational counters or concepts. Disputed ideas in the realm of politics give rise to arguments, not 'concepts'. This fact in itself points to the need for leadership in practical affairs. But what then could act as a guide to political leaders themselves?

Weber was adamant that there could be no science of leadership. However this did not rule out the achievement of clarity (*Klarheit*) about moral choices.[28] A crucial question for the science of politics concerns the conditions under which leaders in possession of clarity might emerge. This question has a singular importance for democracy, since all democracies by definition contain a demagogic component. Demagoguery is not a recipe for confusion in political decision-making – 'it was Pericles, not Cleon, who first bore this title', as Weber reminds us.[29] But it is disposed to gratify the short-term preferences of its audience, above all the moral dogmatism of popular prejudice. Modern demagoguery made possible the emergence of charismatic leadership driven by a single-minded moralising vocation. Moral enthusiasm of this kind poses a threat to prudence, but it can be tamed by the calling of responsibility. Responsibility (*Verantwortlichkeit*) is an essential ingredient of competent political judgement. Political theory by itself is powerless to cultivate such a virtue. However, it can usefully study the conditions of its emergence.

John Dunn once raised the question of how far the legacy of ancient Greece to modern politics is modern politics itself.[30] The question was intended first and foremost as a spur to thinking. In one sense, in its conception the question is an offence against historical intelligence, but it contains the germ of two important truths. The Greeks bequeathed to posterity political theory and democracy, both of which proved impossible to erase from successor civilisations. Certainly the problems of political theory and democracy have been at the centre of Dunn's concerns for a number of decades. The question of what it means to be a political theorist has occupied him since the beginning of his career, and the relationship between democracy and political theory has played a central role among his preoccupations. This

---

[28] *Ibid.*, p. 19.   [29] Max Weber, 'Politik als Beruf' in *ibid.*, p. 54.
[30] Dunn, 'The History of Political Theory', p. 29.

volume draws attention to the ways in which these issues converge on the problem of political judgement. Theory is a tool for the refinement of judgement, but it brings with it the risk of distortion too; democracy amounts to a claim about the equal rights of judgement, but it is continually forced to decide between popular rights and the dictates of reason. For modern politics the contest between theory and democracy persists as an enormously challenging problem, perhaps the central problem that political judgement has to face.

PART I

The character of political judgement

1 | *What is political judgement?*

RAYMOND GEUSS

In his recently published memoirs the former British Ambassador to the United States, Sir Christopher Meyer, describes a dinner party which he attended in Washington in early February 2001.[1] George W. Bush had just been elected – or at any rate inaugurated as – President of the United States, and the members of his new administration were awaiting the first visit of the British Prime Minister Tony Blair.[2] Present at the dinner were several close advisers of the new US President, figures strongly associated with the Republican Right, so-called 'neo-conservatives' such as Richard Perle and David Frum. The conversation quickly moved to Britain's recent decision at the meeting of the Council of Europe in Nice to support closer European defence cooperation. These 'neo-conservatives' thought that Blair had fallen victim to a French plot to harm the USA by introducing a new, independent military force in Europe, which could in principle compete with NATO. Sir Christopher, however, tried to convince them that the projected new form of defence cooperation represented no more than an increase in Europe's ability to discharge subaltern functions *within* a NATO that would continue to be dominated by Washington. The new arrangements, correctly understood, were

---

[1] Christopher Meyer, *DC Confidential* (London: Weidenfeld and Nicolson, 2005), pp. 171–4. I am much indebted to Masaya Kobayashi, Shin Chiba and Naoshi Yamawaki for organising the conference at Chiba University for which this paper was written, and for discussions of this topic. I am also extremely grateful to Istvan Hont for organising a discussion of this paper in King's College, Cambridge, and to him and the other participants of that discussion – Zeev Emmerich, Ross Harrison, Michael Sonenscher, Richard Tuck – for helping me to get clearer on some issues.

[2] This event probably seemed more momentous to Sir Christopher than it did to the members of the new Republican administration in the USA. In fairness, Sir Christopher seems never to have been under any illusions about the asymmetrical nature of the relation between the political elites of the USA and those of its major client state.

therefore not only no threat to the USA; they were in Washington's
own best long-term interest. Sir Christopher then continues:

I found it an uphill struggle to place our initiative in the context which
Blair had intended.

I withstood a full frontal assault from all concerned against our alleged
sell-out to the French ... [One of the neo-conservatives present] argued
that now we were allowing ourselves to be corrupted by political cor-
rectness and socialist Europe. We were, he said, drifting away from our
traditional transatlantic loyalties – look at the threat to fox-hunting, for
Pete's sake!

Some of this was barking mad. But lurking in there was a serious point.
How could even Tony Blair, the most gifted performer of his generation in
the circus of British politics, ride the American and the European horses at
the same time, without falling between two saddles?

The real answer was: with difficulty. At [this] dinner I fell back on the
holy mantra of British foreign policy. There was no choice to be made
between Britain's European and Atlantic vocations. If we were strong and
influential in Europe, this would strengthen our hand in the US. If we were
close to the US, this would redound to our benefit in Europe.

'No, no!' the cry went up around the table, in an unconscious echo of
General De Gaulle, 'Britain must choose.' To this audience of Manicheans
I sounded feeble and temporising, a typical product of the Foreign Office.[3]

This anecdote seems to me to present an archetypical instance of a
'political' disagreement. One of the first features of it that strikes me
is that it has a certain specific historical density. Sir Christopher in
2005 tells the story of a group of people who encountered each other
in Washington in February 2001. At this meeting in 2001 each group
presented, and tried to argue for, a radically different interpretation
of a series of decisions which already at that time lay in the past,
namely the decisions made at the meeting of the European Council in
Nice in December 2000 about European defence. Each of the two different interpretations contains, as an integral part of itself, a divergent
projection about what future we can expect to result from the events
in Nice. Sir Christopher thinks it will strengthen Washington's ability
to project its military power around the world; his neo-conservative
interlocutors deny this strenuously. This disagreement takes place
within the framework of a set of values shared by the two participants
to the discussion, namely the assumption that it is a good thing for

[3] Meyer, *DC Confidential* , p. 174.

the USA to be able to project its power as widely and effectively as possible. This, of course, is an assumption with which it would also be possible to disagree. It seems natural for us to say that the disagreement between Sir Christopher and the neo-conservatives mirrors or results from differences in the respective 'political judgements' each of the two parties make about the project of closer European cooperation on defence.

If one wants to understand what was going on in Sir Christopher's anecdote, one must keep in mind that most of the individuals engaged in this discussion had specific institutional roles which in some cases might give their words extra weight, but which would also require them to be especially circumspect in expressing themselves, and which might even require them on occasion to 'represent' in public an institutional position about which they actually had some private doubts. In his memoirs Sir Christopher is admirably clear about the distinction between his role as a diplomat and thus a member of the Civil Service, and his own private views. He is equally clear about the distinction between either of these and particular policy decisions of the current UK government. Thus, in saying that the UK did not need to choose between an Atlantic and a European 'vocation' he was, as he explicitly says above, voicing the institutional opinion of the British diplomatic corps. When he writes in the passage cited above that this policy was difficult to pursue successfully, I think we can assume that he is speaking in his private capacity, and I think we can be rather sure that Sir Christopher never said to his US interlocutors even in private conversation that, to use his own pungent formulation, Mr Blair's project was to ride them as one of the horses in a two-horse circus act.

The political judgement expressed in a directive to the members of a highly centralised Leninist cadre party has a very different standing and meaning from the 'manifesto' of a contemporary British political party. The abstraction of (mere) opinions or beliefs from their wider context may be highly useful, or even necessary, for certain purposes, but any kind of adequate understanding of political judgements will require reference back to that original full matrix of individual and institutional action. Even when the abstraction is perfectly justified, as it is for most normal cases, one will never know when extracting the judgement from its wider action-context and formulating it as a 'mere' belief will distort it, and in what way it will distort it.

The decision at the conference in Nice was a political act, a choice made by agents empowered to represent recognised states about a future set of courses of collective action, but the later disagreement between Sir Christopher and the neo-conservatives about the retrospective interpretation of that original decision was also a political controversy and not a seminar discussion. I think it is a great failing of much contemporary political philosophy that it tends to focus too exclusively on discussion and also tries to construe discussion on the model of a highly idealised conception of what purely rational or scientific discussion is. Forming and holding opinions and engaging in discussion of those opinions are, of course, important parts of human life, but (a) opinion-formation and discussion are not all there is to politics, and (b) even the formation and evaluation of opinions is comprehensible only in one or another of a number of different wider historical and institutional contexts; most of these contexts will in one way or another be action-orienting. Genuine understanding of any real or envisaged course of action, however, requires one to understand the concrete constellation of power within which it is located.

So in the rest of this chapter I would like to try to elaborate an intentionally rather overdrawn distinction between a political disagreement and a certain ideal-typical account of academic discussion. I will exaggerate slightly in order to bring out some features of the political which philosophers sometimes lose sight of. I wish to emphasise that I am trying to assert a general distinction here *not* between politics and science, but rather between politics and a certain set of philosophical claims that have been made about the nature of rational human discussion.

The political philosophers from whose untender embraces I would like to save politics focus their attention on deliberation resulting in a political judgement, where the process of deliberation is construed as a kind of discussion, the model for which is an idealised version of a Socratic dialogue. This idealised model is characterised by the following eight elements:

1 A judgement is essentially an opinion (or belief), that is, the affirmation or negation in thought of some proposition ('Tabitha has four paws'; 'thou shalt not kill').
2 The content of an opinion is always expressed in language.

3 An opinion is always in the final analysis the opinion of an individual.

4 Those who express opinions in discussion must expect these to be subjected to scrutiny to determine whether or not they are correct or true; this means that the whole apparatus of evaluating truth-claims that has been an obsession of Western philosophy since its origins can be activated in the discussion.

5 Opinions can be investigated atomistically, that is, one can abstract them without remainder and without falsifying them from the context of actions and other opinions in which they are usually embedded, and treat each one in isolation.

6 Participants in the discussion are anonymous; they do not speak *as* bearers of any social roles or offices or with any special authority, but always as naked individuals. The opinions discussed are treated ahistorically, as if it was irrelevant what the person who holds the opinion might have said or done in the past. The only things that are at all important are the considerations each individual participant can bring to bear in the discussion at the moment the discussion is being conducted.

7 'Ethical judgements' formulate a particular 'moral ought' which prescribes once and for all how each individual should act and trumps all other practical considerations.

8 Political philosophy is a part of applied ethics, that is, in discussion ethical judgements are clarified and justified, and they are then applied in the political sphere.

As I said, the above is an ideal-type, that is, a constructed paradigm which is taken to have importance because it gives understanding both of cases that conform to it and of cases that deviate. It is not intended as a description of any reality. Nevertheless, this paradigm seems to me to provide such a distorted view of anything that could reasonably be called 'politics' that it is not a useful starting point for any kind of illuminating analysis. Roughly speaking, each of the eight theses is either false or so misleading that it might as well be false. Traditional philosophy was utterly fixated on the search for a single fundamental concept the analysis of which would allow one to decipher a whole area of human experience, and for a very wide range of human activities philosophers thought they had discovered an Archimedian point in the concept of a 'belief' or an 'opinion'.

I would like to suggest that this traditional approach might stand in the way of a proper understanding of politics. In contrast to the traditional views, I would like to propose two theses. First, if one thinks it is absolutely necessary to isolate a single political concept that was purportedly more central than others, one would be well advised to take not 'belief' or 'opinion' but 'action' or the 'context of action'. Political judgements are not made individually one by one, but always stand as parts of larger sets of beliefs and judgements, and a political judgement is always embedded in a context of *action*.[4] A

---

[4] It has often been noted that the term 'political judgement' is ambiguous in English as between:

 (a) An act of judging made either by a person or a group about what courses of collective action are desirable. For instance, the members of my University Faculty can discuss our curriculum and conclude our discussion by judging that we ought to reduce the number of examinations we require of our undergraduates. This is an action we take at a particular time, i.e. on a particular day in a particular meeting, and it is an action which may turn out to have been a good idea or not.
 (b) A linguistic entity expressing an act of judging. For instance, 'The Faculty Board has decided to reduce the number of examinations' or simply 'The number of examinations will be reduced.'
 (c) The general capacity to make judgements.
 (d) The ability to make *good* judgements.

I wish to suggest that it is a mistake simply to collapse (a) and (b) because I can make a kind of very rudimentary action-guiding judgement without it being the case that I would endorse a specific linguistically formulated proposition. *A fortiori* I can make a judgement without being consciously guided by a particular linguistically formulated proposition. There are, I wish to contend, two correlative mistakes here. One is to over-intellectualise human action, to assume that in order to act I (or we) must have a specific belief or set of beliefs in mind which guide us. Certainly, we are familiar with a phenomenon in animals which we find it natural to describe by attributing to them a proto-judgement, for instance, I say: the cat is treating you as a friend/enemy. This should be taken to indicate to us a certain dimension of very primitive human possibilities, ways of judging that are in some sense prior to linguistic formulation. The other correlative mistake is to overlook the role of language in constituting most human situations, especially those which display any kind of complexity or sophistication. Thus, at the end of World War II the Allies decided to grant to the Kingdom of Italy, as it then was, the status of 'non-allied co-belligerent' in the war against Hitler. The cat may judge that you are a friend without entertaining an appropriate linguistically formulated belief, but it is hard to see how anyone could make any particular judgement about the advisability of granting or withholding the status of 'non-allied co-belligerent' without having something like human language. This, in turn, does not mean one must have a *specific* linguistic item 'non-allied co-belligerent' in order to grant or withhold this status – in fact in English we do not have a *single word*

political judgement is itself specifically directed at focusing, guiding and orienting future action; expressing, or even entertaining, such a judgement is performing an action.[5] Second, 'context of action' would not be a concept that could serve as an essential definition of politics in the traditional sense in which philosophers have sought such a definition. At best, 'context of action' is an open concept with indeterminate contours, and boundaries that can expand and contract depending on a variety of other factors.

It is by no means an unimportant feature of politics that it is a kind of interaction between concrete individuals and groups that have different powers and abilities. Such groups and individuals act, try to pre-empt, counter or control the actions of others and discuss the rationale for and the actual consequences of pursuing a variety of possible and actual courses of action. They do this by appealing to general principles and shared assumptions, blustering, threatening, cajoling and arguing to assert themselves and to further particular policies and orientations towards the world. The people engaged in the discussion are also not anonymous or abstract tokens of universal rationality, but persons who have individual histories, and track records of previously held opinions, actions and associations that are to some degree known to the others.[6] Particularly in the case of politicians who are

---

for that – but it does mean we must have a sufficiently rich stock of appropriate general words to express what we mean. In short, from the fact that *some* linguistic expression is necessary for more sophisticated forms of human interaction to be possible, one must not draw the conclusion that human behaviour can in some sense be reduced to beliefs/language. It is important to recognise both that action and language are connected and that there is a potential looseness of fit between the two. We can have collective hostility to you; to have this enmity it is perhaps necessary that we have *some* linguistic means at our disposal, but it is not the case either that we absolutely must use *this* particular language, or that, in order to act in a particular way, we need exactly to have had some particular, antecedently formulated, linguistically shaped belief in mind to guide us. There is a residual gap or space between language and action, an indeterminateness, which nothing can overcome.

[5] See John Dewey, *The Quest for Certainty* (1929) in Jo Ann Boydston, ed., *John Dewey: The Late Works, 1925–1953*, IV (Carbondale and Edwardsville: Southern Illinois University Press, 1988); and John Dewey, *Human Nature and Conduct* (New York: Random House, 1930).

[6] This is obviously directed at the views held by John Rawls and by Jürgen Habermas who in one way or another believe that one can orient oneself in the world of politics by analysing what would be the object of consensus in an idealised discussion conducted by agents who are deprived of any knowledge of their own empirical singularity or of the contingent historical situation.

known magnitudes the possibility of recalling their past actions, the positions they took and the arguments they used can throw a surprisingly long shadow on a present discussion. This means that agents involved in the interaction will need to think about the consistency of their commitments over time, and about reasons they could publicly give for having changed their views (when they have done so) – reasons that do not do them too much discredit. Thus, everyone present at the Washington dinner party Sir Christopher describes will have known that Richard Perle had been a staunch opponent of any form of arms control agreement with the Soviet Union during the Cold War, and was closely associated in the 1990s with a group called 'The Project for the New American Century'.[7] This group elaborated a plan for US domination of the world by making use of the uncontested military superiority of the US over any possible constellation of conventional enemies which was one result of the collapse of the Soviet Union. One of the central planks of the programme put forward by the Project for the New American Century was the proposal to 'discourage' allies, for example the United Kingdom, from acquiring the military capacity to operate independently of the US. If Richard Perle one day presented himself as an apostle of peace and advocate of genuinely universal disarmament, this deviation from his earlier position would at the very least require him to have some articulable reasons ready to explain why he had changed his mind, or how his new position could be made compatible with the one with which he is so strongly associated. That would not be impossible, but it would be an extra rhetorical task he would have to discharge which might put him at a slight disadvantage in certain discussions. In general participants in a political discussion have internalised at least some minimal historical knowledge about the other participants to such an extent that the past is an essential integral component of the present situation, and one cannot understand what is taking place without knowledge of this historical dimension.

When Richard Perle says to Sir Christopher Meyer that Britain 'must' choose, he is not merely floating for disinterested consideration a speculative hypothesis about historical or contextual necessity, in

---

[7] On Richard Perle and the neo-conservatives, see also James Mann, *The Rise of the Vulcans* (London: Viking Penguin, 2004); and Stefan Halper and Jonathan Clarke, *America Alone* (Cambridge: Cambridge University Press, 2004).

the way in which a biologist might say that all living things must eventually die. Rather, particularly in view of Richard Perle's position as a professional politician and his past, which strongly suggests that he is a bit of a bully, in saying that Britain must choose Perle is most probably trying to influence Sir Christopher's attitude, that is, trying to bring it about that Britain *does* choose. Even *saying* this makes it harder for Britain not to choose, and given Perle's connections he is and is known to be in a position to make it even harder if he wishes. Western philosophers have historically focused on the analysis of beliefs or opinions, have construed these on the model of detached vision and have discussed obsessively the conditions under which such beliefs could be considered to represent the existing world correctly. It is not false to think of a political judgement as a belief, but this is an abstraction, an artificial isolation of one element or component or aspect from a wider nexus of actions and action-related attitudes, habits and institutional arrangements, within which alone the judgement (finally) makes sense.

In addition, although to express the view that 'Britain must choose' might look like a simple prediction, it can also be seen as a kind of threat. What Britain 'must' do is connected to what it 'can' do, and what it politically 'can' do is picked out not by logical or physical necessity, but by what it can reasonably be expected to do without having to pay an exorbitantly high price. The neo-conservatives in the Bush administration, however, wish Britain to choose, and are in a position to impose a price that would make failure to choose unreasonable. In saying that Britain must choose, Richard Perle is perhaps reminding British diplomats of this, signalling his intention to exact this price if necessary and seeking thereby to bring it about that they choose. Although in very many political contexts stating what looks to be a prediction is actually changing the situation, this means not that no prediction is possible in such cases, merely that it must be approached with more care than one needs to use in more straightforward cases of prediction.

It is however by no means the case that attempts to engage in self-fulfilling prophecies will necessarily succeed; an interventive prediction may even backfire, so that what is intended as a self-fulfilling prophecy ends up undermining itself. Diplomats, politicians and national populations can be highly counter-suggestible, and precisely putting this pressure on Britain may convince a majority of

the population that it is best not to allow oneself to be threatened by
a bully. If choose we must, let it be the EU, where at least we have
an institutionally secured set of powers to participate in decision-
making. Whether this reaction of defiance can be maintained or not
depends on a number of different factors. In particular it depends on
the answers to two questions:

(a) What means of coercion does the extortionist actually have at his
    disposal? What could he in principle do to us?
(b) What is the likelihood that the extortionist will actually apply the
    sanctions he threatens us with?

To start with the first question, it should be noted that in many
cases the effectiveness of a threat depends to some extent on the attitude and reaction of the person threatened. The blackmailer's threat
to disclose the contents of some of my correspondence loses its force
if I become indifferent to the publication of the correspondence.
States, of course, have at their disposal means of extreme coercion
the effectiveness of which cannot be blunted simply by a change in
our attitudes, but it seems fair to assume that in February 2001 Perle
did not seriously envisage a series of direct military actions, or even
indirect acts of subversion against Great Britain, and in fact, if he
had been known concretely to have envisaged any such thing, that in
itself would have changed the situation drastically. Short of military
intervention or subversion, however, it would seem that the US government has three possible instruments to hand. First, it can impose
various kinds of economic and commercial sanctions, try to desta-
bilise the currency, etc.; second, it can refuse to supply Britain with
advanced military equipment of various kinds; and third, it can try
to isolate us diplomatically and politically. Economic sanctions might
be very painful, but their effectiveness would depend partly on how
much we were willing to stand. It is at least arguable that we need the
most advanced military systems only if we wish to operate as junior
partners in joint operations with the USA, so if we were willing to
give up some pretensions to Great Power status, we could easily dis-
pense with them. Finally, the idea that the US would be in a position
to isolate the UK politically was a bit of a joke even in 2001. After
all, Blair's reasons for supporting the invasion of Iraq seem partly to
have been his need to cut a vivid figure on the international stage and
accumulate enough influence with the USA to use its power to fuel

his religious fantasies about a never-ending war against Evil. Sources close to Blair, however, have occasionally hinted that another important part of his motivation was his fear that if Britain did not join the USA, Washington would be so isolated politically that the US government would not be able to control its own paranoia and would run amok. So a threat to isolate Britain was not to be taken terribly seriously. On closer inspection, then, none of the three instruments seems utterly irresistible if the UK could keep its nerve.

As far as the second of the two questions is concerned, Perle probably assumed, as General De Gaulle did, that if really forced to choose, there is no question but that Britain would choose a basically Atlantic orientation whatever the damage to our relation with Europe. It is part of Perle's calculation to pretend that he would prefer Britain to be with the European Union rather than a neutral between Washington and the EU, but that pretence is a bluff.

Sir Christopher, as an experienced diplomat, sees through most of what Perle is up to without much difficulty precisely because he does not take the content of what he asserts in isolation and at face-value as a set of propositions to be evaluated for their truth or falsity. Rather he sees them as specific actions in a particular context, and he can interpret them correctly as attempts to influence British foreign policy in a particular way *because* he knows Perle's own history, and that of the groups with which he is most closely associated, and thus he can locate Perle rather exactly in the landscape of contemporary American politics. Meyer, for his part, is trying to bring it about that Perle sees the world in a certain way, in particular that Perle comes to assume that what is politically important is the context Blair intended. Why, though, should Perle and Co. be at all interested in the context Blair *intended*? His policies might well have harmed US interests (as interpreted by Perle) without intending to do so, and Perle might believe that Blair ought to have been able to see that this would be the case. Is politics about intentions or real results? Doesn't the answer to this question depend on a still further context?

Saying that 'Britain must choose' is performing an action which in the context also articulates the attitude of a particular group, the neo-conservatives. This context is partly constituted by a series of historical and institutional facts which one must take account of if one wishes to understand the statement. If one wishes, one can isolate the pure content of this political judgement and formulate it, as it were, as an abstract prediction. This might be a perfectly reasonable and useful thing to do for some purposes, and unobjectionable as long as one remembers that one is artificially extracting the content from a wider context in which it is actually embedded, and as long as one does not forget that what parts of the context are relevant will depend on the particular purpose at hand. This, however, it seems to me, is sufficient to undermine the traditional conception which I outlined above, in which politics is understood on the model of a quasi-academic discussion.

There are two rather different things the term 'political judgement' can mean. First of all, it can refer to a judgement made about a certain domain of the world. Just as a chemical judgement refers to chemical processes, and a biological judgement to the properties of biological systems, a 'political judgement' could be construed as a judgement *about* politics, that is about affairs of state, relations of power, the way in which collective human action was coordinated, or however else one wanted to specify the domain of 'politics', say as opposed to whatever one wanted to oppose it to. Second, one could speak of a political judgement as a judgement not about a certain domain, but rather as a judgement about almost any domain whatever which as a judgement had a certain character. To say that a judgement 'has a political character', however, means that someone can *look at it* in a certain way, namely as an action with implications for further instances or forms of collective human action. So Truman's conversation with Stalin at the Potsdam Conference about the successful testing of the first atomic bomb was a conversation *about* a particular topic, namely a certain experiment with explosive radioactive materials, but it was clearly also a conversation that had a political character, since the point of it was to intimidate Stalin. A historian's description of the Potsdam Conference will contain any number of political judgements in the first sense, but since it is possible to see these judgements, like the judgements Sir Christopher and Richard Perle express in retrospectively interpreting the meeting of the Council of Europe in Nice, under the aspect of their relation to the possibilities of collective human action, they can also be considered 'political judgements' in the second sense. There is, to be completely explicit about this, no reason why an external observer might not wish to look for a political aspect even of actions which are considered by those who perform them to be 'unpolitical', just as there is no reason in principle why I should be disbarred from judging the way the man behind the counter in the post office weighs my letter 'from an aesthetic point of view', even though he has no non-utilitarian intentions. To be sure, if we do this – if we look at the postal worker as if he were a mime or performance artist of some kind – we might not come much closer to an understanding of what he is doing, at any event in *one* sense of 'understanding', but 'understanding' itself is not usually an end in itself, but a means to something else, usually to some kind of action.

As I have tried to emphasise, political judgements occur not generally as isolated individual statements, but as part of sets of beliefs and judgements that are interconnected with forms of individual and institutional action. These sets are Janus-faced, exhibiting two aspects. One aspect makes them look a bit like predictions; the other makes them look like value judgements. They are indeed both at the same time, and regardless of the fact that it might be 'in principle' or 'logically' or 'analytically' possible to distinguish them, in fact these two aspects are so interconnected that in actual political practice they are not separate. In addition, the prediction-aspect and the evaluation-aspect of systems of political judgement are not like the usual models we have and use of either simple prediction or simple evaluation. I have mentioned one important way in which they diverge from our standard models of prediction, namely that they are what some philosophers call 'reflexive', that is they can have a potentially self-fulfilling or for that matter self-undermining property. I would now like to say something about political judgements in their evaluative aspect.

The usual model that is used for classing or grading is one in which I have a set of fixed standards and apply them to candidates for evaluation. The example that is often given is grading eggs or apples.[8] We assume that there are firm and fixed criteria or standards for designating something a 'Grade A' apple: it has a certain size, colour, perhaps a certain degree of ripeness and freshness, it must lack certain disfigurations, etc. The standards will be established relative to a certain fixed human purpose. Grade A apples will be those that have properties which make them especially highly suited to those human

[8] See J. O. Urmson, 'On Grading', *Mind*, 59 (1950), pp. 145–69. This (pre-Wittgensteinean) analysis is still useful as an account of our everyday assumptions.

purposes. These criteria will themselves not be absolutely precise, and
their application to individual cases will rarely be beyond reasonable
disagreement,[9] but one of the usual assumptions we make when discussing this kind of grading is that the process of deciding on the
criteria to be used, and the process of classifying individual instances,
are separate and distinct. The reason for this is that the whole point
of grading things like apples, eggs, timber or undergraduates is to
introduce predictability into life. Grading is supposed to allow us to
know what we are getting. When the grader is classifying, he or she
accepts and applies pre-given criteria; a grader does not change the
goal posts while the game is going on. If this happened, it would
defeat the whole point of grading. That, at any rate, is the conception
implicit in the usual model.

Simple classification or grading of the kind described above, however, is exactly what does *not* characteristically happen in politics. In
politics, simple grading plays an extremely important but distinctly
subordinate role. We collect and use statistics on crime, employment,
productivity, health, but we also constantly question the way the statistics are put together. More generally, political action takes place in
an arena in which the standards for evaluating what is 'success', what
is a good idea, what is a desirable outcome, are themselves always
changing and always in principle up for renegotiation. Thus, on 1
May 2003 George W. Bush announced that the war in Iraq had ended
in 'victory' for US forces, and very clearly presented this as a vindication of his policy of invasion in the interests of 'regime change'.
In conventional terms this was clearly a Grade A military 'victory':
the field army of the enemy was decisively defeated and dispersed,
the command structure utterly dissolved, and the national territory
occupied. Even the further goal of 'regime change' was also attained.
Whatever one might think of the political situation in Iraq after 1 May
2003, the Baathist Party was clearly no longer in control of the apparatus of state power. Is it so obvious, however, that this automatically
counts as a political success?

The prospects of a stable democracy in Iraq do not look very rosy,
but then one would have to be extraordinarily naïve to think that this

---

[9] If Wittgenstein is right, this is a philosophical, not a practical point. Even
apparently fixed everyday 'evaluation' is in fact indeterminate, so our everyday
view of it is incorrect. In politics the real situation is revealed for all to see.

was an important part of the motivation for the invasion anyway. If the real point was to prevent the establishment of any political agency in the Middle East that was independent of the USA, then a democratic Iraq would be a potential danger anyway, because it might at some point be tempted to steer an independent course. So the complete destruction of the country as a viable society capable of setting its own goals and acting on them effectively would be to that extent a success, although one the perception of which would have to be managed carefully given the claims made to justify the war. On the other hand, the price to be paid for the military victory was the weakening of the UN, the diplomatic isolation of the USA, a split in NATO, the generation of thousands of new recruits to a political agenda hostile to the USA,[10] and a significant drain on the US economy because major allies refused to do what they had done in the First Gulf War, namely foot the entire bill for the war. Is it clear that 'regime change' in this sense will be the realisation of a good or will contribute to 'the good life'? Whose good life? Is it clear that it has furthered broad US interests or the wider interests of the populations in Europe, the Middle East and the rest of the world? Was Richard Perle really giving good advice when he counselled invasion? Political success is always subject to re-evaluation in the light of changing circumstances and changing overall conceptions of 'the good life'. There is no reason to think that discussions of what constitutes a good life will ever, certainly not within any finite period of time, end in the kind of normatively binding consensus some philosophers have expected.[11] One thing that seems to have happened in the case of the Second Gulf War is that as a result of action large numbers of people changed the concrete understanding of what would count as 'success' which they antecedently had had. This is not an unusual outcome.[12]

[10] Of course, the *main* self-declared political aim of al-Qaeda is an end to the stationing of US troops in Saudi Arabia. See Bruce Lawrence, ed., *Messages to the World: The Statements of Osama bin Laden* (London: Verso, 2005); or Robert O. Marlin IV, ed., *What Does Al-Qaeda Want?* (Berkeley, CA: North Atlantic Books, 2004).
[11] Again this is directed primarily against Rawls and Habermas.
[12] One of the most deeply illuminating discussions of the differences between everyday grading and the more complex forms of interaction between classing, acting and changing the standards of classing is that to be found in Hegel, particularly in his discussion of the difference between *Verstand* and *Vernunft*. See *Enzyklopädie der philosophischen Wissenschaften* in

Is there, then, nothing but shifting processes of political judgement that comprise changing predictions and infinitely contestable evaluations? Surely, though, one might argue, there are limits to the malleability of concepts like 'success', a 'good outcome', a 'desirable result'. At any rate, life itself, biological survival, sets certain limits to what any of us can construe as a 'good life'. The phenomenon of martyrdom has been familiar in the West since antiquity, and the fact that since World War II we have been confronted with the phenomenon of the coordinated suicide bombing attack means, however, that not even the human desire for self-preservation can be taken unquestionedly as the basis for political valuation.[13] For as long as humans are capable of a moral and social, and not a merely biological, understanding of 'the good life', martyrdom, voluntary self-immolation and suicide attack will remain as human possibilities. This continued openness of 'success' (or 'the good life') to re-evaluation is not, I think, merely a local property of democratic politics, although it is a feature of politics in general which comes most vividly to the surface in democracies. Evaluation in politics will not always be simple, and is almost never definitive. To be sure, if you let yourself be killed as a martyr or kill yourself as a suicide-bomber you close the context for yourself by this action, but what your action means for those of us who survive, and how we will judge it, is still an open question *for us*, which we will try to answer, if we find it pressing enough, by the usual series of complicated acts of interpretation.

Ever since at the latest Thucydides the ability correctly to foresee what was likely to happen has been valued as one of the most important virtues of the politician. This includes the ability not merely to predict or foresee what will happen but also to foresee what *will seem good*, both to oneself and more importantly to 'effective' others, that is to those whose views about what is good/satisfactory count

Werke in zwanzig Bänden, ed. Eva Moldenhauer and Karl Marcus Michel (Frankfurt: M. Suhrkamp, 1970), VIII, pp. 1–168, or the briefer treatment in *Phänomenologie des Geistes* in *Werke in zwanzig Bänden*, ed. Eva Moldenhauer and Karl Marcus Michel (Frankfurt: M. Suhrkamp, 1970), III, pp. 68–81.

[13] See Diego Gambetta, ed., *Making Sense of Suicide Missions* (Oxford: Oxford University Press, 2005), esp. the chapters by Stephen Hopgood (pp. 43–76) and Gambetta (pp. 259–99).

politically.[14] When the war has been lost catastrophically, which policy will have more appeal, one based on a call for *revanche* or one calling for lasting peace at almost any price? The combination of an ability to foresee or predict and an ability to evaluate is not the only important political capacity *tout court*. Obviously, other important traits are persistence, discipline, resourcefulness, the ability to persuade and organise others, etc., but I would like specifically to mention a further, particularly important cognitive-practical ability. There is a distinct ability of practical imagination, inventiveness or creativity, of coming up with new possibilities, or seeing new possibilities or constructiveness, which is very important in politics.[15]

I mean by this, for instance, the sort of ability exhibited by those who organised the attacks on the Pentagon in Washington and the World Trade Center in New York. Someone had to have the utterly ingenious idea of construing civilian passenger aircraft as missiles with suicide hijackers as pilots who would fly them so as to destroy large buildings. More important, however, than this exercise of technical imagination was the kind of *political* imagination that seems to have been at work. We don't know much, or at any rate I don't know much, about the actual planning of these attacks, but to the extent to which one can infer back from the actual results of what was a very well organised operation to the intentions of those who planned it, it seems likely that the planners knew they were about to inflict a deep narcissistic wound on the American psyche, which the population would neither comprehend nor be able to tolerate. The form that reflection took after the attacks – the frantic attempt to answer the question 'why do "*they*" hate "*us*"?' – was sufficiently incoherent to indicate that a deep nerve had been touched. It would not have been difficult, then, to expect the Bush regime to embark on a course of internal repression and foreign military adventure so wild, destructive and dangerous that international public opinion would shift decisively against the USA, which is what happened. So far this strategy, if in fact it was a

[14] I mean 'effective' here in the sense in which economists speak of 'effective demand'.

[15] I am suggesting here a parallel to the distinction sometimes made by aestheticians between the 'genius' who is able to produce works of art that deviate in a way both original and interesting, and the critic or person of taste who is capable of judging works. Kant's discussion of taste and genius in *Kritik der Urteilskraft* is the obvious classic treatment.

strategy and not a mere series of accidents, has been working like a well-engineered Swiss watch. Viewed from the outside, the plan also seems to exhibit great subtlety in utilising American blind spots – the gross ignorance on the part of the population about the rest of the world and their extremely limited ability to see themselves and their actions as others see them – to subvert US military power and cause it to discharge itself in politically self-destructive ways. To come up with this kind of plan requires not merely political judgement, but inventiveness of a high order. The kind of imaginativeness I have in mind might or might not be well grounded, that is, the plan might or might not work; one might or might not approve of the results. An agent may well be capable of coming up with a variety of new suggestions none of which is any good. That is, as I would express it, someone may have political imagination without political judgement. And of course, people may well have both political imagination and judgement without also having a moral sense, or at any rate without exercising that sense.[16]

One of the most interesting aspects of the events of 11 September 2001 has always seemed to me to be the fact that the attacks were carried out wordlessly as far as the international media were concerned. There was no reading out of a set of demands in front of television cameras, no explanation, no public political announcement of any kind; no group immediately fell all over itself to try to lay claim to this tremendous coup. Through their actions themselves the perpetrators expressed a rather clear political judgement about a civilisation based on militarism and economic exploitation *without saying a word*.

---

[16] One might say that there are three 'genuine' dimensions of politics:
   (a) inventiveness – finding new things that work
   (b) prediction, foresight
   (c) trying actively to change people's conception of the good
   and (at least) one very prominent but debased dimension:
   (d*) spin doctoring – trying to cause people to think that outcomes are good by certain accepted standards, which are not, or trying to confuse people about the standards being used.

2 | Sticky judgement and the role of rhetoric

VICTORIA MCGEER AND PHILIP PETTIT

John Dunn has long criticised the easy assumption that in our psychological and political habits of thought we human beings can make ourselves responsive to the lightest breeze of reason.[1] This chapter joins his chorus, focusing on the case of judgement and judgementally sensitive attitudes. We muster evidence that judgement does not come and go as rationality requires; in face of rational demands it proves remarkably sticky. And we argue that there is a case for resorting to the techniques of rhetoric in order to undo that stickiness and to give reason a chance. Rhetoric has a place in the private forum of deliberation, not just in the context of public debate; it can serve in a therapeutic as well as a strategic role.

The thesis about judgement makes a break with the standard approach in which judgement is contrasted with perception. Everyone agrees that perception is sticky in the sense that it often continues to represent things to be a certain way, even when there is irrefutable evidence that that is not how they are; it keeps representing the rod in the water as bent, even when it is clear that the rod is perfectly straight. By contrast with perception, it may seem that judgement is hair-triggered to the demands of evidence; although I continue to see the rod as bent, for example, I will readily judge that it is straight. But we hold that this appearance is misleading and that judgement itself suffers from drag effects akin to those which affect perception. This is what makes a case for the resort to rhetoric.

The chapter is in three parts. In the first we provide an overview of judgement, in the sense in which we are concerned with it here; this, inevitably, is a rather analytical exercise. In the second we marshal support for our claim about the stickiness of judgement, drawing on

---

[1] John Dunn, *The Cunning of Unreason: Making Sense of Politics* (London: HarperCollins, 2000). We benefited from the very helpful comments on an earlier draft that were provided by Richard Bourke and Raymond Geuss.

a representative sample of psychological findings. And then in the third we suggest how rhetoric – long seen as a means of countering the stickiness in other people's judgements – may also serve to counter the stickiness of our own; it may enable us to hear the other side, providing reason and judgement with an indispensable resource. As unreason may be cunning, in the title of Dunn's book, so reason may be uncunning. And the uncunning of reason, by our analysis, creates an opening for the therapeutic use of rhetoric.

What are the political implications of the argument? We cannot explore the full implications here, but three connected lessons stand out. One is that if deliberation about judgement is not sufficient to let reason reign in the private forum, it certainly cannot ensure this in the public. A second is that as rhetoric can serve the cause of reason in the forum of private deliberation, guarding against judgemental stickiness, so it can provide the same service in the public; it need not be merely a tool of spin and manipulation. And a third is that since the public forum of deliberation will typically include the partisans of different viewpoints, it may in that respect score over the private. The publicity of deliberation may let loose unwanted pressures of in-group allegiance but it can also facilitate the forceful presentation of different viewpoints. It can enable participants to live up to the catch-cry of the rhetorical tradition: *audi alteram partem*; hear the other side.[2]

I   The nature of judgement

Judgement and belief

The term 'judgement', as we employ it here, may be used to report a reflectively available event or state. The event is the formation of a belief, say the belief that 'p', in light of distinct beliefs, explicit or implicit, about the evidence for and against 'p'. The state is the belief that is held as a result of that sort of event. We ascribe judgement in the event sense when we speak of someone's making or forming a judgement; we ascribe judgement in the state sense when we speak of the person holding or maintaining a judgement (though more often

[2] Quentin Skinner, *Reason and Rhetoric in the Philosophy of Hobbes* (Cambridge: Cambridge University Press, 1996), p. 15.

we speak here of holding or maintaining a belief). In what follows, we shall sometimes use the term 'judgement' in the event sense, sometimes in the state sense; context will make clear which is involved. There may be other uses of the word 'judgement' besides these two but we shall treat it as a term of art and restrict it to these two senses.

Judgement in the event sense is not the only way in which belief is formed; on the contrary, it represents an unusual mode of belief-formation in which the subject pays attention to evidence: that is, as the phrase suggests, pays attention in an intentional, though perhaps not very reflective manner. Thus the beliefs that are formed as a result of judgements – the beliefs that constitute judgements in the state sense – may be a very small sub-set of the beliefs that are held at any time by a human being.

Many of our beliefs are formed without the exercise of judgement, under pressures that we do not recognise as such. They materialise and mutate in response to perceptual or proprioceptive cues but in a process of which we may have no inkling and over which we have little or no control. Consider the beliefs bearing on the location or orientation of my body, the angle at which to reach for my coffee cup, the direction from which a sound is coming. Such beliefs will come and go within me under the beat of a drum I do not hear. It will be by grace of nature that they are appropriately formed and unformed, not by dint of any attentional effort on my part. While the direction from which a sound is coming will be salient from the difference in the time at which it reaches each ear, for example, I will not have to attend to the time difference in order to know the direction of the sound; indeed I may not even be capable of consciously registering that difference.

Things are very different with judgementally formed beliefs. It is appropriate to speak of our forming a judgement only when we are not involuntarily mainlined in this way by subconscious cues – not hooked up at a level beneath the reach of our awareness and control to the representational requirements of the world. Making a judgement on an issue presupposes an ability to stand back from the current of evidential input and to operate in more reflective, autonomous mode. We will ask ourselves whether all of the evidence is available, how the diffcrent bodies of available evidence measure up against each other, and if they give support to one or another position on the issue. And depending on how our beliefs form in answer to those questions, we will then make a judgement or refuse to make a judgement on the matter raised.

Although only a small sub-set of our beliefs form in response to acts of judgement – although only a small sub-set are properly judgemental beliefs – this does not mean that judgement is only of marginal significance to the beliefs we hold. For while very few beliefs may be sourced in judgement, all of them may be judgement-sensitive.[3] Although not produced by judgement, they may still be subject to judgemental policing.[4]

I normally go about my business in a very unreflective way, forming beliefs on the basis of evidence of which I am barely aware; think, for example, of the way beliefs form within me as to where I am at any moment in the course of driving home from work. Even in this unreflective mode, however, I will be primed to respond to certain cues that things are going awry: say the cue of the unfamiliar look of a street onto which I take a wrong turning. Let these cues appear and they will prompt me to suspend my unreflective belief-formation and have resort to judgement. I will stop the car, pay attention to the landmarks around me and form a judgement as to how I must go from here. While the beliefs that I normally form may not originate in judgement, then, they may still be subject to the discipline of judgement; they may survive only insofar as they do not clash with the judgements I would form were I in more reflective mode.

Human and non-human

Amongst the intentional agents with which we are familiar, judgement is almost certainly the preserve of human beings.[5] Some other animals – or, indeed, robots or other artefacts – may count as intentional agents, but they are not judgemental subjects.

---

[3] T. M. Scanlon, *What We Owe to Each Other* (Cambridge, MA: Harvard University Press, 1998).

[4] It is impossible, of course, for all of our beliefs to be arraigned at once before the court of judgement. Since every judgement presupposes beliefs about evidence, not all beliefs can be put on trial at the same time. Still, this is not to say that any belief is immune from judgemental probing. Every belief can be tested for whether the balance of evidence supports it, but each test has to presuppose the soundness of certain other beliefs.

[5] M. Hauser, *Wild Minds: What Animals Really Think* (New York: Henry Holt and Co., 2000).

To count as an intentional agent, by our lights, a creature must have desires or goals for which it is disposed to act and it must form beliefs about its environment to guide its action, directing it to suitable opportunities and strategies. Such desires and beliefs can be characterised as attitudes towards propositions, with the desire consisting in the targeting of a proposition, with the belief consisting in the acceptance of a proposition, and with the distinction between targeting and acceptance being given by a difference in the direction of fit. An agent will act to make the world fit a targeted proposition and will adjust to make its mind fit a proposition it accepts.[6]

Even a simple system can merit the ascription of propositional attitudes. Consider the little robot that navigates a table top on wheels, scanning various cylinders on the table with bug-like eyes, and moving to set upright any cylinder that falls or lies on its side. Even a system as rudimentary as this can be characterised as accepting propositions to the effect that this or that or another cylinder is upright or on its side and as being disposed with any cylinder on its side to target or realise a proposition to the effect that it is upright once again.

Any creature, even one as simple as this robot, will have to function to a certain minimal level of competence, if it is to deserve the name of agent. The movement of the robot's eyes will have to pick up relevant evidence about the orientation and location of cylinders on their side. Its cognitive processing will have to ensure that it forms a set of consistent representations as to where they are. And those representations will have to interact with its overall goal to generate attempts to set those cylinders back in upright position. In other words it will have to display a minimal level of rationality in evidence-to-attitude, attitude-to-attitude and attitude-to-action relations. Or at least it will have to do this under intuitively favourable conditions and within intuitively feasible limits. We may think that the robot is operating under conditions for which it is not designed – conditions that are not intuitively favourable – if it tends to knock cylinders at the edge of the table onto the ground, rather setting them upright.

Non-human creatures, certainly non-human animals, get to be much more sophisticated agents than the robot imagined. There are a

[6] G. E. M. Anscombe, *Intention* (Oxford: Blackwell, 1957); J. R. Searle, *Intentionality* (Cambridge: Cambridge University Press, 1983); M. Smith, 'The Humean Theory of Motivation', *Mind*, 96 (1987), pp. 36–61.

number of ways in which the robot might be designed to approximate
such animals more closely. It might be built to have a number of goals,
not just a single one; to form beliefs about other objects besides the
cylinders or about other properties besides the location and orientation of the cylinders; and to form dispositions to do things – plans
or intentions – not just in relation to the here and now but also for
situations at a temporal or spatial remove. With these and other developments, it might get to be as flexible and intelligent as a dog or a
chimpanzee.

No matter how complex the robot becomes in such dimensions,
however, it will be unable to form judgements, as we understand
judgement here. It will not be able to attend to bodies of evidence or
to propositions as such; and it will not be able to seek out information on whether certain evidence supports a certain proposition. The
robot may be able to direct its gaze and pay attention to a certain
cylinder, seeking to determine if it is on its side, as a dog is able to
prick up its ears and pay attention to a noise out of a desire to learn if
dinner is being served. But if the robot mimics the capacities only of
non-human animals, then it will not be able to make abstract entities
like bodies of evidence or propositions into objects of its attention. It
will not have achieved the semantic ascent required to be able to form
meta-propositional attitudes – i.e., beliefs and desires about bodies of
evidence or propositions.[7] Hence, it will be unable to ask questions
about the kind of evidence available in any situation, about how far
the different evidential elements fit together, and about whether they
combine to support a certain proposition. In short, it will be unable to
go through the reasoning exercise that is involved, however implicitly,
in forming a judgement.

Language and judgement

We human beings are able to do these things, or so it seems, because
we have access to language. We can utter the words that give expression to a proposition, and we can let them exemplify the proposition

[7] P. Pettit, *The Common Mind: An Essay on Psychology, Society and
Politics* (New York: Oxford University Press, 1993, paperback edn 1996);
P. Pettit, 'Rationality, Reasoning and Group Agency', *Dialectica*, 61 (2007),
pp. 495–519.

as an entity about which we may form a belief: the sentence 'Jane is a good philosopher' can serve, not just to report that state of affairs, but to make the proposition about Jane's philosophical talents salient as an object of attention. Equipped with words, we can attend to such propositions, ask ourselves various questions about them, such as how well supported they are or whether they are consistent with other propositions we accept. And prompted by such questions, we can form beliefs about the properties of those propositions in response.

We routinely make use of this ability to go up a level and form meta-propositional beliefs when we rehearse an argument, as in saying to ourselves: 'p', 'now, if p then q', 'so … q!'[8] Raising suitable questions at the meta-level, we actively engage in forming beliefs about the nature of the propositions we endorse ('are they probable?'; 'are they desirable?') and about the kinds of connections we find among them ('is this an acceptable pattern of inference?'; 'does this conform to *modus ponens*?'). This is not to say that non-linguistic subjects cannot form beliefs in conformity to the *modus ponens* pattern; they may be led by believing that 'p' and that if 'p' then 'q' to believing that 'q'. But they will be unable to form a belief about the requirements of this pattern of reasoning and to police themselves for conformity to those requirements.

The distinctive, human ability to form such beliefs sets us apart from non-linguistic subjects in at least two different respects. First, we can use meta-propositional beliefs to regulate our more basic beliefs, so that these more basic beliefs conform more nearly to patterns of reasoning that we judgementally endorse. And, secondly, in raising the meta-propositional questions that give rise to such beliefs, whole new properties, like probability, desirability, validity – or expressivist counterparts[9] – become available for examination and predication. The robot or any such simple system will have desires, but no beliefs about desirability, as it will have beliefs, perhaps degrees of belief, but no beliefs about probability. Likewise, its belief may form and unform in rough accord with acceptable patterns of inference; but it will have

---

[8] J. Broome, *Reasons: Essays in Honour of Joseph Raz*, ed. J. Wallace, M. Smith, S. Scheffler and P. Pettit (Oxford: Oxford University Press, 2004).

[9] S. Blackburn, *Spreading the Word* (Oxford: Oxford University Press, 1984); A. Gibbard, *Thinking How To Live* (Cambridge, MA: Harvard University Press, 2003).

no beliefs about whether and to what extent such transformations are justified, and so no means of regulating or correcting whatever patterns it follows.

We stressed earlier that it is largely by courtesy of consciously inaccessible and intentionally uncontrolled processing that we, like the robot, manage to be rational in the formation of most of our beliefs and desires and indeed in the formation of intentions to act as they require. This is how we form beliefs, for instance, about the position of the coffee cup and the angle at which we must move our hand in order to grasp it. We transcend that purely autonomic mode of rational processing when we seek out meta-propositional beliefs about propositions themselves and the evidential case for their being true and belief-worthy, and rely on those beliefs to prompt the right beliefs – or, at least, override the wrong ones – at the more basic level. But this transcendence is only partial; it gives our minds a special place in nature but it does not take them beyond nature's bounds.

If meta-propositional beliefs move us, leading us to form suitable judgements, that must itself be due to a level of processing that escapes our awareness and control. If I am moved by certain beliefs about what the evidence supports to make a corresponding judgement, and form a judgemental belief, then on pain of a regress that must be due to a natural process that I do not control.[10] I have to put my trust in my own neural make-up when I assume that any meta-propositional beliefs about consistency, entailment or support that I can induce in myself will have an appropriate effect, leading me to form the judgements for which they argue. While we intentionally marshal the beliefs bearing on what we ought to judge in light of the evidence, we have to rely on our sub-agentially implemented rationality to ensure that as we ought by these lights to judge, so we generally will judge. Even at the most sophisticated level of reasoning and judgement, we surf on swells and tides that ebb and flow within us, shaped by forces that nature, not we, dictate.

---

[10] Lewis Carroll showed us over a century ago that if I am rationally moved by certain premises to endorse a corresponding conclusion, then on pain of an infinite regress that must be because my nature provides the required habit of inference. The lesson underlined here is parallel. See L. Carroll, 'What the Tortoise Said to Achilles', *Mind*, 4 (1895), pp. 278–80.

II Judgemental stickiness

Perception, will and judgement

For all that the foregoing shows, it might be that those of us who operate in the space of judgement, alert to the demands of reason, are capable of a deep and detailed control over our beliefs. We might have a sure feel for when to suspend our more spontaneous, generally reliable habits of belief-formation, forcing ourselves to review the evidence and form a judgement on the relevant issues. And we might have an assured ability to identify where the evidence points, to make the judgement that it supports, and to maintain the belief that judgement puts in place. In a word, we might be paragons of reason, hair-triggered to respond to the evidence and well equipped to maintain that response robustly.

A cursory examination of the differences between perception and judgement may lend some support to this view. It is a commonplace of scientific and folk psychology that while our perceptions are responsive to evidential inputs on the sensory side, they are often resistant to the evidential inputs from collateral sources. They are more or less encapsulated or insulated, as it is often said, against such information.[11] Take the Mueller-Lyer illusion in which two lines of equal length differ in the direction of the arrow heads at either end; one has normal arrow heads at the ends, the other reverse arrow heads. No matter how much collateral evidence is available that the lines are actually equal in length, and no matter how ready we are to accept that evidence, our perceptual system will not adjust accordingly; the lines continue to appear unequal in length. And so it goes for a range of familiar perceptual illusions.

Judgement looks to be very different from perception. Perception is sticky, as we might put it, being subject to representational biases that lock it into certain patterns, even when the evidence shows that those patterns are misleading. But judgement, by contrast, is the very epitome of a light and hypersensitive form of representation. Unlike perception, it is not insulated in principle from any particular sort of evidence. It can be moved by no matter what sort of insight or information, and is capable of leading us to affirm whatever scenario is

---

[11] J. Fodor, *The Modularity of Mind* (Cambridge: MA: MIT Press, 1983).

evidentially supported. In perception, the sun may continue to look as if it crosses the sky, when we know it does not, but judgement is subject to no such limit. Where perception is confined to fixed and inflexible tracks, judgement can apparently soar along any trajectory and light upon whatever hypotheses the evidence happens to support.

While there is certainly a contrast between perception and judgement, this way of presenting it projects a highly misleading image of judgement. Perhaps there are some possible creatures who are as free of judgemental drag and bias as this picture suggests. But we are not those creatures. The one theme that emerges clearly from recent, sustained investigations of cognition is that, just as our perceptual faculties are locked into fixed patterns, so too – in certain ways – are our judgemental faculties. Making evidentially responsive judgements, it turns out, is not easy, and neither is maintaining judgementally formed beliefs. The life of judgement is agonistic, requiring a continuous struggle to escape limiting and warping forces and to keep them at bay in the maintenance of reasoned opinion.

The problem, in a phrase, is that judgement is sticky. It is sticky in two ways. First, the availability of evidence in support of the proposition that p rather than not p – or the proposition that 'p' is more probable than 'not p' – may not actually lead us to make those judgements. And second, even if the evidence does prompt those judgements – even if it overcomes stickiness in this area – still, there is another sort of stickiness that may then come into play. The agent may be unable to internalise fully the belief that the judgement requires or may not be able to sustain that belief robustly, lapsing into thoughts or actions that run against it. Let the evidence fade from view or let other pressures come on stream and the agent will no longer think and act consistently according to his or her judgemental determinations; the agent will not whole-heartedly believe, in the state sense, what he or she judgementally endorses.[12]

The problems we have in mind are easily illustrated.[13] Suppose that someone is an inveterate but inexpert gambler, and is subject to the

[12] V. McGeer and E. Schwitzgebel, 'Disorder in the Representational Warehouse', *Child Development*, 77:6 (2006), pp. 1557–62.
[13] V. McGeer and P. Pettit, 'The Self-regulating Mind', *Language and Communication*, 22 (2002), pp. 281–99; V. McGeer, 'The Moral Development of First-Person Authority', *European Journal of Philosophy*, 16:1 (2008), pp. 81–108.

fallacy of believing that as a run of blacks materialises on a black–red roulette wheel, the chance of a red gets to be higher and higher. Imagine now that this gambler is presented with evidence that, as each spin is an independent event, what happens from one spin to the next is irrelevant for predicting outcomes. The gambler may just be unmoved by that evidence, displaying stickiness at the stage where judgement is formed; the intuition in favour of the gambler's fallacy may be so strong that this evidence does not elicit her judgemental assent. But even if she overcomes stickiness at this point, there is a further point at which it is likely to strike. Sitting at the casino table, the gambler may find that conviction fades from view. In the heat of the moment, her judgementally formed belief becomes cognitively less salient in her, and she continues to operate in ways that signal persistent adherence to the fallacy. Her prior cognitive habits prove too sticky for judgement to dislodge.

There is a natural analogy on this front between the life of judgement and the life of will. As there is weakness of will, so there is weakness of judgement. And as a victory over the weaknesses of will requires sustained efforts at self-control or self-regulation, so something similar is true of what is required for a victory over the weaknesses of judgement. Some theorists of the will imagine that true virtue makes self-regulation unnecessary, inducing a frame of mind in which the siren calls of unreason are simply silenced and the will follows quietly on the paths that reason prescribes.[14] We do not think that this picture of will fits with the facts of human imperfection. And we do not think that the corresponding picture of judgement has any greater claim to accuracy. Just as the person of practical wisdom never passes into the realm where self-regulation is no longer needed, so the parallel lesson holds for all of us in the formation of judgement.

The standard picture of self-control or self-regulation offers a faithful portrait of the best that real human agents can achieve. According to that portrait, self-control is the sort of exercise in which the ploys and strategies recruited to the cause of reason are a mixed and motley bunch; they are as various as the means whereby people can tie their hands and guard themselves against passing temptation.[15] Those who

---

[14] J. McDowell, 'Virtue and Reason', *Monist*, 62 (1979), pp. 331–50.

[15] J. Elster, *Ulysses and the Sirens* (Cambridge: Cambridge University Press, 1979); J. Elster, *Sour Grapes* (Cambridge: Cambridge University Press, 1983).

struggle with the demon drink may have to lock the booze cupboard, only eat at restaurants in which no spirits are served, take devious, bar-avoiding routes between workplace and home. Those who struggle with irritability may have to count to six before responding to mundane queries, arrive in plenty of time at airports and train stations, and avoid too much coffee. Those who find it hard to resist gossiping about their friends may have to shun certain gatherings, force themselves to declare their friendships before gossip gets going, or resort to clowning or self-mockery to change the direction of a conversation.

The profile captured in this picture of self-control is one of moral bricolage, in which any available ploys or wiles – the bric-a-brac of moral psychology – can be employed to overcome or outflank human weakness. Some philosophers see in such moral bricolage nothing but the sad face of human weakness. We see in it the ingenuity of a self-regulating system that has no other way to approach the best in human practice.

As it is with the will, so we think it is with judgement. Here too the stuff of our psychology is not the ideal stuff, by any abstract metric. It can sustain a life in which judgement is formed on reliable lines and sustained to good effect. But it can do this only by virtue of an epistemic agonism: a constant tussle with the gravitational, warping effects of forces that operate behind our backs. The point will become obvious from a quick review of the pressures that tend to push us onto dubious paths.

Problems in judgement formation

The psychological journals abound in lists of the frames, biases and habits that confound the evidence-sensitivity of judgement. We shall restrict ourselves here to illustrating five sets of problems. They affect the revision of existing beliefs, the attribution of attitudes to oneself and others, the capacity to understand the perspective of others, the processing of probabilistic information, and frame-independent thinking. It is important to note that the problems here discussed are merely representative of the pathologies of judgement that cognitive science has begun to document; they do not constitute a comprehensive inventory. Like the tip of an iceberg, they serve to warn of the extensive dangers that lurk in the area.

Revising beliefs

Problems in the revision of existing beliefs are the largest category amongst these five. There is now a stunning variety of studies which show that, whatever evidence is put before us, we display a dogged, unconscious determination not to let it affect our current beliefs. When asked to consider various arguments for their logical validity, we tend to reject valid arguments with conclusions at variance with our beliefs, and to endorse invalid arguments with congenial conclusions. Asked to check hypotheses that we accept, we tend to look for confirming instances, not for counter-examples.[16] And presented with reports that go different ways, we predictably think better of those that fit with our prior beliefs.[17] In the social world, not only are we disposed to make rapid evaluations of others, we also tend to persevere in those initial judgements, often in the teeth of contrary evidence.[18]

Of course, it might not be so very bad that we are loath to revise our existing beliefs and judgements, if psychological studies showed that cognitive biases did not enter into processes of belief formation in the first place. But emphatically, this is not so. The data argue that, notwithstanding our best efforts to be thoughtful and critical judges, we succumb to a variety of evidentially unwarranted epistemic pressures – a few of which we now briefly discuss.

Attributing attitudes

One set of cognitive biases comes with the attribution of attitudes to others – and indeed to ourselves. Beginning with others, the fundamental attribution error, or 'correspondence bias', holds that in explaining what others do, we tend to invoke low-level dispositional explanations – the person is cowardly, or generous, or fair-minded – rather than explanations that refer to pressures of the particular

[16] R. S. Nickerson, 'Confirmation Bias: A Ubiquitous Phenomenon in Many Guises', *Review of General Psychology*, 2 (1998), pp. 175–220.
[17] P. H. Ditto and D. F. Lopez, 'Motivated Skepticism: Use of Differential Decision Criteria for Preferred and Non-preferred Conclusions', *Journal of Personality and Social Psychology*, 63 (1992), pp. 568–84.
[18] L. D. Ross, M. R. Lepper and M. Hubbard, 'Perseverance in Self-perception and Social Perception: Biased Attributional Processes in Debriefing Program', *Journal of Personality and Social Psychology*, 32 (1975), pp. 880–92.

situation of the agent;[19] for example, the pressure to cut a good figure and win the esteem of local observers.[20] E. E. Jones emphasises the significance of this bias: 'I have a candidate for the most robust and repeatable finding in social psychology: the tendency to see behavior as caused by a stable personal disposition of the actor when it can be just as easily explained as a natural response to more than adequate situational pressure.'[21]

The flip side of the fundamental attribution error is shown in explanations of our own behaviour, where we lean – to the contrary – in a situational direction.[22] So strong is this bias that we persist in it even when the situational explanation is not particularly flattering. Where others see us as acting out of bravery, for example, we tend to suppose we act 'bravely' in the situation only because of some chance coincidence of events – e.g. others are watching, we didn't fully anticipate the risks involved, and so forth and so on. Of course, in some of these cases, our own assessments may be more accurate than the assessments others make of us. But that is neither here nor there. Our point remains that, occasional accuracy notwithstanding, the patterns in 'self' and 'other' explanations robustly evince the biases described.

Understanding alien perspectives

Emphasising these biases in understanding others may seem too pessimistic, given that there is one epistemic capacity displayed in dealing with others that has been much celebrated in recent psychology. This is the ability to see things from another's point of view rather than assuming that that point of view will be the same as ours. The false belief test, often invoked in this context, shows that, from about four years on, children are typically able to tell the difference between

---

[19] L. D. Ross, *The Intuitive Psychologist and His Shortcomings: Distortions in the Attribution Process*, vol. X in L. Berkowitz, series ed., *Advances in Experimental Social Psychology* (New York: Random House, 1977).

[20] G. Brennan and P. Pettit, *The Economy of Esteem: An Essay on Civil and Political Society* (Oxford: Oxford University Press, 2004).

[21] E. E. Jones, *Interpersonal Perception* (New York: Freeman, 1990), p. 138.

[22] E. E. Jones and R. E. Nisbett, *The Actor and the Observer: Divergent Perceptions of the Causes of Behavior* (New York: General Learning Press, 1971).

where an object sought by another person actually is, as they happen to know, and where that other person may think it is; given evidence of how the other person was misled, they will ascribe a false belief about the object's location. And that appears to testify to a robust epistemic ability for understanding others that our nature gives us.

Even in this area, however, there is evidence that we have to work hard in order to keep the other's point of view in mind. Competence does not come without attention, even self-regulation. In a series of experiments, Keysar, Epley and colleagues have established a dissociation between our reflective, critical grip on the difference between how things are and how others think they are and our practical, unreflective capacity to act in ways that display a similar sensitivity to the perspective of others.[23]

In one such experiment, there are two parties, a 'director' and a 'participant', and there is a set of shelves between the two, with some items on the shelves being clearly and visibly blocked from the director's view but not from the participant's. For instance, there might be two toy trucks, one large and one small, visible to both director and participant, and a third, even smaller truck visible only to the participant; and both director and participant are made aware of these facts. Now the director asks the participant to move 'the smallest truck'. Since the director can only see two of the trucks, the smallest from his perspective is not the smallest from the participant's. So in order to comply with the director's request, the participant has to discount what she would egocentrically take to be the referent of 'the smallest truck'. Still, the finding of the experiment is that adults often make errors on this test, reaching for what is the smallest truck by their lights, even though they well know – and will readily acknowledge – that this item is not visible to the director. In other words, participants often act in a way that reflects an immediate bias in favour of their own perspective. Moreover, this bias increases with an increase in cognitive load, as when the participants are distracted in some way.

[23] B. S. Keysar, S. Lin and D. J. Barr, 'Limits on Theory of Mind Use in Adults', *Cognition*, 89 (2003), pp. 25–41; N. Epley, C. K. Morewedge and B. Keysar, 'Perspective Taking in Children and Adults: Equivalent Egocentrism but Differential Correction', *Journal of Experimental Social Psychology*, 40 (2004), pp. 760–8.

It does not take much for the participants in this scenario to correct themselves, once they are prompted to reflect. But such prompting often has to come from the outside – e.g. in the form of the director redirecting their attention to the appropriate object. In any case, even when there is self-correction, the fact that the immediate, instinctive response is shaped by the egocentric perspective shows that our adult capacity for 'reading other minds' – though much vaunted in philosophical and psychological literatures – is more fragile and hard won than is often supposed, and requires a struggle against deep-seated dispositional biases in cognition.[24] Our suspicion is that though individuals may readily self-correct or accept corrections from others in epistemically or emotionally uncharged situations, their responses may be quite different in situations where it costs something to concede the validity of another's point of view.

Probabilistic calculation

The area where there is perhaps the most telling psychological evidence of epistemic under-performance is probabilistic judgement. One particular problem here derives from the fact that we are robustly moved by the vividness of a scenario to give it more prominence in our thinking than less vivid but more likely alternatives.

Take a case explored in a famous experiment by Tversky and Kahneman.[25] Participants were asked to consider a description of a woman and to decide which is the more likely: that she is a bank teller; or that she is a bank teller and an active feminist. The description goes like this: 'Linda is thirty one, single, outspoken, and very bright, and she majored in philosophy. As a student, she was deeply concerned with issues of discrimination and social justice, and participated in anti-nuclear demonstrations.' Eighty-five per cent say that it is more likely that Linda is a bank teller and a feminist, ignoring the simple probabilistic principle that it is always more

---

[24] McGeer and Schwitzgebel, 'Disorder in the Representational Warehouse'.
[25] A. Tversky and D. Kahneman, 'Judgements of and by Representativeness' in D. Kahneman, P. Slovic and A. Tversky, eds., *Judgement under Uncertainty: Heuristics and Biases* (Cambridge: Cambridge University Press, 1982); A. Tversky and D. Kahneman, 'Extension versus Intuitive Reasoning: The Conjunction Fallacy in Probability Judgement', *Psychological Review*, 90 (1983), pp. 293–315.

probable that something A obtains – for example, that Linda is a bank teller – than that A and B obtain together: that Linda is a bank teller and a feminist.

The problem here may stem in part from a failure to follow the probabilistic reasoning; but an important source is likely to be the vividness of the image of Linda as a feminist, which we associate with the description of her background. There is ample experimental evidence of this problem of misleading vividness, and everyday experience testifies strongly to its influence. We are all familiar with it in the statistically unreasonable fear that many people have of flying, given the terrifying prospect of falling from the sky. And we can immediately understand the dramatic effect of an example invoked by George H. Bush in his debate with Michael Dukakis, when they were contenders in the 1988 US presidential election. As governor of Massachusetts, Dukakis had maintained a regime of comparatively lighter criminal sentencing than was common in other States. Despite the fact that the crime figures for Massachusetts compared favourably with those elsewhere in the USA, that evidence was entirely eclipsed when Bush drew attention to a particular, heinous crime that the more lenient measures had made possible. The shocking vividness of the rape and brutal beatings committed by convicted felon Willy Horton, while on furlough under a Massachusetts State programme, entirely swamped the epistemic impact of the statistical record and set back Dukakis' campaign.

Escaping frame

The final set of problems that we would like to mention is associated with the phenomenon of framing, as it has come to be known. The most famous case here, again due to Amos Tversky and Daniel Kahneman,[26] is one in which participants were asked to make a judgement between different programmes for dealing with an Asian disease that is threatening the United States and is expected to kill 600 people.

---

[26] A. Tversky and D. Kahneman, 'The Framing of Decisions and the Psychology of Choice', *Science*, 211 (1981), pp. 453–8; A. Tversky and D. Kahneman, 'Rational Choice and the Framing of Decisions', *Journal of Business*, 59 (1986), pp. 251–78.

As between programmes A and B, 72 per cent favoured A, 28 per cent B:

A: 200 people will be saved.
B: There is a one-third probability that 600 people will be saved and a two-thirds probability that no one will be saved.

As between programmes C and D, however, 78 per cent favoured D, 22 per cent C.

C: 400 people will die.
D: There is a one-third probability that nobody will die and a two-thirds probability that 600 people will die.

But programme A is identical with programme C, and programme B with programme D. The description or framing of the programmes makes all the difference in determining how participants judge.

This particular experiment has been a model for many later investigations. The upshot of those studies is that we are deeply and incorrigibly frame-sensitive in our first take – indeed, in later takes too – on any issue. Even when we know better, we often have to fight intuition to think and act in accord with our more tutored judgements. How the different sides in the issue are presented fixes how we understand the question, and how we understand the question has a powerful influence on the judgement that we are then inclined to make.[27] In the alternatives presented, A rather than B puts the focus on lives saved, as does D rather than C. And it is that focus, that shaping of attention, which primes most participants to prefer A to B and, inconsistently, D to C.

Judgement is sticky

The lesson, we think, is clear. We do not operate in the free space of reason when we seek out the judgements we think are defensible. We are subject to silent forces that are as powerful and unrelenting as gravity and that curve the space of reason in ways that it is difficult for us to detect. The contrast between perceptual and judgemental

[27] F. Schick, *Understanding Action* (Cambridge: Cambridge University Press, 1991).

representation is misleading. Neither operates with the spontaneity that Kant celebrated; each is subject to its own inbuilt limitations and pressures. Recognising this, we have to see the challenges in the formation and maintenance of judgement as akin to the challenges we all acknowledge in the formation and maintenance of will. We are not by nature the enlightened masters of where our judgement goes; having been selected for survival, not for insight, our natural instinct is a wayward ally in the struggle for truth.

III   Rhetorical therapy

Hear the other side

It may be of interest in the context of epistemic agonism to think again about the tradition of rhetoric, as that was established in the classical and the Renaissance worlds. Rhetoric was presented in this tradition as providing resources of persuasion whereby one might hope to convince others of one's point of view. The positive assumption was that the judgements of others are sticky and can be moved only with the help of special techniques of persuasion. The discipline of rhetoric was developed out of the attempt to identify the best techniques. These might be used insincerely to persuade others of a viewpoint one does not hold but they are also useful in communicating a viewpoint to which one is sincerely attached.

To our knowledge, no one in the tradition of rhetoric comments on the need for self-persuasion. The assumption appears to have been that the resources of rhetoric are not necessary in the internal forum, only in the external. The default idea must have been that one can move oneself to judge according to the evidence without recourse to special techniques of persuasion. Rhetoric may be needed in public debate, as one strives to make one's viewpoint accessible to others – assuming sincerity in defending that viewpoint – but rhetoric will have no role to play in the forum where one debates with oneself.

If we grant that the intrapersonal formation of judgement is subject to the same stickiness that appears in interpersonal exchange, then rhetoric assumes a new guise. It begins to look like a discipline that one may use in one's own case, in order to overcome psychological obstacles to the reasoned exercise of judgement: a therapy one can practise in personal, inevitably agonistic reasoning. The methods of rhetoric may serve as means for escaping some pathologies of judgement and for exercising an epistemically useful form of self-persuasion. They can provide a degree of protection against the psychological pitfalls we have been documenting both for those who are unaware of the problems and for those who know of them: knowledge, it turns out, is no more a guarantee of judgemental virtue than it is of practical virtue.

Despite its often dubious reputation, rhetoric was celebrated in the period of its prominence for a range of insights that have something to teach about how to succeed in the struggle for judgement. Those insights were rehearsed with enthusiasm by classical figures like Aristotle, Cicero and Quintilian and by a range of authors in the 300 years or so leading up to the rise of science in the seventeenth century and the subsequent demise of rhetoric as a discipline worthy of scholarly attention and practical study.[28] While these authors were invariably focused on the interpersonal context where others need to be persuaded, we think their insights also have relevance for how we conduct our intrapersonal affairs.

The central axiom of rhetoric can be summarised very simply: in persuading others of our point of view, it is often not enough just to make a good case for that point of view; it is also necessary to move or bend your hearers, letting them feel the force of what you have to say.[29] Dr Johnson chided one interlocutor with the comment: 'Sir, I have found you an argument; but I am not obliged to find you an understanding.'[30] The remark typifies an Enlightenment mentality – not that Johnson was in other respects a luminary of that movement – and stands directly opposed to the assumptions of the earlier tradition. On that earlier way of thinking, the understanding that makes conviction possible is hard to come by. And so anyone who seriously wants to persuade another has to take on board the lessons of rhetoric about what is required for generating such understanding in others.

[28] Skinner, *Reason and Rhetoric in the Philosophy of Hobbes.*
[29] K. Burke, *A Rhetoric of Motives* (Berkeley: University of California Press, 1969), p. 73.
[30] J. Boswell, *Life of Samuel Johnson* (1791) (Chicago: Encyclopaedia Britannica, 1951), IV, p. 545.

We think that the fallibility of judgement, and the agonistic efforts required for the formation and maintenance of reliable opinion, means that the basic axiom of rhetoric applies in the intrapersonal as well as in the interpersonal context. We human beings may have to rely on rhetoric, not just in seeking to persuade others, but also in trying to think matters through on our own. The methods of rhetoric may be necessary aids to hearing the other side, in the catch-cry of the tradition. They may provide essential strategies for giving every side a fair hearing and for finding our way, by the dim light of reason, along unfamiliar and – often for that very reason – unfetching tracks.

Rhetorical aids to enlightenment

The methods of rhetoric that are of interest in the current context are those that have to do with *elocutio*, as it is called in the textbooks: presentation, as we might say. The tradition distinguishes different ways in which an argument, once identified and structured, can be put forward with a view to engaging and affecting the minds of an audience. There are different accounts in the tradition of these modes of presentation, and different interpretations in contemporary commentary, but it is not misleading to distinguish between three families of strategies employed to improve the design and force – the *ornatus* – of an argument. These may be described as rhetorical schemes, rhetorical tropes and, to use a term with no pedigree in the tradition itself, rhetorical techniques.[31]

Rhetorical schemes focus on the ordering of words: for example, on the effects that may be achieved via alliteration, repetition, climax and the like. They are of obvious utility in mocking the views of others, as in references to chattering classes, charmed coteries or Semillon socialists. But they are not likely to be of great importance in helping us to get our own views in perspective and to give a fair hearing to rival opinions. Here tropes and techniques promise to be the crucial aids.

Tropes involve the use of particular words and concepts in non-literal ways, as in metaphor and, on some interpretations, irony.

[31] R. A. Lanham, *A Handlist of Rhetorical Terms* (Berkeley: University of California Press, 2nd edn, 1991).

Other examples include metonymy in which one object is used to pick out another, as when 'Westminster' refers to the British parliament; and synecdoche, in which a part is used to pick out a whole (or vice versa) – 'the crown' refers to the monarch or more generally to government.

Techniques involve not just the transformed use of particular words or concepts but the casting of whole passages in an unusual key. One example would be the allegory in which a story is told that bears by parallel on some context under discussion. Another would be sustained mockery or sarcasm in relation to a particular person or point of view. And yet another would be the extended attempt to redescribe a situation so that where it previously looked good or bad, now it is given a changed valence; what had seemed like cowardice is recast as a form of bravery, what had looked like a failure to inform is reconstrued as modesty about committing to a not quite established narrative.

If we consider the different deficiencies of judgement that we illustrated in our earlier discussion, it should be clear that one way of guarding against them, both in seeking to persuade others and in seeking to persuade ourselves, is by the use of such rhetorical tropes and techniques.

A main problem, so we saw, arises with the difficulty all of us experience in letting go of prior, perhaps long-established habits of thought. We give the benefit of doubt to things we already hold and change our minds only reluctantly and with difficulty; we are subject to forces of judgemental inertia and attachment. How to cope with this inbuilt hostility to the new and unfamiliar? One obvious way would be by drawing on resources of metaphor to cast the novel theses in terms that make them look more homely; another by developing a redescription of the claims that trouble our cautious, stick-in-the-mud minds, giving them a more acceptable cast; yet another by seeking out aspects of our adherence to the older views that invite a certain ridicule, if only for the doggedness of our attachment to them.

The rhetorical tradition of educating the young to debate in public, taking up any point of view they are asked to defend, can be seen as a way of training them to be able to adjust flexibly in the way required for combating judgemental inertia. If we are unable to give colour to points of view we do not hold, if those standpoints are always going to assume a drab and alien profile for us, then we can have little hope of moving ourselves by argument. We will naturally slip into whatever ruts or grooves come first on our path and will roll along, uncritically and unshakeably, on our predetermined way. If we are to be able to reason effectively in the internal forum then we must be able to remonstrate with ourselves, agonising over the epistemic challenges presented. We must not think that calm contemplation will deliver the goods. If we find ourselves able to maintain such calm, then that is likely to be a sign that we have not really reached out to the other point of view. We have not heard the other side.

A second set of problems identified in the psychological literature arises with the attribution of attitudes to ourselves and others. These problems stem from the difference in how we tend to interpret our own behaviour and that of others – the difference revealed in the fundamental attribution bias – as well as the difficulty we find in taking another's point of view. Here there may be no better antidote to our natural habits than to nurture use of the rhetorical technique of allegory and parable. We may not often have occasion to employ that technique in full dress but we would benefit enormously from seeking, in the spirit of the strategy, to keep alive an imaginative sense of how it is with others and how it may be that they are led to act as they do. The friend who seems to have given up on us, the colleague who appears untrusting, the neighbour who presents as downright hostile, the sycophant who finds us relentlessly charming; these figures may assume more likely profiles in light of some imaginative reconstrual.

The difficulty of overcoming our habitual stereotyping of others can hardly be overestimated. Consider the study by Dale Miller and Deborah Prentice into habits of undergraduate drinking.[32] The study revealed that the students each believed that others drank a relatively large quantity because they preferred that level of consumption and disapproved of drinking less. However, speaking for themselves, the students each maintained that they shared neither this general preference nor the general attitude of disapproval. Why then did they drink? The explanation in every student's case was their fear of not

---

[32] D. T. Miller and D. A. Prentice, 'Collective Errors and Errors about the Collective', *Personality and Social Psychology Bulletin*, 20 (1994), pp. 541–50; D. T. Miller and D. A. Prentice, 'The Construction of Social Norms and Standards' in E. T. Higgins and A. W. Kruglanski, eds., *Social Psychology: Handbook of Basic Principles* (New York: Guilford Press, 1996).

living up to their own stereotypical assessments of others' behaviour: the conviction that others drank out of a settled disposition for being a certain kind of drinker (the fundamental attribution error), and a concern with attracting disesteem or even ostracism for not fitting into the group as a drinker of that type. If people can be evidentially insensitive and empathetically unimaginative to the point of sustaining a norm of which no one approves,[33] then we know that the malaise runs deep.

The third general area where we commented on the psychological evidence of our judgemental fallibility was in our estimates of probability and, more generally, in our dealing with framing effects. This may be the area where we are most vulnerable in the judgements we make and it is significant that it connects with perhaps the most powerful technique advertised in the tradition of rhetoric: that of strategic redescription.[34] The lesson of redescription is that the only way to cope with framing effects is to learn the habit of reframing, the only way of coping with presentations that marginalise probability is to learn to cast things in a manner that puts statistical facts back at centre focus. The idea is to fight fire with fire, looking for such a wealth of alternative frames that every side is given a fair hearing on any issue, and there is a better chance of making a balanced judgement.

Rhetoric recast

These, of necessity, are rather tentative thoughts about the particular ways in which rhetoric may serve the cause of judgement. But we hope that the general thesis is attractive. Achieving the insight for which we look in judgement, and holding robustly onto such understanding, does not come as naturally as many traditional views of thinking suggest. We have to fight for freedom from the drag effects that bend judgement away from the tracks of evidence and for the ability to resist those effects as they pull us back into older habits of thought. This requires the deployment of all the strategies we can

---

[33] P. Pettit, 'Error-Dependent Norms' in G. Eusepi and A. Hamlin, eds., *Beyond Conventional Economics: The Limits of Rational Behaviour in Political Decision-Making* (Cheltenham: Edward Elgar, 2006).

[34] Skinner, *Reason and Rhetoric in the Philosophy of Hobbes*, ch. 4.

muster in our support, and rhetoric is a rich source of advice on the arsenal of weapons available in this fight.

Quentin Skinner points out that the Latin rhetorical term 'ornatus' was also the word for the armoury of the soldier and that theorists of rhetoric thought of it as essential to victory in any war of words.[35] If the line of thought pursued here is sound, such *ornatus* may also be necessary to the personal fight that each of us has to wage with ourselves in order to win and secure the gains of sound judgement.

Without the resources that rhetoric puts at our disposal, then, we may not be able to conduct and sustain our reasoning to reliable effect. And if that is true for reasoning with ourselves, it is certainly true of reasoning with others. While there will certainly be contexts where rhetorical persuasion has a non-epistemic, non-edifying appeal – contexts where it amounts to manipulation – that is not its only use. In winning the way to insight we will often have to exercise persuasion in order to get a good sense of the alternatives on offer, and in order to secure our attachment to the viewpoint that judgement selects. And that will be as true of the case where we reason with others as it is true of the case where we reason with ourselves.

The point we are defending here is not particularly novel, though it may give a novel cast to rhetoric. Think of the argument that when we philosophise we are often at the mercy of intuition pumps: models that make certain ways of thinking unavoidable – both for good and for ill.[36] Or think of the broader Wittgensteinian lesson that philosophy is often best advanced by a therapy in which examples and reminders and analogies are multiplied, and abstract argument is put aside. The claim we are defending is that this sort of lesson may apply outside the realm of philosophy as well as within. In order to think well on our own or with others, we will often have to invoke a therapy that releases us from *idées fixes*, blind spots, obsessions and other pathologies of judgemental life. And rhetoric directs us to methods of persuasion that promise to serve us well in that role. It may not be the only source of such lessons but it is likely to be an important one.

[35] *Ibid.*, p. 49.
[36] D. Dennett, *Elbow Room: The Varieties of Free Will Worth Wanting* (Cambridge, MA: MIT Press, 1984).

Rhetoric is not essentially designed to get in under the radar of reason and shape people's minds in subversive, non-rational ways. Nor is it essentially designed, as more sympathetic commentators suggest,[37] to move people by *ad hominem* considerations, finding for every audience the customised reasons that will work best on their minds. While rhetoric may certainly be employed to such cynical or tactical purposes, its use in the service of reason can be avowed on all sides and may count in that sense as a more central function. In giving colour and life to rival standpoints, rhetoric serves as a therapy against being captured in any single point of view. It helps to ensure that no insight is lost, no judgement missed, for lack of exposure to the persuasive, imaginative appeal of different propositions.

[37] B. Garsten, *Saving Persuasion: A Defense of Rhetoric and Judgement* (Cambridge, MA: Harvard University Press, 2006).

Theory and practice: the revolution in political judgement

RICHARD BOURKE

Introduction: enlightenment and revolution

The role of political judgement is a subject rich in confusion.[1] The confusion is a product of antagonism. Distinct accounts of the relationship between political theory and practice reached a pitch of mutual antipathy during the aftermath of the French Revolution. Opposing philosophical positions became increasingly associated with rival political commitments as the experience of revolutionary turmoil deepened. A crucial matter in contention among competing political sects was the connection between enlightenment and politics itself. This question had been debated since the latter half of the seventeenth century in terms of the relationship between philosophy and government.[2] How best to conceptualise this relationship was a matter of dispute giving rise to sharply divergent affiliations. Stipulating how judgement bridged the gap between theory and practice depended upon general assumptions about how philosophy should serve politics. Should it set out moral principles in terms of which existing political

---

[1] I am grateful to David Bromwich, Roger Cotterell, Karuna Mantena, Henning Ottmann and Wilhelm Vossenkuhl for comments which helped me to sharpen the argument presented here, and to audiences at the University of Munich, Yale University and the University of Chiba where earlier versions of this chapter were delivered.

[2] The debate has a longer pedigree still. See Richard Tuck, *Philosophy and Government, 1572–1651* (Cambridge: Cambridge University Press, 1993). Standard eighteenth-century attempts to fathom the relationship between philosophy and government sought to understand it developmentally in terms of longer-term conjectural histories of society. From this perspective, the Enlightenment itself might usefully be seen as revolving around debates about the history of enlightenment – or around rival genealogies of the relations between theory and practice. My point here is that after the American Revolution, and more particularly after the French Revolution, the stakes involved in deciding upon the terms of trade between theory and practice intensified dramatically.

arrangements could be evaluated, or should it strive to predict the
probable consequences of actions pursued under differing kinds of
political system? The main advocates of the answers to these questions
became ideologically polarised by the end of the eighteenth century.
Divergence bred hostility; hostility brought confusion. The absence of
current consensus on how political judgement should be understood is
a product of this process of ideological struggle.

A twentieth-century historian turned philosopher once tried to erect
a political theory on the assumption that any theory must subtract
from the subtlety of practice. Writing in 1947 with both the Butler
Education Act and the work of Friedrich von Hayek in his sights,
Michael Oakeshott set out to ridicule attempts to provide a recipe
for 'practical knowledge'.[3] The aim of advancing political reform by
seeking to implement a comprehensive scheme for social improvement seemed to Oakeshott at once monstrous and forlorn – a cas-
ualty of the determination to rationalise prudence into a technique,
inaugurated by the heirs of Machiavelli.[4] But despite his posture of
magisterial disdain, Oakeshott soon found himself running in cir-
cles. Judgement, he argued, was not a method but a kind of 'connoisseurship'. Yet connoisseurship, or a 'taste' for politics, of the kind
that Oakeshott approved comprised nothing other than a capacity for
applied practical understanding. Practical understanding of this sort
was simply a form of political technique rooted in a social context
more to Oakeshott's liking.[5]

---

[3] Michael Oakeshott, 'Rationalism in Politics' (1947) repr. in *Rationalism in
Politics and Other Essays* (1962) (Indianapolis: Liberty Press, 1991), p. 29.
Although von Hayek is singled out for criticism in Oakeshott's essay (p. 26), he
is clearly the lesser target. For a resort to 'reasonableness' instead of 'rationalism'
as an appropriate guide to politics, see Michael Oakeshott, 'Scientific Politics',
Cambridge Journal, 1:6 (March 1948), pp. 347–58; Michael Oakeshott,
'Rational Conduct', *Cambridge Journal*, 4:1 (October 1950), pp. 3–27, rev. edn
in *Rationalism in Politics and Other Essays*; and Michael Oakeshott, 'Political
Education' (1951) in *Rationalism in Politics and Other Essays*.

[4] Oakeshott, 'Rationalism in Politics', p. 30: 'it was not Machiavelli himself,
but his followers, who believed in the sovereignty of technique'. Cf. Michael
Oakeshott, 'The Tower of Babel' (1948) in *Rationalism in Politics and Other
Essays*.

[5] Oakeshott, 'Rationalism in Politics', pp. 15, 29, 41. A fuller account of
Oakeshott's position would have to relate his doctrine of political connoisseurship to his notion of distinct 'modes' of experience and the conversational
(as opposed to systematic) character of relations between them. On this, see

It would be foolish to ignore the suggestion that the relationship between theory and practice is problematic. Dissonance between the two has commonly been held responsible for the violent collision between facts and values characteristic of revolutionary upheaval.[6] But we can surely do better than Oakeshott in explaining the character of the collision. This chapter develops an explanation by clarifying the issues that have been at stake among opposing views of the role of political judgement from the French Revolution down to the end of the twentieth century. It proceeds by reopening the pivotal debate on the relation between philosophy and politics which erupted after 1789. But it begins with older traditions of argument that ultimately fed into that debate. After setting out the constitutive elements of classical thought that underlay the project of an Enlightenment science of politics, I focus on the conflict between moral and historical prudence as this came to a head in the ideological polemics staged in the 1790s.

This conflict has been variously epitomised over the course of the last two centuries. It has been described in terms of a collision between morality and politics; it has been cast as a confrontation between enlightenment and established opinion; and it has been set out in terms of an antithesis between cosmopolitanism and patriotism. These pairs of contrasts have in turn been regularly connected to one another. Their relations were first systematically examined in the 1790s by Immanuel Kant. In a polemical contribution to the September issue of the *Berlinische Monatsschrift* in 1793, Kant mounted a comprehensive assault on what he presented as a rising tide of Prussian and Hanoverian empiricism directed against the dignity of theory. Kant

Michael Oakeshott, 'The Voice of Poetry in the Conversation of Mankind' (1959) in *Rationalism in Politics and Other Essays*. For a full account of Oakeshott's thinking in this connection, see Efraim Podoksik, *In Defence of Modernity: Vision and Philosophy in Michael Oakeshott* (Charlottesville, VA: Imprint Academic, 2003), Part I.

[6] For variations on this theme in post-war scholarship, see J. L. Talmon, *The Origins of Totalitarian Democracy: Political Theory and Practice during the French Revolution* (London: Martin Secker and Warburg, 1952); Isaiah Berlin, 'Two Concepts of Liberty' (1958) repr. in *Four Essays on Liberty* (Oxford: Oxford University Press, 1969); John Dunn, *Modern Revolutions: An Introduction to the Analysis of a Political Phenomenon* (Cambridge: Cambridge University Press, 1972); Bernard Williams, 'Saint-Just's Illusion' in *Making Sense of Humanity and Other Philosophical Papers* (Cambridge: Cambridge University Press, 1998).

defended the role of judgement as enabling the passage from theory to practice in experimental science, in moral conduct and in political life alike. Orientating oneself in science or technology without recourse to general rules of procedure was equivalent to muddling through the world of affairs in the absence of the slightest guide to action. Scientific procedure shorn of theoretical abstraction is condemned to absolute confusion, Kant contended; in a similar vein he claimed that political judgement bereft of normative principles reduces to a hapless struggle for power.[7]

The Kantian analogy between judgement in natural science and in political affairs might be seen as advancing the claims of enlightenment against arbitrary prejudice. The analogy, however, is fundamentally flawed since power is not enlightened merely by the acquisition of knowledge. It is the case that the limitations of the analogy are implicit in Kant's treatment. But they are never made explicit – indeed, if anything, they are occluded. The implicit limitations are evident in Kant's distinct handling of the figure of the economic and political expert on the one hand and that of the sovereign legislator on the other. Cameralist advice, Kant makes clear, is refined by the addition of new empirical insights; but he also argues that sovereignty can never be rendered more just by an increase in the knowledge of public utility.[8] Thus on a Kantian prospectus the conduct of public administration shares with the application of technology the possibility of improvement by means of the experimental method. The cause of justice, however, is never served by the most exhaustive exercise of empirical prudence. In fact, the legitimation of sovereignty on the basis of expert judgement amounts from Kant's perspective to an apology for despotism. At the

[7] Immanuel Kant, *Über den Gemeinspruch: Das mag in der Theorie richtig sein, taugt aber nicht für die Praxis (1793) und Zum ewigen Frieden: Ein philosophischer Entwurf (1795)*, ed. Heiner F. Klemme (Hamburg: Felix Meiner Verlag, 1992), pp. 3–6. Kant begins by framing his intervention as a response to the avowed Burkeanism of August Wilhelm Rehberg, Friedrich von Gentz and Christian Garve. He then proceeds to focus his arguments against the moral and political principles of Garve, Hobbes and Moses Mendelssohn.
[8] *Ibid.*, pp. 3, 31. The kinds of expert exhibited by Kant include the agricultural economist (*Landwirt*) and the public official (*Kameralist*) (p. 3). That the common welfare is not reducible to empirical utility is clearly asserted: 'The phrase, *salus populi suprema civitatis lex est*, retains its irreducible value and respect; but the public well-being that must above all be considered is precisely that lawful constitution which secures to each their freedom through laws' (p. 31).

same time, a bid to enlighten authority by the coercive judgement of the people is a recipe for destructive revolution.[9]

Modern theories of political judgement for the most part take their bearings from the legacy of Kantian critical philosophy. Kant's influence has been felt in two dimensions. First of all, attempts to construct a modern science of politics have drawn inspiration from the Kantian project of demarcating science through a systematic criticism of metaphysics. From Neurath to Popper, the objective of political reform was constructed on the analogy of scientific method. On this worldview, social progress is assumed to depend on the methodical criticism of dogma.[10] This simplified version of a genuinely Kantian approach verges on a parody of enlightenment in general, where enlightenment is understood as a commitment to subjecting political authority to intellectual scrutiny.[11] The widespread success that has attended this way of proceeding has given succour to the second dimension in which the distorted legacy of Kant has held sway over political philosophy. This is the idea that the criticism of authority is most appropriately pursued by passing moral judgement on the exercise of power.

[9] *Ibid.*, pp. 22, 34: government devoted eudaimonistically to the welfare of the people is 'the greatest despotism thinkable' (p. 22); the resort to coercive popular rights against the state involves recourse to 'complete lawlessness' (p. 34).

[10] I have selected both Neurath and Popper here as rival representatives of the Viennese 'Enlightenment's' scientific challenge to superstition and backwardness as exemplified by Ernst Mach, *Erkenntnis und Irrtum: Skizzen zur Psychologie der Forschung* (Leipzig: J. A. Barth, 1905), pp. 454–5. For Neurath's commitment to rationalism in the field of social choice, see his 'Die Verirrten des Cartesius und das Auxiliarmotiv: zur Psychologie des Entschlusses', *Jahrbuch der philosophischen Gesellschaft an der Universität zu Wien* (1913), pp. 57–67; for his charge that Popper was a pseudo-rationalist, see his 'Pseudorationalismus der Falsifikation', *Erkenntnis*, 5 (1935), pp. 16–22. Popper himself took Neurath to task for his understanding of scientific method in *The Logic of Scientific Discovery* (1935) (London: Routledge, 1992), pp. 76–9; he set out to expose Neurath's utopianism in *The Poverty of Historicism* (1936–45) (London: Routledge, 1957, 2002). For a more sympathetic understanding of their shared project, see Popper's 'Memories of Otto Neurath' in Otto Neurath, *Empiricism and Sociology*, ed. Marie Neurath and Robert S. Cohen (Dordrecht: D. Reidel, 1973), p. 53.

[11] For the presentation of *fin de siècle* Viennese progressive intellectual culture as exemplifying Enlightenment or 'late Enlightenment' (*Spätaufklärung*) characteristics, see Friedrich Stadler, 'Spätaufklärung und Sozialdemokratie in Wien, 1918–1938' in Franz Kadrnoska, ed., *Aufbruch und Untergang: Österreichische Kultur zwischen 1918 und 1938* (Vienna, Munich and Zurich: Euroverlag, 1981).

In the pages that follow, I defend the argument that both of these preconceptions about the nature of political judgement promote an inadequate grasp of the reality of orientating oneself in politics. The first approach is basically architectonic in character, construing practical judgement as a branch of theoretical reason. It is tempting to see this conception as deriving originally from Socrates insofar as it treats political problems as examples of more general problems of knowledge. But the second approach undoubtedly is of Socratic provenance insofar as it seeks to solve political problems through moral judgement.[12] My focus is on the simplification that inevitably accompanies this second approach to politics. In collapsing political problems into forms of moral argument, political judgement is reduced to the judgement of intentions. Historical judgement, which relates intended actions and their unintended consequences, is replaced by the activity of moral prudence.

I   Morals and politics: Socrates to Popper

Kant understood the business of politics to be concerned with the well-being of states. The maintenance of their well-being was enjoined upon their sovereigns as a duty of right (*Rechtspflicht*). This judgement of duty had to be based on moral theory, not on the calculation of practical benefits. *All* would be lost, as Kant put it dramatically, if political rights were confused with projected utilities.[13] Practical judgement was thus identified with the faculty of moral reason rather than with historical understanding. Kant did claim that the enlightenment of moral reason would be a matter of historical process rather than an achievement of the moral faculty itself. Nonetheless, the severe reduction of political theory to the effective use of the *faculty* of judgement persisted through the annals of neo-Kantian analysis. To the extent that reliance on this faculty did not entail estimating courses of action by way of reference to outcomes judged to be probable (*wahrscheinlich*) in accordance with previous experience, it ruled out the involvement of historical reasoning.[14] Even where modern attempts to solve the riddle of practical judgement have not resorted to the

---

[12] On this, see Raymond Geuss, 'What is political judgement?' in this volume, pp. 29–46.
[13] Kant, *Über den Gemeinspruch*, p. 5.   [14] *Ibid*.

standard procedure of seeking to resolve political problems through moral reasoning, they have concerned themselves with a search for seemingly more serviceable 'faculties' – the faculty of aesthetic judgement is one example – thus forgetting the first lesson of historical prudence: namely, that political understanding is not advanced by the philosophical scrutiny of a mental faculty.[15]

John Dunn has written that prudence should stand at the centre of political analysis. From that position it can 'steady and deepen' our understanding of public affairs.[16] Prudence here is another word for judgement in practical matters. But practical matters can be understood in either moral or political terms. If we are to elucidate the role that prudence ought to play in the world at large we therefore need to be clear about whether we are using the word in its moral or political sense. There is a long philosophical tradition of treating practical reason within the framework of moral theory. Prudence, or *phronêsis*, from Aristotle onwards has for the most part been interpreted in the sense of reasoning practically in the field of ethics.[17] But this curious restriction should prompt us to consider how practical reason might be more appropriately understood in relation to political affairs.

---

[15] See Ronald Beiner, *Political Judgement* (London: Methuen, 1983). Cf. Hannah Arendt, *Lectures on Kant's Political Philosophy*, ed. Ronald Beiner (Chicago and London: University of Chicago Press, 1982). Also relevant in this context is Hans-Georg Gadamer, *Wahrheit und Methode: Grundzüge einer philosophischen Hermeneutik* (1960) (Tübingen: J. C. Mohr, 1972), I, i, 1.

[16] John Dunn, 'Reconceiving the Content and Character of Modern Political Community' in *Interpreting Modern Political Responsibility: Essays 1981– 1989* (Cambridge: Polity Press, 1990), p. 214. The argument is more fully developed in John Dunn, *The Cunning of Unreason: Making Sense of Politics* (London: HarperCollins, 2000), pp. 180–208.

[17] For practical reasoning in moral life see Aristotle, *Nicomachean Ethics* III (1111b5–1113a2), VI and VII, and *De Anima* III, 7. For scholarly opinion on Aristotle's discussion of the topic, see Richard Sorabji, 'Aristotle on the Role of Intellect in Virtue', *Aristotelian Society Proceedings*, 74 (1973–4), pp. 107–29; David Wiggins, 'Deliberation and Practical Reason' in Amélie Oksenberg Rorty, ed., *Essays on Aristotle's Ethics* (Berkeley, Los Angeles and London: University of California Press, 1980); R. B. Louden, 'Aristotle's Practical Particularism' in J. P. Anton and A. Preuss, eds. *Aristotle's Ethics: Essays in Ancient Philosophy*, IV (Albany, NY: State University of New York Press, 1991); P. Gotlieb, 'Aristotle on Dividing the Soul and Uniting the Virtues', *Phronesis*, 39 (1994), pp. 275–90. For an overview of the subject in Greek thought, see Terence Irwin, 'Prudence and Morality in Greek Ethics', *Ethics*, 105 (January 1995), pp. 284–95; Julia Annas, 'Prudence and Morality in Ancient and Modern Ethics', *Ethics*, 105 (January 1995), pp. 241–57.

The Aristotelian conception of *phronêsis* as moral judgement ultimately derived from a Socratic arrangement of priorities.[18] The ethical turn in philosophy with which Socrates is usually credited should not simply be contrasted with earlier philosophical cosmologies: it should also be distinguished from specifically political forms of inquiry.[19] It was Plato who gave momentum to the privilege accorded in subsequent traditions of thought to an ethical interpretation of the function of practical reason. In the *Republic* and the *Laws* alike, the science of legislation was charged with regulating communal life in accordance with a philosophical norm of justice. The presumption was that theory (*logos*) could show how justice depended on philosophy's government of power – or, in practice (*ergon*), how the world of human affairs could best approximate that arrangement.[20]

Phronêsis in Plato is a branch of moral science. This interpretation of the role of practical reason can be distinguished from a perspective in which judgement is understood as a form of historical prudence. Practical reasoning in this sense sets out to understand the systematic relationship between deliberate intentions and accidental

---

[18] The Socratic origin of the classical debate about *phronêsis* is spelled out by Aristotle himself. See Aristotle, *Nicomachean Ethics* VI (1144b15–1144b25) and VII (1145b20–1146b5). Aristotle's engagement with Socrates occurs in the midst of his clarification of the role of *phronêsis* in moral judgement. Commentators standardly remark upon Aristotle's revision of Socrates; but his own sense of his continuity with his predecessor is equally important: 'Socrates in a way examined the matter correctly' (1144b19).

[19] As exemplified, for example, by Solon: see his elegy on the advent of tyranny among the Athenians as an unintended consequence of human action – not a result of simple moral failure or of divine retribution – as recorded in the *Universal History* of Diodorus Siculus. The relevant Solonian verses are reproduced in *Greek Elegiac Poetry*, trans. Douglas E. Gerber (Cambridge, MA: Harvard University Press, 1999), pp. 125–7.

[20] On the theory (*logos*) of philosophical statesmanship, see Plato, *Republic*, 471e1–473d9; for the approximation of theory (*logos*) to practice (*ergon*), see Plato, *Laws*, 636a–b; for a clear statement of the combination of virtue (*aretê*) and knowledge (*epistêmê*) required for the government of a just polity, see Plato, *Politicus*, 301d. For recent discussion of the development of Plato's political thought, see Christopher Rowe, ed., *Reading the Statesman* (Sankt Augustin: Akademia Verlag, 1995); André Laks, 'The Laws' in Christopher Rowe and Malcolm Schofield, eds., *The Cambridge History of Greek and Roman Political Thought* (Cambridge: Cambridge University Press, 2000); Christopher Bobonich, *Plato's Utopia Recast* (Oxford: Oxford University Press, 2002); Malcolm Schofield, *Plato: Political Philosophy* (Oxford: Oxford University Press, 2006).

outcomes. Its purpose is to generalise about political reasons and causes rather than to establish ethical norms – to account for the conditions of social and political agency instead of framing the parameters of moral responsibility. Thucydides exemplified the perspective of historical reason: his aim was to present the 'truest explanation' for the political events he was narrating.[21] It was Xenophon who tried to make historical explanation serve a general political theory. To succeed in his purpose, he needed to itemise the circumstances that favoured the emergence of talented leaders. He insisted against both Socrates and Plato that political judgement was a practical skill rather than a subject of scientific study.[22] However, even the most outstanding practitioner of politics is at the mercy of the constitution inside which they are constrained to operate. As Xenophon is at pains to emphasise in the *Cyropaedia*, for all his overwhelming practical genius Cyrus unintentionally generated the collapse of his own regime. The message of Xenophon's narrative is clear: historical study must discover the institutional arrangements that best support the pragmatic skills required to win from men their willing obedience.[23] So while the Platonic project strove to establish a moral science of prudence, Xenophon endeavoured to systematise historical prudence. By common consent both enterprises failed. Plato diverted political judgement into moral science while Xenophon was left meditating on the tragedy of human frailty.

The standard textbook versions of the thought of Plato and Aristotle underline the decisive differences between their respective projects. To this extent the common view dovetails with Aristotle's design.[24] Their differences of course are fundamental, not to say obvious. But the overlap is arguably just as important. Practical reason (*phronêsis*) in Aristotle remains concerned with moral deliberation. Prudence is contingent not on political organisation but on the ethical disposition

---

[21] Thucydides, *Historiae*, ed. H. S. Jones (Oxford: Oxford University Press, 1900), 2 vols., I, XXIII, 6. My phrase 'truest explanation' renders Thucydides' *alêthestatên prophasin*, which could equally be taken in the sense of 'fundamental cause' – more fundamental, that is, than either protagonist appreciated, and so more basic than their separate intentions.

[22] Xenophon, *Oeconomicus* XXI, 8–12.   [23] Xenophon, *Cyropaedia* I, i, 3.

[24] For Aristotle's view that Plato developed a modified version of Socratism to be distinguished from Aristotle's own project, see Aristotle, *Nicomachean Ethics* VII (1145b30): 'There are some [e.g. Plato] who accept the [Socratic] doctrine in some respects.'

of the ruler.[25] The *Nicomachean Ethics* underlines this point by an exercise in creative etymology: the word 'moderation' (*sôphrosunê*) is a neologism – Aristotle tells us – whose meaning has the sense of 'conserving prudence' (*sôzousa tên phronêsin*).[26] Prudent judgement is a function not of a moderate regime but of the moral moderation of the statesman.[27] This vision of enlightened statesmanship continued to attract supporters down to the eighteenth century, and beyond; but it was also seriously challenged by the constitutional theory of the Enlightenment.

Montesquieu's famous comment to the effect that it is pointless scolding political reality for its failure to oblige the aspirations of moral criticism should be seen as a negative verdict on the method of collapsing political analysis into moral prudence, as exemplified by Aristotle.[28] The alternative approach, developed in *The Spirit of the Laws*, was to examine the circumstantial relations between human desires, social attitudes and political institutions with a view to establishing empirical laws governing those relations.[29] In the absence of discovering laws of sufficient generality to guide historical prudence, political analysis would be forced to depend on pragmatic skill for the conduct of affairs, as occurred in Xenophon. In that case, the

[25] Aristotle, *Nicomachean Ethics* VI (1141b24–30), on the architectonic nature of the mental faculty of practical wisdom. Cf. Plato, *Politicus*, 292c–d, on knowledge rather than regime form as the distinguishing feature of a polity.

[26] Aristotle, *Nicomachean Ethics* VI (1140b10–15). Aristotle's example of a commonly accepted prudent man is Pericles, distinguished for his capacity to establish the best opinion as to how to promote a good life.

[27] Cf. *Politics* III (1281b1). Where 'the people' (*plêthos*) is statesman, the justice of the arrangement is defended in terms of the collective *phronêsis* of the many (*hoi polloi*).

[28] Charles-Louis Montesquieu, 'De la politique' in *Œuvres complètes*, ed. Roger Caillois (Paris: Gallimard, 1949), 2 vols., I, p. 112: 'Il est inutile d'attacquer directement la politique en faisant voir combien elle répugne à la morale, à la raison, à la justice.'

[29] Montesquieu, *De l'esprit des lois* in *ibid.*, II, p. 238: 'C'est ce que j'entreprends de faire dans cet ouvrage. J'examinerai tous ces rapports: ils forment tous ensemble ce que l'on appelle l'ESPRIT DES LOIS.' A fuller analysis of Montesquieu's method would have to take account of the way in which the 'rapports' he discovers are derived, as David Hume saw, from Malebranchian metaphysics, and so cannot properly be described as empirical relations. See David Hume, *Enquiries Concerning Human Understanding and Concerning the Principles of Morals*, ed. L. A. Selby-Bigge and P. H. Nidditch (Oxford: Oxford University Press, 3rd rev. edn 1975), p. 197n.

judgement of how to sustain optimal political arrangements would be reduced to a matter of superior skill in public administration. Alexander Pope had defended this option with heroic simplicity in the 1730s, 'For Forms of Government let fools contest;/Whate'er is best administer'd is best.'[30] Pope was merely adapting the Aristotelian formulation: 'of the correct constitutions there are three, and the best must be the one that is administered by the best'.[31]

Taking up the question of whether politics could be reduced to a science in 1742, David Hume cited these lines from Pope as capturing a set of assumptions about political organisation which needed to be challenged.[32] Whilst putting an end to debate about 'Forms of Government' had its attractions for Hume as a prophylactic against party strife in the domestic politics of Walpolean Britain, a resolution of the kind would in reality be an argument in favour of the unlimited prerogative of rulers. 'All absolute governments must very much depend on the administration', Hume observed.[33] Under this type of government the quality of rule was identical to the quality of execution. There was no competing organ of state to block the executive's decisions, and for that reason no political means of offsetting the autonomy of its resolutions. As a result, the designs of the government would simply track the prejudices of its ruler. Political judgement would be confined to the moral prudence of the chief administrator. This meant that the application of the doctrine of moral prudence to

---

[30] Alexander Pope, *Essay on Man*, ed. Maynard Mack (London: Methuen, 1950), Book III, lines 303–4.

[31] Aristotle, *Politics* III (1288a30–35).

[32] David Hume, 'That Politics May Be Reduced to a Science' (1742) in *Essays Moral, Political and Literary*, ed. Eugene F. Miller (Indianapolis: Liberty Press, 1985, 1987), p. 14: 'It is a question with several, whether there be any essential difference between one form of government and another? and, whether every form may not become good or bad, according as it is well or ill administered?' For the wider intellectual context of the Humean science of politics, see Duncan Forbes, *Hume's Philosophical Politics* (Cambridge: Cambridge University Press, 1975); James Moore, 'Hume's Political Science and the Classical Republican Tradition', *Canadian Journal of Political Science*, 10 (1977), pp. 809–39; Robert Mankin, 'Can Jealousy Be Reduced to a Science? Politics and Economics in Hume's *Essays*', *Journal of the History of Economic Thought*, 27 (March 2005), pp. 59–70; Istvan Hont, *Jealousy of Trade: International Competition and the Nation-State in Historical Perspective* (Cambridge, MA: Harvard University Press, 2005), ch. 4.

[33] Hume, 'That Politics May Be Reduced to a Science', p. 15.

political life was a recipe for promoting the management of public affairs by the unimpeded will of the principal magistrate.

However, as Hume went on to argue, historical analysis could be used to demonstrate the political imprudence of entrusting the affairs of state to the unregulated judgement of a supreme ruler. The demonstration would be based on certain *a priori* principles, and Machiavelli could be drawn upon to illustrate the procedure: 'There is an observation in MACHIAVEL ... which I think, may be regarded as one of those eternal political truths, which no time nor accidents can vary.'[34] The observation in question appears in chapter 4 of *The Prince*, relating to the conquests of Alexander. As Hume saw it, Machiavelli's treatment highlighted the fact that moderation in politics is always the wiser course of action. But more importantly it underlined how moderation in public life could not be made a function of moral prudence.

As Machiavelli had emphasised, the Persians endured their slavery under the yoke of Alexander because they had been accustomed to despotic rule by Darius and his predecessors. But such slavery, Hume argued, does not pay: neither the ruler nor the ruled stand to benefit from the arrangement. Not only does the yoke of a despot annihilate public spirit, it also fails to offer security against the onset of revolution. Among 'eastern' governments military satraps pose a constant threat to public order, whereas the 'milder' European monarchies secure the allegiance of their noble families and thereby consolidate the stability of the regime.[35] Gentle government, as against despotic rule, is therefore better equipped to serve the goal of peace through moderation. Two conclusions, Hume explained, immediately follow: first, moderation can be justified on the grounds of reason of state; but second, moderation should be understood as a product of political restraint imposed upon the exercise of power. The regulated intercourse between political forces rather than the quality of a ruler's moral disposition secured a society against the kind of abuse brought about by the unimpeded application of governmental power. As Hume put it: 'Legislators, therefore, ought not to trust the future government

---

[34] *Ibid.*, pp. 16–17, 21. It is clear that Hume does not mean necessary truths deductively inferred: he is thinking in terms of law-like generalisations about human affairs ascertained by means of historical investigation.

[35] *Ibid.*, pp. 22, 24.

of a state to chance, but ought to provide a system of laws to regulate the administration of public affairs to the latest posterity.'[36]

Hume's analysis depends on Xenophon as much as it is derived from Machiavelli.[37] But his point, in any case, is clear: historical study surveys particular cases so as to provide the material for generalisations which can be used in turn to guide political judgement. However, the most important claim was contained in the conclusions of Hume's argument following on from the application of historical prudence. The key result was that political science should not be treated as a form of applied moral reasoning, which in truth could lead to nothing better than the wise administration of a philosophical ruler or benevolent despot. Instead, a true science of politics should seek to understand how the effects of average moral shortcomings among the members of a society could be counteracted by the impact of the constitutional regulation of opposing political forces on public life. For the study of politics the implication was striking: namely, that the standard philosophical preoccupation with the moral virtues ought to be subordinated to a science of systematic political relationships made available through the application of historical prudence.

Commenting favourably in 1980 on the return of moral reasoning to the centre of theoretical debate about politics in the United States since the publication in 1971 of John Rawls' *A Theory of Justice*, Albert Hirschman regretted the historical separation of what he termed an 'analytical-scientific' style of reasoning about society from the method of evaluating political theory in terms of morals. Hirschman identified what he took to have been a tradition of political thought extending from Machiavelli to Montesquieu as bearing responsibility for this separation, culminating in the impoverishment

---

[36] *Ibid.*, p. 24.

[37] *Ibid.*, pp. 22–23n. Hume draws on the evidence supplied by Xenophon's *Cyropaedia* (II, i, 9) to advance the thesis – against Machiavelli ('the FLORENTINE secretary, who seems to have been better acquainted with the ROMAN than the GREEK authors, was mistaken') – that Persian society had originally contained a powerful nobility until the reforms of Cyrus the Great. The point of the *Cyropaedia* seems to have been to try to illustrate the consequences which followed on from Cyrus' decision to extinguish the historic privileges of the *homotimoi* (nobility). Hume's treatment of Machiavelli should be seen as a reworking since it is not obvious that *The Prince* assumes moderation to be a reason of state.

of political understanding.[38] Over a third of a century after this reorientation was supposedly introduced into political philosophy by the quasi-Kantian contractualism of Rawls, it is surely time to question the validity of Hirschman's judgement.[39] His proposal to reintegrate normative and social scientific modes of analysis risks substituting moral criticism for political restraint and so accidentally rehabilitating the pretensions of enlightened despotism against which Humean theory had been deployed.

I take Dunn's appeal to the virtue of prudence in public life as forming part of a plea for a science of politics which rejects the resort to political moralisation promoted by the traditions of Anglo-American moral philosophy that rose to dominate political theory over a generation ago. This sort of appeal has been hampered throughout the course of the past half-century by a set of arguments that have cast doubt on the pretensions of political analysis to qualifying as any kind of theoretical science. The ethical turn in political philosophy is to this extent connected to alarm about the grandiose claims of theory. It was Karl Popper who led the way in stigmatising this grandiosity.[40] But having rejected the ambition to develop a theoretical science of

[38] Albert O. Hirschman, *Essays in Trespassing: Economics to Politics and Beyond* (Cambridge: Cambridge University Press, 1981, 1984), pp. 287, 295–6. Hirschman begins by targeting the agenda implied in the Montesquieu fragment, 'De la politique', cited above.

[39] For a critical perspective on attempts to establish political philosophy on the model of an 'applied ethics', see Raymond Geuss, 'Introduction' in Raymond Geuss, *Outside Ethics* (Princeton, NJ: Princeton University Press, 2005), p. 7; on Rawls in particular, see Geuss, 'Neither History nor Praxis' in *ibid.*, pp. 29–39.

[40] Popper drew strength from Friedrich von Hayek's endorsement of his project in this regard. See F. A. von Hayek, 'Economics and Knowledge' in Hayek, *Individualism and Economic Order* (Chicago and London: University of Chicago Press, 1948), p. 33n; F. A. von Hayek, *The Counter-Revolution of Science: Studies on the Abuse of Reason* (Indianapolis: Liberty Press, 1952, 1979), p. 384. But in reality their arguments significantly diverged from one another. Incremental planning is as problematic if not as destructive as grand planning in Hayek's vision. Popper's criticisms were directed against the crystallisation of Hegelianism in figures of both the right and the left from Spengler to Mannheim. Hayek on the other hand was following Carl Menger and Ludwig von Mises in targeting the 'pragmatism' of the German historical school of political economy. For Menger's specifically focused indictment of *Pragmatismus*, see Carl Menger, *Untersuchungen über die Methode der Sozialwissenschaften, und der politischen Oekonomie insbesondere* (Leipzig: Duncker and Humblot, 1883), pp. 201–4; for Hayek's debt to Menger, see

politics, Popper succeeded inadvertently in collapsing political rule into a species of moral administration. Hume had countered precisely this reduction by means of an appeal to political theory against applied political skill. However, Popper reverted to a pre-Humean perspective which assumed that government behaviour was best modified by 'piecemeal' improvements in its operation through incremental refinements in the application of public power. Popper characterised his endeavour as a revolt against the despotism of holistic schemes of social science, but actually he constructed a model of enlightened administration in which the dimensions of the element of enlightenment were scaled down.[41]

This result is all the more astonishing given Popper's declared aim of calling the proto-scientific designs of political philosophy in the form of Platonism, positivism and utopian socialism to account.[42] It was the more modern versions of the age-old aspiration to a science of society that he was particularly keen to expose. He traced this modern tendency, designated by the term 'historicism', back to the intellectual programme of the Enlightenment – 'perhaps the greatest of all moral and spiritual revolutions of history'.[43] But his account of the dangers that beset a science of politics is as problematic as the solution proposed by Hirschman. The inadequacy of Popper's account is best illustrated by going back over the genealogy which he himself supplied for the emergence of the spurious scientific claims of modern historicism – claims which he took to have guided the progress of totalitarianism in recent history.[44]

Bruce Caldwell, *Hayek's Challenge: An Intellectual Biography of F. A. Hayek* (Chicago and London: University of Chicago Press, 2004).

[41] See Popper, *Historicism*, pp. 80–1, on the piecemeal 'technologist' or 'scientific politician'.

[42] For Popper's own autobiographical description of the forces to which he was opposed, see Karl R. Popper, *Unended Quest: An Intellectual Autobiography* (London: Routledge, 1974, 2002), pp. 30–9. For Popper's intellectual development, see Malachi Haim Hacohen, *Karl Popper: The Formative Years, 1902–1945* (Cambridge: Cambridge University Press, 2000).

[43] Karl R. Popper, 'Preface to the Second Edition', in *The Open Society and Its Enemies* (London: Routledge and Kegan Paul, 1945, 3rd rev. edn 1957), 2 vols., I, p. ix.

[44] Many of the positions criticised by Popper in *Historicism* are more fully identified with specific figures in Felix Kaufmann's *Methodenlehre der Sozialwissenschaft* (Vienna: Julius Springer Verlag, 1936), esp. pp. 129–53, on which Popper drew. For navigating a path through the *Methodenstreit*, Popper

Historicism is presented in *The Open Society and Its Enemies* as the great peril destined to subvert modern civilisation if left unopposed. The habit of thought guiding historicism found expression both in nationalism and in National Socialism in the twentieth century, but the style of reasoning itself arose out of the aspiration to found a science capable of being applied to the advancement of human welfare. This ambition may have been 'admirable', but it was also 'dangerous', in Popper's terms.[45] The very rationalism of the undertaking left the project vulnerable to irrationalism since the objective far exceeded what social science could in fact achieve. A science of society, unlike a science of physical nature, could not predict the future. Historicism, however, did precisely try to anticipate and manipulate the future by subjecting social processes to a theory of inevitable change. This doctrine of inevitability was supported by a method of selecting facts to suit the theory. This practice, in Popper's estimate, was rather an example of superstitious prejudice than a case of scientific explanation.[46] So the question remained of how such superstition could be counteracted.

It could not be opposed by a genuinely demarcated science, according to Popper, since social processes were not amenable to scientific explanation in any way remotely comparable to theoretical physics.[47] An explanation of the kind would have to deduce particular events from generalising laws, whereas historical explanation is concerned to account for specific occurrences on the evidence of antecedent events. Abstract or universal generalisations cannot sensibly be made to explain or 'cover' the raw materials of historical data, which

was also indebted to Viktor Kraft, *Die Grundformen der wissenschaftlichen Methoden* (Vienna: Verlag der Österreichische Akademie der Wissenschaften, 1925). For the idea of a 'Historicist' genealogy connecting Plato to Hegel, Popper drew on M. B. Foster, *The Political Philosophies of Plato and Hegel* (Oxford: Oxford University Press, 1935).

[45] Popper, *Open Society*, 'Preface to the Second Edition', I, p. ix.

[46] Popper, *Historicism*, pp. 105–9. Cf. Karl R. Popper, 'Truth, Rationality, and the Growth of Scientific Knowledge' in Popper, *Conjectures and Refutations: The Growth of Scientific Knowledge* (London: Routledge, 1960, 1963); 'Prediction and Prophecy in the Social Sciences' (1948) in *ibid.*; 'Utopia and Violence' (1948) in *ibid.*

[47] Popper, *Open Society*, II, 261 ff. On theory construction in Popper, see Herbert Keuth, *The Philosophy of Popper* (Cambridge: Cambridge University Press, 2005), pp. 51–108. On Popper's own formulation of his divergence from Henri Poincaré and Pierre Duhem, see *Historicism*, pp. 121–2n.

consist of an endless stream of incomparable events.[48] By virtue of the uniqueness of each individual circumstance, history is resistant to any process of 'theorisation'.[49] This conclusion landed Popper in a curious position. It obliged him to present the management of political affairs as a matter of incremental empirical adjustment. However, this is exactly what he did not want to argue. After all, he had set out to defend a project of viable political reform.[50] Yet reform is simply impossible without an assessment of probable outcomes – without reliance on historical prediction. Having denied this possibility, Popper is left championing the cause of critical inquiry against the hegemony of political and metaphysical superstition.

This was a fine critical gesture against authority, but it was hardly a credible theory of how to curtail the abuse of power. It was a retreat from, rather than an advance on, David Hume. Still, Popper was disposed to think of it as a development of Kant. As a gesture, it amounted to a partisan appeal to what Popper mistakenly took to have been the core agenda of the Enlightenment.[51] This appeal was more rhetorical than instrumentally focused insofar as it was destitute of the elements of a programme of action: in the end, Popper merely summons the enlighteners of the world to unite against the combination of prejudice and power.[52] This call has been misidentified as a definite political project because it capitalised on positive-sounding idioms of the Enlightenment. But in the process of trading promiscuously on this resource, Popper impoverished the fund on which he

---

[48] Popper, *Historicism*, p. 71, where he is drawing on Heinrich Gomperz, *Weltanschauungslehre* (Jena: Diederichs, 1908), 2 vols.

[49] Popper, *Historicism*, pp. 98–120, where the main targets are Comte and Mill – the former's holism and the latter's inductivism. Cf. Carl G. Hempel, 'The Function of General Laws in History' in *Aspects of Scientific Explanation and Other Essays in the Philosophy of Science* (New York: The Free Press, 1965). Popper's views on causation and explanation were originally set out in *The Logic of Scientific Discovery*, pp. 38–40. For the claim that Hempel derived his ideas from Popper, as evidenced by his review of *Logik der Forschung* in *Deutsche Literaturzeitung*, 8 (1937), pp. 310–14, see Popper, *Open Society*, II, p. 264n. For discussion of the general model, see Alan Donagan, 'The Popper–Hempel Theory Reconsidered' in William H. Dray, ed., *Philosophical Analysis and History* (Westport, CT: Greenwood Press, 1966).

[50] Popper, *Open Society*, I, pp. 1–3.

[51] Karl R. Popper, 'Kant's Critique and Cosmology, I: Kant and the Enlightenment' in Popper, *Conjectures and Refutations*.

[52] Popper, *Open Society*, 'Preface to the First Edition', I, p. vii.

drew. He distorted the contribution which the Enlightenment science of politics actually made.

This distortion, however, was not the original work of Popper: its genesis lay in the period before 1789. But after that date, opposing schemes for the development of a science of politics drew yet more radically apart. Popper was an inheritor of that polarity. So equally were Oakeshott, von Hayek, von Mises, Lukács, Cassirer and Horkheimer, each of whom took his bearings from some version of the idea of an 'age of reason' and an 'age of reaction' in terms of which they interpreted the trajectory of modern history from 1648 to 1848. The resulting schism will not be repaired by recounting the original process of polarisation. But it can be better understood. Understanding it must take account of the intensification of ideological antagonism from 1790 onwards. A conspicuous figure in this development was Edmund Burke, who remained central to the controversy over the significance of the Revolution from Tocqueville and von Savigny to Menger and Taine. Recovering Burke's defence of how judgement should be used to form a bridge between theory and practice marks a crucial stage in recapturing the distinct positions canvassed during the early period of revolutionary struggle. It will also help us choose between the alternatives.

II Patriotism and cosmopolitanism: Burke and Price

Burke took the opportunity twice in his *Reflections on the Revolution in France* to object to the sentiments expressed in a couple of open letters written by Richard Price's nephew, George Cadogan Morgan. Both letters were originally composed in July 1789 and then published in separate issues of the *Gazetteer* – on 13 August and 14 September respectively. The questionable use that Burke made of Morgan's letters prompted Price himself to respond in defence of his nephew in the Preface to the fourth edition of his published sermon, *A Discourse on the Love of Our Country*, the third edition of which had provoked Burke into writing the *Reflections* in the first place. Morgan, who had recently been invited to preach as a dissenting minister in Hackney, made an expedition to France in the summer of 1789, arriving in Paris on 9 July in time to witness at first hand the spectacle of the fall of the Bastille less than a week later. In one of the letters later published in the *Gazetteer*, he describes the scene on 27 July, when Louis XVI was greeted in Paris to the cries of both *vive la Nation* and *vive le Roi*, as 'one of those appearances of grandeur which seldom rise in the prospect of human affairs'.[53]

Burke mistook this tribute to the events of 27 July for a salute to the forced retreat of the royal family from Versailles on 6 October. Price himself had championed what in his eyes had had the appearance of a providential marvel on 27 July – 'I could almost say ... *mine eyes have seen thy salvation*' – only to be accused by Burke, along with Morgan, of revelling in the humiliation of the King and Queen of France on 6 October.[54] In fact, as Price protested, he had been celebrating the earlier reception of the monarch by the people of Paris 'as the restorer of their liberty'. So too had Morgan, as demonstrated by the fact that both his letters had been 'dated in *July* 1789', as Price now emphasised.[55] But while the intentions of Price and Morgan were indeed distorted by the *Reflections*, it seems that Burke's allegations were based less on deliberate misrepresentation than on plain misunderstanding. This misunderstanding had important consequences for how Burke chose to cast the relationship between enlightenment and politics in the 1790s. That choice in turn has been decisive for subsequent attempts to develop a theory of judgement within the framework of political rather than moral science.

Burke is unlikely to have read the dates placed at the head of Morgan's letters: he most probably first encountered the minister's views in the form of excerpts from the offending articles included in an anonymous pamphlet that appeared in 1790 under the title *A Look to the Last Century*.[56] Moreover, the language used by Morgan and

---

[53] This line from Morgan's letter of 14 September is quoted in Edmund Burke, *Reflections on the Revolution in France*, ed. J. G. A. Pocock (Indianapolis: Hackett Publishing, 1987), p. 57n. Unless otherwise explicitly stated, all references below are to this edition of the *Reflections*. A passage from the letter of 13 August is quoted in *ibid.*, p. 76n.

[54] Richard Price, *A Discourse on the Love of Our Country, Delivered on Nov. 4, 1789 ... Commemorating the Revolution in Great Britain* (London: 4th edn, 1790), p. 49. Burke cites this passage from Price in *Reflections*, p. 57.

[55] Richard Price, Preface to the Fourth Edition, in Price, *A Discourse*, pp. vii–viii.

[56] Anon., *A Look to the Last Century: or, the Dissenters Weighed in their Own Scales* (London, 1790). The suggestion, which seems to me almost certainly correct, that Burke's source for the Morgan quotation comes from this pamphlet was originally put forward in D. O. Thomas, 'Edmund Burke and the Reverend Dissenting Gentlemen', *Notes and Queries*, 29 (1982), pp. 202–4.

Price to describe the king's reception on 27 July hardly matches the more moderate interpretation subsequently supplied by Price in the Preface to the fourth edition of his *Discourse*. Originally, Price had spoken of a 'king led in triumph' to surrender himself to the population of France.[57] Morgan was more expressive still: he presented a picture of the French monarch *'dragged in submissive triumph by his conquering subjects'*.[58] Burke's notoriously indulgent depiction of the treatment of Marie Antoinette immediately before her escape to the Tuileries with her husband on 6 October should be understood for what it was: an extravagant response to what looked like the extraordinary provocation offered by figures like Morgan and Price in casting an incident of popular outrage as an act of righteous retribution.

But instead of simply mimicking the histrionic postures that both Burke and Price adopted in 1790 by choosing to rationalise the behaviour of only one of the two participants in the controversy over the significance of 1789 as has been the wont of most of the historiography on this episode to this day, we should try to appreciate the reactive dynamic into which these figures were thrown. Few have doubted that Burke's presentation of the treatment of Marie Antoinette on the morning of 6 October as confirming that 'the glory of Europe is extinguished for ever' was hyperbolical; but it would be strange to conclude on that basis that Price's reaction to the events of 27 July as almost revealing the *'salvation'* of the Almighty was a dispassionate and balanced intervention.[59] We need to restore the sense of exuberance, the feeling of alarm and the mounting suspicion entertained by the various British and French spectators of the early stages of the Revolution if we want to account for the extremes into which opposing reactions were seduced.

This interpretative generosity is not only required to make sense of the psychological processes that accompanied the progress of the Revolution. It is essential if we are to recover the precise character of the arguments advanced in defence of rival positions developed in response to events as they unfolded in the summer and autumn of

---

[57] Price, *A Discourse*, pp. 49–50.

[58] Anon., *A Look to the Last Century*, p. 122.

[59] Burke, *Reflections*, p. 66; Price, *A Discourse*, p. 49. In the Preface to the Fourth Edition of *A Discourse*, p. viii, Price singled out Burke's elegiac strains on the departed glory of Europe for ridicule.

1789. Debate over the significance of the Revolution in France was immediately conducted in terms of a discussion of the relation of theory to practice. The early stages of the Revolution exhibited to Price himself, for example, the prospect of a bounteous future guaranteed by the judicious management of that very relation: the utility of 'philosophy in forming governments' had in effect been demonstrated, Price argued, by the triumphant deliverance of July 1789. Burke's pronouncements against the 'intriguing philosophers' of dissent in England and the inspired theorists of enlightenment in France were accordingly taken by Price as proof of a 'frantic ... zeal' on his antagonist's part for the most retrograde forms of superstition.[60] Price, however, was wide of the mark.

Scholarship has not uniformly accepted Price's verdict, but it has taken at face value the exaggerated position assumed by Burke as part of a strategic response to the kind of ideological project that he associated with Price. Burke's apparent denunciation of theory in relation to practice illustrates the point. The most recent authoritative biographical study of Burke identifies one of the three core principles that informed its subject's critical reaction to developments in France by November 1789 as 'a distrust of theory'.[61] It is easy to quote Burke to this effect. For precisely that reason, the perception of him as an agitator against the influence of 'theory' on political organisation has featured prominently in the history of the reception of his thought.[62] But the fact is that the *Reflections on the Revolution in France* represents a defence of the use of theory in giving direction

[60] Burke, *Reflections*, p. 10; Price, *A Discourse*, p. viii. For the eccentricity of Price's position in the wider context of Enlightenment thought, see Frederick Dreyer, 'The Genesis of Burke's *Reflections*', *Journal of Modern History*, 50:3 (September 1978), pp. 462–79.

[61] F. P. Lock, *Edmund Burke II: 1784–1797* (Oxford: Oxford University Press, 2006), p. 247. Cf. *ibid.*, pp. 323, 330.

[62] An endless array of examples can be found from the eighteenth to the twenty-first century. See, for example, James Mackintosh, *Vindiciae Gallicae* (1791) in *Vindiciae Gallicae and Other Writings on the French Revolution*, ed. Donald Winch (Indianapolis: Liberty Press, 2006), pp. 50–3; John Morley, *Edmund Burke: A Historical Study* (London: Macmillan, 1867), p. 151; Leslie Stephen, *History of English Thought in the Eighteenth Century* (London: Smith Elder and Co., 2nd edn, 1881), 2 vols., II, pp. 223–7; Harold Laski, *Edmund Burke* (Dublin: Falconer, 1947), p. 11; Carl B. Cone, *Burke and the Nature of Politics* (Lexington: University of Kentucky Press, 1957–64), 2 vols, II, p. 319; Conor Cruise O'Brien, 'Edmund Burke: Prophet against the Tyranny of the Politics of

to the conduct of affairs. The important thing is to see how Burke's argument worked in this regard. Of course, this requires some sense of what he was arguing against. It also demands an appreciation of the rhetorical compromises he was forced to make in order to advance his own agenda.

Price's *Discourse on the Love of Our Country* can easily be read as an unexceptional call for a balanced combination of patriotic loyalty with cosmopolitan zeal. This harmony, it was claimed, should be employed in pursuit of religious and political reform. Towards that end, Price began by arguing that immediate domestic and national allegiances are not founded on Christian principles as such: Christ taught that strangers were equally our brothers, implying that the compass of human sympathy should recognise no bounds. Nonetheless, local forms of patriotism ought to be seen as a wise provision of providence for conveying human beings towards the lofty ideals of 'truth, virtue and liberty' since, in the absence of concrete social attachments, we would lack all incentive for moral action. But in identifying ourselves with such proximate versions of high ideals as are embodied in the fabric of the environment around us, we ought equally to strive to extend the circle of our affections beyond the narrow limits of local yet imperfect affiliation to encompass a wider universal benevolence. In the effort to realise this 'Religion of Benevolence', as Price describes it, we must certainly befriend our own country, 'but at the same time we ought to consider ourselves as citizens of the world'.[63]

Faced with this invocation of Christian brotherhood, two important questions arise. First, at what point should patriotic allegiance be sacrificed to cosmopolitan imperatives in Price's scheme of political value? The cosmopolitan ideal of universal justice diffused throughout society by the progress of enlightenment challenged the legitimacy of existing patriotic arrangements. But at what point should a new political dispensation of the kind that philosophical innovation might prescribe tip the balance against an established order? In the final additions to his *Theory of Moral Sentiments*, Adam Smith concluded that an answer to this question would require 'perhaps, the highest effort' of political judgement which a reforming legislator might have

Theory' in Edmund Burke, *Reflections on the Revolution in France*, ed. Frank Turner (New Haven and London: Yale University Press, 2003).
[63] Price, *A Discourse*, pp. 8, 11.

to apply.[64] But this superior effort of practical wisdom would depend on finding an answer to our second question: what price should be paid in promoting a cosmopolitan agenda? How should one assess the risk involved in dismantling a functioning state of affairs in the hope of forwarding the cause of justice?

Burke was profoundly suspicious of the content of this kind of hope. Price had spoken with conviction about his acute sense of the 'favourableness of the times' to his own and his associates' exertions in the service of liberty.[65] Burke doubted that the magnitude of Price's expectations was founded on any credible sense of practical possibility. But he also suspected that millenarian hope was a cover for desperation. Disappointed expectation could grow bitter and destructive. Burke presumed that with Price it already had. The moderate advocacy of a programme of dissent in 1780s Britain occluded, in Burke's view, the true grandiosity of its ambition. Heterodox clergy like Price and Priestley, in league with aristocrats like the Earl of Shelburne, the Duke of Grafton and Earl Stanhope, were threatening to capsize the constitution of their country for the sake of doubtful gains.[66]

Fusing religious and political purposes, 'political theologians' like Priestley combined with 'theological politicians' like Shelburne for the propagation of reforming schemes whose seeming modesty increasingly belied their all-encompassing ambition.[67] Deceit and subterfuge had become their accepted method of procedure. Discreet plans for the reform of representation masked the aim of drastic constitutional overhaul; moderate proposals for toleration were intended as instruments of ecclesiastical subversion. Priestley seemed to prove the point: on the one hand he professed himself opposed to '*violent*' change, but on the other he was happy to welcome 'the fall of the civil powers'.[68]

---

[64] Adam Smith, *The Theory of Moral Sentiments* (1790), ed. D. D. Raphael and A. L. Macfie (Indianapolis: Liberty Press, 1982), pp. 233–4.

[65] Price, *A Discourse*, pp. 49–50; cited in Burke, *Reflections*, p. 47.

[66] See Peter Brown, *The Chathamites* (London: Macmillan, 1967); Derek Jarrett, *The Begetters of Revolution: England's Involvement with France, 1759–1789* (Totowa, NJ: Rowman and Littlefield, 1973); Burke, *Reflections*, p. 219n; J. C. D. Clark, 'Introduction' to Edmund Burke, *Reflections on the Revolution in France*, ed. J. C. D. Clark (Stanford, CA: Stanford University Press, 2001), pp. 58–60.

[67] Burke, *Reflections*, p. 10.

[68] Joseph Priestley, *A Letter to the Right Honourable William Pitt ... on the Subjects of Toleration and Church Establishments* (London, 1787), pp. 40, 6;

Burke cited this line from Priestley in the *Reflections*. It seemed to
him to illustrate what he termed the spirit of 'rapture' which united
Unitarian radicals in Britain with enlightened legislators in France.[69]
This unity of spirit was matched by a similarity of purpose. Both were
to be advanced by a deliberate understatement of objectives: behind
the show of virtue lurked a revolutionary *arcanum* whose true aim
was to forward a deluge of destruction.

Burke did not immediately light upon this idea of a secret but deliberate programme of annihilation evident in the progress of French
affairs. It took him until four months after the fall of the Bastille to
decide on whether the ferocity apparent in some of the proceedings
across the Channel was incidental or integral to the flow of events. In
a letter to Lord Charlemont dated 9 August 1789, he openly mused
over developments since the spring.[70] Was the spread of fear and violence an accidental explosion, or was it definitive of the character of
the Revolution? Within months he had decided: any chance of renovation now seemed utterly forlorn. By the time he came to finish the
Reflections in September 1790, Burke was clear that the accumulated
impact of reforms since May 1789 had succeeded only in destroy-
ing every possible instrument of improvement. But this result was
unsurprising, Burke further noted. The prime movers in the National
Assembly had learned the art of government from philosophical masters for whom ways and means in politics were the merest distraction
from their goals: 'To them it was indifferent whether ... changes were
to be accompanied by the thunderbolt of despotism or by the earth-
quake of popular commotion.'[71]

There can be no doubt that Burke blended the deliberate designs
of revolutionary leaders, the unintended consequences of legislative

---

Joseph Priestley, *The Importance and Extent of Free Inquiry in Matters of
Religion: A Sermon* (Birmingham, 1785), p. 11; Joseph Priestley, *An History
of the Corruptions of Christianity, in Two Volumes* (Birmingham: J. Johnson,
1782), II, p. 484. On millenarianism in Priestley's political thought, see Martin
Fitzpatrick, 'Joseph Priestley, Political Philosopher' in David L. Wykes and
Isabel Rivers, eds., *Joseph Priestley: Scientist, Philosopher, and Theologian*
(Oxford: Oxford University Press, 2008).

[69] Burke, *Reflections*, p. 9. The passage from Priestley cited in Burke, *Reflections*,
p. 50 is also cited in Anon., *A Look to the Last Century*, p. 113.

[70] *The Correspondence of Edmund Burke*, ed. T. W. Copeland *et al.* (Chicago
and Cambridge: University of Chicago Press, 1958–78), 10 vols., VI, p. 10.

[71] Burke, *Reflections*, p. 98.

action, and the objectives of diverse partisans of reform together into a single premeditated process that swept France in 1789. It is right to note the extent to which blanket judgements of the kind contributed to the process of polemical escalation characteristic of the Revolution's trajectory. But Burke's responsibility in this regard does not provide a justification for muddling his political intentions after the fact, nor for confusing his commitments with his propagandising methods. Burke's purpose can best be ascertained by the way he characterised his opponents. His hostility towards *philosophes* was particularly directed at Voltaire, Rousseau, Turgot and Helvétius. Deism, democratic republicanism, physiocracy and moral materialism were most prominent among his targets. The diffusion of these doctrines not only had bred contempt for the idea of ethical restraint in Burke's judgement, but also had fostered a culture of intellectual conceit.

The outstanding representatives of this tendency in the *Reflections* were Rabaut Saint-Étienne, the Abbé Sieyès and Condorcet. But Burke did not ascribe the conceit that he believed to have characterised their designs to an attempt to put theory into practice. Instead, in Burke's mind the problem with revolutionary fervour was that it lacked a political theory of any kind. The language of Saint-Étienne resonated for Burke with the moral enthusiasm of Priestley. A frenzy of abolition seemed to guide their search for an enlightened humanity lodged beneath the accumulated corruption of ages. What 'convulsion' in the political world should not be welcomed, Priestley had wondered back in 1782, if it were attended by so desirable an effect as the final purification of Christianity? For Rabaut Saint-Étienne, just seven years later, moral renovation was likewise to be accessed via destruction: 'tout détruire; puisque tout est à recréer'.[72] Burke misread the malevolent intent behind this rhetoric of purgation. But he accurately understood the devastating consequences that would follow from any attempt to 'deduce' reforms from the premise of moral revolution instead of trying to infer improvements with the aid of historical prudence.

---

[72] Priestley, *An History of the Corruptions of Christianity*, II, p. 484. The passage is cited in Burke, *Reflections*, p. 50. The same paragraph is also cited in Anon., *A Look to the Last Century*, p. 113. The phrase from Saint-Etienne is cited in Burke, *Reflections*, p. 147n.

Burke was acutely conscious of the fact that the project of moral revolution was being conducted under the auspices of 'enlightenment'. The rhetorical strategy of the *Reflections* was to concede the use of the term to his opponents whilst restating what he took to have been the substantive point of a science of politics as elaborated by Hume and Montesquieu. Montesquieu had insisted that a purely moral enlightenment could offer no security against the abuse of power: power could only be checked by an opposing power.[73] Burke specifically criticised the argument put forward in *The Spirit of the Laws* to the effect that an intermediary nobility was adequate to the task of harmoniously regulating power in a state.[74] But he endorsed the underlying contention that power could only be moderated by the coordination of opposing forces in civil society. The question was how these forces could be collaboratively conjoined without neutralising one another. But it seemed obvious that the moral illumination of power was the least dependable route to moderation.

Morgan's letter of 13 August 1789 had compared the spirit of French agitation during the previous month to 'the most *enlightened and liberal amongst the English*'. Burke commented: 'If this gentleman means to confine the terms "enlightened" and "liberal" to one set of men in England, it may be true. It is not generally so.'[75] Since Price, Priestley and Rabaut Saint-Étienne chose to pick out the project of cosmopolitan illumination by use of the term 'enlightenment', Burke responded by charging 'prejudice' and 'superstition' with a positive influence on human affairs. This strategy carried with it considerable risk. On the one hand Burke had a serious point to

---

[73] Montesquieu, *De l'esprit des lois*, I, ii, 4. On this facet of Montesquieu's thinking, see Bernard Manin, 'Checks, Balances and Boundaries: The Separation of Powers in the Constitutional Debate of 1787' in Biancamaria Fontana, ed., *The Invention of the Modern Republic* (Cambridge: Cambridge University Press, 1994). On this topic in the history of Enlightenment constitutionalism, see David Wootton, 'Liberty, Metaphor, and Mechanism: "Checks and Balances" and the Origins of Modern Constitutionalism' in David Womersley, ed. *Liberty and American Experience in the Eighteenth Century* (Indianapolis: Liberty Fund, 2006).

[74] Burke, *Reflections*, pp. 162–3. On Burke's criticisms of Montesquieu in connection with his ideas about intermediary powers, see Richard Bourke, 'Edmund Burke and the Politics of Conquest', *Modern Intellectual History*, 4:3 (November 2007), pp. 403–32.

[75] Burke, *Reflections*, p. 76n. This passage from Morgan's letter is also cited in Anon., *A Look to the Last Century*, p. 123.

make: since prejudice is ineliminable from social life, it is vital that we discover the best means of enlightening it. But at the same time Burke's posture was deliberately ironic: it is clear that he took one of the great achievements of modern history to reside in the escape from superstition. But this irony was lost amid the polarities of the Revolution. That leaves us having to recover the main plank of his argument about the role of judgement in the relationship of theory to practice.

III Natural right and civil reform: Burke and Kant

'Far am I from denying in theory', Burke insisted in the *Reflections*, '... the *real* rights of men.'[76] Rights in Burke's sense are considered 'real' if they are entitlements or powers recognised in civil societies. They identify permissions in connection with social relations. They have no meaning in abstraction from the relationships they define. A theory of civil rights therefore involves a systematic conception of the character, distribution and balance of powers that constitute a functioning society. Any attempt to reform this distribution will require a minutely sensitive application of the science of political causation. Reform entails a reorganisation of prevailing obligations as these are embodied in definite social and political relationships. It is necessarily accompanied by a rearrangement of the balance between rival claims to power. It must therefore proceed on the basis of knowledge of the probable consequences of the impact of such readjustment on existing entitlements and preferences. To justify a reconfiguration of civil rights by reference to some speculative norm of justice is the business of a metaphysics of morals. This activity involves the application of moral judgement to the current disposition of affairs. Moral theory of the kind can be safely exercised within the confines of philosophical inquiry, but it cannot be left to impose its conclusions upon a political state of affairs by right of conquest.[77]

---

[76] Burke, *Reflections*, p. 51.
[77] For an account of the intellectual origins of revolutionary crisis within Enlightenment politics as deriving from the extrapolation of moral criticism into philosophical history, see Reinart Koselleck, *Kritik und Krise: Eine Studie zur Pathogonese der bürgerlichen Welt* (Frankfurt am Main: Suhrkamp, 1959, 1973). The work was originally intended as a study of Kant.

Burke captured this sentiment by citing a couplet from Book I of the *Aeneid* in which Neptune sends a message to the rebellious Aeolus for his part in stirring up a storm against Aeneas and his returning band of Trojans: 'illa se iactet in aula/Aeolus et clausa ventorum carcere regnet' – 'Let Aeolus bluster in that hall/and rule in the closed prison of his winds.'[78] Aeolus corresponds here to the tempestuous energy of moral enthusiasm liberated from the constraints imposed by circumstantial reality. Abstract norms might be harmlessly debated in the context of academic disputation, but they cannot be indifferently let loose upon existing power relations. The application of new values to a society inevitably introduces new relationships into an established equilibrium of forces. A fresh political departure of the kind risks fomenting anxiety, suspicion and resentment among the settled orders of a state. Innovation in the field of the theory of morals can raise a storm against existing ethical dogmas without precipitating any kind of crisis in social relations. But political innovation in the name of moral principle can only succeed on condition of its pragmatic viability.

A theory of politics, as opposed to a theory of morals, comprises a systematic understanding of the conditions underlying this pragmatic viability. To advance the claims of such a theory is not to conclude that values are irrelevant to politics, nor that norms can only be justified empirically. Burke's point instead is that political progress depends on the exercise of historical rather than moral prudence.[79] Political reasoning is not a matter of applying normative judgements to determinate actions. It involves applying consequential analysis to interdependent actions. Towards that end, it proceeds by factual observation and counter-factual evaluation.[80] It is constantly obliged

[78] *Ibid.*, p. 51. The lines from Virgil can be found at *Aeneid*, I, lines 140–1.

[79] For the opposite and to my mind misguided view, see Francis P. Canavan, 'Edmund Burke's Conception of Reason in Politics', *Journal of Politics*, 21:1 (February 1959), pp. 60–79.

[80] On the importance of counter-factual considerations to historical explanation, see Michael Scriven, 'Causes, Connections and Conditions in History' in William H. Dray, ed., *Philosophical Analysis and History* (Westport, CT: Greenwood Press, 1966). On the centrality of counter-factual analysis to political judgement, see John Dunn, 'Conclusion' in John Dunn, ed. *West African States: Failure and Promise – A Study in Comparative Politics* (Cambridge: Cambridge University Press, 1978), pp. 214–16. Cf. Geoffrey Hawthorn,

to conjure, project and assess historical probabilities.[81] In that effort, it is forced to discount what Burke termed 'the delusive plausibilities of moral politicians'.[82] Burke's meaning here is condensed, but nonetheless clear. Political judgement trades in probabilities. Pragmatic judgements of probability infer projected outcomes from a concatenation of causes. They do not infer probable consequences from moral preferences.

Cosmopolitan debate about moral preferences may happily be allowed to flourish in academic life, but it cannot be permitted to supplant patriotic norms merely on the assumption of the moral appeal of its proposals. For this reason, as Hume had already argued in 1754, to 'tamper ... or try experiments merely upon the credit of supposed argument or philosophy, can never be the part of a wise magistrate'.[83] It is of course possible, Hume went on, to introduce improvements into a commonwealth by estimating current arrangements against a model version of a constitution, and then cautiously proceed to reduce 'theory to practice'.[84] But in the case of a proposal for the complete replacement of existing arrangements, where the counterfactual analysis of probable historical outcomes must take account of limitless possibilities, the science of government can only function by exercising its presumption in favour of established political precedent – or, as Hume put it: 'An established government has an infinite advantage, by the very circumstance of its being established.'[85]

This appeal to the advantage of a settled pattern of arrangements is not an example of gratuitous or pious conservatism, but a reasonable conclusion of applied practical reasoning. As Burke similarly

---

Plausible Worlds: Possibility and Understanding in History and the Social Sciences (Cambridge: Cambridge University Press, 1991, 1993), p. 15.

[81] The kinds of probability in question are historical not statistical probabilities: they must offer at once contingently sufficient and contextually meaningful explanation. On both these conditions, see Max Weber, 'Objektive Möglichkeit und adäquate Verursachung in der historischen Kausalbetrachtung', Part II of *Kritische Studien auf dem Gebiete der kulturwissenschaftlichen Logik* in Johannes Winckelmann, ed., *Max Weber: Gesammelte Aufsätze zur Wissenschaftslehre* (Tübingen: J. C. B. Mohr, 1922, 1985). Cf. H. L. A. Hart and Tony Honoré, 'Preface to the Second Edition' of *Causation in the Law* (Oxford: Oxford University Press, 1959, 1985), pp. 13–25.

[82] Burke, *Reflections*, p. 33.

[83] David Hume, 'Idea of a Perfect Commonwealth' (1754) in *Essays Moral, Political and Literary*, p. 512.

[84] *Ibid.*, p. 513.   [85] *Ibid.*, p. 512.

recognised, to dissolve the fabric of an interconnected system of government is not simply to engage in trying out improvements. It is to dismantle an intricate structure of political power. Total political deconstruction can only be justified in the certain expectation that improvements will be made by the use of methods that are adequate to the task. This requires astonishing powers of calculation operating on responsive political material to succeed. Since the objects of social and political reform are rarely so obliging, the wise magistrate will bank where possible on tried expedients. With the example of a revolution in France before his eyes, Burke concluded in this spirit that 'it is with infinite caution that any man ought to venture upon pulling down an edifice which has answered in any tolerable degree for ages the common purposes of society, or on building it up again without having models and patterns of approved utility before his eyes'.[86]

Burke's point was that a total moral renovation of intricately coordinated political structures should be restricted to a process of mental trial and error. However, the force of his analysis was easily underestimated, as Kant's response to arguments contained in the *Reflections* would soon make clear. So too was the significance of Hume's argument for reform. Price cited the 'Idea of a Perfect Commonwealth' in his *Discourse on the Love of Our Country* in defence of the recently publicised electoral system of France.[87] The assumption was that political science could be justified by the quality of its ethical aspiration. Hume's point, of course, had been the reverse of this.[88] But the question remained for many of Hume's opponents whether in the process of elaborating a science of politics he had undercut the foundations for a science of right; whether he had in effect lost sight of the cause of justice in an effort to serve the interest of expediency. When Kant came to argue in the 1790s that the fundamental rights of states and citizens could be justified not in terms of a science of empirical principles but only in terms of a science of rational obligation, he chose to direct his remarks against Hobbes' doctrine of state and against the Burkean theory of resistance, although Hume could have served just

---

[86] Burke, *Reflections*, pp. 53–4.   [87] Price, *A Discourse*, p. 44.

[88] Hume, 'Idea of a Perfect Commonwealth', p. 514: 'All plans of government, which suppose great reformation in the manners of mankind, are purely imaginary.'

as well to exemplify the problems Kant associated with the notion of a right of rebellion justified in terms of necessity.[89]

Kant objected to the idea found in Burke that moral metaphysics was a delusive guide to politics and should consequently be confined within its sphere. In his 1793 essay on *Theorie und Praxis* Kant took exception to what he saw as the offensively conceited notion that moral theory should be confined within the academy, reproducing for his own purposes the very line from the *Aeneid* that appeared in Burke's *Reflections* as a satire on the idea of abstract right. Kant turned the tables on Burkean presumptuousness: the man of affairs is merely getting ahead of himself in consigning the philosopher to the schools – presuming to declare, as Burke had done, 'illa se iactet in aula!'[90] Political theory is legitimate only as a theory of pragmatic right, not as a theory of practical utility. It could not function, as Kant later put it, on the basis of 'enlightened concepts of political prudence'.[91] An enlightened understanding of practical utility could analyse contingent relations between constitutional powers. But it could not identify *necessary* restraints upon branches of government since only relations of obligation were truly 'necessary'.[92]

Two years later, in *Zum ewigen Frieden*, Kant extended this argument in response to the 'hollow boast' publicised by Mallet du Pan in his *Considérations sur la Révolution de France* of 1793. Experience of the Revolution had convinced the Genevan royalist of the truth of Pope's notorious saying – 'For Forms of Government let fools contest;/

---

[89] Immanuel Kant, *Über den Gemeinspruch*, pp. 20–40. Kant's comments on Hobbes appear on p. 37, and about the right to rebel from necessity on p. 33n; his apparent reference to Burke appears on p. 6. For the view that Burke is indeed Kant's direct target here, see Paul Wittichen, 'Kant und Burke', *Historische Zeitschrift*, 93 (1904), pp. 253–5. For Hume's connection with these themes in Kant's mind, see Immanuel Kant, *Kritik der praktischen Vernunft* (1788) in *Werke*, VII, ed. Wilhelm Weischedel (Frankfurt am Main: Suhrkamp, 1956, 1977), p. 173. For Burke's doctrine of a right of resistance deriving from necessity, see *Reflections*, pp. 16, 26–7. Cf. David Hume, *The History of England, From the Invasion of Julius Caesar to the Revolution of 1688* (London, 1778), 6 vols, V, p. 544.

[90] Kant, *Über den Gemeinspruch*, p. 6.

[91] Kant, *Zum ewigen Frieden*, p. 52: 'nach aufgeklärten Begriffen der Staatsklugheit'. For Kant's attempt to absorb and correct the Platonic ideal of philosophical monarchy, see Otfried Höffe, *Kant's Cosmopolitan Theory of Law and Peace* (Cambridge: Cambridge University Press, 2006), pp. 144–9.

[92] See Kant, *Kritik der praktischen Vernunft*, pp. 165–73.

Whate'er is best administer'd ist best' ('Laß über die beste Regierung Narren streiten; die bestgeführte ist die beste'). Kant retorted that du Pan's implicit claim either was a straight tautology, identifying the best constitution as 'the best'; or else was plain false, equating the best form of government with the best ruler. Kant responded tartly: 'Wer hat wohl besser regiert als ein Titus und Marcus Aurelius, und doch hinterließ der eine einen Domitian, der andere einen Commodus zu Nachfolgern.'[93] Kant elaborated his position by explaining how political right depended on the constitutional regulation of political power rather than on the capricious will of a ruler. However, the question was what agency could secure the regulation of a state in such a way that the opposition of interests on which constitutional government depended was protected short of allowing this opposition to degenerate into factional struggle.

Kant tackled this issue by arguing that a popular democracy was not susceptible to political regulation since only a representative (*repräsentativ*) system of government could sustain the separation of powers that was the hallmark of a legitimate constitution. As Kant saw it, a legitimate (or republican) form of government must be based on the separation of legislative and executive power. But he did not conceptualise that separation in terms of an opposition of interests so much as in terms of a delimitation of principles. This delimitation distinguishes the principle of executive action, which puts particular decisions into effect, from the principle of legislative will, which strives to serve the well-being of the whole. It is this last principle that 'obliges' executive power in the name of public right. But Kant failed to show how this obligation could operate as a practical constraint without betraying its moral worth as an obligation.[94]

Burke had set out to illustrate how the political worth of an obligation is determined by the extent to which it acts as a contingent constraint rather than as a moral compunction. Any attempt to regulate political power must begin by taking human beings as they are. It must then project how they will be once their original dispositions have

---

[93] Kant, *Zum ewigen Frieden*, p. 63n: 'Who governed better than a Titus or Marcus Aurelius, though the one left a Domitian and the other a Commodus as his successor?'

[94] See Immanuel Kant, *Die Metaphysik der Sitten* (1797) in *Werke*, VIII, ed. Wilhelm Weischedel (Frankfurt am Main: Suhrkamp, 1956, 1977), p. 439.

been modified by the circumstances that define their civil condition. As these conditions must be various, so the interests connected with them will diverge from one another. A programme of systematic political reconstruction must compose this diversity into a representative interest by the reconciliation of differences. But it must also protect the integrity of each distinct condition by providing them with sufficient defensive force.[95]

The purpose of a science of politics is to illustrate how individual judgement can be minimised by directing the machine of politics through the arrangement of its springs and levers. These mechanical components are tangible political forces that need to be harnessed, juxtaposed and reconciled to one another. Power is restrained by the competing influence of rival power, not by moral deference to political norms. The security of any system of antagonistic forces depends upon the rapport between its parts. Since any such rapport is a concrete historical achievement it is amenable to causal explanation. Despite the fact that explanation of this kind is the fundamental requirement of political analysis, political philosophy remains predominantly concerned with the issue of moral justification. I conclude this chapter with a contemporary example of this tendency. The aim here is not to diminish the significance of moral judgement in the estimation of ethical choices but to recover the importance of historical prudence in the evaluation of political processes.

Conclusion: history and legitimacy

Ronald Dworkin set out in the 1970s to put the question of justification at the centre of legal and political theory. The idea behind this approach was that moral theory could supply a proper foundation for the conduct of law and politics. Dworkin set about explaining the theoretical foundations of jurisprudence by contrasting his own preferred mode of vindicating political and legal judgements with two opposing theories of legitimacy. To begin with he advanced his case against utility-based forms of moral reasoning, which Bentham in particular was taken to represent. Next he sought to refute duty-based theories of legitimacy, of which he considered Kant to be an exemplar. In opposition to both these approaches Dworkin deployed

---

[95] Burke, *Reflections*, pp. 162–3.

a rights-based theory, exemplified by a style of argument which he associated with Thomas Paine.[96]

Power is justified for Dworkin in terms of the principles it can be commanded to respect. In cases where power is curtailed out of respect for duties, it is not obliged to recognise the individuals it constrains as independent centres of moral action but rather enforces their 'conformity' to absolute norms of behaviour.[97] At the same time, where power is answerable to nothing other than existing standards of utility, it cannot be called to account by basic moral values. The utility in question can be measured either positivistically as the declared will of sovereign authority, or socially as a requirement of the general welfare. It is clear that Dworkin associated legal positivism with Jeremy Bentham and H. L. A. Hart. However, he assumed that the doctrine of social utility had both Benthamite and Burkean exponents.[98] He seemed to believe that for Burke only customary utility could be pleaded against the rights of institutional authority, whereas with Paine public decisions could be limited by appeal to a framework of fundamental values. Dworkin's basic point was that where power is justified by an appeal to either duty or utility, it cannot be obliged to protect individual rights of a kind that it ought in principle to guarantee.

Fundamental rights function somewhat differently in Dworkin's legal theory and his political one. As regards his theory of adjudication, which stands at the centre of his philosophy of law, rights ground principles which in turn grant legal entitlements that transcend the decrees of the popular will. But in his theory of political obligation, a due regard for rights prescribes constitutional arrangements which provide for an independent judicial process secured against arbitrary

---

[96] Ronald Dworkin, 'Justice and Rights' (1973) in *Taking Rights Seriously* (London: Duckworth, 1977, 2000), pp. 171–3. For a discussion of the remaining utilitarian elements in Dworkin's scheme, see H. L. A. Hart, *Essays in Jurisprudence and Philosophy* (Oxford: Oxford University Press, 1983, 2001), pp. 208–21.

[97] Dworkin, 'Justice and Rights', p. 172. It is in these terms that Dworkin differentiates his political theory from Kant's. While it may be difficult to justify this interpretation of Kant, this fact need not affect the wider cogency of Dworkin's position.

[98] *Ibid.*, 'Introduction', pp. ix, x.

injustice by the integrity of its underlying principles.[99] The doctrine of political justification therefore depends upon the robustness of the theory of adjudication. But the question arises whether it is plausible to argue that basic principles like that of equality of concern and respect before the law are a gift of moral prudence – or, as Dworkin put it, a gift of 'conscientious judgement' – to modern systems of government.[100] Theories of moral justification played a crucial role in distinguishing legal from theological authority in early modern Europe. They still play a vital role in orientating public debate in morally charged political cultures like that of the United States of America today. But even in political environments where righteousness does not trump interests absolutely, justification will play an ineliminable part in the conduct of debate. Yet this cannot supply any kind of basis for a science of politics.

It is no part of the purpose of this chapter to try to evaluate the moral theory in terms of which Dworkin expected he could validate legal and political practice. My intention has instead been to argue that a science of government cannot be erected on the foundations of moral theory. Attempts to bolster such a construction have uniformly collapsed constitutional theory into political morality. If this course is to be avoided, the science of government must begin by resorting to historical prudence as a basis on which to make pragmatic judgements. In a fragment which he composed on the 'Laws of England' around 1757, Burke marvelled at the emergence of judicial power in the midst

---

[99] For Dworkin's account of adjudication, see *ibid.*, 'Hard Cases' (1975); for his constitutional theory see *ibid.*, 'What Rights Do We Have?' (1977), 'Political Judges and the Rule of Law' (1978) repr. in *A Matter of Principle* (Oxford: Oxford University Press, 1985, 2001), esp. pp. 23–32, and 'Liberalism' (1978) in *ibid.* For Dworkin's more recent and revised statements on these themes see, respectively, Ronald Dworkin, *Law's Empire* (Oxford: Hart Publishing, 1986, 1998); Ronald Dworkin, *Sovereign Virtue: The Theory and Practice of Equality* (Cambridge, MA: Harvard University Press, 2000).

[100] For Dworkin's characterisation of judicial intervention in the constitutional processes of liberal democracies as guided by 'conscientious judgment', see *Law's Empire*, p. 399. For his earlier response to the charge of Platonism against this understanding of the constitutional regulation of political behaviour, see 'The Forum Principle' (1981) in *A Matter of Principle*, p. 71. For the claim that the *procedures* of debate underwrite the commitment to *principle* that defines the rule of law (or *Rechtstaat*) as understood by Dworkin, see Jeremy Waldron, 'The Rule of Law as a Theatre of Debate' in Justine Burley, ed., *Dworkin and His Critics* (Oxford: Blackwell, 2004).

of 'the ambition and violence of mankind'. But his point was that the triumph of 'the first principles of Right' over partiality and despotism was a contingent product of European culture, underwritten by peace, prosperity and enlightenment.[101] Moderate government was a historical achievement, not an effect of moral prudence.

Burke doubtless thought that the progress of justice in modern Europe had been invisibly guided by the hand of providence. But he also thought that providential design could only be recognised after the fact. Since providence was inscrutable from the vantage point of human intelligence even though it operated through the agency of human desires, its concrete results ought for practical purposes to be regarded as a product of historical contingency.[102] For Carl Menger, it was this perspective that testified to Burke's significance as a political thinker. As Menger saw it, Burke had followed in the tracks of Montesquieu in directing historical study towards the analysis of the unintended (*unreflectirte*) consequences.[103] History is the outcome of blind collision between countless human intentions. Where this collision has contributed advantageously to the promotion of human welfare, it is tempting to think of this happy result as brought about by cunning. It is a feature of the moralising impulse that forms a part of human psychology that the unplanned results of historical action are belatedly invested with deliberate purposiveness. Accidental conjunctions are standardly reconceptualised as a product of design. Despite this historical illusion, we are still capable of realising that uncoordinated combinations of human actions, although they may give rise to beneficial results, would be better described as unreasoned than as cunning.[104]

A science dedicated to explaining political action proceeds by discovering predictable patterns of relations among these irrational combinations of forces. Historical prudence provides the basic

---

[101] Edmund Burke, 'Fragment on the Laws of England' (*c.* 1757) in *The Writings and Speeches of Edmund Burke I: The Early Writings*, ed. T. O. McLoughlin and James T. Boulton (Oxford: Oxford University Press, 1999).

[102] For a discussion of this important component of Burke's thought, see Rodney W. Kilcup, 'Burke's Historicism', *Journal of Modern History*, 49:3 (September 1977), pp. 394–410.

[103] Menger, *Untersuchungen*, pp. 201–14. Cf. Carl Menger, *Die Irrthümer des Historismus der Deutschen Nationalökonomie* (Vienna: Alfred Hölder, 1884), pp. 84–5.

[104] See Dunn, *The Cunning of Unreason*, pp. 19–47.

method of investigation. As Weber saw, such an approach must begin by rejecting the kind of moral teleology that had infected historical jurisprudence and political economy in Germany from Savigny to Schmoller. Under the influence of Hegel and Adam Müller, Weber claimed, the epigones of the historical school had transformed Enlightenment social *Theorie* into a form of *Theodizee*.[105] One distinguishing feature of theodicy is that it moralises history. The same habit of thought encourages us to moralise the use and abuse of power. But experience shows that appeals to political morality are not sufficient to restrain the ambition or reduce the corruption of power. The well-being of citizens is better secured by the judicious application of schemes for regulating competition among opposing political forces than by subjecting the general welfare to the judgement of enlightened rulers, or to the imaginary rigours of a science of public right. Modern political philosophy has managed successfully to revive the perspective of ancient prudence in subordinating politics to ethics. Historical prudence should seek to revise this inversion by liberating political analysis from the hegemony of moral judgement.

---

[105] Max Weber, 'Knies und das Irrationalitätsproblem', Part III of *Roscher und Knies und die logischen Probleme der historischen Nationalökonomie* in *Weber: Wissenschaftslehre*, p. 140.

Trust, judgement and consent

4 | *On trusting the judgement of our rulers*

QUENTIN SKINNER

I

John Dunn has not only been one of the leading interpreters of John Locke's political theory in our time; he has also become an increasingly deep admirer of what he describes as the soundness and sober realism of Locke's political stance.[1] Dunn's strong sense that Locke has something of vital importance to tell us here and now was by no means his initial reaction to the *Two Treatises of Government.* When in 1969 he published his classic monograph, *The Political Thought of John Locke,* he declared in his Preface that 'I simply cannot conceive of constructing an analysis of any issue in contemporary political theory around the affirmation or negation of anything which Locke says about political matters.'[2] Dunn had already begun to reconsider this verdict some time before he formally recanted it in an essay of 1990 entitled 'What Is Living and What Is Dead in the Political Theory of John Locke', in which he characterised his original response as 'peculiarly ill-considered'.[3] He had already maintained in his Introduction to *Rethinking Modern Political Theory* in 1985 that Locke's view of political power 'has a trenchancy and a relevance' that are in some respects 'unmatched by any other major political thinker',[4] and in the same collection of essays he went so far as to add that we have good reason to treat Locke's conception of political philosophy as exemplary for our times.[5]

[1] John Dunn, *Interpreting Political Responsibility: Essays 1981–1989* (Cambridge: Polity Press, 1990), pp. 24, 43.
[2] John Dunn, *The Political Thought of John Locke: An Historical Account of the Argument of the 'Two Treatises of Government'* (Cambridge: Cambridge University Press, 1969), p. x.
[3] Dunn, *Interpreting Political Responsibility,* p. 9.
[4] John Dunn, *Rethinking Modern Political Theory: Essays, 1979–83* (Cambridge: Cambridge University Press, 1985), p. 4.
[5] *Ibid.,* p. 34.

What is it about Locke's vision of politics that has made Dunn speak of it with such increasing warmth? The answer can be found in two important essays in which he draws on Locke's insights to help him formulate his own views about the relationship between government and the governed. One of these discussions, ' "Trust" in the Politics of John Locke', appeared in *Rethinking Modern Political Theory* in 1985; the other, 'Trust and Political Agency', appeared in *Interpreting Political Responsibility* in 1990. In the first of these essays Dunn already argues that the sober realism he admires in Locke is embodied above all in his recognition of 'the inescapable asymmetry of power between ruler and ruled which precludes the latter from exercising direct and continuing control over the former'.[6] This commitment is restated in the second essay, in which Dunn lays particular emphasis on the inevitability of this asymmetry and the foolishness of refusing to recognise it. We need 'fully to acknowledge the reality of the distinction between leaders and led'; to admit the need for 'trust in the relation between ruler and ruled' is simply 'an eminently realistic assessment of the irreversibility of a political division of labour'.[7]

Dunn's later discussion goes still further in building on this insight. He now stresses that to accept this distinction, and hence to accept the discretionary nature of the sovereignty conceded to our rulers, is not merely realistic but right. 'Men and women need in their rulers a power of agency which they can themselves only marginally control.'[8] Those in political authority 'must be in some ways released from the control of those over whom they govern' and 'accorded the discretion and the coercive power that they need'.[9] The appropriateness as well as the inescapability of discretionary power is presented as perhaps the most central lesson to be learned. As Dunn had already affirmed in his earlier essay, it is part of what is exemplary in Locke's view of sovereignty that he sees so clearly that 'discretion is intrinsic to its use'.[10]

Dunn infers that the basic aspiration of any political system concerned with human flourishing must be that of 'establishing and sustaining structures of government and responsibility which in some measure merit and earn trust'.[11] Here we not only reach what Dunn

---

[6] *Ibid.*, p. 51.   [7] Dunn, *Interpreting Political Responsibility*, pp. 40–1, 42.
[8] *Ibid.*, p. 40.   [9] *Ibid.*, p. 36.
[10] Dunn, *Rethinking Modern Political Theory*, p. 52.
[11] Dunn, *Interpreting Political Responsibility*, p. 32.

takes to be Locke's core commitment; we also come close to the bedrock of his own political thought. This in turn helps to explain why, in his more recent writings, Dunn has spoken so forcefully about the rationality of trust. As he wrote in an essay published in 1996, 'the question of whom to trust and how far is as central a question of political life as it is of personal life', so that 'the rationality of trust will always be the most fundamental question' to be addressed.[12] The fact that contemporary political theory has in Dunn's view 'essentially given up on this question' is one reason for his scornful dismissal of so many current practitioners of the subject.[13]

The specific section of Locke's political theory that Dunn is echoing in these pronouncements is chapter 14 of the *Second Treatise of Government*, the chapter entitled 'Of Prerogative'. It was not the least original feature of Dunn's monograph of 1969 that he devoted so much space to examining this aspect of Locke's constitutional thought. (It is worth observing that the other most influential interpretation from the same period, C. B. Macpherson's *Political Theory of Possessive Individualism*, failed even to mention it.) Dunn assigns a separate chapter to discussing prerogative rights, offering a finely crafted analysis of Locke's contention that a monarch's prerogatives may be said to constitute, in Dunn's summary, 'a reservoir of authority, which is imputed to him by sociological necessity, because legislative activity is inherently incapable of providing for the full complexity of actual social circumstances'.[14]

While Dunn gives a detailed account of what the *Second Treatise* says about prerogative right, he has little to tell us about the place of Locke's argument on the spectrum of political debate in his time. By contrast, Locke himself is keen to draw attention to the polemical nature of his claims, explicitly noting that his analysis is designed to refute the contentions of 'some Men' who have been criticising the royal prerogative.[15] But who were these men? And what particular view of the prerogative was Locke seeking to discredit in responding to their case? My first aim in what follows will be to attempt (in section II) to answer these questions, thereby supplying a sketch of

[12] John Dunn, *The History of Political Theory and Other Essays* (Cambridge: Cambridge University Press, 1996), pp. 95, 98.
[13] Dunn, *The Political Thought of John Locke*, p. 95.   [14] *Ibid.*, pp. 148–9.
[15] John Locke, *Two Treatises of Government*, ed. Peter Laslett (Cambridge: Cambridge University Press, 1988), II.14, para. 163, p. 377.

the historical context missing from Dunn's account, and in this way adding a footnote to his analysis of Locke's argument. I shall then attempt (in section III) to deploy this historical evidence to reconsider the theoretical commitment that Dunn has developed out of his reading of Locke. Locke's account of prerogative, I shall suggest, has the effect (and perhaps the intended effect) of occluding a series of claims about discretionary power that we very much need to keep in sight. Once we succeed in identifying the position that Locke's analysis hides from view, we may feel less inclined to applaud his defence of discretionary powers with quite the enthusiasm that Dunn has urged.

II

The place of the royal prerogative within the English constitution was already a serious subject of debate at the beginning of the seventeenth century. But the first moment at which the issue arguably became the central question in dispute between crown and Parliament was at the time of the presentation of the Petition of Right to Charles I in 1628.[16] One use of the prerogative to which both houses of Parliament took exception was that, as they reminded the king, 'divers of your subjects have of late been imprisoned without any cause showed'.[17] A further abuse cited in the Petition was the use of prerogative powers to impose levies on the people in the absence of parliamentary consent. This policy had already led to quarrels in the previous reign, when James I had exacted customs dues and other 'impositions' on his own authority, and a renewed outcry had arisen when Charles I raised a Forced Loan in 1626. The Petition explicitly denounces these expedients, complaining that 'your people have been in divers places assembled and required to lend certain sums of money unto your Majesty' contrary to their statutory rights.[18]

As the wording of the Petition makes clear, Parliament saw two distinct objections to these and similar misuses of the prerogative.

---

[16] My discussion in this section of the revolutionary period draws on Quentin Skinner, *Hobbes and Republican Liberty* (Cambridge: Cambridge University Press, 2008), pp. ix–xii, 82–6.

[17] S. R. Gardiner, ed., *The Constitutional Documents of the Puritan Revolution 1625–1660* (Oxford: Clarendon Press, 1906), p. 67.

[18] *Ibid.*, p. 67.

One was that the crown's policies involved direct interference with the people's 'rights and liberties according to the laws and statutes of this realm'.[19] A large number of people were being 'compelled against their will', and thereby 'molested and disquieted'.[20] The other objection reflected an even deeper anxiety about their liberty. As the Petition put it, the exercise of such discretionary powers, in particular the power to imprison without charge, is incompatible with the standing of the English people as *liberi homines* or freemen. 'No freeman may be taken or imprisoned or be disseised of his freeholds or liberties' except 'by the lawful judgement of his peers, or by the law of the land.'[21] If, in other words, the crown possesses such discretionary powers, the king cannot be said to be ruling over a nation of free subjects.

These invocations of the concept of a 'freeman' or *liber homo* carry us back, as the Petition duly notes, to the language of Magna Carta.[22] They also carry us back to a legal text that many parliamentary spokesmen viewed with the highest reverence, the pioneering treatise on common law produced by Henry de Bracton in *c.* 1260 under the title *De legibus et consuetudinibus Angliae.* Bracton introduces the concept of the *liber homo* in chapter 6 of his opening book, in which he anatomises the different types of *personae* and proceeds to ask 'what is liberty?' and 'what is servitude?'[23] 'To put it as briefly as possible', he begins, 'the first division of persons is that all men are either *liberi homines* or else are slaves.'[24] Moreover, even if you only submit yourself to a condition of vassalage, this may also be said to have the effect of taking away your standing as a freeman, because it likewise means that you are 'bound to a certain degree of servitude'.[25]

To be a vassal or a slave, Bracton goes on, is to live 'subject to the dominion of', and hence in a state of dependence upon, the will of

---

[19] *Ibid.*, p. 69.   [20] *Ibid.*, pp. 66, 68.   [21] *Ibid.*, p. 67.

[22] *Ibid.*, p. 67. For the *liber homo* in the first printed edition of Magna Carta see Richard Pynson, ed., *Magna Carta* (London, 1508), ch. 15, fo. 3ᵛ; ch. 30, fo. 5ᵛ; ch. 33, fo. 6ʳ.

[23] Henry de Bracton, *De legibus et consuetudinibus Angliae, libri quinque* (London, 1640), 1. 6. 1, fo. 4ᵛ: 'Quid sit libertas'; 'Quid sit servitus.'

[24] *Ibid.*, 1. 6. 1, fo. 4ᵛ: 'Est autem prima divisio personarum haec & brevissima, quod omnes homines aut liberi sunt, aut servi.'

[25] *Ibid.*, 1. 6. 1, fo. 4ᵛ: '[villanus] quodam servitio sit astrictus'.

someone else.[26] If your property is at the disposal of such a master, then you are a vassal; if your person is additionally at their mercy, then you are a slave. From these definitions it follows, as Bracton notes in chapter 9, that what it must mean to be a *liber homo* is *not* to be dependent on the will of a master, but to be capable of acting *sui iuris*, 'according to your own right'.[27] 'Everyone', as Bracton summarises, 'is *sui iuris* who is not subject to the power of another', so that everyone who is *sui iuris* enjoys the status of being a *liber homo* or freeman.[28]

Bracton's contrast between freedom and slavery furnished the vocabulary in which the concept of individual liberty was discussed throughout the debates between crown and Parliament in the opening decades of the seventeenth century. We already encounter the distinction in Sir Thomas Hedley's great speech to the House of Commons in 1610, in which he questioned the prerogative right of the crown to impose levies without parliamentary consent. Hedley's key contention is that 'in point of profit or property of lands and goods, there is a great difference betwixt the king's free subjects and his bondmen; for the king may by commission at his pleasure seize the lands and goods of his *villani*', whereas if he seizes the property of free subjects by a similar exercise of his arbitrary will, the effect will be to introduce 'a promiscuous confusion of a freeman and a bound slave'.[29] We come upon the same line of argument in the Parliament of 1628, particularly in the protests over Charles I's exaction of the Forced Loan two years earlier. Sir Dudley Digges opened the debate by denouncing those who say that 'he is no great monarch' who cannot take 'whatsoever he will'. Any king, he retorts, who 'is not tied to the laws' and rules merely according to his will is nothing better than 'a king of slaves'.[30] Later in the debate Sir John

---

[26] *Ibid.*, 1. 6. 3, fo. 4ᵛ: 'Est quidem servitus ... qua quis dominio alieno ... subiicitur.'

[27] *Ibid.*, 1. 9. 1, fo. 6ʳ: 'omnis homo aut est sui iuris, aut alieni'.

[28] *Ibid.*, 1. 9. 2, fo. 6ʳ: 'Sui iuris autem sunt omnes, qui non sunt in aliena potestate.'

[29] Elizabeth Read Foster, *Proceedings in Parliament 1610* (New Haven, CT: Yale University Press, 1966), II, p. 192. For a full analysis of this speech see Markku Peltonen, *Classical Humanism and Republicanism in English Political Thought 1570–1640* (Cambridge: Cambridge University Press, 1995), pp. 220–8.

[30] Robert C. Johnson *et al.*, eds., *Commons Debates 1628, volume 2: 17 March–19 April 1628* (New Haven, CT: Yale University Press, 1977), p. 66.

Eliot echoed his argument, stressing once more that the very fact of being 'liable to the command of a higher power' is what takes away our liberty as subjects.[31]

After the bruising attacks of 1628, and after the brief and chaotic parliamentary session of 1629, Charles I and his advisers resolved to abandon Parliament and impose a system of personal rule. They were able to sustain this policy for nearly eleven years, but by the autumn of 1639 the crown's financial embarrassments had become so acute that a new Parliament had to be called. Meanwhile the government's efforts to manage without parliamentary subsidies had given rise to even more controversial uses of the royal prerogative, the most hated of which had been the extension of the 'ship money' paid by the kingdom's seaports into a general levy in the later 1630s. As a result, the so-called Short Parliament that finally met in April 1640 reverted with even greater urgency to discussing the subversion of liberty. Speaker after speaker denounced the use of the prerogative to 'make void the lawes of the kingdome', to 'impeach the Liberty of the Subject contrary to the Peticion of right' and to introduce a general condition of servitude.[32]

Charles I initially decided on an immediate dissolution, but his financial difficulties proved so intractable that he found himself unable to avoid summoning a new Parliament, which duly met in November 1640. Refusing the crown's pleas for a subsidy, the members fell yet again to denouncing what Sir John Holland described as 'the late inundations of the prerogative royal, which have broken out and almost overturned our liberties'.[33] Sir John Culpepper warned that if the king can 'impose what and when he pleases, we owe all that is left to the goodness of the king, not to the law'.[34] Lord Digby concluded that 'our Liberties, the very spirit and essence of our weal, which should differ us from slaves, and speak us Englishmen, are torn away'.[35]

---

[31] *Ibid.*, p. 72.

[32] Esther S. Cope and Willson H. Coates, eds., *Proceedings of the Short Parliament of 1640* (London: Offices of the Royal Historical Society, University of London, 1977), pp. 136, 137, 140, 142–3.

[33] William Cobbett and T. C. Hansard, eds., *The Parliamentary History of England, from the Earliest Period to the Year 1803 … volume 2: AD 1625–1642* (London, 1807), p. 648.

[34] *Ibid.*, p. 655.   [35] *Ibid.*, p. 664.

This was also the moment at which Henry Parker, the most formidable proponent of the parliamentarian cause, stepped forward with his tract entitled *The Case of Shipmony*, which he issued at the beginning of November 1640 to coincide with the opening of the Long Parliament.[36] Like Culpepper, Parker objects that the imposition of ship-money presupposes that 'the meere will of the Prince is law', and that 'he may charge the Kingdome thereupon at his discretion, though they assent not'.[37] If the king is able to claim such discretionary powers, then as subjects we depend not upon the law, to which we have given our consent, but merely upon the will of the king. As Parker insists, however, to depend upon the arbitrary will of anyone else is to live in servitude. He accordingly concludes that, if it is left to the king's 'sole indisputable judgement' to 'lay charges as often and as great as he pleases', the effect will be to turn us into 'the most despicable slaves in the whole world'.[38]

The claim that the royal prerogative enslaves the nation thereafter became one of the leading arguments deployed against the monarchy throughout the revolutionary decade of the 1640s. We already come upon it in the earliest works written in defence of Parliament after the formal declaration of war in August 1642. If we turn, for example, to Richard Ward's *Vindication of the Parliament* of October 1642, we find him inveighing against the king's evil counsellors for persuading him that his will is law.[39] To allow the king 'to rule by his owne *Will*', Ward replies, will be 'to introduce and reare amongst us an *Arbitrary Government*'. But to live under the arbitrary will of another, and thereby 'stand at his mercy', will be to fall into the condition of 'miserable and wretched slaves'.[40]

During the mid-1640s the Levellers began to turn these objections against Parliament, arguing that its conduct of the war showed it to be no less arbitrary in its dealings than the king himself. These were the accusations hurled at the two Houses by Richard Overton

---

[36] For a full analysis see Michael Mendle, *Henry Parker and the English Civil War: The Political Thought of the Public's 'privado'* (Cambridge: Cambridge University Press, 1995), pp. 32–50.

[37] [Henry Parker], *The Case of Shipmony Briefly Discoursed* (London, 1640), pp. 5, 17.

[38] *Ibid.*, p. 21.

[39] [Richard Ward], *The Vindication of the Parliament and their Proceedings* (London, 1642), p. 12.

[40] *Ibid.*, p. 28.

in his *Arrow against All Tyrants* of October 1646. If, Overton objects, Parliament assumes power over us in such a way as to be able 'to do with us as you list', then we shall no longer be a free people.[41] We shall instead be settled, as Parliament is currently settling us, into a condition of bondage and thraldom, unable even to live like men.[42]

The same claims remained crucial to the Independent spokesmen who, towards the end of 1648, began to press for the vanquished Charles I to be put on trial for his life. Among these writers, incomparably the most important was John Milton, who started to write his *Tenure of Kings and Magistrates* at the moment when the House of Commons, purged of its moderate Presbyterian elements, finally resolved to charge the king with treason against his people. Milton never deigns to mention Charles I by name, but he launches a passionate attack on the type of discretionary power that the king had claimed to exercise. Any nation, he proclaims, that lives 'in the tenure and occupation of another inheriting Lord', whose government 'hangs over them as a Lordly scourge', lacks any title to be regarded as a free people. They 'may please thir fancy with a ridiculous and painted freedom, fit to coz'n babies', but in truth they are living 'under tyranny and servitude' in conditions 'no better then slaves and vassals born'.[43]

It needs to be emphasised that what these writers abominate is not the misuse of discretionary power but its mere presence within the constitutional fabric of any legitimate state. They all insist that, even if such powers are employed with unwavering benignity to promote the common good, this piece of good fortune does nothing to alter the fact that those who live under such regimes are living in dependence and hence in servitude. As Richard Ward puts it in his *Vindication*, anyone who possesses the arbitrary power of a master over a dependant can always exercise it 'either to impoverish or enrich, either to kill him, or keepe him alive'.[44] But even if the master chooses to keep his dependant alive and make him rich,

---

[41] Richard Overton, *An Arrow against All Tyrants* in Andrew Sharp, ed., *The English Levellers* (Cambridge: Cambridge University Press, 1988), pp. 56–7.

[42] *Ibid.*, pp. 56–7.

[43] John Milton, *Political Writings*, ed. Martin Dzelzainis (Cambridge: Cambridge University Press, 1991), p. 32.

[44] [Ward], *The Vindication of the Parliament*, p. 28.

the dependant remains at the mercy of the master and consequently remains a slave. Richard Overton expresses the same commitment in his attack on the House of Commons in his *Arrow against All Tyrants*. It is open to Parliament, he concedes, to make use of its arbitrary powers 'to save us or to destroy us' and hence 'for our weal' as easily as 'for our woe'.[45] But even if it employs its powers entirely for our weal, they remain arbitrary in nature and consequently leave us in bondage and thralldom.[46]

Of all these writers, no one articulated this argument with greater force than Milton in his two major political tracts of 1649. He first speaks in these terms in his *Tenure of Kings and Magistrates,* in which he reaffirms that, even if there is nothing in the least 'illegal, or intolerable' about the exercise of discretionary power, the mere fact of its being discretionary means that it leaves us enslaved. So long as we live under an 'inheriting Lord', we cannot boast of being a free nation, for we are living 'under tyranny and servitude; as wanting that power, which is the root and sourse of all liberty'.[47] The same argument recurs in *Eikonoklastes*, Milton's highly personal attack on Charles I and his government, which he published later in the same year. As before, he concedes that it may be possible for an absolute monarch to provide his subjects with 'all things conducible to well being and commodious life'. But he then declares that if the enjoyment of these things depends upon 'the gift and favour of a single person', the community 'cannot be thought sufficient of it self, and by consequence no Common-wealth, nor free'. No such regime amounts to anything better than 'a multitude of Vassalls in the possession and domaine of one absolute Lord'.[48]

This line of attack on the royal prerogative was finally consolidated in the period after England officially became a republic in May 1649, when it reappeared as a leading theme in such explicitly republican works as Marchamont Nedham's *Excellency of a Free State* of 1656, James Harrington's *Oceana* of the same year and John Milton's *Readie and Easie Way to Establish a Free*

---

[45] Overton, *An Arrow against All Tyrants*, p. 56.   [46] *Ibid.*, pp. 56–7.
[47] Milton, *Political Writings*, p. 28.
[48] John Milton, *Eikonoklastes* in *Complete Prose Works of John Milton, ed.* Merritt Y. Hughes (New Haven, CT: Yale University Press, 1962), III, p. 458.

Commonwealth of 1660.[49] These writers continue to attack the misuse of discretionary powers, usually equating such behaviour on the part of our rulers with the exercise of tyranny. As with the propagandists of the 1640s, however, their main concern is with the very presence of such powers within free commonwealths, whether these powers are exercised for good or for ill, and they proceed to denounce the enslaving consequences of such constitutional arrangements in two connected ways.

The principal objection they continue to raise is that the relationships of domination and dependence entrenched by the existence of discretionary powers are intolerable in themselves. The reason is that those who live at the mercy of others forfeit the essential attribute of human agents.[50] To have freedom of action is to be able to act as your will and reason dictate.[51] But as soon as you become subject to the power of someone else, you are no longer able to do or forbear according to your independent will. When you now act, you do so by the leave and hence with the implicit permission of the master or ruler under whom you live. As Harrington expresses it, you are controlled by someone else.[52] Slaves are never free, in short, because they are never free of their master's or ruler's will; their pattern of conduct is nothing other than a reflection of what their master or ruler may prove to be willing to tolerate.

The basic claim of these writers is thus that the presence of discretionary power serves in itself to make us slaves. As they willingly admit, however, it is highly unlikely that anyone could be a slave for long without coming to appreciate the implications of their predicament. As a result, they go on to develop a further argument about the lack of liberty suffered by those condemned to servitude. They argue that, as soon as you recognise that you are living under a ruler with discretionary powers, this awareness will have the effect of imposing further and more specific constraints on your freedom of action. You

[49] On the 'commonwealth' political theory of the 1650s see Jonathan Scott, *Commonwealth Principles: Republican Writing of the English Revolution* (Cambridge: Cambridge University Press, 2004), pp. 151–69.

[50] This paragraph draws on Skinner, *Hobbes and Republican Liberty*, pp. xi–xii.

[51] James Harrington, *The Commonwealth of Oceana*, ed. J. G. A. Pocock (Cambridge: Cambridge University Press, 1992), p. 19.

[52] *Ibid.*, p. 20.

will now be inclined to shape and adapt your behaviour in just such a
way as to try to minimise the risk that your ruler may choose to intervene in your life in a detrimental way.

Milton takes up this second theme with particular ferocity in his
Readie and Easie Way of 1660. Treating the impending restoration
of the English monarchy as a return to just such a condition of servitude, he paints a disgusted picture of the servility that will inevitably result. There are deeply reprehensible forms of conduct, he
first observes, that people living in slavery find it almost impossible
to avoid. Not knowing what may happen to them, and desperate to
avoid their ruler's rage, they will tend to behave in appeasing and
ingratiating ways, becoming 'a servile crew', engaging in 'flatteries
and prostrations', displaying 'the perpetual bowings and cringings
of an abject people'.[53] At the same time, there are various lines of
conduct they will find it almost impossible to pursue. We can never
expect from them any noble words or deeds, any willingness to speak
truth to power, any readiness to offer frank judgements and be prepared to act on them.[54] Such is the abject condition under which all
monarchs with discretionary powers condemn their subjects to live.

III

I have been tracing one element in the constitutional theory developed
by the enemies of absolute monarchy – the enemies stigmatised by
Thomas Hobbes in *Leviathan* as the 'Democraticall writers'. These
are the writers, Hobbes sardonically adds, who profess to believe
'that the Subjects in a Popular Common-wealth enjoy Liberty; but
that in a Monarchy they are all Slaves'.[55] John Locke is no less aware
of these theorists, and is scarcely less opposed to their contentions
about prerogative right. He certainly knew Harrington's *Oceana*,
which he bought when it was republished in 1700.[56] He also owned a

[53] John Milton, *The Readie and Easie Way To Establish a Free Commonwealth* in
Complete Prose Works of John Milton, ed. Robert W. Ayers (New Haven, CT:
Yale University Press, rev. edn, 1980), VII, pp. 407–63, at pp. 425, 426, 428.
[54] *Ibid.*, p. 428.
[55] Thomas Hobbes, *Leviathan, or The Matter, Forme, & Power of a Commonwealth Ecclesiasticall and Civill*, ed. Richard Tuck (Cambridge: Cambridge
University Press, 1996), ch. 29, p. 226.
[56] John Harrison and Peter Laslett, *The Library of John Locke* (Oxford: Oxford
University Press, 1965), item 1388, p. 151.

complete collection of Milton's political tracts,[57] and he even includes an apparent allusion to Milton's *Tenure of Kings and Magistrates* in his chapter 'Of Prerogative' in the *Second Treatise*.[58] There seems little doubt that Locke numbered these theorists among the 'some men' who claim that prerogative powers amount to nothing more than a means of doing harm to the people, and he opens his chapter on the royal prerogative by responding directly to their objections in vehemently anti-republican terms.

There is simply no alternative, Locke begins by announcing, but to accept the need under all systems of government for certain forms of discretionary power:

Where the Legislative and Executive Power are in distinct hands, (as they are in all moderated Monarchies, and well-framed Governments) there the good of Society requires, that several things should be left to the discretion of him, that has the Executive Power.[59]

After this resounding opening, Locke proceeds to underline the two separate judgements he has made. First he reiterates that such discretionary powers are indispensable. 'Many things there are, which the Law can by no means provide for, and those must necessarily be left to the discretion of him, that has the Executive Power in his hands.'[60] Next he reaffirms that this arrangement is entirely in line with the public good. 'Nay, 'tis fit that the Laws themselves should in some Cases give way to the Executive power.'[61]

As Locke makes clear, he is not simply speaking of a power to supplement the laws, although that is of course included. He is speaking of a right to act against the law, to override and set it aside. The capacity he has in mind is that of acting wholly 'according to discretion'; not merely 'without the prescription of the Law' but 'sometimes even against it'.[62] This authority, he explains, is essentially what he means by prerogative, which he takes to include an ability on the part of

---

[57] *Ibid.*, item 1994, p. 189.
[58] Milton, *Political Writings*, p. 28, and Locke, *Two Treatises of Government*, II.14, para. 163, p. 376, both speak of 'the root and source' of tyranny and liberty.
[59] Locke, *Two Treatises of Government*, II.14, para. 159, p. 374.
[60] *Ibid.*, II.14, para. 159, p. 375.   [61] *Ibid.*, II.14, para. 159, p. 375.
[62] *Ibid.*, II.14, para. 160, p. 375.

rulers 'to do several things of their own free choice, where the Law
was silent, and sometimes too against the direct Letter of the Law'.[63]
The prerogatives of rulers, in other words, are completely insulated
from the power of the people, and Locke explicitly maintains that the
people have no right to judge whether these prerogatives are being
justly or properly used. As he bluntly insists, the people simply 'cannot be Judge' of 'when this Power is made a right use of'.[64]

Locke concedes that, in speaking in these terms, he may appear
to be describing a purely arbitrary form of authority. He not only
observes that the wisest princes have generally been permitted to exercise their prerogative with so much latitude that they may indeed be
said to have 'had some Title to Arbitrary Power'; he also agrees that,
if we think of this power as a right to act 'for the harm of the people,
if they so pleased', then it unquestionably deserves to be condemned.[65]
As Dunn has shown in a fascinating account of the place of clientage in Locke's own moral and social formation, Locke was highly
sensitive to the insults and injustices that can arise from the wilful
and capricious exercise of such unregulated powers by patrons and
masters over servants and other dependants.[66] Furthermore, Locke
is in full agreement with the democratical writers that, in political as
well as in private life, to be subject to this form of power is what it
means to live in servitude. Chapter 4 of the *Second Treatise* is entitled
'Of Slavery', and in that discussion Locke unequivocally concludes
that anyone who puts himself 'under the Absolute, Arbitrary Power
of another' must be said to *'enslave himself'*.[67]

Locke is vehemently insistent, however, that the prerogatives of
rulers cannot possibly be classified as instances of such arbitrary
power.[68] The reason is that '*Prerogative* can be nothing, but the
People's permitting their Rulers, to do several things of their own
free choice' for 'the publick good'.[69] With characteristic repetitious-
ness, he continually reaffirms that prerogative is nothing other than
a right to act at discretion for the good of society, for the benefit of

[63] *Ibid.*, II.14, para. 164, p. 377.   [64] *Ibid.*, II.14, para. 168, p. 379.
[65] *Ibid.*, II.14, paras. 165–6, pp. 377–8.
[66] Dunn, *Rethinking Modern Political Theory*, pp. 13–33.
[67] Locke, *Two Treatises of Government*, II. 4, para. 23, p. 284.
[68] On Locke and the 'non-arbitrary' see Lena Halldenius, 'Locke and the Non-
Arbitrary', *European Journal of Political Theory*, 2 (2002), pp. 261–79.
[69] Locke, *Two Treatises of Government*, II.14, para. 164, p. 377.

the community, for the good of the people.[70] He finally lays it down that 'prerogative' can actually be defined as *'nothing but the Power of doing publick good without a Rule'*.[71] Such a capability cannot in principle be arbitrary, and ought to be positively welcomed as a valuable addition to any constitutional structure, and not merely as an inevitable feature of all systems of public power. He goes so far as to add that 'a good Prince, who is mindful of the trust put into his hands, and careful of the good of his People, cannot have too much *Prerogative*, that is, Power to do good'.[72]

Locke presents this argument as a complete rebuttal of the democratical writers and their attack on prerogative rights. As will by now be evident, however, he wholly fails to come to grips with their basic anxiety. He assumes that, so long as such powers are employed for the public good, they are inherently rightful in character.[73] But this fails to meet the fundamental objection of the democratical writers: that so long as these powers are discretionary, we are left at the mercy of those who have the right to wield them. As a result, even if their intentions are entirely benign, we are left in a state of dependence on their goodwill, and thus in the condition of slaves. What the democratical writers are arguing – and it is not clear if Locke is simply failing or deliberately refusing to see their point – is that the obligation to trust our rulers to exercise their prerogatives for the public good, when we have no means of preventing them from failing in that trust, is what renders the mere existence of such powers intolerable. To permit the creation of such powers is to establish relationships of domination and dependence, and the presence of any such relationships in civil associations has the effect of reducing us to servitude.

Nor was this invocation of the language of slavery mere hyperbole. As we have seen, the democratical writers had two specific objections to the presence within any constitutional system of discretionary powers: first, and most seriously, that they take from us our standing as human agents; and secondly, that they are bad for the character, encouraging as they do the cultivation of craven and obsequious behaviour. These are powerful and inescapable criticisms, and there

---

[70] *Ibid.*, II.14, para. 159, p. 374; para. 161, p. 375; para. 166, p. 378.
[71] *Ibid.*, II.14, para. 166, p. 378. [72] *Ibid.*, II.14, para. 164, p. 377.
[73] *Ibid.*, II.14, para. 159, p. 374; para. 162, p. 376.

is a strong case for saying that it is a serious weakness not merely of
Locke's response to the democratical writers, but of the entire liberal
tradition that has looked to Locke as its patron saint,[74] that it has
failed to recognise – as a number of political theorists have begun to
point out[75] – the distinctive ways in which relationships of domination
and dependence serve in themselves to limit civil liberty.

To raise this doubt about the adequacy of Locke's response to the
democratical writers is not to deny that, at least in one important
respect, he had the better of the argument. He is surely on strong
ground in concluding that, under any political system of any complexity, some element of discretionary power will be ineliminable.
Furthermore, the reason he gives for this conclusion reads no less
convincingly today than when he first penned it. We need to grant
such discretion, he maintains, because governments cannot operate
efficiently in the absence of a high degree of speed and flexibility of
executive response. Legislative assemblies cannot always be sum-
moned and persuaded to make their decisions with sufficient dis-
patch. Even when they are assembled, they may not always be able
to foresee what laws may be most useful to the community. And even
when they legislate, the laws they enact may turn out not to provide
the full directions that may be needed, or else may prove too rigid to
cope with changing circumstances.[76]

The question to ponder, however, is not whether we are bound to
accept the need for some such powers. Obviously we are bound to do
so, and it might even be wondered if the point needs to be underscored
with quite so much emphasis as Locke – and indeed Dunn – both give
to it. The more interesting question to ask is about the spirit in which
this concession should be made. Here again Locke speaks without

[74] As, for example, John Rawls does in John Rawls, *A Theory of Justice*
(Cambridge, MA: Harvard University Press, 1971), p. viii.
[75] See, for example, Philip Pettit, *Republicanism: A Theory of Freedom and
Government* (Oxford: Oxford University Press, 1997); James Tully, 'The
Agonic Freedom of Citizens', *Economy and Society*, 28 (1999), pp. 161–82;
Halldenius, 'Locke and the Non-Arbitrary'; Iseult Honohan, *Civic
Republicanism* (London: Routledge, 2002). I have contributed to this dis-
cussion myself: see Quentin Skinner, *Liberty before Liberalism* (Cambridge:
Cambridge University Press, 1998); Quentin Skinner, 'A Third Concept of
Liberty', *Proceedings of the British Academy*, 117 (2002), pp. 237–68; Skinner,
Hobbes and Republican Liberty.
[76] These are the considerations brought forward in Locke, *Two Treatises of
Government*, II.14, paras. 159–60, pp. 374–5.

hesitation. As we have seen, he believes that we should 'acquiesce', as he puts it, in the need for such powers as a straightforward recognition of political necessity. 'Many things there are, which the Law can by no means provide for, and those must necessarily be left to the discretion of him, that has the Executive Power.'[77] This too is Dunn's response, and more firmly even than Locke he expresses it in the tones of someone reminding us of the inescapable facts of political life. 'We have no option but to take the concentration of power in human societies as given.'[78] To trust our rulers to act at their discretion is 'an eminently realistic assessment of the irreversibility of a political division of labour', and this assessment in turn reveals 'the soundness of Locke's insight into what politics is really about'.[79]

Once we see, however, that the mere existence of such powers has the effect of limiting our liberty, we may begin to wonder if these calls for a 'realistic' acquiescence in their ineliminability represent the right response.[80] Consider, for example, the extent of the discretionary authority enjoyed by the executive in the United Kingdom as a result of the gradual handing over of the royal prerogative to the government of the day. Some of the resulting powers stem from the original duty of the crown to guard the boundaries of the realm. They currently include the right to grant and withhold passports, to expel foreign nationals, to prevent them from entering the country, and more generally to judge whether the country is in a state of emergency. Of even greater importance are the executive powers that stem from the historic right of the crown to regulate relations with other states. These include the right to deploy the armed forces, to ratify the terms of international treaties and, until very recently, to declare war and peace.

These survivals of the royal prerogative are very far from being a dead letter in contemporary British political life. In March 2003, Tony Blair as Prime Minister made use of the prerogative of war and peace to join the invasion of Iraq, allowing Parliament only an advisory

---

[77] Locke, *Two Treatises of Government*, II.14, para. 159, pp. 374–5.
[78] Dunn, *Interpreting Political Responsibility*, p. 31.
[79] *Ibid.*, pp. 40–1, 43; cf. also Dunn, *Rethinking Modern Political Theory*, p. 52.
[80] On the appropriateness of 'acquiescence' see Locke, *Two Treatises of Government*, II.14, paras. 164 and 165, p. 377; on this response as the 'realistic' one see Dunn, *Interpreting Political Responsibility*, pp. 40–2.

vote on the issue. In February 2005 the Home Secretary, Charles Clarke, invoked the security of the kingdom to withhold passports from two British men who had been released from Guantánamo Bay. Meanwhile all ministers of the British crown continue to be appointed under prerogative powers, without any possibility on the part of the people's representatives in Parliament to question or even to discuss the appointments being made.

What attitude should we adopt towards the continuing presence of these and other discretionary powers? I have been focusing on the Lockean answer, according to which we need to acquiesce in them, even if we may not approve of their specific use, on the grounds that they are indispensable to the effective functioning of modern government. But perhaps we might do better to focus on the contrasting answer of the democratical writers, especially if we aspire to be democrats ourselves. We might do better, that is, to question the fixity implicit in claims about 'what politics is really about', and demand instead to be told which of these powers are truly ineliminable and why this is supposed to be the case. We might also be well advised to make it clear that we will not necessarily accept the answers offered by our rulers to a question so closely touching their capacity to get away with doing what they like. It is arguable, in short, that the right response is not to acquiesce in these powers at all, but rather to insist on their reduction to an absolute minimum, to watch over their continuing exercise with the deepest suspicion, and to protest in the strongest possible terms against any extension of their use.

By contrast with these Leveller sentiments, Locke is unequivocal in responding that a good ruler 'who is mindful of the trust put into his hands, and careful of the good of his People, cannot have too much *Prerogative*'.[81] With the prospects for liberty darkening, however, it is worth asking if Locke may not be altogether too sanguine a guide. Perhaps a better watchword for our present times might be the one that the democratical writers liked to express in the words of the Psalmist: 'Put not your trust in princes.'[82]

[81] Locke, *Two Treatises of Government*, II.14, para. 164, p. 377.
[82] Psalms 146.3.

5 | Adam Smith's history of law and government as political theory

ISTVAN HONT

I The burden of judgement: Dunn, Kant and Locke

In all his work John Dunn has insisted that political judgement must be regarded as a central issue of political theory. Nonetheless, only a few political theorists work explicitly on this topic.[1] Among them Dunn is perhaps the only one who stands entirely outside the Kantian tradition. This is a striking fact, for Kant's contribution is widely regarded as foundational for the understanding of judgement (moral, aesthetic and political) in modern thought. Judgement is usually defined with reference to Kant's pithy characterisation of it in his *Critique of Judgment* as 'the ability to think the particular as contained under the universal',[2] as the link between theory and practice. 'It is obvious', Kant claimed in his essay 'On the common saying: That may be correct in theory, but it is of no use in practice', that 'between theory and practice there is required … a middle term connecting them and providing a transition from one to the other', an 'act of judgment by which a practitioner distinguishes whether or not something is a case of the rule'.[3]

---

[1] See Ronald Beiner, *Political Judgement* (Chicago: University of Chicago Press, 1983); Peter J. Steinberger, *The Concept of Political Judgement* (Chicago: University of Chicago Press, 1993); Ronald Beiner and Jennifer Nedelsky, eds., *Judgement, Imagination, and Politics: Themes from Kant and Arendt* (Lanham, MD: Rowman and Littlefield, 2001). Leslie Paul Thiele, *The Heart of Judgement: Practical Wisdom, Neuroscience, and Narrative* (Cambridge: Cambridge University Press, 2006) deals with practical rather than specifically political judgement, but chapter 1 presents a brief intellectual history of practical judgement in the work of Plato, Aristotle, Cicero, Machiavelli, Kant, Nietzsche, Dewey, Heidegger, Gadamer, Arendt, Derrida, Lyotard and Rorty, which also touches upon the political aspects of judgement.

[2] Immanuel Kant, *Critique of Judgement*, trans. Werner S. Pluhar (Indianapolis, IN: Hackett, 1987), 'Introduction', Section IV, p. 18.

[3] Immanuel Kant, 'On the common saying; That may be correct in theory, but it is of no use in practice', in Kant, *Practical Philosophy*, trans. Mary J. Gregor (Cambridge: Cambridge University Press, 1996), p. 279.

Kant's essay conveyed a double-edged message about the problem of judgement. At first Kant asserted that there was an ineliminable gap between theory and practice which could not be closed by developing a theory of judgement. Judgement as such could have no rule, for a rule was precisely a theory, requiring a further judgement for its implementation as practice. This would lead to infinite regress.[4] In Kantian terms, a theory of judgement was an oxymoron.

Kant's second message, which constituted the main thrust of his essay, mitigated the scepticism of the first. It was wrong, he argued, to conclude from the stubborn presence of a gap between theory and practice that moral and political theory had no value for real life and had to be replaced by a prudential calculus of the myriad contingent conditions that influenced practice. To demonstrate his point in politics, Kant compared Hobbes' prudential theory of sovereignty to the resistance theories of Hobbes' opponents. He entitled the section of the essay which dealt with political judgement 'Against Hobbes'.[5] By this, Kant did not mean to endorse the right to revolution upheld by Hobbes' opponents. On the contrary, he agreed with Hobbes that sovereignty was either absolute or nothing, and gave a thorough thrashing to the traditional constitutionalist theories of resistance. The idea of an original contract, he claimed, was not historically accurate, nor could it offer proper practical guidance for citizens who found it difficult to cope with the coercive powers of the state.

Nonetheless, Kant insisted that Hobbes was wrong to maintain that sovereigns had no duty to control their judgements, and could regard them as infallible. They had an obligation to recognise the idea of a social contract not as a challenge to their authority, but as a litmus test of their own duties. Just as the categorical imperative gave each agent an a priori test for the morality of an intended individual action, a hypothetical contract could guarantee the legitimacy of the

---

[4] *Ibid.*

[5] *Ibid.*, Part II. 'On the relation of theory to practice in the right of the state', pp. 290–304. For Dunn's critical thoughts on Kant's contractualism and his denial of the right of resistance see his 'Political Obligations and Political Possibilities', in John Dunn, *Political Obligation in Its Historical Context: Essays in Political Theory* (Cambridge: Cambridge University Press, 1980), pp. 293–4, and more expansively in 'Contractualism', in John Dunn, *The History of Political Theory and Other Essays* (Cambridge: Cambridge University Press, 1996), pp. 58–60.

sovereign's judgements, prohibiting legislation that could harm the
people, but permitting all other legislative decisions. 'Harm' in this
context is understood in Kant's own idiosyncratic non-eudaemonist
way: people are harmed when their freedom, equality or independence is undermined or infringed, not when their happiness is reduced
or threatened. Rulers must desist from any measure that could not in
principle be the object of free agreement by the people. Conversely,
if a reform plan was capable of passing the test of the hypothetical
social contract it could safely become law. Thereby, Kant claimed,
theory showed its mettle. His conclusion reinforced his Hobbesian
theory of sovereignty. The prudential judgements of sovereigns could
always be erroneous or sub-optimal. But if the measures they planned
were not self-contradictory by the standards of hypothetical popular consent, they could legitimately be enforced. The people had no
right to resist them, no matter how much they themselves judged the
reforms, individually or severally, as injurious, repugnant or not being
in their interest.[6]

Kant's amendment to Hobbes became the source of the most
influential strand of late twentieth-century political theory when
John Rawls in his *A Theory of Justice* applied it to the possible
introduction of social democracy in the United States of America.[7]
Dunn has never shared Rawls' underlying optimism concerning
the tractability of political judgement via contractarian thought
experiments.[8] The urgency of Dunn's call for reconsidering political judgement is best understood by realising that he shared Kant's

[6] Kant, 'On the common saying', p. 298.
[7] John Rawls, *A Theory of Justice* (Cambridge, MA: Harvard University Press, 1971). For context see Samuel Freeman, 'Motivations Underlying Rawls's Lifework' and 'Historical Influences' in Samuel Freeman, *Rawls* (London: Routledge, 2007), pp. 8–14, 14–28. Freeman emphasises Rawls' disappoint-ment with Christianity, and with theodicy in particular, as a reason for his revival of the doctrine of social contract as a secular alternative. On Rawls' role in American constitutionalism and impact on it, as opposed to academia, see Frank I. Michelman, 'Rawls on Constitutionalism and Constitutional Law' in Samuel Freeman, ed., *Cambridge Companion to Rawls* (Cambridge: Cambridge University Press, 2002), pp. 394–425. On the relevance of theodicy for modern Western thought, and the inherent difficulties involved in finding an alternative to it, see Raymond Geuss, 'Art and Theodicy' in Geuss, *Morality, Culture and History: Essays on German Philosophy* (Cambridge: Cambridge University Press, 1999), pp. 78–115.
[8] Dunn, 'Contractualism', pp. 60–3.

anxiety about judgement in 'On the common saying: That may be
correct in theory, but it is of no use in practice', but not his conclusions. Dunn's first major work, *The Political Thought of John
Locke*,[9] often proceeded along the same lines as Kant's critique
of the resistance theory of Hobbes' constitutionalist opponents.
Although always deeply sympathetic to Locke as a person and as
a thinker, Dunn's dissertation was not an apology of Locke but a
devastating critique.[10]

Like Kant, Dunn explicated the logical structure of Locke's con-
tractarianism and highlighted its flimsiness and inconsistency. He
repeatedly demonstrated the erroneousness of the belief that for Locke
consent would have constituted the general ground of political obligation. Rather, Dunn pointed out in an eerily Kantian vein, consent was
a logical requirement of Locke's theory of legitimate authority and no
more than the occasion for the issue of obligation to arise.[11] The reason for this was the peculiar nature of Locke's view on the location
of the only true source of authority for fallen men. 'There is no such
category in Locke's political theory', Dunn explained, 'as authority
which is both intrinsically human and legitimate.' Hence Locke's pol
itical thought lacked a theory of sovereignty in any conventional sense.
Instead, 'all legitimate authority everywhere and always exercised by
one human being over another is an authority conferred upon him
ultimately by God'.[12] Therefore, Dunn concluded, Locke's political
theory was irredeemably Christian. Through his highly flexible theories of trust and broad executive prerogative Locke did successfully

[9] John Dunn, *The Political Thought of John Locke: An Historical Account of
the Argument of the 'Two Treatises of Government'* (Cambridge: Cambridge
University Press, 1969).
[10] Dunn sees Locke's life as the paradigm case of a political theorist who fully
accepts his duty, see 'What Is Living and What Is Dead in the Political Theory of
John Locke?' in John Dunn, *Interpreting Political Responsibility* (Cambridge:
Polity Press, 1990), pp. 9–25, particularly p. 25. Locke's courageous struggle
for honest theory is also emphasised in John Dunn, *Locke*, Past Masters series
(Oxford: Oxford University Press, 1984); Dunn, 'Trust and Political Agency'
in *Interpreting Political Responsibility*, pp. 26–44, especially pp. 36–41; and
Dunn, 'Measuring Locke's Shadow' in Locke, *Two Treatises of Government
and A Letter Concerning Toleration*, ed. Ian Shapiro (New Haven, CT: Yale
University Press, 2003), pp. 257–85.
[11] John Dunn, 'Consent in the Political Theory of John Locke' in *Political
Obligation in Its Historical Context*, p. 31.
[12] Dunn, *The Political Thought of John Locke*, p. 127.

update traditional constitutionalism to approximate the requirements of Hobbesian theory, and this was no insignificant achievement. On the most fundamental points, however, Locke simply failed to find a secular answer to Hobbes' prudential politics. Locke did provide a rule for political resistance, but foundered on the issue of judgement.[13] To put resistance into practice, Locke required agents to ground their judgements, i.e. their application of the rule of resistance to concrete circumstances, in an 'appeal to heaven', to their Christian conscience as guided by moral obedience to God.[14] Hence Lockean resistance theory could not work reliably without presupposing Christian agency. As Dunn has never tired of pointing out, Locke deemed a stable atheistic polity to be impossible and excluded atheists from toleration.[15] They were dangerous because they were incapable of steady and reliable judgement.

Dunn never reached out for Kant, because from Locke's disastrous failure he drew the direct conclusion that we lack any secular

[13] See John Rawls' recognition of this in his *Lectures on the History of Political Philosophy*, ed. Samuel Freeman (Cambridge, MA: Belknap Press of the Harvard University Press, 2007): 'These questions have no precise answers and depend, as one says, on judgment. Political philosophy cannot formulate a precise procedure of judgment; and this should be expressly and repeatedly stated. What it may provide is a guiding framework for deliberation to be tested by reflection ... This is a paradigm case of what I have called "the burdens of judgment"' (p. 135). On Rawls' idea of the burdens of judgment, see his *Justice as Fairness: A Restatement*, ed. Erin Kelley (Cambridge, MA: Harvard University Press, 2001), pp. 35–6; also John Rawls, *Political Liberalism* (New York: Columbia University Press, 1993), pp. 54–8. Once Rawls fully realised the implications of the burdens of judgement, he gave up on his ideal of a well-ordered society: see Freeman, *Rawls*, p. 410. For a critique of Rawls' project see Raymond Geuss, 'Neither History, nor Praxis', in Raymond Geuss, *Outside Ethics* (Princeton: Princeton University Press, 2005), pp. 29–39.

[14] Locke, *Two Treatises of Government*, student edition, ed. Peter Laslett (Cambridge: Cambridge University Press, 1988), *Second Treatise*, §168, pp. 379–80, as a condition for judging the appropriateness of resistance and possibly civil war; see also §§20–1 (p. 282), §176 (p. 386), §§241–2 (p. 427).

[15] Locke, *A Letter Concerning Toleration*, ed. James H. Tully (Indianapolis, IN: Hackett, 1983), p. 51: 'Those are not at all to be tolerated who deny the being of God. Promises, covenants, and oaths, which are the bonds of human society, can have no hold upon an atheist. The taking away of God, though but even in thought, dissolves all. Besides also, those that by their atheism undermine and destroy all religion, can have no pretence of religion whereupon to challenge the privilege of a toleration.'

political theory that could defeat Hobbes.[16] Famously, Dunn stated that secular political theory had practically nothing to learn from Locke, and he never really withdrew this judgement.[17] He seems to accept Hobbes' view that the problem of political judgement can be solved only in practice by a twofold state monopoly. The state has a monopoly of power, but power is also used to enforce an effective monopoly of judgement. Dunn's Hobbism, however, is a reluctant one. He anxiously highlights the need for further thinking about political judgement, because he ultimately distrusts a purely prudential politics, even if he cannot see what a robust alternative might be. In many ways Dunn wants to nudge us away from Hobbes. Constitutionally he is a theorist of the modern representative republic.[18] He also wants us to have a political theory, which, unlike those of Hobbes and of Locke, accepts and understands capitalism. Dunn's later work is an unceasing search for a theory of judgement and political obligation that is appropriate to our time and can actively and productively complement a mitigated Hobbesian account of the modern representative and commercial republic. [19]

[16] Although Dunn was persistently critical of any attempt to import ethics into politics and hence of twentieth-century American Kantianism, the seventeenth-century English grounding of his thought also prevented him from developing a more radical and comprehensive critique, as exemplified by Raymond Geuss's position, based on Hegel, Marx and Nietzsche, which is expressed most emblematically in his essay entitled 'Outside Ethics', in *Outside Ethics*, pp. 40–66. As a consequence, Dunn is perhaps best described as assuming the stance of an early modern sceptic, who extrapolates this idiom directly into early twenty-first-century political thought.

[17] Dunn, *The Political Thought of John Locke*, 'Preface', p. x. For a balancing act, but no real contrition or revision, see 'What Is Living and What Is Dead in the Political Theory of John Locke?' and 'Measuring Locke's Shadow'.

[18] John Dunn, 'The Identity of the Bourgeois Liberal Republic' in Biancamaria Fontana, ed., *The Invention of the Modern Republic* (Cambridge: Cambridge University Press, 1994), pp. 206–25; Dunn, *Setting the People Free: The Story of Democracy* (London: Atlantic Books, 2005), ch. 3, 'The Long Shadow of Thermidor', pp. 119–47.

[19] John Dunn, *The Cunning of Unreason: Making Sense of Politics* (London: HarperCollins, 2000), ch. 10, 'Doing Better: Fantasy and Judgement', pp. 339–63; Dunn, *Setting the People Free*, ch. 4, 'Why Democracy?', pp. 149–88. On Dunn's appreciation of Hobbes see 'Political Obligation' in Dunn, *The History of Political Theory*, pp. 68–81; Dunn, *Cunning of Unreason*, pp. 41–6, 68, 86–9; Dunn, *Setting the People Free*, pp. 61–4.

II The principle of authority: the Lockean challenge and Smith's history of law and government

The purpose of this chapter is to redirect this search for a viable post-Hobbesian and post-Lockean form of political thought towards the political theory of Adam Smith and to point out possible genealogical lineages between Locke and Smith. Smith fits Dunn's bill readily. He eschewed theology, was neither a contractarian nor a utilitarian, and located himself generally in a Hobbesian moral lineage while also sharply criticising Hobbes.[20] Last, but not least, he thought long and deeply about the compatibility between commerce and political theory.[21] Smith's achievement, of course, did not escape Dunn's attention. Smith, Dunn readily acknowledged, was exceedingly well positioned to move us on from Hobbes and Locke. He obviously had done so in the field of political economy. But was this also true about his political theory? Dunn is more sceptical on this point, because he is not sure what kind of political theory, if any, Adam Smith had.[22] This is the issue that this chapter aims to throw some light on.

Dunn is not alone in doubting whether Smith was a political theorist. Those who study his political economy realise that he had many political concerns. But they nonetheless claim that by denigrating the importance of the form of government he sidelined many traditional concerns of political thought.[23] Those who focus on his four-stages

[20] Adam Smith, *The Theory of Moral Sentiments*, ed. D. D. Raphael and A. L. Macfie (Oxford: Oxford University Press, 1976), pp. 315–18. Henceforth *TMS*.

[21] On this issue see Istvan Hont, *Jealousy of Trade: International Competition and the Nation-State in Historical Perspective* (Cambridge, MA: Belknap Press of the Harvard University Press, 2005), 'Introduction', Part I, pp. 1–77 and John Dunn, 'The Economic Limits of Modern Politics' and 'Capitalism, Socialism and Democracy: Compatibilities and Contradiction' in Dunn, ed., *The Economic Limits to Modern Politics* (Cambridge: Cambridge University Press, 1990), pp. 15–40, 195–219.

[22] There is also doubt about Smith's status as a moral theorist. Smith's contemporaries, with the exception of Hume, frequently claimed that *The Theory of Moral Sentiments* was a failure because it did not elucidate the central question of moral theory, namely the origin of the distinction between right and wrong, good and evil, virtue and vice. Rather, they argued, Smith's book was a theory of 'good breeding', of moral socialisation and politeness, not of morality itself.

[23] Donald Winch, 'Adam Smith's "Enduring Particular Result": A Political and Cosmopolitan Perspective', in Istvan Hont and Michael Ignatieff, eds., *Wealth*

theory of history often see him as a proto-Marxist and economic determinist.[24] Here the accusation is that Smith replaced political theory with historical sociology. We have known since the late nineteenth century, from the publication of the first set of student lecture notes of the jurisprudence lectures Smith gave at the University of Glasgow, that Smith was interested in certain aspects of English political thought and attacked Locke's theory of political obligation in some detail.[25] His spectacular attack on Locke's theory of express and tacit consent could indeed be regarded as a hallmark of Smith's political theory. There are, however, two problems with this argument. The first relates to Smith's originality. Had Smith developed this critique of Locke himself, this part of his thought alone would earn him a place in modern textbooks of the history of political thought. Alas, he borrowed them from David Hume. As Duncan Forbes put it trenchantly, though somewhat unkindly, the student note-taker could have saved himself a lot of effort by simply inserting a note 'see Hume's *Essay on the Original Contract*'.[26]

The second issue is raised by those who are less interested in originality, but rather think that it is the content of Smith's Humean attack on Locke that disqualifies him from being a political theorist. They accept that Hume and Smith did refute Locke conclusively, by proving that the legitimate origins of the state did not and could not lie

and Virtue: The Shaping of Political Economy in the Scottish Enlightenment* (Cambridge: Cambridge University Press, 1983), pp. 233–69.

[24] Roy Pascal, 'Property and Society: The Scottish Contribution of the Eighteenth Century', *Modern Quarterly*, 1 (1938), pp. 167–79; Ronald Meek, 'Smith, Turgot, and the "Four Stages" Theory', *History of Political Economy*, 3 (1971), pp. 9–27; Knud Haakonssen, *The Science of a Legislator: The Natural Jurisprudence of David Hume and Adam Smith* (Cambridge: Cambridge University Press, 1971); Andrew S. Skinner, 'Adam Smith: An Economic Interpretation of History' in A. S. Skinner and T. Wilson (1975), in *Essays on Adam Smith* (Oxford: Clarendon Press, 1975); Andrew S. Skinner, 'A Scottish Contribution to Marxist Sociology' in I. Bradley and M. Howard, eds., *Classical and Marxian Political Economy* (London: Macmillan, 1982), pp. 79–114.

[25] Adam Smith, *Lectures on Jurisprudence*, ed. R. L. Meek, D. D. Raphael and P. G. Stein (Oxford: Oxford University Press, 1978), 'Report of Lectures 1762–3', pp. 315–17 and 'Report of Lectures 1766', p. 402. Henceforth referred to as *LJ* (A) and *LJ* (B), respectively.

[26] Duncan Forbes, 'Sceptical Whiggism, Commerce and Liberty', in Skinner and Wilson, *Essays on Adam Smith*, p. 181.

in either express or tacit consent.[27] Nonetheless, this view construes Locke's theory of consent as the epitome of early modern normative theory and therefore sees Smith's rejection of it as a regrettable retreat from the normative foundations of political theory. By accepting and repeating Hume's critique of Locke without any further comment, Smith had virtually no alternative but to retreat into either political sociology or a kind of proto-utilitarianism. This is also Dunn's view. He agrees with Hume and Smith that Locke's contract theory, even if understood as a theory of trust, cannot be saved. But he sees Locke's theological politics as a noble and tragic effort to measure up to the problem of political obligation, no matter how intractable the problem proved to be. Dunn quite explicitly asserts that he is unable to find an equivalent moral courage in most of Smith's engagement with politics,[28] particularly when looked at separately from his political economy – an admitted masterpiece, but in a different field of inquiry.

The relationship between Smith and Locke might look somewhat different, however, if one paid more attention to the theoretical context of Smith's rejection of Locke's theory of consent as the foundation of political obligation. In his Glasgow lectures Smith presented two principles which he claimed were both necessary for understanding the theory of government. These two principles were public utility and authority.[29] As Hume had shown, the two principles had been separated during the political upheavals of seventeenth-century England and had crystallised subsequently into the rigidly opposed principles of Britain's two political parties, the Whigs and the Tories.[30]

[27] A. John Simmons, *On the Edge of Anarchy: Locke, Consent, and the Limits of Society* (Princeton, NJ: Princeton University Press, 1993), ch. 7, 'The Critique of Lockean Consent Theory', pp. 197–216. Dunn complains that Hume misread Locke, see his 'From Applied Theology to Social Analysis: The Break between John Locke and the Scottish Enlightenment' in Hont and Ignatieff (eds.), *Wealth and Virtue*, p. 129.

[28] Dunn, 'From Applied Theology to Social Analysis', p. 133. It is difficult to see the evidence for Dunn's assumption that Smith broke with his alleged complacency only near the end of his intellectual life.

[29] *LJ* (A), pp. 318–21 and *LJ* (B), pp. 401–3.

[30] David Hume, *Essays Moral, Political and Literary*, ed. Eugene F. Miller, revised edition (Indianapolis, IN: Liberty Classics, 1987): 'Of Parties in General', pp. 54–63; 'Of the Parties of Great Britain', pp. 64–72; 'Of the Original Contract', pp. 465–87; 'Of Passive Obedience', pp. 488–92; 'Of the Coalition of Parties', pp. 493–501.

Smith's characterisation of these principles as party positions closely
followed Hume's. He endorsed Hume's claim that the apparently
severely conflicting principles of the two parties ought to be reunited
in a new dualistic theory (and he probably also agreed with Hume
that the future of British politics lay in a coalition of the two parties). Smith presented public utility as the principle of republicans,
resistance theorists and, in party terms, the Whigs. Smith depicted
Locke (together with Algernon Sidney) as the inspiration of the Whig
party doctrine, which he identified with an overstated version of the
principle of utility.[31]

Smith's main preoccupation, however, was not with the utility
side of the two principles of government. Like Hume, he readily recognised that the principle of utility was just another name for the
time-honoured principle of *salus populi suprema lex esto* (which
was emblazoned on the cover page of eighteenth-century editions of
Locke's *Two Treatises*).[32] This was not a hugely problematic principle,
if indeed it was problematic at all. Nor was the idea that consent
was in principle the correct foundation of rightful government hugely
contentious. As Hume clearly declared in the *Treatise of Human
Nature*, the difference between him and Locke was not in the basic
doctrine, for they both defined a legitimate state as based on consent
and the principle of *salus populi*. Rather, the bone of contention was
the philosophical and pragmatic identification of the kind of consent
and the kind of agency that was in play. This, however, was more of
a philosophical than a political disagreement.

At bottom Locke was sound on the principle of utility. Where he
really stumbled, as Dunn pointed out, was the principle of authority.
It is a commonplace today that Locke's *Two Treatises* ought to be read
not as an abstract analytical work on politics but as a tract for the time
and as a specifically tailored attack on Sir Robert Filmer's defence of
absolute political authority in his *Patriarcha*.[33] Hume already clearly

---

[31] *LJ* (A), pp. 315–16, 323, 370.
[32] See, for example, *Two Treatises of Government*, ed. Thomas Hollis (London:
A. Millar and others, 1764), cf. Locke, *Second Treatise*, §158 '*Salus Populi
Suprema Lex*, is certainly so just and fundamental a Rule, that he, who
sincerely follows it, cannot dangerously err' (p. 373). On the Hollis edition see
Peter Laslett, 'Introduction', in Locke, *Two Treatises*, ed. Laslett, p. 11.
[33] See Dunn, *The Political Thought of John Locke*, ch. 6, 'Sir Robert Filmer',
pp. 58–83.

recognised that this was Locke's context and emphasised that the reason why Locke overstated his own case was because the divine right theorists whom he was opposing had already presented him with a grossly exaggerated argument. Locke complained that Filmer's patriarchalist theory of divine right monarchy was a crass innovation and until it emerged in England in the seventeenth century it had been unknown not only outside England, but even within the country.[34] Hume and Smith in turn levelled the same accusation against Locke, claiming that his doctrine of contract, as based on either express or tacit consent, was a peculiarly English invention that was unknown elsewhere in Europe.[35] The difficult task was not simply demolishing Locke's ideas about the role of consent in politics, but reconfiguring Locke's peculiar balance between utility and authority without swinging too much to the authoritarian side.

For Hume any rehabilitation of Filmer's authoritarianism was out of the question. He loathed even the much milder principle of authority of the Tory party, the doctrine of passive obedience,[36] and doggedly tried to develop a rounded theory of political allegiance with a proper emphasis on the importance of authority, first in the *Treatise*,[37] then in his essays,[38] and finally in the *History of Great Britain*.[39] Smith also thought that it was Locke's theory of authority, not his contractarian interpretation of public utility, that primarily required revision. He went even further than Hume in this direction and made the task of developing a new principle of authority the central task of post-Lockean political theory. If one wants to discover the content of

---

[34] Locke, *First Treatise*, §§3–5, pp. 142–3.

[35] David Hume, 'Of the Original Contract' in *Essays*, pp. 486–7. For Smith, see *LJ* (A), pp. 316–18; *LJ* (B), pp. 434–5.

[36] Hume, 'Of Passive Obedience', in *Essays*, pp. 488–92.

[37] David Hume, *A Treatise of Human Nature*, ed. David F. Norton and Mary J. Norton (Oxford: Oxford University Press, 2000), Bk 3, Pt 2, Sections 7–10, 'Of the Origin of Government', 'Of the Source of Allegiance', 'Of the Measures of Allegiance', 'Of the Objects of Allegiance', pp. 342–62.

[38] Hume, 'Of the Origin of Government', *Essays*, pp. 37–41.

[39] See Hume's outburst in a footnote on the origins of the doctrine of passive obedience: 'The patriarchal scheme is nonsense. The original contract is opposed by experience. Men are unwilling to confess, that all government is derived from violence, usurpation or injustice, sanctified by time, and sometimes by a seeming imperfect consent'; David Hume, *The History of England from the Invasion of Julius Caesar to the Revolution of 1688*, ed. William B. Todd, 6 vols. (Indianapolis, IN: Liberty Classics, 1983), V, p. 563.

Smith's political theory one needs to reconstruct his views not on the principle of utility but, first and foremost, on the theory and history of authority.

Locke famously stated that history could never be a true source of normativity, for the past cannot bind the present or future. Nonetheless, in order to rebut Filmer's perennial absolutism he had to shift the ground of argument to history. He developed his own history of early government in Chapter VIII of the *Two Treatises*, 'Of the Beginning of Political Societies', which immediately followed the much better known Chapter VII, 'Of Political and Civil Society', the chapter that was the immediate target of Hume's and Smith's critique.[40] In Chapter VIII Locke described government as arising without any express and legally articulated consent. The birth of political society in which express consenting did play a crucial role was for him not the beginning but the end of the story. Locke described this history as the rise of government in the state of nature, and he defined the state of nature as the jural condition, in which a society operated without institutionalised and centralised forms of judicial or political judgement.[41] Theoretically, in order to answer Filmer on the question of ultimate origins, Locke maintained that in the state of nature each individual possessed an executive right of punishment. In his history, however, he emphasised that single individuals had the greatest of practical difficulties in exacting such punishment. Actual punishment in the early stages of mankind was communally enacted justice of a nascent kind. The formation of government therefore could be depicted as the slow emergence of judicial power.

Locke's conjectural history of governmental authority was grounded in the idea that while human beings had to be considered as jurally and normatively equal, in fact they were unequal in both physical and mental ability.[42] These natural inequalities, plus additional differences in age and experience, facilitated the emergence of leadership in early societies. Natural authority, Locke explained, led to executive power of a weak sort. Fathers of extended families

---

[40] *Second Treatise*, §§95–122, pp. 330–49.
[41] See Dunn's repeated emphasis that Locke's state of nature is not a piece of conjectural history, sociology or anthropology. Besides being jurally defined, it is a piece of theology; see Dunn, *The Political Thought of John Locke*, pp. 97, 103, and in general ch. 9, 'The State of Nature', pp. 96–119.
[42] *Second Treatise*, §54, p. 304.

continued in their leadership role even after their strictly parental function had ceased. Later, as larger social units were formed, the fathers became chieftains of tribes and eventually of the federations of tribes, called nations. How did judges emerge in these circumstances? As Locke pointed out, communities were threatened existentially much more from the outside, by other communities, than by the domestic criminality of individuals. Hence the idea of leadership, the rule of man over man, first originated from attempts to deal with issues of external security which necessitated the creation of military command.[43]

Judicial power could be created more easily once military leadership had already been established. Judging became an added function of military chiefs who were already in possession of executive or federal power. At first their offices were elective, but over time they were often transformed into hereditary positions. All these developments could easily be construed as consent-based. They were not forced on the population by anything other than difficult circumstances. Leadership arrangements were accepted voluntarily, for they answered a common need and were instruments of public utility, the *salus populi*. This kind of consent developed historically, through customary practice, because for ages there were no express stipulations that office-holding should be conditional on performing a genuine service for public utility. Rule by natural authority, Locke emphasised, was based on naïve trust and unguarded ignorance of the looming danger of cumulative and eventually irreversible corruption.[44]

Locke was obviously not a theorist of an original contract when thinking about the historical emergence of government.[45] What he claimed was that the corruption of early governments could be reversed only through active resistance and revolution. Historically, the principle of utility or *salus populi* was increasingly betrayed by rulers who systematically abused the initial trust invested in them by substituting their own private interest for the common good. What they abused was executive and judicial power. Both had to be curtailed

---

[43] *Ibid.*, §108–9, pp. 339–41.   [44] *Ibid.*, §107, pp. 338–9.

[45] See Laslett's remark that the term 'contract' does not appear more than about ten times in the entire *Second Treatise*; it is 'compact' or often mere 'agreement' that creates a society, a community or political power. In §97 the phrase is 'original compact'; 'Introduction', in Locke, *Two Treatises*, ed. Laslett, pp. 113–14.

by expressly redefining their purpose and specifying clear limits to their legitimate use. This was achieved through the creation of legislative power. For Locke, corruption was inevitable because it was the effect of economic development. Natural authority and naïve unconditional trust were feasible only while social and economic life were simple and relatively non-conflictual. As money was invented, wealth accumulated and property rights proliferated, the incidence of social conflict increased dramatically. With it grew the opportunity for abusing power.[46] This part of Locke's history of government in the *Two Treatises* is even more sketchy than the rest, because it was not strictly necessary for defeating Filmer's Adamite theory of the beginning of authority. Locke simply hinted at the causal mechanism that was in play, but he did not describe the prehistory of the move from natural to political government in any detail. Fallen men were inherently corruptible and their tendency for corruption was further aided and abetted by the rise of private property, which multiplied the opportunities for possessiveness and injustice.

Against the rot of economic progress there were no inbuilt natural defences in human nature. The invention of money broke all the natural limits of primitive society. Without them corruption could be rolled back only by criminalising and punishing its political excesses through publicly stated and incontestable legal regulations that were applied to all, rulers and ruled alike. The invention of this kind of legislation required a revolution, the establishment of a new kind of regime based on express consent, in which the legislative was supreme and was assigned the task of controlling corruption. Such a government was the *civitas*, commonwealth or political society. Once the codification of the principle of utility as supreme law was established, the actual form of limited government was less important. It could be monarchical, aristocratic, democratic, or a mixture of these. The essence of the new regime was in its clearly stated limits. If the *salus*

---

[46] Dunn, *The Political Thought of John Locke*, pp. 117–18. The invention of money is in *Two Treatises*, Ch. V, 'Of Property', §36–7, pp. 293–4. Through money any limitations on consumption according to the 'intrinsick' or use value of things could be overridden, amplifying the covetous desire of 'having more than Men needed'. The impact of this on politics (in Chapter VIII), was as great as the dramatic reshaping of the economy (in Chapter V), even if Locke did not explicitly correlate the two in detail, although in Chapter VIII §108, p. 339, there are hints of this view.

populi was disregarded, resistance to government was possible, not only in fact, but legitimately, by right.

If Smith genuinely wanted to replace Locke's political theory, he had to deal with this theoretical history of government and adapt it to his own thoughts on the relationship between authority and utility. Readers of Smith's *Theory of Moral Sentiments* and his *Wealth of Nations* noticed that he sporadically raised issues connected to this theoretical area. From these books alone, however, it is not entirely obvious whether he ever managed to develop a consistent and extended answer to Locke. We need to notice, however, that Smith had meant to write a third major book. When he published his moral theory in 1759, at the very end, literally on the last page, he included a trailer for his next book. In the last section he treated the practical rules of morality, an issue which is at the heart of the problem of moral judgement. Smith categorically rejected the 'frivolous accuracy' of casuistry, extrapolation from previous instances of moral action, as a proper approach to improve judgement. The weakness of casuistry, he emphasised, was most obvious if one studied the ways in which judicial judgement gradually improved over the course of human history. If doing justice had been abandoned to the verdict of those who were or felt injured, chaos would have ensued, preventing the emergence of stable social order. For secure society to exist, the provision of justice had to be brought under the umbrella of authority, requiring the appointment of judges who served everybody impartially and equally, and the creation of rules to guide their decisions in such a way that these decisions became consonant with natural equity.

Each nation developed positive laws for this purpose, but these laws themselves needed to be guided by a more foundational understanding of the general or natural rules of justice and judgement. The improvement of judgement, Smith claimed, required the development of natural jurisprudence or 'a theory of the general principles which ought to run through and be the foundation of the laws of all nations'.[47] Ancient thinkers, like Plato and Cicero, failed to construct any such system. It was only in modern Europe that systems of

---

[47] Both casuistry and jurisprudence were attempts to provide rules for judgement: 'It is the end of jurisprudence to prescribe rules for the decisions of judges and arbiters. It is the end of casuistry to prescribe rules for the conduct of a good man.' (*TMS*, p. 330.)

natural jurisprudence were developed, first and foremost by Grotius, in his 'treatise on the laws of war and peace'. It was at this point that Smith announced his own ambition most clearly. 'I shall in another discourse endeavour to give an account of the general principles of law and government, and of the different revolutions they have undergone in the different ages and periods of society, not only in what concerns justice, but in what concerns police, revenue, and arms, and whatever else is the object of the law.'[48] I suggest that this immensely ambitious enterprise was Smith's attempt to solve the problems associated with the principle of authority, which both Hume and he diagnosed as the true underlying weakness of Locke's political philosophy.

Although we know that Smith never abandoned this vast project, he unfortunately never finished the book that would have presented it in a definitive form.[49] He had a manuscript, but on his deathbed he asked the executors of his will to destroy it after he had passed away, which they duly did.[50] The basic outline of his theory, if by no means all the detail, is nonetheless recoverable. Today we possess two sets of extensive student notes of the lectures on jurisprudence which Smith gave at the University of Glasgow in the 1760s. It has been noticed that sentences that introduce his announcement of the plan of his uncompleted third major work are identical to sentences in these student notes.[51] It is, therefore, a safe assumption that he presented early versions of his planned book in lecture form to his students in Glasgow. Once we recover the outlines of his book from the lecture notes, it becomes visible that both in the *Theory of Moral Sentiments* and particularly in the *Wealth of Nations* Smith actually published significant chunks of his planned work in a fairly polished form. It is reasonably clear that Book III of the *Wealth of Nations* comes from Smith's planned treatise on the general principles of law and

---

[48] *TMS*, p. 342; the sentence printed in 1759 was repeated word for word in the sixth edition of the book, published in 1790, see *TMS*, 'Advertisement', p. 3.

[49] For the last mention of the project still not having been abandoned see the letter of Smith to the duc de la Rochefoucauld, 1 November 1785, in *The Correspondence of Adam Smith*, ed. E. S. Mossner and I. S. Ross (Oxford: Clarendon Press, 1977), p. 287 and the 'Advertisement' of the sixth edition of *TMS* in 1790, see above. In 1785 Smith reported that the 'materials ... are in a great measure collected, and some Part of it is put into tolerable good order'.

[50] See Ian Simpson Ross, *The Life of Adam Smith* (Oxford: Clarendon Press, 1995), pp. 404–5.

[51] See *LJ* (B) p. 397 and editorial note 9 in *TMS*, p. 342.

government, as well as a great deal of the material that he presented about law and the state in Book V of his *magnum opus*.

The lecture notes also allow us to see that the work of John Millar, the only pupil in Smith's jurisprudence class in Glasgow who became a published academic in a closely related field, contains extensive paraphrases of Smith's thoughts on the history of law and government. Millar's first book, with the revealing title *The Origin of the Distinction of Ranks*, was described by its author as an attempt to construct a theoretical history of authority.[52] It was unmistakably and even slavishly based on Millar's own notes from Smith's Glasgow lectures. After Smith's death, Dugald Stewart, who was entrusted with the task of delivering the official memorial lecture about Smith, turned to Millar to obtain a description and brief interpretation of Smith's great unfinished project. Millar suggested that when planning and writing the book Smith was 'endeavouring to trace the gradual progress of jurisprudence, both public and private, from the rudest to the most refined ages, and to point out the effects of those arts which contribute to subsistence, and to the accumulation of property, in producing correspondent improvements or alterations in law and government'.[53]

Smith's theoretical history of law and government is both complex and detailed, traversing the entirety of European socio-legal development.[54] Its shape, however, emerges quite clearly even from

---

[52] John Millar, *The Origin of the Distinction of Ranks*, ed. Aaron Garrett (Indianapolis, IN: Liberty Fund, 2006). According to the editor, the question Millar was trying to answer was: 'What is the nature of authority? How does it change and why?', p. ix. The first edition of *Ranks* came out in 1771. Millar's 'Lectures on Government' of the same year was clearly a derivative of the history of law and government part of Smith's own lecture courses, see *Ranks*, ed. Garrett, Appendix 3, pp. 288–9.

[53] Dugald Stewart, *Account of the Life and Writings of Adam Smith, L.L.D.*, ed. I. S. Ross, in Adam Smith, *Essays on Philosophical Subjects*, ed. W. P. D. Wightman, J. C. Bryce and I. S. Ross (Oxford: Oxford University Press, 1980), pp. 274–5.

[54] A magisterial account is in John Pocock's work on Gibbon, see 'Adam Smith: Jurisprudence into History' in *Barbarism and Religion*, II, *Narratives of Civil Government* (Cambridge: Cambridge University Press, 1999), pp. 309–29, and 'European Enlightenment and the Machiavellian Moment, the Scottish Narrative: David Hume and Adam Smith' in *Barbarism and Religion, III, The First Decline and Fall* (Cambridge: Cambridge University Press, 2003), pp. 372–98. Knud Haakonssen also provided an excellent overview in *The Science of the Legislator: The Natural Jurisprudence of David Hume and*

the meagre and programmatic information I presented above. It had two distinctive features which are important when considering it in relation to Locke. First, its starting point was a history of natural authority and it conceived the early history of mankind as lacking the office of judges and the institution of courts. Smith's history patiently tracked the history of legal organisation, from having no judges at all to the emergence of full legislative sovereignty. The family resemblance to Locke's theory of natural government is very strong throughout. The Lockean sequencing of Smith's theoretical history of the early phase of law and government becomes clear when one considers Smith's opposition to Rousseau's ideas on the same topic. When Smith encountered Jean-Jacques Rousseau's *Discourse on Inequality*, he noticed Rousseau's Hobbist assertion that before the social contract there could be neither government nor courts. As Rousseau put it, 'to say that the Chiefs were chosen before the confederation was established, and that the Ministers of the Laws existed before the Laws themselves, is an assumption not worthy of serious refutation'.[55] Smith dismissed both these notions brusquely. There were first chieftains, then government. Also, the rise of judges preceded both the idea and the practice of legislation. 'Laws are ... posterior to the establishment of judges',[56] he told his Glasgow students, and his history demonstrated the close correlation between the rise of government and the emergence of judicial institutions. In both cases he assumed a gradual, natural historical build-up. As for Locke, in Smith's theory legislative power was the last arm of government to develop.

The second distinctive feature of Smith's history is that he clearly made a determined effort to relate the development of both law and government to economic development. What Smith's rejection of Locke's consent theory of authority committed him to was the dismissal of the Lockean interpretation of the birth of the last historical stage, namely the suggestion that constitutional government and absolute legislative power were the results of a revolution

Adam Smith (Cambridge: Cambridge University Press, 1981), ch. 7, 'Smith's Historical Jurisprudence', pp. 154–77.

[55] J.-J. Rousseau, 'Discourse on the Origin and the Foundations of Inequality among Men', in Rousseau, *The* Discourses *and Other Early Political Writings*, trans. Victor Gourevitch (Cambridge: Cambridge University Press, 1997), p. 176.

[56] *LJ* (A), p. 314.

against corrupt executive power, which was *post factum* legitimised by an express promise of allegiance. Such an ur-revolution and the subsequent foundational promising of allegiance, Smith claimed, either never happened, or if it perhaps had, could not be recalled by anyone. A certain type of constitutional regime did in fact emerge in European history in general, and in Britain in particular, but not through this kind of revolution. This was a more general issue than resistance to James II or the justification of the Glorious Revolution. James could be dismissed because he broke the already existing rules of English politics. Resistance and revolution were possible, because England was already a legitimate constitutional regime. In fact, this was already Locke's tacit assumption in the *Two Treatises*.[57] Hence it was the rise of the English constitutional regime before the Glorious Revolution that primarily needed an explanation. This implied a need for a credible history that could fill the enormous gap that Locke left between his history of early governments and the emergence of the English constitutional crisis of the seventeenth century. It was this formidable task that Smith decided to take on.

Since Locke suggested that it was the rise of the economy that corrupted the trust that allowed the early career of government, Smith had to find an answer to this particular hypothesis. In order to make the causation from economic growth to governmental change visible in each stage, he created a step by step explanation of the ways in which the growth of the economy had influenced and changed authority and power relations over the whole period between hunting-gathering societies and modern commercial civilisation. This is the origin of Smith's 'four-stages' history of the mode of subsistence, charting the progress of mankind from hunting-gathering to pastoralism, to agriculture and eventually to commercial society, which became the backbone of his history of judicial and governmental authority. The end result was Smith's famous reversal of Locke's theory, namely that commerce in modern England and Europe had not ruined but rather created modern liberty.[58] Thereby he reversed Locke's grand

[57] See Dunn, *The Political Theory of John Locke*, pp. 130–1.
[58] See Istvan Hont, 'Adam Smith and the Political Economy of the "Unnatural and Retrograde" Order' in *Jealousy of Trade*, pp. 453–88, and also the 'Introduction' to *Jealousy of Trade*, pp. 99–111.

historical valorisation of the negative effects of luxury, at least as far
as it influenced politics in modern European history.

III   Wealth as a source of authority

The third and fourth parts of this chapter focus on two important
issues that arise in the substantial material which Smith was preparing for incorporation into his book. In dealing with them, my aim is
to illustrate the power of Smith's theorising and its potential for developing a post-Lockean mode of political theory. Both topics relate to
the role that Smith assigned to wealth in his explanation of political authority. The first concerns the contribution wealth made to the
development of authoritative leadership, while the second concerns
the influence of wealth on the initial development of republican constitutionalism. When Locke listed age and ability as the grounds of
natural authority, he simply reproduced a commonplace that had
existed in Western moral and political thought at least since Plato
and Aristotle. However, in Book V of the *Wealth of Nations*, Smith
listed not two but four grounds of authority.[59] His first two items
were also personal superiority and age. But to these he also added
superiority of fortune and superiority of birth, and he explained that
these two latter qualities historically often overshadowed the first
two qualifications. The fourth item, high birth, simply expressed
the perceived additional authority which old wealth had over new.[60]
Wealth as a source of authority, Smith noted, was the target of inces-
sant moral and political 'complaint of every period of society which
admitted of any considerable equality of fortune'.[61] It was often seen
as an epiphenomenon of inequality and symbolised precisely the sort
of political corruption that Locke complained about. Nonetheless,
it was this third item on the list which Smith regarded as the most
important and the key to the history and theory of authority.

In his Glasgow university lectures Smith instructed his students
to consult *The Theory of Moral Sentiments* if they wished to grasp
his views on authority. He asked them to read his chapter on the
nexus between wealth and social deference, entitled 'Of the origin
of Ambition, and of the distinction of Ranks'.[62] In it Smith explained

[59] *WN*, II, pp. 710–14.   [60] *WN*, II, p. 713.   [61] *WN*, II, p. 712.
[62] *LJ* (B), p. 401.

how wealth attracted admiration and respect, and thereby created authority for its possessors. Our tendency to sympathise with the rich and shun the poor, he claimed, was a consequence of our natural disposition to feel more for the joy than for the sorrow of others. Smith drew heavily on Hume's chapter 'Of our esteem for the rich and powerful' in the *Treatise of Human Nature*,[63] but he went significantly further in developing the political consequences of this personality trait. A critical tone pervaded his entire discussion which became even more pronounced with the addition of a new chapter on the same topic in the sixth and last edition of the *Theory*, entitled 'Of the corruption of our moral sentiments, which is occasioned by this disposition to admire the rich and the great, and to despise or neglect persons of the poor and mean condition'.[64] This was evident in Smith's scathing critique of the mediocrity of the personnel of modern governments, in his critique of syrupy modern politeness, and in his denunciation of luxury consumption as a form of status seeking. However, the real political bite of the chapter was in Smith's thoughts on the role that the admiration of wealth played in upholding governmental authority.

Resistance theorists assume that what makes revolutions difficult is the reluctance of the powerful to give up their privileges. Smith, however, presented the real political problem not so much as the desperate clinging of the wealthy to power, but as overcoming the deference of the poor to the rich and powerful. This predilection, he claimed, was often so powerful that it thwarted revolutions and reforms even when such changes would have been clearly in the interest of the lower ranks of society. Smith was a staunch defender of the Glorious Revolution. In his lectures he described James II as a silly king who, having recklessly embarked on an abrupt change of the religion of England, also openly broke the fundamental laws of the land.[65] Still, it was difficult to remove him from office. In the *Theory of Moral Sentiments* Smith complained that 'compassion for James II when he was seized by the populace in making his escape on ship-board, had almost prevented the Revolution, and made it go on more heavily than before'.[66] This was not a unique case. As Smith reported with

---

[63] David Hume, *A Treatise on Human Nature*, ed. David Fate Norton and Mary J. Norton (Oxford: Oxford University Press, 2000), pp. 231–6.
[64] *TMS*, pp. 61–6.   [65] *LJ* (B), pp. 435–6.   [66] *TMS*, p. 53.

obvious disgust, on the popular level 'all the innocent blood that was shed in the civil wars, provoked less indignation than the death of Charles I'[67] and he conjectured that it was this deeply corrupt mood that made the Restoration of the monarchy in 1660 so easy. Smith concluded that the mechanism of sympathy which lurks behind the ascendancy of the rich and powerful has often provided the principle of authority with stronger support than the psychological support given to the principle of utility by calculations of prudence. The implication was clear: 'That kings are the servants of the people, to be obeyed, resisted, deposed, or punished, as the public conveniency may require, is the doctrine of reason and philosophy, but it is not the doctrine of Nature.'[68] Deference could sustain the authority of the rich and powerful even when prudential calculations of utility pointed in the opposite direction.

Smith was making a point here about judgement, not about power relationships. Loyalty to the rich was based on sentimental admiration and not on the logic of deep social and economic structures. The modern world was not, as might at first appear, the historical stage in which power based on wealth was most rampant. Wealth played a more important role in the period when significant and lasting social and economic inequalities first arose. This was during the period of the shepherd mode of subsistence, when private property in livestock emerged. Smith associated shepherd polities with Asia and described them as military regimes based on despotic executive power.[69] In such circumstances wealth underpinned both authority and power. Rule among the earlier hunter-gatherers was based on the natural authority of ability and age alone. These early regimes, Smith explained, were very shaky because the men in authority in fact lacked any significant power. Shepherd societies were the first genuine governments because their leaders possessed both authority and power.[70] Their power flowed from their wealth. Once private property was possible, personal wealth and inequality could be made stable, creating a pivotal dependency of the poor on the rich. In *The Theory of Moral Sentiments* Smith described in detail how in modern politics the sentimental loyalty of the poor to the rich acted as a crucial stabiliser. Smith saw this as particularly important, because

[67] *TMS*, p. 53.   [68] *TMS*, p. 53.   [69] *LJ* (A), p. 202.   [70] *LJ* (A), pp. 215–20.

it was at odds with the underlying power relations. Modern polities were more benign than earlier ones because in a commercial society the poor depended on the rich far less for their subsistence than they did in shepherd societies. Modern deference was not a faithful mirror of prevailing property relations, and hence of the balance of power, but diverged from it in this important respect.

Smith subscribed to the doctrine of politics which claimed that rule normally could not be based on physical force alone, but rested far more on opinion than on direct coercion.[71] That is why the observation that wealth confers much less power in modern times than in earlier societies does matter.[72] For Smith the transition from despotic pastoral politics to constitutionalism was not the result of a political revolution against the corrupting powers of wealth, as Locke implied. Instead, it was brought about by economic change and the consequent shift away from the property arrangements which made the poor highly dependent on the rich towards regimes with far less personal and economic dependence. Modern society was not truly egalitarian, but was still far more egalitarian than preceding social formations. Smith's analysis of changes in the systems of economic and personal dependency was the backbone of his history of modern Europe, the foundation of his explanation of the transition from feudalism to modern regimes of liberty and commercial society.

This kind of analysis permeated Smith's entire theoretical history of law and government. However, it was one thing to show that the distribution of property in modern societies was far more equal than it had been previously. It was quite a different task to explain how private property could come about legitimately at all. Smith did not

---

[71] Hume, 'Of the First Principles of Government', in *Essays*, pp. 32–6.

[72] See Smith's remark in *WN*, I, p. 48, about the category error of equating modern market power with the political power that wealth used to convey to the rich through dependency relations in earlier societies: 'Wealth, as Mr. Hobbes says, is power. But the person who either acquires, or succeeds to a great fortune, does not necessarily acquire or succeed to any political power, either civil or military. His fortune may, perhaps, afford him the means of acquiring both, but the mere possession of that fortune does not necessarily convey to him either. The power which that possession immediately and directly conveys to him, is the power of purchasing; a certain command over all the labour, or over all the produce of labour which is then in the market' (*Leviathan*, ed. Richard Tuck (Cambridge: Cambridge University Press, 1996), p. 62). Although the point is very important, Hobbes' remark in fact conveys quite a different meaning from that which preoccupied Smith.

have at his disposal Locke's labour accession theory of property, because he regarded it as deeply flawed.[73] He needed a historical and causal rather than a purely jural explanation of how private property was created. In the *Wealth of Nations* Smith claimed that significant inequality in property holding could never have been stabilised without the simultaneous emergence of the state to protect it. Shepherd inequality could survive only because rich rulers invented and used the state to protect themselves from the poor. This explanation was not quite sufficient. It still left open the question how the inequalities in wealth that needed the protection of the state could have arisen in the first place. Smith needed to fill in the missing historical and logical link between rule based on natural authority alone and the first shepherd states in which authority was assisted by power based on wealth. To suppose that this step was accomplished by violence would have violated Smith's assumption that domination based on violence alone could never remain stable. However, Smith showed, leaders whose rule was based on natural authority did not need to use force to acquire the wealth that made their position secure and lasting.

Wealth was transferred to them voluntarily by their clients. Military rulers and judges were showered with gifts by the grateful beneficiaries of their activities.[74] These gifts were a sign of respect towards such leaders, creating a custom whereby gifts were expected from those who wanted to avail themselves of such leadership services. Thus, when the transition to private property took place, wealth was already readily available to the natural rulers of early societies without any recourse to violence. The admiration of the rich, then, is not simply a feature of modern societies and commercial regimes. The moral psychology that Smith identified in his theory of sympathy operated throughout history. With all its potential weaknesses, it offered Smith a way out of the suggestion that the history of government and its corruption can be explained in a moralising way, as in Locke's *Treatise*, by blaming luxury on the '*amor sceleratus habendi*, evil concupiscence' of fallen men.[75] It allowed Smith to bypass what Hume called the 'philosophical chymistry' of the selfish system, which reduced

---

[73] See Hume's sharp criticism of Locke's labour theory of the acquisition of property through accession, *Treatise*, p. 324, note 72.

[74] *LJ* (A), p. 212.   [75] Locke, *Second Treatise, Ch.* VIII. §111, pp. 342–3.

complex moral and cultural phenomena to effects of selfishness.[76] Smith built a more sophisticated explanatory machine, whose essence was anything but linear economic determinism.

IV   Luxury and the history of ancient and modern liberty

My second topic relates to Smith's reflections on the rise of legislative power, which he took to be as important and decisive a watershed in the history of government as Locke had. Smith saw its first emergence in a very special early case of the transition from the shepherding to the agricultural-commercial stage of the mode of subsistence. The shepherding stage was far more important for Smith than the hunting-gathering one, because this was the stage in which property and government first arose.[77] It was also important because modern Europe had emerged from a historical process prompted by the conquest of the Western Roman Empire by German shepherding nations. Following Montesquieu, Smith wanted to show how the Germans gradually developed a modern legal system of liberty and transformed their feudal states into modern political regimes based on agriculture and commerce. The shepherd state consisted almost entirely of executive power, with only rudimentary forms of judicial power in place. In them there was no notion of the legislative power of government. This developed only with the coming of agriculture and commerce. In pure versions of the four-stages theory, the mode of living determined the form of property rights, and property rights determined the kind of judicial and political institutions which were needed to regulate them. Smith, however, was not constructing either an entirely universal or a purely jurisprudential theory of politics. He was explaining the rise of modern European politics in general and the making of the modern English political constitution in particular. He had to take a position in the great debate about the

---

[76] David Hume, *An Enquiry concerning the Principles of Morals*, ed. Tom L. Beauchamp (Oxford: Oxford University Press, 1998), Appendix 2, 'Of Self-Love', p. 165. Smith accused Rousseau of using at least some philosophical chemistry in his republican discourse, see 'A Letter to the Authors of the *Edinburgh Review*' in Smith, *Essays on Philosophical Subjects*, p. 251.

[77] *LJ* (B), p. 404. For interpretation see J. G. A. Pocock, *Barbarism and Religion*, vol. 3, *The First Decline and Fall* (Cambridge: Cambridge University Press, 2003), pp. 372–99.

ideological origins of post-feudal European politics, which pivoted around the issue whether modern liberty stemmed from the classical Greco-Roman heritage or was an outgrowth of the Gothic legacy of medieval Europe.

Smith knew perfectly well that European history had to be divided into ancient and modern history. Accordingly, there were two transitions from the shepherd to the agricultural stage. The first happened in Greece, Rome and Carthage, which all became sophisticated agricultural and commercial states. Ancient development, however, fell victim to shepherd military power, to the German conquest of the Western Roman Empire. Accordingly, Smith divided his history of European law and government into two sections, the histories of ancient and modern liberty. He discussed the transition from the shepherd to the agricultural stage in Europe two times and demonstrated that fully fledged political regimes with legislative power also emerged twice. It was the ancient transition to agriculture and commerce in Europe that first created what Locke called political government, i.e. the commonwealth or *civitas*, and Smith described as a republic. He portrayed the rise of ancient republics as premature and highly specific.[78] It was not a part of a global or continental socio-political transformation, but an avant-garde development that remained surrounded by the shepherd nations in Asia and Europe, who eventually destroyed it. A more widespread and final transition from the shepherd stage to agriculture and commerce occurred only in modern European history. While the two European transitions had important similarities, they also had different political outcomes.

[78] Smith's modern history became Book III of the *Wealth of Nations*, which made the publication of the entire edifice of his theoretical history of law and government very difficult. Accordingly, after 1776 he primarily planned to publish the ancient part. As John Millar described to Dugald Stewart, 'he had heard him sometimes hint an intention of writing a treatise upon the Greek and Roman republics'. This was an extremely well-versed topic in the eighteenth century. Therefore Millar, who knew Smith's material well, and used it in his own lectures and writings extensively, told Stewart about the originality of Smith's planned book: 'after all that has been published on that subject, I am convinced, that the observations of Mr Smith would have suggested many new and important views concerning the internal and domestic circumstances of those nations, which would have displayed their several systems of policy, in a light much less artificial than that in which they have hitherto appeared' (Stewart, *Account of Smith*, p. 295).

In ancient Europe the first transition from shepherding to agriculture was determined by geographical luck. The early Greeks, a shepherd nation, conquered the fertile landmass of Attica which had clear natural borders, allowing easy defence. Traditional shepherd life in this restricted and hilly territory ceased to make sense. Its fertility allowed the Greeks to replace it with the sedentary practice of agriculture.[79] Increased productivity in agriculture and external security led to rapid economic development. The Greeks developed both artisanal industry and commerce. Material progress had momentous social and political consequences. The wealth of the Greeks, Smith argued, necessitated strong defence. Hence their politics started to change not only according to the demands of economic progress, but under the pressure of the security problem Greek prosperity gave rise to. Attica's sea frontier was unprotected, and the best defensive response against pirate attacks was to usher the whole population into a well-protected walled settlement. Thereby the Greeks invented the agricultural city-state. It was urbanisation that changed Greek politics so dramatically.

In the city none of the tribal chieftains could dominate the others and establish a despotic, i.e. shepherd-style, monarchy. The limited space of the city also made the vast inequality that characterised nomadic communities impossible. In his history of ancient republics Smith demonstrated how the Greek republic went through monarchical, aristocratic and democratic phases. To distinguish Theseus' monarchy in Athens from Asiatic monarchies, he described it as a republican monarchy,[80] for the shepherd military monarchies of Asia belonged to a pre-republican stage of socio-economic development. The next step, Athenian democracy, was born as the balance of power mirrored the increasingly egalitarian balance of property. For Smith democracy had its economic or material roots in crowded urban living. It was urban equality that led to a government of laws. With

---

[79] This was not the normal terrain for the development of the agricultural stage in the mode of living as measured by world historical standards. Agriculture first developed in Egypt, Bengal and China, around the Nile, the Ganges and the Yangtze rivers, see *WN*, I, pp. 34–6; the origins of the passage are in *LJ* (A), pp. 158, 223, and *LJ* (B), pp. 408–9, where Smith also specifically emphasised Attica as an exception, and most closely in the 'Second Fragment on the Division of Labour', in *LJ*, p. 585.

[80] *LJ* (A), p. 258.

economic growth, Smith explained, the incidence of conflict over property and commercial contracts started to rise. The increased need for judicial services was first satisfied by communal institutions, rather than by chieftains, or individual men in general, since nobody yet trusted the judgement of single judges. The judicial assemblies later became legislative assemblies. An even more elaborate judicial system arose in Rome. Through Roman legal history Smith could demonstrate conclusively that the creation of a political society, which according to Locke had to be based on legislative supremacy, was the achievement of ancient republicanism. From here Smith had gone on to develop a history of the modern version of this kind of political unit, showing that it was the history of the English courts that produced the best parallel instance of legal growth in modernity. This was the kind of history that Locke ought to have included in his *Two Treatises*, but did not. First, however, Smith had to explain why the original European republics, the Greek *polis* and the Roman *civitas*, declined and vanished.

The security problem which had given rise to republics was also the cause of their demise. Republics became islands of liberty in a sea of peoples governed by shepherdic authority. Because of their economic and social advancement, republics were destined to become rich. They became prima facie targets for conquest, the standard mode of wealth acquisition by pastoral people. The cards were stacked against republics. They were small and primarily consisting of a city and its immediate surrounding territory. Shepherd states, on the other hand, were large and populous. Eventually they looted and destroyed the republican bridgeheads of social and economic advancement that developed in European antiquity. It was at this point, when discussing the loss of ancient liberty, that Smith deployed a classificatory scheme that bears close resemblance to ones that were first deployed in the early modern republicanism of Machiavelli and Harrington. Republics had two modes of solving their security problem, Smith asserted. They could become either defensive or conquering republics.[81] Athens was the archetype of the first, Rome of the second.

[81] *LJ* (A), pp. 228–9, 233–5; *LJ* (B), pp. 411–14, 426. For Machiavelli, see *Discourses on Livy*, trans. Harvey C. Mansfield and Nathan Tarcov (Chicago: Chicago University Press, 1996), Book II, chs. 1–4, particularly Chapter 4, 'Republics Have Taken Three Modes of Expanding', pp. 135–8; Harrington's

Machiavelli expressed a preference for states that grew in territory, such as Rome, over defensive ones, which for him were exemplified by the Etruscan federation. Smith showed this preference as futile. Both kinds of ancient states had disappeared, even if Roman decline took longer to run its course than the demise of Greece. Smith's first concern was to show that a purely defensive republic was impossible, primarily because of inevitable changes in military technology. The material origin of republics was in the idea that a fortified city could withstand attacks from a shepherd army. Over time, however, the military initiative swung to the attackers and fortifications lost their pivotal martial importance. More importantly, there was an incompatibility between economic development and warfare. The republic, as a political formation with an urban core, was an advanced economic formation, encouraging the growth of arts and commerce. These occupations made the population disinclined to wage war. Smith saw this as a general rule for all republics. Stopping economic development, however, was not an option to city-based republics. Sparta could do it, but Sparta was not really a commercial republic.[82] Smith explained the longevity of ancient republics by their use of slavery. Economic development, commerce and the arts were carried on by slaves. This made it possible to use the republican citizenry for warfare for a significantly longer period.

For Smith there was no predestined reason for a republic to become a defensive or a conquering one. The character of a republic was decided by its citizenship policy. Restrictive or exclusive policies of citizenship resulted in a defensive republic, inclusive policies in an expansive republic.[83] Eventually, however, the fate of conquering republics was the same as that of the defensive ones. For Smith, Machiavelli's reason for preferring the Roman option, namely that expanding empires made the acquisition of wealth for public flourishing, for republican *grandezza*, much easier, was quite meaningless.[84]

---

phrase was republics or commonwealths for 'increase' or 'preservation', see James Harrington, *The Commonwealth of Oceana*, in *The Political Works of James Harrington*, ed. J. G. A. Pocock (Cambridge: Cambridge University Press, 1977), pp. 180–2, 273–8, 320–5; see also Pocock, 'Historical Introduction', pp. 18–19, 71.

[82] *LJ* (A), p. 231.   [83] *LJ* (A), p. 235; *LJ* (B), p. 412.

[84] For interpretation of Machiavelli's preference for *grandezza* see Quentin Skinner, *Machiavelli*, Past Masters (Oxford: Oxford University Press, 1981),

Such external acquisition of wealth for Smith was the characteristic of shepherd states. The transformations taking place in Rome's economic organisation, however, were much deeper than growing rich on the spoils of conquest. Hence the sort of military greatness Rome pursued became just as incompatible with commerce and manufacturing as Greek military policy. Here Smith was traversing the same intellectual territory that Montesquieu had covered in his *Considerations on the Causes of the Greatness of the Romans and Their Decline*. Montesquieu argued that when the socio-economic foundations of the Roman republic changed, Rome should have turned itself into a kind of monarchy that was fully compatible with commercial foundations and the social inequality produced by the extensive division of labour, rather than persevering with the half-monarchical, half-republican arrangement of the Roman Principate.[85] Similarly, Smith's main interest in discussing Rome was to investigate the repercussions of the conquest strategy on the internal political constitution of the republic.

Rome's destruction was postponed for centuries through the success of its strategy of eliminating the security problem of the republic by pre-emptive warfare. Shepherd states were conquering states. The appropriate defence posture was to respond in kind and to become a conquering republic. The strategy of conquest created a huge military presence within the republic. The political cost was enormous. It caused Rome to relapse into a pre-republican, essentially shepherdic political form, i.e. military government. The republic became bastardised. Rome became a half-monarchical, half-republican military government. Smith described this as a transformation of republican politics by a conquest from within. The republic was conquered by its army. Despite this political militarisation, great differences remained between imperial Rome and Asiatic military governments. Rome was a post-republican

pp. 50–65, 73–4; 'Republican Virtues in the Age of Princes', in Quentin Skinner, *Visions of Politics*, II, *Renaissance Virtues* (Cambridge: Cambridge University Press, 2002), pp. 149–51, and David Armitage, 'Empire and Liberty: A Republican Dilemma' in Martin van Gelderen and Quentin Skinner, eds., *Republicanism: A Shared European Heritage*, II, *The Values of Republicanism in Early Modern Europe* (Cambridge: Cambridge University Press, 2002), pp. 29–46.

[85] Montesquieu, *The Greatness of the Romans and Their Decline*, trans. David Lowenthal (Ithaca, NY: Cornell University Press, 1968).

military state that preserved, and indeed further developed, the civil government of the republic. Its military despotism, which represented a confused reversion to a type of Asiatic shepherd state, coexisted with a strict regime of republican civil laws.[86] The Principate was a mixed state, a combination of a domestic republican private sphere with a commercial and manufacturing base and a shepherd–military super-structure. This continuing development of a republican private sphere made Rome increasingly vulnerable militarily. Securing Rome would have required, Smith pointed out, a professional army based on the div-ision of labour. The substitute solution, to outsource national defence to shepherd mercenary militias, was a disaster. It left Rome defenceless once the shepherds turned against their masters.

Smith relied heavily on Renaissance and post-Renaissance repub-lican political theory to construct this account of the decline of the ancient republics. It was a central tenet of this discourse that luxury destroyed Rome by undermining its civic character and military prow-ess. Clearly, this was a kind of economic interpretation of history. Did Smith subscribe to it? He did mention that Rome was destroyed by luxury in his *Lectures on Rhetoric and Belles Lettres*, when teaching his students that historical or genetic explanations must not regress indefinitely. Normally one could terminate complicated historical explanations by providing them with a baseline whose validity was widely accepted. Since the idea that Rome declined because of its luxury was just such a seemingly incontestable truth, it was possible to use it as a baseline for explaining the demise of the late Roman republic.[87] Smith could have cast doubt on this thesis and argued that it was false, but he did not. His sophisticated analysis of the ancient economy was far superior to the moralistic attacks on luxury by many of his contemporaries, both Christian and republican. Nonetheless, his explanation of the demise of ancient republics still amounted to

---

[86] *LJ* (B), pp. 413–14, *LJ* (A), pp. 240–2.

[87] Adam Smith, *Lectures on Rhetoric and Belles Lettres*, ed. J. C. Bryce (Oxford: Clarendon Press, 1983): 'we naturally demand how it came to pass that a people once so strictly virtuous and sober should have degenerated so much, [Sallust] tells us that it was owing to the Luxury introduced by their Asiatick conquests. This altogether satisfies us; as those conquests and their circum-stances however interesting appear no way connected with the matters in hand' (pp. 92–3). Later in the lectures Smith remarked on 'the circumstances by which [Sallust] represents the Luzury of the Romans and their depraved moralls are such as attend Luxury in every country' (p. 110).

a version of the idea that it was luxury that undermined classical republican politics.

It is often argued that Smith's emphasis on the economic basis of politics came from the jurisprudential character of the four-stages theory. True, Smith's discussion of ancient republican Europe was framed by the four-stages theory. Nonetheless, his history of European law and government was not simply or even mainly jurisprudential. His economic explanations of the ancient republic followed the drift of the republican analysis of politics, including the emphasis on the political and military consequences of luxury. If Smith came to conclusions about modern politics that flew in the face of republican argument, this was not simply due to a preference for jurisprudence over civic humanism. Rather, he turned republican political analysis into modern political science, as much as he turned natural jurisprudence into theoretical history. Instead of separating the two or replacing the one discourse by another, he combined them. The idea that wealth and luxury dominate politics and law was present in both. Smith forged a new modern republican, or liberal, idiom in which the two predecessor discourses reinforced each other.

This becomes even clearer if one considers, however briefly, the modern part of Smith's history of European law and government. This is the better-known part, because it became Book III of the *Wealth of Nations*. The story here is different from the ancient one. After the Gothic shepherds overran Europe, they settled in the ex-provinces of the Roman Empire, in large territorial units that later became the medieval kingdoms. The Germans represented the politics of shepherds. Once they settled down in Europe, they created feudalism, a mongrel kind of polity that consisted of the superimposition of shepherd military government over a nascent agricultural stage, based on the permanent settlement of the population within well-delineated tribal or national borders. Feudal government was based not on a city, but on a scattered population. In city-states political participation was localised. In a dispersed community a new system of political communication had to be invented. This was the origin of representation as a mode of conducting modern, as opposed to ancient, government.

When the Roman military empire was destroyed by the German tribes, no remnant of ancient political republicanism survived. When Smith talks about the importance of medieval towns in early modern European history, it is crucial to notice that he does not equate them politically with ancient city-states, nor does he assume that the logic and institutions of city-state politics could simply be transferred to the large territorial kingdoms which were the main scene of Europe's development. Smith knew the republican city-state legacy of the Renaissance perfectly well. Nonetheless, he insisted that the little republics of Renaissance Italy and a few other isolated republican developments in Europe, such as Switzerland and the Netherlands, were not the key to explain the rise of modern liberty. These republics were isolated occurrences in feudal and early modern Europe. The republican city-states of Italy were a product of the country's feudal anarchy.[88] The fortified cities that survived from the Roman Empire not only preserved their intramural civil liberty but also enjoyed a defensive military advantage over the feudal aristocracy who resided in the anarchical countryside. Eventually the towns conquered the country around them, becoming little republics. When the nobility of the country moved into the city, an urban-centred political regime arose. A republican order that embodied not just civil but political liberty came into existence.

These city republics became famous and important for Europe's progress because they amassed enormous wealth and became the economic leaders of Europe. They were, Smith claimed, at least two centuries ahead of the rest of Europe in terms of economic development.[89] This was the real base of their *grandezza*. Their wealth, however, was not simply the result of a natural social and economic growth, or of political advantage. It was an outcome of a confluence of causes. One was geography, the Mediterranean position of Italy, between East and West. Another was the enormous war profits that were gained from providing economic and logistical assistance to the Crusades, a unique ideological–military event whose causes stood outside any regular pattern of social and economic advancement.[90]

---

[88] *WN*, I, pp. 403–4.
[89] *LJ* (A), p. 288: 'the Italians, who had at this time in the 14th century made as great advances in arts and emprovement as the rest of Europe arrived to in the 16th'.
[90] *WN*, I, p. 406.

Smith applied his general theory of the decline of ancient republics to the Renaissance ones too. As they became rich and economically advanced, they were bound to decline militarily.[91] Those who understood the history of the ancient republics wanted to stop the development of manufacturing in their city-states, as Machiavelli's hero Castruccio Castracani did in Lucca, but if they succeeded they only rendered their own republic backward and insignificant.[92] The rich and successful ones were weakened militarily by their luxury and commercial–manufacturing mode of living. The lack of slavery in modern republics implied that the general population had to be busy conducting the daily functions of economic life. Hence there were no significant instances of democracy in Renaissance Italy. There were only aristocracies, because political participation by working artisans would have been very time-consuming.[93] The same applied to the military. Yet again, military technology advanced, making the defence of walled cities and the conduct of modern warfare increasingly difficult. The republican militias were no match for the professional monarchical armies of Europe. Eventually, Smith concluded, the small Italian city republics perished by war and declined into relative insignificance, just as their ancient predecessors had.

In fragmented Italy, where the extreme weakness of national feudal rule created a power vacuum, towns could become city-states. Where no such power vacuum existed, cities throughout Europe remained the bastions of civil but not political liberty.[94] For Smith this was the significant fact. The civil society of the towns played an important role in the transition to modern European politics as a catalyst for the political and economic change of large territorial political units. How the economy and legal structure of the towns that had survived from the ancient world aided and abetted (and subsequently led) the conversion of the large post-Roman nations of the medieval period into properly modern statehood is a well-known story, even if not always a well-understood one. It was, however, only half of Smith's explanation of modernity. The other half was his demonstration of

[91] *LJ* (A), p. 231.
[92] *WN*, I, p. 407. For how republicanism in Lucca eventually retreated to the opera house, see Peter N. Miller, 'Stoics Who Sing: Lessons in Citizenship from Early Modern Lucca', *Historical Journal,* 44 (2001), pp. 313–39.
[93] *LJ* (A), p. 289.   [94] *WN*, I, p. 404.

the reasons why the towns could impact so effectively on the feudal socio-political system of the post-Roman era. For constitutional politics to arise, this post-shepherdic polity had to dissolve. Smith's story of the republics of the ancient world was that of liberty gained and then lost. His modern history was a mirror image of the ancient. It started with the condition of ancient liberty being lost and showed how something similar, in legal if not political terms, could emerge anew. The pattern was a triad: liberty gained, lost and regained.

How could liberty be regained from the destruction of Rome and from the subsequent rule of feudalism? Smith distinguished three revolutions or cataclysmic changes in ancient European history. All three were instances of military defeat.[95] A similar fate befell the small republics of Renaissance Italy. However, European feudalism was not destroyed in this way. The Goths destroyed Rome. The medieval Gothic polity, however, did not fall through military defeat by some new equivalent of the Goths. There were no new waves of barbarian conquerors, no further wanderings of nations from the East. Nor was feudalism terminated by any internal political revolution in the modern sense, although Smith called the demise of feudalism a revolution, in the old sense of the word that implied a major turning around of affairs. This revolution that terminated feudalism was not the result of violence. In fact, Smith's explanation was very similar to his earlier analysis of the reasons that led to the decline of ancient states. Like its ancient predecessors, feudalism was also destroyed by luxury.

As a successor to the Asiatic shepherd state, feudalism exemplified the conjunction of authority and power in its state form. The vast inequality that characterised feudal regimes carried with it a direct form of dependency of the poor on the rich. The military power wielded by the rich was also based on the exchange of economic support for the military service of the poor. Luxury destroyed the strength of this symbiotic arrangement. As more and more opportunities arose for the rich to increase their prestige by spending their income on luxury goods, they foolishly grasped at those opportunities, and in order to do so they dismissed their military retinues, telling them to fend

[95] WN, II, pp. 702–5. The first was the conquest of Greece and Persia by the Macedonians. The fall of Carthage and the subsequent ascendancy of Rome was the second. The third was the fall of the Western Empire of Rome to the Germans.

for themselves in some other way. In his lecture notes Smith listed the influence of the Church as another important contribution to regaining Europe's liberty. The Church, he claimed, wished to increase its following among the poor and hence supported their demands for greater equality. This story, however, almost disappeared from the later version. In the *Wealth of Nations* Smith firmly stated that it was luxury that destroyed the medieval feudal order.

Smith had to solve a number of difficult problems if he wished to run with this theory. He had to determine where the luxury goods came from, since he knew that, under the post-shepherdic regime of Rome's conquerors, Europe's agricultural economy had continued to languish for a very long period.[96] Post-Roman Europe was not at all like Athens or Rome, where the development of the city and the arts went hand in hand. As Smith recognised, luxury appeared in medieval Europe via the Roman cities that survived the Gothic holocaust and kept trading, both regionally and between East and West. As an ultimate twist of history, the shepherd states that were founded on the ruins of Rome were themselves destroyed by this poisonous legacy of Rome. The Goths destroyed Rome when it was fatally weakened by luxury, but the Roman cities that survived the Gothic conquest successfully injected their luxury into the political system of their conquerors.

Their continued provision of luxury goods slowly destroyed the feudal elite, thereby opening the way for the rise of the modern constitutional state.[97] Thus the re-enactment of the sad story of ancient luxury led to a happy ending in early modern Europe. As Smith explained, this was not a straightforward playing out of the

---

[96] The problem in question is known in modern historiography as the Pirenne thesis, first formulated in the early twentieth century; for its most famous expositions see Henri Pirenne, *Medieval Cities: Their Origins and the Revival of Trade*, trans. Frank D. Halsey (Princeton, NJ: Princeton University Press, 1925) and Henri Pirenne, *Mohammed and Charlemagne*, trans. Bernard Miall (London: G. Allen and Unwin, 1939); for a recent revision see Michael McCormick, *Origins of the European Economy: Communications and Commerce, 300–900* (Cambridge: Cambridge University Press, 2001).

[97] *LJ* (A), p. 264: 'the nobility necessarily fell to ruin as soon as luxury and arts were introduced ... The nobility came to ruin before any system of liberty was established. The luxury which followd on the arts ruind their power ... the power of the nobles has allways been brought to ruin before a system of liberty has been established, and this indeed must always be the case. For the nobility are the greatest opposers and oppressors of liberty that we can imagine.'

logic of the four-stages theory of history. This was a story which was retrograde, that is, the other way round.[98] Luxury was inherited from the commercial developments of a previous cycle of European development. As it was infused into the primitive agricultural society of the feudal era, it gave a dynamism to that economy and enabled it to change itself into an appropriate base for a post-feudal polity. The political story ran along a similar trajectory. The march of luxury led to a victory of the Roman civil liberty of the towns over the lack of freedom in feudalism and absolutism. The legal regime that reflected a more advanced economy triumphed over the political residue of less advanced economic stages of history. This was the modern appropriation of the civil republicanism that survived the termination of the Roman Republic and continued to exist throughout the Principate and the post-Roman towns. In early modern Europe it became the legal regime of the new socio-economic stage based on agriculture, commerce and manufacturing, and deeply influenced the politics of large territorial states. The ancient republics were early and isolated advances to the third and fourth stage of the mode of subsistence, while the rest of the world remained in previous stages. This first experiment failed. The second time round the whole of Europe transited to legality and the advanced economy. The contagion could spread even further. As Smith explained, modern Europe had a military advantage over all the less developed societies of the world. The whole of mankind could eventually reach the same level of development, he thought, even if this would lead to the eventual dissipation of both the military and economic advantage of Europe.

This sophisticated argument about Europe's retrograde development under the influence of luxury had close ties to the explanation of authority which Smith offered in *The Theory of Moral Sentiments*. It explained why the feudal elites, having recently emerged from the shepherd mode of life, were so vulnerable to luxury. Their luxury

---

[98] WN, I, p. 380: The 'natural order of things ... in all the modern states of Europe, been, in many respects, entirely inverted ... The manners and customs which the nature of their original government introduced, and which remained after that government was greatly altered, necessarily forced them into this unnatural and retrograde order.' The term 'retrograde' was used frequently in Smith's essay on 'The History of Astronomy' in Adam Smith, *Essays on Philosophical Subjects*, ed. W. P. D. Wightman and J. C. Bryce (Oxford: Clarendon Press, 1980), pp. 57, 60–1, 63, 66, 72–3, 81.

was the kind of prestige consumption that characterised all shepherd states. It was an exercise in demonstrating authority and thereby garnering and solidifying political obedience. It was politics, although not the kind of politics that depended on using physical force, but one that operated on the terrain of opinion. For baubles and trinkets, for acquiring wealth as a source of authority, the feudal elites abandoned their real levers of power. Smith did not argue that medieval populations recoiled from revolution because of their admiration of the rich and powerful. Rather, he demonstrated how elites destroyed themselves when they bought into the same underlying psychology and shored up their authority by ostentatious prestige displays, even when they knew that the expenditure and the economic transformation it engendered could ruin them. Political change happened, on the whole, not because of a revolution against a corrupt ruling class, but through the self-destruction of elites. These elites consistently undermined their own power base by failing to understand the intricate intertwining of power and authority in their own feudal political culture.

Smith tried to provide a complete theoretical history of European politics from its early beginnings to his own time, in order to close the gaping hole in Locke's account of how commerce corrupted politics to such a degree that the damage could be repaired only by revolution. Locke's consent theory of political obligation was designed to protect and support this conclusion. Smith's response to Locke lies in his history and theory of the influence of wealth and economic development over European politics from the ancient republics to modern European commercial society. Only by fully understanding its content and implications can we ascertain whether Smith could offer an alternative to Locke's normative political theory. Smith's ambition as a political thinker was breathtaking. Secular political theorists can lose nothing and stand to gain a great deal both by taking Smith seriously as a political thinker and by abandoning the attempt to try to pigeon-hole his work as mere historical sociology.

If we heed John Dunn's call to refocus our efforts in political theory on the issue of political judgement, in the very broad and political sense that he suggests, we have to move on from a choice between Hobbes and Locke, representative sovereignty or resistance theory, as the primary framework for understanding the history of modern political thought. John Dunn would probably agree that the Kantian suggestion to put a partial safety net under the problem of political judgement needs to be integrated, however belatedly, into his quest for a post-Lockean political discourse. We should, however, proceed along a different road from the one that was travelled by modern Kantians in the late twentieth century. A good way to integrate Kant's thoughts on political judgement into this debate would be to compare Kant's own ideas on political reform systematically with those of Smith. When one reads the material that survives from Smith's theoretical history of European law and government alongside Kant's essay 'On the common saying: That may be correct in theory, but it is no use in practice', one is struck by the tremendous synergy between these two bodies of work.

A good starting point for such a comparison would be to compare the component elements of Kant's essay with Part VI Chapter II 'Of the Order in which Societies are by nature recommended to our Beneficence' of *The Theory of Moral Sentiments*, which appeared in the last edition of the book, in 1790.[99] In this chapter Smith breaks down patriotism into two components, the safeguarding of the basic order of society based on political obligation, and the desire to improve society and increase its happiness and welfare.[100] Smith is preoccupied with controlling judgement relating to the second, insisting that it must not ever breach the duties involved in the first. In this respect Kant and Smith move along the same trajectory, and Kant's solution is perhaps superior, because Smith relies argumentatively on Plato's comparison between endangering the *polis* through failed initiatives for reform and parricide in the *Crito*.[101] However, Kant allows sovereigns the freedom to act on their reform impulses once basic safeguards against the harm caused by reforms to the society's legal infrastructure are in place, while Smith argues against

---

[99] *TMS*, pp. 207–34.   [100] *TMS*, p. 231.

[101] *TMS*, p. 233. Plato's maxim in Smith's text ultimately refers to *Crito*, 51c: 'Both in war and in the law courts and everywhere else you must do whatever your city and country command, or else persuade them in accordance with universal justice, but violence is a sin even against your parents, and it is a far greater sin against your country' (trans. Hugh Tredennick), although Smith actually refers to Plato's *Crito* through Cicero's citation of it in *Epistulae ad Familiares*, English translation as *Letters to Friends*, ed. and trans. D. R. Shackleton Bailey, Loeb Classical Library (Cambridge, MA: Harvard University Press, 2001), Letter 20 [I.9] 'Cicero to Lentulus Spinther' (Rome, December 54), para. 18, pp. 137–8.

any form of enlightened despotism, and provides a powerful analysis of the psychology and power relations involved in judgements that lead to social and economic experiments. Behind his ideas stands his theoretical history of law and government and the strategy for economic reform that was built on it in the *Wealth of Nations*. In 'On the common saying' Kant hints at protectionism and economic nationalism as consequences of his safety net of protecting the citizens of modern societies against the consequences of modern trade,[102] while Smith concludes that such a judgement ignores the history of Europe, in which commerce and liberty grew hand in hand. Kant's idea was most consistently developed by Fichte, in his 1800 book on *The Closed Commercial State*,[103] the best historical example of implementing Kant's idea of a hypothetical contract in the terrain of modern political economy. The contrast between Fichte's economic model, based on the concept of right and guaranteeing the right to work, and Smith's is striking and needs to be fully understood, not simply as a divergence in understanding political economy, but in

[102] Kant, 'On the common saying', p. 298n.
[103] J. G. Fichte, *Der Geschlossene Handelsstaat: Ein philosophischer Entwurf als Anhang zur Rechtslehre und Probe einer künftig zu liefernden Politik* (Tübingen: J. G. Cotta, 1800), reprinted in Fichte, *Ausgewählte Politische Schriften*, eds. Zwi Batscha and Richard Saage (Frankfurt am Main: Suhrkamp, 1977). Excerpts from the *Closed Commercial State* were translated in H. S. Reiss, ed., *The Political Thought of the German Romantics, 1793–1815* (Oxford: Blackwell, 1955). On Fichte's political economy, see Adam Müller, 'Ueber einen philosophischen Entwurf von Hrn Fichte, betitelt: *Der geschloßne Handelstaat*', *Neue Berlinische Monatsschrift* 6 (1801), 436–8; Gustav Schmoller, 'J. G. Fichte: Eine Studie aus dem Gebiete der Ethik und der Nationalökonomie' in *Zur Litteraturgeschichte der Staats- und Sozialwissenschaften* (Leipzig: Duncker und Humblot, 1888); Marianne Weber, *Fichtes Sozialismus und sein Verhältnis zur Marx'schen Doktrin* (Tübingen: Freiburg i. B. and Leipzig: J. C. B. Mohr (P. Siebeck), 1900); Ernst Bloch, 'Fichtes geschlossener Handelsstaat oder Produktion und Tausch nach Vernunftrecht' in Bloch, *Das Prinzip Hoffnung* (Frankfurt am Main: Suhrkamp, 1973), pp. 642–7; Werner Krause, 'Fichtes ökonomische Anschauungen im Geschlossenen Handelsstaat', *Wissen und Gewissen: Beiträge zum 200. Geburtstag Johann Gottlieb Fichtes 1762–1814*, ed. Manfred Buhr (Berlin: Akademie Verlag, 1962); Andreas Verzar, *Das autonome Subjekt und der Vernunftstaat: Eine systematisch-historische Untersuchung zu Fichtes Geschlossene Handelsstaat von 1800* (Bonn: Bouvier, 1979); Richard T. Gray, 'Economic Romanticism: Monetary Nationalism in Johann Gottlieb Fichte and Adam Müller', *Eighteenth-Century Studies*, 36 (2003), 535–57; see also Douglas Moggach, 'Fichte's Engagement with Machiavelli', *History of Political Thought*, 14 (1993), 573–89.

terms of political theory. In many ways John Rawls' adaptation of Kant to social democracy in the United States was a merger between the Kantian and Smithian approaches and failed for that reason. The problems involved in this can be rethought productively if one realises that behind the *Wealth of Nations*, as indicated by its third book, there is Smith's history of law and government with its novel theorising of the relationship between the principles of authority and utility as a guide for judgement. Contrasting and synthesising Kant and Smith, to be sure, would oblige us to look at Smith not merely as a historical sociologist, political economist and natural jurist, but as a theorist of authority and liberty, a major and original political thinker in his own right.

6 Marxism in translation: critical reflections on Indian radical thought

SUDIPTA KAVIRAJ

Introduction

Any observer of the modern world of politics is likely to notice an interesting and puzzling fact to which social scientists and political theorists have not given sufficient attention. Today's world shows a bewildering variety of actual political institutions – from tribal chieftainships, to assorted monarchies, to the diverse range of modern democracies. Yet, the language deployed in describing, evaluating and analysing them is remarkably uniform, drawn primarily from the range of judgements that emerged from analyses of the political history of modern Europe. To appropriate Mill's phrase for our purposes, human beings' language about politics is much narrower than the actual diversity of their experience. This carries an interesting implication for the study of political ideas. It suggests that although in other locations of the world people are purportedly running socialist parties or liberal governments and working democratic systems, these qualifying adjectives frequently mean something appreciably different from the meanings they bear in their original Western contexts.[1] As a result, the study of political language becomes a demanding yet exciting discipline – its task being to stalk and capture strange practices masquerading under familiar names. It is true that the early work of John Dunn that came

[1] Although the contextualist study of political theory, for which John Dunn argued forcefully in his early works, was primarily confined to the analysis of the Western canon, this is an obvious extension of its methodological principles – if we begin to study political ideas in other cultural settings. See John Dunn, 'The Identity of the History of Ideas' (1968) repr. in *Political Obligation in Its Historical Context: Essays in Political Theory* (Cambridge: Cambridge University Press, 1980).

closest to appreciating this complex subterfuge was not primarily or exclusively directed at this problem: its central purpose was to convey a deeply felt concern that the resources of contemporary Western political theory were inadequate for an understanding of the world in which the West lived.[2] But by implication it was poorly equipped for meeting the challenges beyond the frontiers of the West. Long before the current fashion for emphasising the fact that we live in a globalised world in which causalities and influences swirl uninterruptedly across vast tracts of the earth, the fates of Western and other cultures were entwined through complex relations of compulsion and emulation, of hard and soft power, through European colonialism and native resistance. For a considerably longer period than merely the last fifty years or so, the world has been unified through the use of an increasingly shared 'language' of politics learnt by the rest of the world through its absorption of the Enlightenment. Terms like liberal, democratic, socialist, communist and Marxist acquired a strangely untroubled currency as means of depicting the political institutions, movements and aspirations of people in vastly different cultures. To understand what 'Western' political theory – in its varying forms – has done in the world is therefore to move beyond the local history of Western societies.

There is a second reason why it is appropriate to enquire into the uncharted territory of modern India's political languages. India has been arguably one of the success stories of the export of Western ideas for organising political life.[3] Despite the existence and the easy accessibility of an ancient civilisation, an astonishingly successful mixture of the Hindu and Islamic cultural traditions, India's modern

---

[2] John Dunn, *Western Political Theory in the Face of the Future* (Cambridge: Cambridge University Press, 1979).

[3] I do not think the present revival of colonial nostalgia is backed by compelling political reasoning. Its success relies rather heavily on its similarity to the ambition of the last US administration to assume the role of the successor to British dominion of the world in the nineteenth century. Unfortunately, some strands in British political commentary have fallen for this enticement, and there is a tendency to portray British imperial domination as a rather early combination of the functions of the Department of International Development and the British Council – intent only on spreading the knowledge of Shakespeare and democracy. My argument is not the same as the celebratory thought that Indian democracy has succeeded obviously because of the long British tutorship – which seems to have failed rather spectacularly in the neighbouring areas of Burma, Pakistan and large segments of Anglophone Africa.

political life has been resolutely untraditional. After the collapse of
the revolt of 1857 against British colonial power, there was no serious
attempt to revive traditional political imaginaries.[4] The Congress, the
primary vehicle of India's national struggle against British rule, and
the strands which contested its dominance – like the Muslim League,
or the Hindu nationalist movement – all drew the fundamental elements of their political imagination from modern European political
ideals of nationalism, constitutionalism and representative government.[5] None of them seriously contemplated a return to traditional
political organisation. The Indian story is also peculiarly apt for a
discussion of Dunn's ideas, because he has, at least since the decisive
decline of communist states in the 1980s, tried to make sense of the
reasons why liberal democracy has slowly secured its ascendancy over
a rival vision of egalitarian society – without in the process resorting to a simplistic or morally triumphalist explanation.[6] While being
alert to this undeniable historical fact, he has avoided three common forms of thinking about it: neither viewing a capitalist economy
as embodying in some sense a 'natural' form of human economic
organisation which was somehow bound to flower whenever artificial traditional controls were lifted; nor attributing this development
to the incontestable moral superiority of the capitalist economy; nor

---

[4] It appears justified, against some nationalist interpretations suggesting that
1857 represented the first stirrings of Indian nationalism, to see it as the last
stirrings of a more traditional conception of political rule – though it was certainly fuelled by resentment against government by alien rulers. Some of these
controversies have been revived again in the controversies regarding William
Dalrymple's study of the rebellion, *The Last Mughal: The Fall of a Dynasty,
Delhi 1858* (London: Bloomsbury, 2006).

[5] I do not mean they were equally impelled by nationalist and democratic ideals; but they were all equally involved in working out different positions on
questions about what a nation was, what kind of representation was justified,
whether democracy was an acceptable form of government – which all yield
equally modern, if not equally pleasant, answers.

[6] See particularly his very insightful comments on Marxism as a theory of modern politics, where, against usual trends, he suggests that its critique of modern
capitalism remains deeply compelling, but its failure was mainly in successfully conceiving an alternative economic form of modern life. Particularly
important in this connection are: John Dunn, *The Politics of Socialism: An
Essay in Political Theory* (Cambridge: Cambridge University Press, 1984)
and John Dunn, 'Capitalism, Socialism and Democracy: Compatibilities and
Contradictions' in John Dunn, ed., *The Economic Limits to Modern Politics*
(Cambridge: Cambridge University Press, 1990).

concluding from the present that the current dominance of capitalist economy and liberal democracy must continue on historical cruise control into an indefinite future. What makes his thinking about the current situation interesting and complex is his attribution of this historical development to contingencies of political life, and his conviction that despite the current absence of any serious ideological challenge to liberalism, it is hard to deny the truth of at least one component part of the socialist critique: that given the levels of productivity contemporary economies can achieve, it is hard to justify the capitalist unconcern for the distributive inequalities that afflict the present organisation of world politics.[7] In Dunn's view, the classic socialist criticism of 'poverty in the midst of plenty' – or, to correct this somewhat, the persistence of poverty in the face of an evident potential for plenty – remains a fundamental cause for political alarm. It is essential, on this view, to see the premature deaths of thousands of children in Africa from preventable or reducible disease as completely unnecessary, rather than as a regrettable but necessary part of the proper functioning of an unstoppable machine. For Dunn, the failure of socialism is not primarily due to the implausibility of its indictment of capitalist economies, but to its failure to devise an institutional form to supplant them with something practically superior.

Interestingly, the historical trajectory of Indian politics parallels this process unfolding on a world scale. In the fifties, after independence, actors in the Indian political universe spoke a predominantly Western language, and the main political parties and individual agents defined their positions in terms of the modern language of politics deriving originally from Europe – including liberal supporters of unrestricted capitalism,[8] socialist advocates of a 'mixed economy',[9] communist projects for a radical overthrow of what they rather gratuitously called 'the bourgeois state' in favour

---

[7] For a lucid and powerfully persuasive argument from an economic point of view on global economic iniquities, see Joseph Stiglitz, *Globalisation and Its Discontents* (New York: W. W. Norton, 2003) and his more recent *Making Globalization Work* (New York: Simon and Schuster, 2006).

[8] The Swatantra Party, literally meaning the Free Party.

[9] This position is represented, strictly speaking, by the Nehruvian centre of the Congress Party, though Congress included people who subscribed to a large variety of ideological positions.

of a utopian egalitarian economic order,[10] and even some admirers
of the power and impressive discipline of German Fascism.[11] It is
interesting that even the rulers of the 'princely states', delicately supported by British rule, did not produce any credible advocacy of a
return to monarchical government.[12] It is true that the 'democratic'
alternative eventually won out in India – in fact, somewhat earlier
than the fall of international communism. By the late 1960s, Indian
radical politics was already conceding defeat to liberal democracy
in two rather peculiar ways. From the mid-1960s, the organised
communist movement, which might have emerged as a serious chal-
lenger to Nehru's government, was already fragmenting into smaller
and fractious pieces which shifted their political energies to mutual
destruction rather than opposition to 'bourgeois' parties. Secondly,
in a more subtle process of imaginative defeat, the most effective sections of the fragmenting radical movement secretly accepted a complete absorption into ordinary electoral politics – banishing serious
social change to the level of pure rhetoric.[13] The most effective section of the Indian left became a party which was both impeccably
Stalinist in its ideology and impeccably electoralist in its political
practice. More recently it has owned up to its imaginative exhaus-
tion by simply accepting the current equation of the establishment
of shopping malls with the achievement of economic growth. In this
chapter, I hope to show how Dunn's powerful diagnosis of the current situation facing Western political theory applies with equal force
to the Indian situation as well. The recent spurt in the Indian economy after liberalisation has not disposed of the traditional problem

[10] The Communist Party of India.
[11] Hindu nationalists often openly spoke with admiration about German Nazism –
attracted presumably by their discipline, which, in their view, Indians chronically
lacked, and the ethnic conception of a nation united by language, religion and
culture – which they desired for India. Such admiration for German discipline
and defiance of British domination of the world was more widely shared in colonial India, and the Hindu nationalists' admiration for the Nazis came from the
pre-war era.
[12] For an interesting analysis of the grounds of British admiration for these 'natural rulers' see David Cannadine, *Ornamentalism* (London: Penguin Books,
2001), especially chapters 4 and 5.
[13] It was a rather badly kept secret, as the evidence of their electoral character was writ large on every aspect of their practice; in annual conferences,
however, they continued to indulge in a strange ceremony of affirmation of
improbably Stalinist principles.

of 'plenty in the midst of poverty' (to adapt the phrase to Indian conditions) – of American-style condominiums rising from a sea of slums. But socialists, for their part, have not been able to provide any answer to the seductions of either the economic practices of capitalism or the political structures of liberal democracy. This chapter does not attempt to develop a comprehensive explanation for this complex history. Instead it offers some observations on the characteristic problems that have beset the 'translation'[14] of radical socialist ideas into an Indian context. It is hoped that this will contribute to an explanation of the baffling failure of egalitarian politics in a society of deep and degrading inequality.

I Two approaches to the history of ideas

There is a fundamental distinction between two ways of thinking about the grounds of persuasion in the history of ideas: the first is a general rationalist approach associated with Enlightenment thought, probably best articulated in Kant and in what might be termed a 'critical' Marxist view.[15] In the Althusserian tradition, the latter perspective is assimilated to Feuerbach as distinct from Marx himself. But in any case the true originator of the humanistic approach is Kant, whose way of thinking about intellectual persuasion informs much of liberal theory. This tradition of thought rests on the assumption of the presence of a universally available apparatus of rational thinking in all human beings, such that moral principles, if they are correctly enunciated, would be clear in their meaning and compelling in their practical implications to all human beings independently of their

---

[14] Translation, in this case, is a vague term, indicating a resemblance to the activity of literary writers in converting a text from one language to another. In the case of political theory, the conversion has to negotiate many layers of complexity – of two *conceptual* languages, two cultures, different historical trajectories. To call the process a 'translation' is a preliminary notice of the difficulties, not an entirely clear programme. It is necessary to understand more clearly what exactly is involved in the process of this 'translation'.

[15] In a sense, it is wrong to attribute this notion too closely to Marx: elements of such a view are fairly common in earlier social thought – for example, in the sardonic reference to conditions of persuasiveness of theories in Thomas Hobbes' closing remarks in *Leviathan*, ed. C. B. Macpherson (Harmondsworth: Penguin Books, 1968), p. 729: 'For such Truth, as opposeth no man's profit nor pleasure, is to all men welcome.'

position in social structures or their location in culture. Against this –
as Althusser showed persuasively in *For Marx* – Marx, as early as the
Economic and Philosophical Manuscripts, set out the view that the
persuasiveness of a set of ideas depended on historical and situational
factors like *class*.[16] The conclusion drawn from the analysis presented
in the crucial fragment on 'Estranged Labour' in the Manuscripts suggests that rational assent to abstract ideas is mediated by an apparatus
of reflection that is deeply anchored in the social experience of thinking subjects.[17] Social experience in Marx's Europe was fundamentally
decided by class; but we can read this proposition more generally, and
emphasise the social mediation of rational plausibility, rather than the
historically specific form it takes in mid-nineteenth-century Europe.
This implies that the 'rational plausibility' of a political idea is much
more deeply mired in the social ecologies of thinking than Kant was
prepared to suppose. This distinction is reflected in the way in which
liberals and Marxists have thought about the manner in which their
ideas might be applied to or spread within societies outside the modern West. Liberal theory is usually less worried about cultural and
historical differences; Marxist theory, on the other hand, has been
seriously concerned about historical differences in social structures,
and the consequent problem of whether and how various social groups
might find ideals plausible. Interestingly, whenever Marxist groups
have successfully extended egalitarian principles to a very different
context from the West European one – as in the case of Russia or
China – there was a prior attempt to tackle the complex of questions
raised by the 'historicity' of this theory. Broadly, these two conceptions of theory can be labelled a contextless-universal and a contextual theory of political persuasion.

It is possible then to distinguish between three different views of
what persuades actors and groups to accept a particular body of social
theory. The first asserts that adherents to theory are convinced by the
rational arguments about social justice, which should be acceptable to
all reasoning individuals irrespective of their social location. On this
view, a correct or a true theory should be reasonably acceptable to

---

[16] Louis Althusser, 'On the Young Marx' in *For Marx*, trans. Ben Brewster
(London: Allen Lane, 1969).
[17] Karl Marx, 'Estranged Labour' in *Economic and Philosophical Manuscripts*,
trans. Martin Milligan (Moscow: Progress Publishers, 1974), pp. 61–74.

all. A second universalist view would claim that a true theory would convince all reasonable persons because of its scientific character, entirely independent, unlike the first case, of its moral appeal. A third view, which Marx himself and some Marxists after him have put forward, would hold that the persuasiveness of social theories has a strong link to social positionality; and that Marxist theory is persuasive to the working class because it views the social world and its conflicts from a point of view which parallels their experience in capitalist society. Clearly, there is a dissonance between the second and the third conception of theoretical persuasion; and both Marx himself, and Marxists after him, have appealed to these two different, if not contradictory, positions. A central feature of this third view is the connection this sets up between social experience and the plausibility of a theoretical view. This implies that a theory is unlikely to appeal to a group of political actors if it does not square with the way they picture their own social experience. If the argument is taken seriously that the persuasiveness of political theory owes something to its alignment with social experience, this raises an important question for cases where Marxism, or any Western-derived theory, is used to analyse a non-Western social structure. Inside Western Europe, it is possible to make a strong argument that the angle of vision of radical theory is aligned perspectivally to the social experience of the industrial proletariat. But how should this be 'translated' into the different social ecology of an Indian society which is historically and culturally different, and where the impulses of modernity are still rudimentary? This is the first point of translation. Indian intellectuals attracted to the egalitarian ideals of Marxism are faced with a translation problem: how should the demand for equality be translated into the terms of historically existing social discourse?

II   Principles in history: universalism in Indian Marxism

In a sense, some theoretical guidance about this crucial judgement could be drawn from Marx's own intellectual trajectory. In his own self-interpretation, Marx consciously moved away from the abstract egalitarianism of earlier socialist thought to a historicising version of egalitarian ideals. To be practically effective, egalitarianism had to pass through a historical translation. Egalitarian politics needs to be based on the precise historical character of existing social conflicts ('the structure of contradictions'). Equality can make sense to people, and produce effectual politics, only if two conditions are met: if the abstract principle – equality – is 'translated' into a register of historical sociology, and if it can be linked to the every-day self-interpretation of political agents. If these are viewed as specific methodological demands of Marx's political thought – namely, how something abstract like social theory could be made to produce entirely practical effects – then the ways in which Indian Marxists thought about their social world and acted on it politically begin to appear rather surprising.

On account of this methodological imperative, Marxist analyses of politics proceed from a description of 'a mode of production' or a 'social form'. Social formations, in most historical societies, are based on class stratification, or an always historically specific architecture of social inequality. Radical politics implies taking part in social conflict in favour of egalitarianism, while conflicts themselves occur around fundamental divides between social groups specific to a given social form. To get the social geography of groups right is to gain a correct picture of the form of society in question. In the abstract, Indian Marxists were alert to this methodological requirement; but they proceeded to advance their analysis in a highly peculiar fashion. Obviously Indian society was passing through rapid and fundamental social transformations. Understanding political possibilities required an accurate picture of *two* social forms – the one that prevailed before the arrival of modern processes and institutions, and the form into which Indian society might evolve in the future. Indian Marxists assumed that from Marx's theoretical picture of Western European capitalist economies they possessed a reliable picture of what future Indian society would look like. But the central question of how to characterise pre-modern Indian society within the conceptual language of Marxist social theory remained. If the egalitarian political project entailed acting upon existing lines of social cleavage and conflict – on the side of the disadvantaged – it was necessary to understand what, given the specific character of Indian society, these groups were and how they habitually acted in the world. This would certainly involve taking into account, in thinking critically about the society, the self-conceptions of subaltern social groups.

In identifying the appropriate form of society, Indian Marxists followed two lines of reasoning – both of which were 'universalist' in character, but to different degrees. An inventory of all possible social formations in human history was drawn from Marx's reflections on long-term historical processes. On three specific occasions in his intellectual career, Marx was seriously engaged in thinking about the possible range of social forms – in early texts like *German Ideology* and the *Communist Manifesto* between 1846 and 1848; in middle-period texts like the famous introduction to *A Contribution to the Critique of Political Economy* and the *Grundrisse* between 1857 and 1858; and in the late-period correspondence with Engels and Vera Zasulich, which included speculation about Germanic and Slavonic 'social forms'.[18] For nearly three decades – from the 1940s to the 1960s – Indian Marxist thinking vigorously engaged with these texts and their theoretical preoccupations. These debates had to labour under some serious textual constraints. Marx's letters from the late period were not very well known, and his ethnographic notes had not yet been published in English. Consequently, their readings were obliged to focus on the works from the early- and middle-period texts.

Two main lines of argument emerged from this trawl through Marx's texts in search of the determination of the form of society in India prior to the entry of colonial modernity along with the world capitalist market.[19] The boldest but less sophisticated version of the first conception, illustrated by S. A. Dange's *India: From Primitive Communism to Slavery*,[20] assumed that the series of social forms outlined in the *Communist Manifesto* not only provided the list of

[18] Karl Marx and Friedrich Engels, *The German Ideology* (1846), trans. S. Ryazanskaya (Moscow: Progress Publishers, 1976), ch. 1, particularly pp. 38–41; Karl Marx and Friedrich Engels, *The Communist Manifesto* (1848), trans. Samuel Moore (London: Penguin Books, 2004), Ch. 1; the passages dealing with Marx's speculations about various social forms in *Grundrisse* (1857–9), trans. M. Nicolaus (Harmondsworth: Penguin Books, 1973); Karl Marx and Friedrich Engels, *A Contribution to the Critique of Political Economy* (1859), trans. S. W. Ryazanskaya (Moscow: Progress Publishers, 1970), p. 21. The fragments from the *Grundrisse* and the later correspondence were collected with an influential introduction by Eric Hobsbawm: see Karl Marx, *Pre-capitalist Economic Formations*, trans. Jack Cohen (New York: International Publishers, 1965).
[19] A more detailed examination of these arguments can be found in my 'On the Status of Marx's Writings on India', *Social Scientist*, 124 (September 1983), pp. 26–46.
[20] S. A. Dange, *India: From Primitive Communism to Slavery* (Bombay: People's Publishing House, 1951).

all possible social forms in human history; Marxist historians were further determined to demonstrate that each society went through every single one of these forms. Dange, therefore, strove to prove that Indian history obediently passed from a 'primitive communist' phase of classless early settlements to a slave society, before its mandatory evolution into 'feudalism'. Because of the conjunction of these two beliefs, I call this design a *strong* universalism. It was universalist in two distinct but mutually reinforcing ways. First, the sequence of forms in the *Manifesto* was a design of 'universal history', applicable to all societies; secondly, every single stage in the sequence had to apply to all societies. In subsequent periods of its evolution, from the 1960s, Marxism began to influence serious academic historical scholarship, and some of the excesses of this early version of strong universalism were significantly modified. The evident awkwardness of such extreme conceptions led Marxist scholars to search for alternative ways of characterising Indian society.[21] Still reluctant to place caste at the centre of their historical sociology, historians of a later generation softened the universalism by abandoning Dange's doctrinaire insistence that Marxist historians were committed to showing that the history of all societies necessarily passed through all of the European stages. In its place, Marxists began thinking about possible ways of *refining* the historical category of feudalism.[22]

There were probably two logical reasons why Indian Marxists wished to retain the concept of feudalism: first, for capitalism to have arisen in modern India, the social formation that preceded capitalism in the conventional Marxian sequence had to be designated feudalism; but secondly, the social form in any case deserved

---

[21] For a detailed examination of the Indian Marxist historical debates, see Harbans Mukhia, 'Marx on Pre-colonial India' in Diptendra Banerjee, ed., *Marxian Theory and the Third World* (New Delhi: Sage Publishers, 1985); Diptendra Banerjee's essay 'Marx on the "Original" Form of India's Village Community' is focused on the neglect of the hypothesis of an 'Asiatic mode of production', and reaches a different conclusion. See also Diptendra Banerjee, 'In Search of a Theory of the Pre-capitalist Modes of Production', in the same volume. For the first examination of some of these questions, which set the terms of the discussion, see Irfan Habib, 'Potentialities of Capitalist Development in the Economy of Mughal India', *Enquiry* (Winter 1971), pp. 1–56.

[22] See Victor Kiernan's excellent and wide-ranging 'History' in David McLellan, ed., *Marx: The First 100 Years* (London: Fontana Paperbacks, 1983), pp. 57–102.

to be called feudalism because of the empirical similarities between the extant features of Indian society and those of European feudalism. However, this second argument gradually faded on account of adverse empirical evidence. Nonetheless, after a long interval, a sort of consensus eventually emerged among Marxist historians, leading them to call the previous social form by the agreed name, 'Indian feudalism'.[23] This distinction between European or classical feudalism and an increasingly differentiated Indian version was useful in advancing historical research, because it protected historians from the temptation of denying altogether facts that lacked any European equivalents, or from bending individual cases so as to render them similar to European precedents. Conceptually, this solution remained problematic, because it evaded the question of how the pre-modern Indian social form diverged from the European one. It could designate a mere sub-genre of a general structure of feudalism by the addition of the term Indian, or it could suggest that the Indian pre-modern form was fundamentally different. However, in the second case, it would be quite inappropriate to settle on the term feudalism. In this connection, it is interesting to note the peculiarity of the phrasing of Harbans Mukhia's question: was there feudalism in Indian history? If feudalism was a European social structure, how could it 'be' Indian? Here Mukhia was in fact changing the question by problematising one of its key conceptual components: should, he was asking, the pre-modern Indian form be designated 'feudalism'?

III   Two concepts of class in Marx's thought

The conceptual strategies adopted by weak universalism did not solve the central problems involved in identifying specifically Indian forms of society. As is well known, traditional Indian society was based on a form of stratification known as the caste system – a hierarchy

---

[23] For a classic statement of the case, see R. S. Sharma, *Indian Feudalism* (Calcutta: University of Calcutta Press, 1965). Notably, a range of distinguished historians who use Marxist theory in different ways – from Irfan Habib to Ranajit Guha – concurred in using the category 'feudalism'. For a more general analysis of this trend and the difficulty this produced for Marxist historical theory – as feudalism became alarmingly capacious, and bore the burden of describing nearly all forms of pre-capitalist societies in the world – see Kiernan, 'History'.

of inflexible, ascriptive groupings fixed by birth – which regulated economic production, social status and access to cultural goods. The fundamental problem of Marxist analyses of Indian society was to find a way of describing the structure and dynamics of caste given the resources of Marxist historical theory. Generally, Indian Marxists assumed that to speak of the reality of castes was to fall out of this conceptual language altogether. Caste was generally regarded as an epiphenomenal fact of consciousness: while the underlying structural reality was the presence of feudal classes of the European kind. Caste and class were mutually exclusive categories, as they came from two distinct and competing languages for the description of social reality. Analyses in terms of caste could not be joined, interconnected or subsumed within analysis in terms of class. Debates between Marxist social science and its detractors thus took the form of a collision between the exponents of caste and the exponents of class – a dispute in which social anthropologists sought to explain Indian politics by explanatory reference to castes, and Marxists by class. Yet, there was no conceptual necessity for posing the problem in this particular way. Indian communists ignored a possible second move that could be derived easily from a reading of Marx's writings on history.

Clearly, there are two distinct applications for the term class in Marx's historical writings. The idea of class constantly appears and it performs a crucial function in his detailed economic studies of capitalism after 1857–8. But it also occurs in those writings that are concerned with analysing social formations other than those of capitalism. In Marx's works the term class carries more than one sense, as textual commentators have long recognised. 'Class' is used in Marx's writings on the capitalist economy of the modern West in a specific, narrow sense – to refer to the form of social stratification that is specific to modern capitalist economies. On this definition classes are relatively stable groups determined by their relation to the society's mode of production, unified by similar income, occupations and enjoyment of social power, with relatively open boundaries which individual members could cross according to their changing economic circumstances. Class, in the language of modern sociology, would be an 'open' stratification system, unlike the entirely fixed and closed system of feudal hierarchy. Quite evidently, then, there is a wider, more generic conception of class – a placeholder – which figures in Marx's more general statements about history. To take the simplest contrast, for Marx feudalism was also a 'class society', though class within feudal society operated in quite a different way. If class always and only meant the stratification system specific to capitalist economies, to claim 'all history is the history of class struggle' would then imply that all history was the history of capitalism.

In statements like these, then, Marx used the term class in a more general sense, to include classes that functioned in ways different from the classes of capitalist societies. We can designate these two senses as class (1) and class (2). If, then, there are two conceptions of class in Marx – a generic and a capitalist one – it follows that the general category must have the character of an underdetermined concept, a blank conceptual place where a determinate category might be developed. The few contrastive discussions in Marx's works which compare 'class' in capitalism with 'class' in feudal or slave societies show a clear appreciation of this difference. At times Marx says that it would be more appropriate to use the concept of 'estates', the term Hegel prefers in the *Philosophy of Right*, precisely to avoid this confusion. Estates would avoid some of the defining characteristics of class in a capitalist society, and could become one of the concepts which could fit into the more abstract and general conception of class. It was possible, if the logic of conceptualisation in Marx was viewed in this fashion, to make room for a theorisation of caste as a specific, historically located system of social stratification within a *general* theory of class, an option Indian communists by and large ignored.[24]

---

[24] Of course, Indian Marxists did not think exactly identically on the issue of basic social stratification, and some authors attempted to bring caste into a broadly Marxist analysis of society. An early example of such an attempt is Bhupendra Nath Dutta's *Studies in India's Social Polity* (Calcutta: Purabi Publishers, 1934). D. D. Kosambi continued to use the historical category of 'feudalism' but brought in interesting conceptual inflections and refinements, for instance in his *Introduction to the Study of Indian History* (Bombay: Popular Book Depot, 1956). In the fifties, the immense practical initiatives of J. Nehru and B. R. Ambedkar were influenced by their reading of a literature which stressed class inequality; and in more recent analysis of social conflict some analysts, like Gail Omvedt, have stubbornly insisted on the reality of caste. But the continuing difficulty of Marxist thinking in negotiating the problem of caste epistemically is shown by the 'conversion' of many former Naxalite activists to a 'dalit' political platform. Ambedkar, the most insistent critic of the caste system, and its most implacable enemy, demonstrated a distance and hostility to Marxism as a general theory – and particularly its application by Indian socialists – precisely because of the neglect of the fact of caste. Interestingly, Ambedkar did not characterise himself in Europic

Caste could be theorised as a historically and culturally specific form of class (1).

IV   The strange disappearance of caste

To borrow from linguistics, Indian Marxists saw class as a kind of universal grammar of social inequality, not as a historically regional form specific to European capitalism. Their inability to distinguish between the two senses of class – class (1) and class (2) – compounded this problem, and turned the caste–class debate into singularly unpropitious terrain. For one thing, it meant that Marxists were forced to insist on a much more developed state of a capitalist society in India than was remotely plausible to assert in the 1950s. This also meant the passing of a significant political opportunity. Among the various political groups active in Indian society, the Marxists were undoubtedly the most seriously committed to the reduction and eventual abolition of social inequality. But their misleading sociology directed them to abolish entirely the wrong form of inequality. Conceptual difficulties of this kind made Indian socialist discourse a rather contorted way of thinking about equality. On the one hand, leftists were most deeply committed to an end of inequality in Indian society; on the other, their sociological writings, which had the function of understanding the bases of social power, and consequently of inequality, were strangely indifferent to the primary form in which Indians actually experienced inequality in social life. With some few exceptions, Marxist writers rarely sought to engage with the problem of viewing caste as the primary stratificational structure of the traditional Indian social form.[25] In the 1980s, Arun Bose untypically called on Marxists

descriptions like 'socialist' or 'communist', but adhered to a more abstract affiliation to egalitarianism, recognising both his fundamental commitment to a liberal political equality and a strong sense that, in a society like the Indian, a Tocquevillian extension of egalitarianism from one sphere to another was highly likely. See his valedictory address to the Constituent Assembly of India in Valerian Rodrigues, ed., *The Essential Writings of B. R. Ambedkar* (Delhi: Oxford University Press, 2004).

[25] Two atypical writers who wrote about caste stratification among early Marxist authors were D. D. Kosambi and Bhupendra Nath Dutta. Kosambi's historical work exerted wide influence, but not to encourage others to theorise the problem of caste. B. N. Dutta's work on the early evolution of caste society was entirely neglected, unlike his better-known analysis of land relations.

to combine the resources of Marxism with an anthropological study of caste along the lines already pioneered by Louis Dumont.[26] But he met with little response. Even academic strands of Marxism, which were far more scrupulous about the systematic collection and analysis of social stratification, neglected the study of caste relations, although, by the 1970s, large parts of Indian society were engulfed in intense, often violent forms of electoral caste politics. One of the odd features of the well-known debate about the 'development of capitalism in agriculture', which paid close attention to changes in patterns of agricultural production and sources of economic power in rural India, was that it gave relatively little attention to the operation of caste-based inequality.[27]

Consequently, the nature of sociological analysis determined, in a rather interesting fashion, the political efficacy of radical movements. To anticipate later arguments, one of the primary features of India's political sociology is that there exists no single 'India' to analyse: sociologically and politically, the 'idea of India' has a second-order quality. Political agents do not directly inhabit a space called India, they must inhabit more local spaces – with their peculiar historical, sociological and cultural attributes – in order to inhabit the space called India. Owing to this segmented aspect of Indian society, the primacy of class analysis drew radical politics inevitably towards those parts of India where this sociology could apply with some felicity; and it was hardly surprising that these were the industrialised metropolitan regions. Of course, communist politics acquired political influence in these areas for a more directly political, less epistemically detached reason. Trade union organisations were initially established by communist activists, and consequently communists possessed wide electoral support together with a street presence in these cities. It is likely, however, that the epistemic inclination towards class analysis gave them a sharper understanding of social conflicts than their competitors.

The cost radical politics had to pay for this epistemic inability to see any form of stratification other than class was an attenuated grasp of India's vast countryside. Communist social analysts were

---

[26] Arun Bose, *India's Social Crisis* (Delhi: Oxford University Press, 1985).

[27] For a selection of essays from the long-running debate, see Utsa Patnaik, ed., *Development of Capitalism in Indian Agriculture* (Delhi: Oxford University Press, 1990).

committed to one of two awkward positions. The first of these was
the idea that class stratification existed in all social milieux, but without the agents themselves being aware of that fact – a form of argument which had a long life in modern social theory, particularly in
the Marxist tradition. If confronted with the factual ubiquity of caste
structures, Marxists could easily have recourse to a 'false consciousness' argument. Social agents did indeed believe and act as if caste
relations captured some kind of reality; but class could nonetheless
be shown to represent a deeper, more fundamental grid of underlying
social relations – 'underlying' in both senses in which Marxists would
use this notion. Class was an underlying reality in the sense that it
exerted a more fundamental causal pressure on political conduct; but
also in the sense of its not being immediately accessible to the agents
themselves. In analysing social reality, Indian Marxists often used all
the resources of this kind of 'depth ontology' common to nineteenth-
century social science. Caste was reduced, misleadingly, to a matter of
consciousness. Caste-consciousness thus turned into something 'epiphenomenal', present to the consciousness of the agents, but super-
seded by the superior philosophical vision of Marxist social scientists,
exactly like the famous cases of natural science inversion of common-
sense pictures of the world. One important result of this was a curious
transposition of the real and the ideal: while ordinary Indians could
persistently complain about the oppressive everyday reality of caste
inequality, radical commentators could look condescendingly at their
inability to see through the *appearance* of caste to the 'reality' of
classes, giving rise to a double gratification: that of being intellectually
subtler than the common peasant, while at the same time putting this
higher rationality in the service of their social emancipation – a pleas-
ing conjunction of cognitive and moral superiority.

This substitution of caste by class as a hyper-real, underlying reality
had a further consequence. In effect, Marxism was an incisive theory
about modern capitalism. Applying first its descriptive and then its
explanatory categories to different social forms transposed the real
and the unreal in a still different sense, and laid bare a radical epistemic malaise afflicting much of modern social science. Marxism, as
part of modern social science, employed categories that resulted from
a distillation of the historical experience of the modern West – the
temporally and spatially particular history of the capitalist economy.
This is not surprising in view of the intimate connection between

experience and cognition in social life. If we accept that European history is written into these categories in some sense, their unproblematic application to India gives rise to serious problems of factual misrecognition. This meant that historical experience operated inside the categories as a form of conceptual gravitation – tending to drag analyses of distinct societies into a persistent but distorting resemblance to European history, in the process conferring upon European experience and its history the status of apparent 'normalcy'. An implicit European reference works from the heart of the conceptual apparatus of modern social sciences, turning it 'naturally' towards Euro-normality, much as the magnetic properties of a compass needle always make it point north.

European history is the natural north of modern social science. To use the term state is instantly to evoke the Weberian state, that is, the modern European one. To speak of a society is to use its default meaning of a modern Western sense of a collection of individuals. To use these concepts in any other sense is hard and requires a further conscious process of evacuation of the European connotation naturally lodged inside the concept. The Marxist error of transposing class for caste acts as an illustration of this wider tendency in social science thinking. It was this pervasive form of thinking that made the transposition of caste into class possible – turning the European condition of class into the *natural* form of stratification, turning caste into something strange that required elaboration. Retrospectively, this can be seen as a bizarre kind of strangeness, created by an epistemic property built into the apparatus of fundamental concepts, as if a kind of self-relation to Europe was buried deep in the ordinarily inaccessible core of its very categories: a kind of ineradicable conceptual 'unconscious', a subtle, silent history sitting inside the concepts and pulling explanations in the direction of Europe. It is as though all other historical forms had to apologise for their existence.

Serious reflection on this problem of course shows that this is not a problem peculiar to Marxist theory, but a more general difficulty involved in applying social scientific theories to non-European societies and their earlier history. But the case of Indian Marxism brings into particularly clear relief the problem of theory in relation to political agency. It could be argued that Marxists did not entirely neglect factual properties of the caste system on the ground – at least not its economic characteristics. Characterising these pre-capitalist social relations as *feudalism*, Marxists were evidently trying to capture in their conceptual net precisely those features – such as the existence of non-market compulsions on agricultural labour.[28] But the use of the concept of feudalism did not solve the problems involved because, despite partial similarities, caste is stubbornly different from the structure of feudal 'estates', and the substitution of feudal social relations for a caste order worked as a strange substitution of one social ontology for another. At most, an approach through categories of European feudalism gave communists something caste-like to analyse, not caste itself. Feudal society was also a system of closed stratification, primarily determined by birth: but it did not possess the detailed rules of endogamy, prohibitions on social interaction, and religious associations that the caste order had. The situation became even more problematic when the arrival of independence inaugurated an era of serious liberal-democratic politics. Marx's political sociology expected from political agents a strong sense of historical realism. Effective politics required that political initiatives 'reflected' or connected to real social cleavages in society. Democratic political institutions introduced an even more stringent requirement of political intelligibility into this scene. Political ideals required a genuine connection with the intentions of ordinary political agents; and to link up with their intentions in the political world, ideals had to connect to their existing patterns of self-interpretation. If ordinary agents in Indian society interpreted their location in society in terms of caste, and perceived injustice as caste inequality, to ignore that central fact was to miss entirely any potential connection with their intentions. By applauding their own acuity, their ability to penetrate to the underlying depth ontology of social relations, which ordinary political agents could not grasp in their pre-scientific common sense, Marxists in fact alienated their politics from the ordinary people's sense of what real cleavages in Indian society were.

V Textualisation of the world

This does not imply that the historical analyses of Indian Marxism did not involve serious intellectual labour; but it is to suggest that

---

[28] For examples of such analysis of feudalism, see the essays in *ibid*.

this labour assumed a peculiar form, and despite the undeniable rationalism of Marxist thinking, it bore some resemblance to the techniques of traditional Brahminical learning. One of the major drawbacks of Brahminical learning could be described in terms of its *textualisation* of the world. Some forms of Brahminical learning were obsessively textual in a peculiar sense: knowledge in any particular field required mastery over often arcane and difficult textual material. It required the double mastery of an esoteric language, often rendered into particularly exacting form in its search for conceptual exactitude and logical rigour, and of highly complex modes of argument specific to individual *sastras* (systems of knowledge). Eventually, in many cognitive fields, the textual, propositional world took over from the referential world which the texts were about, often giving rise to systems of ideas which became irrefutable because of their lack of reference to reality. Learning came to be regarded as mastery not of the world outside, but of the shadowy, wordy world inside texts which, instead of making the real world available, actually obscured it. If a peasant asked a learned Brahmin for advice about planting seeds for the propitious growth of his crops in the next season, the Brahmin would have taken this request seriously as a cognitive question. Usually, he would immerse himself in treatises which provide complex, internally consistent calculations, with demanding internal rules of procedure: he might produce a precise conclusion at the end, suggesting that sowing should occur between 3.17 and 4.53 on a particular day of the month because there is a conjunction of the relevant planets, producing particularly propitious conditions for the flourishing of a specific crop. What is remarkable in this procedure is that this involves mastery of a 'science' in the true sense – an interconnected, structured body of knowledge, which requires genuine intellectual effort to acquire and to bring under cognitive control. The intellectual labour of the scholar is not delusive: it is real intellectual labour, requiring a host of necessary skills; and often additionally this depends upon mastery of esoteric languages like Sanskrit. As a cognitive system, its only fault is that it bears little connection to the real process of agricultural production. Parallel examples could be found among the Brahminical practices of advising families about the future prospects of harmony and happiness in a projected matrimony.

The procedure followed by the early Indian Marxists evinced a surprising similarity to this traditional form of truly esoteric scholarship. Certainly, for Indian intellectuals detailed grasp of the events and processes – often, to be perfectly pedantic, the dates – of distant European history was an immense intellectual challenge: first, the facts of that history were accessible only through the grasp of an erudite literature written in English; secondly, Marxists had not merely to know the factual stratum of that history, but also to process it through an unusually complex interpretative inversion; and finally, fluency in Marxist historiography required mastery of a difficult, unfamiliar conceptual language made additionally difficult by the peculiarity of Hegelian terminology and vagaries of translation. Although Marxism claimed, on the one side, to be the conceptual language of the 'downtrodden', in actual fact it became a cognitive form which contained forbidding elements of erudition and esotericism. Marxist intellectual debates had a way of turning eventually into fractious, ill-tempered contests of primarily textual erudition. Arguments were won or lost by the degree of familiarity and exegetic facility in Marx's or later Lenin's texts. A late example of this textualisation can be found in a contribution by the economist Paresh Chattopdhyay to the 1970s debate about the 'development of capitalism in agriculture'. Characteristically the paper was titled in wholly gratuitous German, 'Anti-Kritik' – which sought to disprove the judgements of another economist, Utsa Patnaik, not by referring to economic facts of agricultural production in Haryana or Bihar, or other Indian regions where the green revolution had taken place, but by allegedly incontestable evidence drawn from Marx's writings on capitalism – preferably from the more obscure, less accessible, later editions of his texts.[29] Historical practices are known to be remarkably resilient; and it might be an interesting project to apply the Marxists' mistrust of 'transparency' in intellectual practice to their own collective work. Marxists certainly did not wish to emulate or to continue 'Brahminical' traditions of cognitive practice: but if we disregard what they thought about the way they thought, some of these deep patterns of behaviour do nonetheless appear strangely 'Brahminical'.

---

[29] It is interesting to note the title, because it named an article written in English, for a predominantly Indian audience: the purpose of the use of German was exactly similar to the Brahminical use of Sanskrit to add scholastic emphasis to perfectly ordinary ideas.

VI Generalisation, averaging and composition

The peculiar singularity of India poses a challenge to all kinds of political imagination and demands a general solution. A complex and stratified political reality demands some intellectual resolution. This can be attempted in three different ways – by generalisation, by resort to the notion of an average, and by composition. In a complex, internally segmented field of political relations, composed of say five sub-fields of A, B, C, D, E, the first and often the most tempting intellectual move is towards *generalisation*[30]– in other words, to claim the properties of one segment to be the common properties of all. This is particularly easy in cases where the location of the observer of political trends and sociological facts limits his vision within that horizon. Indian political analysis has often been plagued by the force of much plausible but inappropriate generalisation. A famous controversy about caste or class, waged between Marxists and academic sociologists in the 1960s and 1970s, often demonstrated 'generalising' arguments from both sides of the debate – claiming that either caste or class could explain *all* segments of Indian politics without any recalcitrant residue. Optimistic generalisations of this kind came apart very quickly in the face of reality. Inattention to caste politics cost radical parties dearly in their attempt to spread from the industrialised to the agrarian parts of the subcontinent. On the other hand, the success of a predominantly class-orientated politics can hardly be denied in cases like Kerala and West Bengal, despite attempts by some academic political sociologists to reduce communist success in Kerala and Andhra Pradesh, in a manner precisely reminiscent of communist analysis, to an underlying causal efficacy of caste.[31]

In other disciplines and cognitive contexts where qualitative analysis is appropriate, scholars can capture some aspects of a complex reality through an average, which has the advantage of yielding a singular judgement about a complex reality that is not misleading. But here the distinction between politics and disciplines like economics

---

[30] This is not the strict meaning of generalisation in inductive logic, but what I mean here should be sufficiently clear, and sufficiently common to students of politics.
[31] Donald Zagoria, 'The Social Basis of Indian Communism' in Richard Lowenthal, ed., *Issues in the Future of Asia* (New York: Praeger, 1969).

comes to stand out clearly. Economists, faced with two regions with
significantly different rates of income, can resolve this into a serviceable truth in terms of averages. The average, though distinct from the
real income of either region, will indicate something meaningful, in
specific contexts, about both regions. Interestingly, political analysis
does not have an equivalent of 'averaging'. Politics in West Bengal
is primarily driven by a class-orientated ideology of the Communist
Party of India (Marxist) and its coalition partners. In contiguous
Bihar, political initiatives – both electoral and violent – are primarily
pursued in terms of caste groups and their historically shifting coali-
tions. It is impossible to perform an exercise like 'producing an average' to create a composite picture of this reality of eastern India. The
truth about east Indian politics is the cognitively inconvenient fact
that the two states experience politics of irreducibly different types,
for which an 'average' cannot be found.

What I want to call *composition* (or *collocation*) is not exhausted
by a simple registration of diversity, which would imply the non-
existence of any broad framework capable of holding the segments
together. Some commentators endorse exactly this kind of simplification of political reality in India in asserting that political life, together
with its underlying social structures, is so different across the regions
that it makes no sense to think in terms of *any form of singleness*,
however indirect or attenuated that might be. Yet that would be
an evident mistake. To take a simple and startling example, if the
states in the Indian federal union were to become independent states,
there is a great likelihood that many would turn into non-democratic
regimes. West Bengal, under overwhelming communist power, would
probably have moved closer to a 'people's democracy', instead of a
'bourgeois' one, with its citizens enjoying the vastly different rights
of the populations of the former Soviet Union or present-day China.
Similarly, it is probable that various other states, because of overwhelming dominance of single leaders, or the statistically unbeatable
dominance of particular social groups, would have turned to other
forms of non-democratic rule. Indeed, sometimes it is possible to
identify trends within Indian federalism of precisely such entirely one-
sided social or political dominance. A common argument in political
theory – running through a long and distinguished Western tradition
from Montesquieu to Guizot – asserts that one condition of successful democracy is an underlying sociology in which no fundamental

social group or 'principle' acquires incontestable supremacy.[32] In Indian democracy, the presence of a countervailing power sometimes works extra-regionally. In its sixty-year democratic history, India's deeply segmented society ensured that a balance of countervailing power be maintained between its various groups. In the early period of wall to wall dominance by the Congress Party, internal representation of different regions, social groups, religious communities and ideological strands ensured that none of these groups actually enjoyed overwhelming dominance: all sections viewed their defeats as transient and thus retained an interest in democratic processes.

Examined closely, the overwhelming dominance of the Congress *party*, which has given rise to much reproachful commentary on the part of Western observers, was a thin screen behind which a bustling, highly complex system of *social competition* thrived – with each constantly opposing, restricting and balancing the other. Subsequently, from the late 1960s, after Congress dominance had progressively diminished, opposition *state* governments have tended to serve to balance the power of the *central* governments, such that political groups were never, except in some persistently difficult cases,[33] entirely exposed before the power of electorally entrenched regimes. Sometimes this is reflected in a comic spectacle: political leaders who evidently enjoyed dictatorial control of their regional parties or states acted as apparently ingenuous defenders of democracy, because each dreaded falling under the control of others and realised that the only way in which several dictators could cooperate was on the basis of strict equality. All these instances demonstrate that the fact that these segmented regions are parts of an overarching frame of Indian political institutions is a consideration of some importance. To state this more abstractly, the politics of state A is of course partially determined by its *internal* political sociology and political economy, but its being part of India is an important *relational* property of its politics. Politics in any state or sociological segment[34] is thus a product of the

---

[32] François Guizot's *History of the European Civilisation* (Harmondsworth: Penguin, 1997) offers an argument of this kind in explaining the development of modern European democracy.

[33] The case of the state of Punjab during the period of violent militancy illustrates some of these difficulties.

[34] Obviously, the boundaries of these sociological and political-economic segments do not coincide with the boundaries of states of the Indian federation;

internal characteristics of its sociology and the relational properties derived from the fact of their being part of a vast, intricate but causally significant Indian political system. In political terms, the *singleness* of India has a *second-order* quality that ought not to be confused with the more insistent, immediate causal impulsions of regional and local sociologies of power; but it would be a significant error to discount it as distant and therefore causally ineffectual.

Conclusion: judgement and political efficacy

In retrospect, there can hardly be any doubt that radical politics in India, despite its considerable resources – intellectual energy, political idealism, skilful organisation – failed to be particularly efficacious when compared to the messier and less elevated politics of the Congress. Nehru's political initiatives, after independence – not when he was a Marxist, but when he had ceased to be one – were, in the long run, surprisingly successful in making possible an unpredictable, unprecedented but at the same time undeniable transformation of some primary relations of Indian society.[35] In a broad sense, these two forms of politics – Communist radicalism and Nehruvian reformism – constituted the two major strands comprising the drive towards egalitarianism in recent Indian history. Both faced the serious challenge of having to figure out how to translate modern Western ideals of equality into the very different Indian historical context.[36] Both could be said to have made an attempt to translate an abstract principle of equality into the language of Indian history. There is hardly any doubt now that the more ambitious, radical Marxist version was far less

and also, in the nature of things, these segments often end in 'frontiers' rather than in linear 'boundaries'.

[35] There is a considerable political literature on historical interpretations of Indian democracy; see Rajeev Bhargava, 'Democratic Constitution for a New Republic' in Francine Frankel *et al.*, eds., *Transforming India* (Delhi: Oxford University Press, 2002); Sunil Khilnani, *The Idea of India* (Harmondsworth: Penguin, 1997); Pratap B. Mehta, *The Burden of Democracy* (Delhi: Penguin Books, 2004).

[36] This is not meant to deny that there were movements of social reform and critical thinking about social inequality in the pre-modern Indian tradition; but it seems to me undeniable that the primary inspiration for a politics of equality came from India's absorption of European political ideals.

successful than the liberal one represented by Nehru and Ambedkar.[37] This is a fascinating and crucial contrast, essential for understanding the prospects of translational attempts for modern Western political imaginaries across the world – a cognitive project that John Dunn's work has done a lot to clarify. What was common between communists and the radical liberals was the Enlightenment ideal of equality, and a shared belief that the instrumentality of the modern state was the primary and the only historically adequate instrument to achieve this end. The key difference lay in moral optimism, and in distinct cognitive techniques. The techniques were often quite opposite: for instance, both strands of egalitarian initiatives sought to use the concepts of caste and class – but in opposing ways. The Marxist tradition had to note the factual existence of caste as social practice, but subsumed it as a relatively minor part of a general class analysis.[38] Ambedkar, the pre-eminent intellectual of caste liberation in modern India, subsumed class into an analysis which asserted the analytical primacy of caste structures.[39] The difference in historical efficacy of these two forms of politics appears to be connected to the nature of their historical judgements. Radical political theorists appeared to believe that class analysis was a universal tool of social explanation, and they narrowed down their reflections further by ignoring the more general conception of class in Marx's theory. This obliged Marxists to interpret egalitarian politics in terms of *class* equality – obviating, in a sense, the primary need for a translational conception of political theory. The transfer of political theory became too mechanical, and, to inhabitants of rural Indian society, barely intelligible. By contrast, the really interesting case is Nehru's shifting position on the meanings of equality in India. His early thinking, symbolically condensed into the famous speech to the Indian National Congress

---

[37] It is essential, for political realism, to stress the unpopular point that Ambedkar, undoubtedly the pre-eminent leader of the dalits in modern India, was critically reliant on Congress support and Nehru's dominance inside the Congress. A gathering impulse of hagiographic exaggeration of Ambedkar's single-handed impact on Indian society through its constitution does serious damage to an unexcited assessment of causes and consequences in political history.

[38] Reducing it often, and unhelpfully, to a form of 'false consciousness'.

[39] See Ambedkar's essays on Indian society generally in Valerian Rodriguez, ed., *The Essential Writings of B. R. Ambedkar* (Delhi: Oxford University Press, 2004).

in 1936, closely followed the more orthodox Marxist understanding of Indian politics – with an exclusive emphasis on class inequality.[40] After he assumed office, quite a startling change occurred in Nehru's thinking, reflected in the fading emphasis on pure class in the most significant institutional arena of the Constituent Assembly.[41] Equally remarkable is his crucial decision to rescue Ambedkar from political obscurity and install him in a position of crucial authority in the constitution-making process. Ambedkar at the time was a relative outsider, having alienated Congress opinion by his strenuous hostility to Gandhi's ideas on untouchability. Inclusion of Ambedkar inside the intellectual elite that had the rarest of historical opportunities to shape the contours of fundamental institutions of Indian politics was a critical move.

Through the work of Nehru and Ambedkar, liberal reformist politics in independent India offered a different *translation* of the ideal of equality: by implication, suggesting that political ideals had first to go through a process of abstraction from their specific European historical form into a *general* principle, to be adapted or translated into the relevant form demanded by a different, non-European history. To be sure, this rendering of the principle of equality was less radical than the communist version: it acquiesced in restricting the principle of equality only to the *political* sphere, and abandoned, at least for a time, the more morally ambitious goal of eliminating inequality altogether. Two crucial judgements were involved in this translation – a *sociological* judgement that caste was the primary experiential form of social inequality, and a *historical* judgement that this needed to be tackled by the state. Like Tocqueville, Nehru and Ambedkar believed that historically the taste for equality would tend to extend from the political to other spheres, particularly the economic.[42] In the shorter term,

[40] I emphasise this side of his thinking for the sake of the present argument: after the Moscow trials, Nehru was clearly troubled by the emerging nature of the Soviet regime and started rethinking his position on the indispensability of democratic political institutions – which increasingly set him apart from communists.

[41] For an excellent general analysis of its debates, see Granville Austin, *India's Constitution: The Cornerstone of a Nation* (Oxford: Clarendon Press, 1964).

[42] This connection is more evident in the case of Nehru; see, for instance, his 'Draft Resolution for the Avadi Session of the Indian National Congress' in *Selected Works of Jawaharlal Nehru* (Delhi: Oxford University Press, 2000),

however, their translation of the modern ideal of political equality into Indian history appears to have been remarkably successful. The relative success of Indian democracy seems to have something to do with a successful translation in political theory. In political theory, as in literature, translation remains a partially obscure process, but the consequences of successful translation are easy to read – alike in texts and in social history.

Second Series, XXVII, pp. 255–61, and his speech to the Avadi session, 'Socialistic Pattern of Society' (21 January 1955) in *ibid.*, pp. 279–83; but there is a remarkably similar reading of the historical future in Ambedkar's valedictory speech to the Constituent Assembly of India.

PART III

Rationality and judgement

7 | *Pericles' unreason*

GEOFFREY HAWTHORN

It is one of John Dunn's distinctive claims that those who make political judgements cannot be sure of what they are doing and that those who reflect on them will be unsure of what they find. We describe our own judgements and reflect on those of others in the language of intentions and consequences and speak as if we could capture these. 'But we cannot do so in practice. To so do is simply beyond our powers … when we speak and think in these terms, we can very seldom (perhaps never) be doing more than guessing what we are doing. We act in hope and fear, in speculation driven by varyingly pressing motives. We cannot act on knowledge, or, indeed, in large measure, even on comprehension.'[1]

This is right. Political judgement is a species of practical reasoning, reasoning that the world has to fit. It will usually rest on shreds of theoretical reason, reason that fits a world, or has done. But it is not itself knowledge. It cannot be known to be true or false either in advance of the outcome it strives to achieve or after the outcome is known, even if we can be sure that the outcome is indeed its own. The best that one can say of it is that it is reasonable in the circumstances in which it is proposed. Nor are political judgements easy to comprehend. Their reasoning can be complex and obscurely connected. When driven by what Dunn nicely calls the cunning of unreason, they can be more or less completely opaque. But this is not to say that it is difficult to see what in a general way reasoned judgements in politics should contain, and I shall come to that. Nor is it to say that identifying the kinds of unreason at work in such judgements, as distinct from how one or another kind does its work, will always prove elusive. One such kind is the unreason of power itself. This can both concentrate a reasoning mind and confuse it, and may at times altogether occlude

---

[1] John Dunn, *The Cunning of Unreason: Making Sense of Politics* (London: HarperCollins, 2000), pp. 243–4.

it. There is interest therefore in reflecting on the final and immensely consequential judgement of a man of power who has been said, with authority, to have judged rather well.

Thucydides is a writer who encourages one to think hard about practical political judgement, and does so with a scepticism not unlike Dunn's own. Yet he gives every sign of believing – one should rather say of this austere man that he gives no sign of not believing – that in the years before the start of 'the war between the Peloponnesians and the Athenians' in 431 BC, Pericles, 'the first man of his time' in Athens, acted with great intelligence and good judgement. In so far as one can read Thucydides' work as a drama, Pericles is its hero.[2] As with many heroes, we learn less about him as a man than we do about others in the story. But Pericles himself knew exactly how he wanted publicly to appear: as a patriot, he declared to citizens sceptical of his refusal to engage the by then twice-invading Spartans, uncorrupt, and 'inferior to no man in judging what is necessary and explaining it'. Some have looked beyond Thucydides' own judgement of the man to see his entire story as 'a vindication of Pericles' foresight'.[3] Quite apart from the fact that Thucydides is not well seen to have been vindicating anything, this, I suggest, can only be

---

[2] Thucydides on Pericles at 2.65. An early reading of his book as a kind of drama, published in 1907, is Francis M. D. Cornford, *Thucydides Mythistoricus* (London: Routledge and Kegan Paul, 1965). This can be read as a tragedy; for a recent review, David Bedford and Thomas Workman, 'The Tragic Reading of the Thucydidean Tragedy', *Review of International Studies*, 27 (2001), pp. 51–67; notably subtle and perceptive. C. W. Macleod, 'Thucydides and Tragedy' in *Collected Essays* (Oxford: Clarendon Press, 1996), pp. 140–58. In these readings, however, the tragedy is usually said to be Athens', not Pericles'. They can overlook the fact that Thucydides gives good reasons to believe that the Athenians' defeat in the Sicilian campaign could have been averted, and that there is reason to believe that they were by no means bound eventually to be defeated in the war itself; for example Ian Morris, 'The Athenian Empire (478–404 BC' (2001), www.stanford.edu/group/sshi/Conferences/2000–01/empires2/morris.pdf. Also note 13.

[3] Thucydides at 1.1.1, 1.139.4, 2.65.4, Pericles on himself at 2.60.5–7, compared with other Athenian leaders by John H. Finley, *Thucydides* (Cambridge, MA: Harvard University Press, 1942), p. 203, who is not alone in finding that only Hermocrates could match him, and who remarks on Thucydides' story as a vindication of Pericles' foresight at 308. I take the quotations from the translation that Jeremy Mynott is preparing for the Cambridge University Press. I am grateful to him for this generosity and continuing conversations on Thucydides, and to him, Helen Thompson and the editors for invaluable comments on a draft of this chapter.

perversely correct: Pericles himself ignored his foresight, and without good political reason.

Later fifth-century Greek *poleis* are not the kind of state on which Dunn has concentrated his thoughts on political judgement. Indeed Athens can only disputably be described as a state at all. But it did have procedures of selection for rulers and for rule itself that were independent of those who exercised it. What we would think of as its foreign policy (although not only its foreign policy) was considered by the council of 500, directed by a board of ten *strategoi*, political generals, each of whom was elected annually, and decided in the assembly. Pericles was elected fifteen times. The generals usually came to their position with clients and supporters and some experience of public life and war; they listened more or less attentively to the mood of the assemblies they tried to control; and to an extent that remains as unclear as it can be in modern states, they also conferred with each other about what to do. 'Only the naive or innocent observer can believe that [any] came to a vital assembly meeting armed with nothing but his intelligence, his knowledge, his charisma and his oratorical skill.[4] But in the absence of elaborate institutions, the generals' judgements were more exposed and often, though by no means always, more consequential than those of leaders now. In virtue of this and the comparatively simple scope of ancient politics, their qualities are easier to see.[5]

---

[4] M. I. Finley, *Politics in the Ancient World* (Cambridge: Cambridge University Press, 1983), p. 76; a contrary view, A. J. Holladay, 'Athenian Strategy in the Archidamian War', *Historia*, 27 (1978), p. 422.

[5] My understanding of Athenian politics in the fifth century is very much that of Walter Eder, 'Aristocrats and the Coming of Athenian Democracy' in *Democracy 2500: Questions and Challenges*, Colloquia and Conference Papers no. 2 (Dubuque, IO: Archaeological Institute of America, 1997), S105–S140, www.tu-berlin.de/fb1/AGiW/Hospitium/Eder.htm, strengthened and refined by the work of Charlotte Hartley in the Department of Politics at Cambridge. Eder suggests that it is not surprising, given its origins in aristocratic competition for power over the *polis*, that the *demokratia* (probably first described as such in the 460s) remained a mixed regime at least until the reforms of 404–3 and arguably beyond. Dunn's self-knowing remark in the course of an elegant account of it, that 'what we most want to believe is that Athenian democracy somehow worked because it should have done', is to be set beside his simple but equally important observation of the distance between an account of a politics that accepts 'its own aspirations and pretensions' and one that 'attempts instead to pin down what actually happens': John Dunn, *Setting the People Free: The Story of Democracy* (London: Atlantic Books, 2005), pp. 38, 29.

Like all leaders of states in which leaders are held, however imperfectly, to account, Pericles had three central purposes. He had to secure and maintain his position against other contenders for power within the state. He had to maintain the security and prosperity of the state (and to an appropriate and convenient level, its citizens also) against other states. And he had to offer a persuasive legitimation of how he did both. In explaining how modern states maintain their positions against others, students of 'international relations' have often tended to resort to the workings of what Dunn describes as 'highly skilled and utterly morally unanchored instrumental calculation'. They have been proudly 'realist' in what they regard as an anarchic world. But they have not always been able, in Machiavelli's jibe, to endure all the political reality there is.[6] The simpler realists have often ignored the fact that those directing the foreign policy of many modern states (including, most obviously, those directing the presently most powerful of them all) have not always been able to insulate themselves from battles for power within the state or from their own legitimation. Thucydides does not do this, and by his account, the generals in Athens could certainly not do so. Pursuing Athens' foreign policy in what had come to be described as the democracy, a form of rule that Pericles was to do much to strengthen and on which much of his own power and authority depended, could not be a matter of politically insulated calculation alone. Nor, I shall explain, could it be reliably rational, although one can argue about how much Pericles' final unreason owed to the fact that it was unleashed in this particular form of rule.

Leaders nevertheless led, and for most of his career Pericles does appear to have led Athens effectively. He had defeated his political opponents with the ostracism of Thucydides son of Melesias in 443. By the middle of the 430s, he had constructed as secure a position for the city and himself as he could reasonably have hoped to do. An

---

[6] Dunn, *The Cunning of Unreason*, p. 107, Machiavelli's jibe at p. 108. On the origins of models of rational choice in strategic theory, Ron Robin, *The Making of the Cold War Enemy: Culture and Politics in the Military–Industrial Complex* (Princeton: Princeton University Press, 2001). On the wider political context of the intellectual history, Martti Koskenniemi, *The Gentle Civiliser of Nations: The Rise and Fall of International Law 1870–1960* (Cambridge: Cambridge University Press, 2001). Self-described 'classical' realists, often acknowledging Thucydides, do allow for the play of internal politics, but they do not abandon the presumption of reason in the pursuit of 'national' interests. Also note 31.

expedition against the Persians in Egypt in 454 had ended in disaster; 8,000 citizens, perhaps one out of five or six adult men, are thought to have been lost.[7] Defeats to the north and south of Attica in the 450s and the first half of the 440s in what some historians have called 'the first Peloponnesian war' had indicated the limits of Athens' expansion on land; rebellions at Erythrae, Miletus and Euboea (in 441–40, on Samos also) had also shown that a great deal of effort was required to keep control of the empire there was. Expanding it, Pericles realised, was out of the question. By the end of the 440s, Kagan suggests, Athens was in Bismarck's phrase a 'saturated power'.[8]

Pericles had perhaps had a hand in the peace that Athens may have made with Persia in 449 and the peace that it did make with Sparta in 445. The Athenians, it is true, were to go on to found a new city, Thurii, in Italy, and another, Amphipolis, on the northern shore of the Aegean (which Thucydides – the son of Olorus and writer – was later to play a part in losing), in the second acquiring a useful source of timber and gold and some strategic advantage. Pericles himself had also led a pointedly extravagant fleet to the Black Sea to support Greek colonies there, impress barbarians, and ensure the continuation of grain supplies from the steppes. But these were not attempts seriously to extend Athens' empire at the expense of Sparta or its allies, and the one or two new conquests Athens made within Greece itself can be regarded (even if some there did not choose to do so) as minor consolidations.[9] By the mid 440s, the city's financial reserves were sufficiently good, its income from 'tribute' in the existing empire and from taxes (both now being more stiffly imposed) sufficiently high, and its security, it seems, sufficiently sure, to allow Pericles to embark

[7] Kurt A. Raaflaub, 'Warfare and Athenian Society' in Loren J. Samons II, ed., *The Cambridge Companion to the Age of Pericles* (Cambridge: Cambridge University Press, 2007), pp. 96–124, p. 114.

[8] 'Empire' is the usual translation of the *archê* that Athens' original *hegemonia* had become, but the use of the term has been curiously unexamined: Morris, 'The Athenian Empire'; Donald Kagan, *The Outbreak of the Peloponnesian War* (Ithaca, NY: Cornell University Press, 1969), p. 107.

[9] G. E. M. de Ste Croix, *The Origins of the Peloponnesian War* (London: Duckworth, 1972), pp. 315–16, gives a good summary of Pericles' restraint. A striking late instance of this is Athens' acceptance of the pro-Spartan judgement of the oracle at Delphi in 433, that Thurii, in which civil strife had broken out, had been founded by Apollo and was thus pan-Hellenic (*ibid.*, pp. 154–66); Russell Meiggs, *The Athenian Empire* (Oxford: Clarendon Press, 1972), p. 368.

on a flamboyant building programme in the city itself. 'To say that the Athenians built the Parthenon' and transferred the cult of Athena to a lavish new statue on the Acropolis 'to worship themselves', remarks Lewis, 'would be an exaggeration, but not a great one.' Having restricted Athenian citizenship to those with two native-born parents rather than one, Pericles could also afford a degree of what we would call welfare. Lewis captures the man well. 'Pericles was not a modest man, and there was nothing little about his ideas.'[10]

How then did this seemingly saturated and now prosperous power, under such a politically successful and apparently prudent 'first man', find itself by 431 at war with the state with which, just fifteen years before, it had signed a thirty-year peace?[11] There have been three sorts of answer. The first is that Pericles' defensive strategy for Athens was inherently unsustainable. His own former ward, Alcibiades, was to scorn it at the second of two assemblies in March 415 in defence of the decision to send an expedition to Sicily that had been taken at the first. 'It is not an option for us to set some careful limit to the empire; on the contrary, since we are in this situation we are forced to take active initiatives against some cities and keep our grip on others, because there is a danger that if we do not take others into our empire we shall fall into theirs. *You* cannot take the same passive view as other states might' – he told the assembly, presumably referring to Sparta – '... unless you are going to change your style of life to be like theirs' (6.18.3). The second answer is that both sides

<hr />

[10] D. M. Lewis, 'The Thirty Years' Peace' in D. M. Lewis *et al.*, eds., *Cambridge Ancient History*, V, *The Fifth Century BC* (Cambridge: Cambridge University Press, 1992), pp. 139, 146.

[11] I here disregard the view that Thucydides was writing about *stasis*, civil or internal war within one community rather than a war (or wars) between communities that we now think of as states. Jonathan J. Price, *Thucydides and Internal War* (Cambridge: Cambridge University Press, 2001). This view can be deployed to strengthen the claim that he was lamenting the collapse of that 'simplicity of spirit ... such an important part of true nobility ... laughed to scorn and vanished, [with] people ... largely divided into opposite and mutually suspicious camps' (3.83.1), across the Greek world and not just within the *poleis*, and thus the wider claim that it is disquiet about the collapse of a single moral community that pervades his work. Whatever the merits of this view, the *poleis* undeniably valued their *autonomia* as *poleis* and, where possible, sought power over others. On the presuppositions guiding relations between what she regards as distinct Greek states, see Polly Low, *Interstate Relations in Classical Greece: Morality and Politics* (Cambridge: Cambridge University Press, 2007).

made mistakes in the later 430s. The Spartans later agreed that they
had. 'They considered ... that the offence [by 431] had been more
on their own side, both on account of the attack of [their allies] the
Thebans on Plataea [an ally of Athens] in time of peace' – which
Thucydides regards as the first engagement of the war itself – 'and
also of their own refusal to listen to the Athenian offer of arbitration'
after they had themselves voted for war (7.18.2; the Athenian offer
and the Spartan refusal at 1.144.2, 1.145). In Athens, some opinion
at the start of the war attributed its cause to restraints on trade that
Athens itself had imposed on Megara, a small state that was strategically placed on the isthmus between Attica and the Peloponnese and
had come into Sparta's league after rebelling against Athens in 446.
Commentators have since argued that Athens could have afforded to
relax these restrictions when the Spartans offered peace if it were to
do so (1.139.1).[12] The third answer is Thucydides' own. Sparta's fear
of Athens' power, he says, was leading to war, and everyone knew it
(1.23.6, 1.33.3, 1.44.2). The public pretexts disguised a deeper conviction. Everything that happened before the fighting began, Stahl
reads Thucydides to be saying, was conditioned by the certainty on
all sides that it would.[13]

   The first answer, Alcibiades', was probably wrong. The Athenians
did go to Sicily and there suffered as great a defeat as they had in
Egypt forty years before. Few of the many who went, Thucydides
remarked of both campaigns, were to return. But it is not clear that
Sicily confuted Alcibiades' view that, to survive, the empire had to
extend. Nicias, who was left in charge of the Sicilian expedition, pursued a tactic that Alcibiades had himself recommended. It was clear in
advance of the event that it was not the most sensible of the three that
were proposed. That was Lamachus', which was to attack Syracuse
at once. But Lamachus deferred to Nicias and Alcibiades, and Nicias,
perhaps fearing the reaction back in Athens if he followed his own,
which was not to press an attack at all, followed Alcibiades' after
Alcibiades himself had been arrested on a separate charge and taken

[12] For example Kagan, *The Outbreak of the Peloponnesian War*, p. 324, and my
   argument below.
[13] Hans-Peter Stahl, *Thucydides: Man's Place in History*, trans. David Seward
   (Swansea: Classical Press of Wales, 2003), p. 40. Stahl characterises the
   certainty as 'emotional'. As I explain, this is not wrong, but politically
   incomplete.

off the expedition. Even then, despite the Spartan support for Syracuse that had been engineered by the now renegade Alcibiades, had Nicias' own command been more vigorous and alert, and had the inventive Demosthenes, sent out later to help him, not allowed his troops on a crucial night to become confused, the Athenians might not have lost the campaign. Athens was not again to attempt to extend its empire. Its naval operations between 413 and 404 were directed to maintaining the one that it had and the passage for grain down from the Black Sea.[14] Yet even if one might find a way of agreeing with Alcibiades that no empire can exist in equilibrium, Pericles had known before the war that even with the considerable resources available to him at that time, resources greater than those that were to be available at the start of the Sicilian campaign, it could not safely expand.[15] Not only had its forces been decisively beaten in Egypt and Boeotia in the 450s. In the difficult year of 446, Euboea had revolted, Megara had taken the opportunity to break away, and the Spartans had marched up to Athens itself. Pericles knew that he could only ever achieve what he could with the Athenian navy, and that that was required for protecting the merchant fleet, containing rebellion in the existing empire, and bringing in the tribute. Nicias, opposing Alcibiades in the argument about whether to go to Sicily, was to make much the same

---

[14] Ironically, Athens' defeat at Aegospotamoi in the Hellespont in 404 was said (by Xenophon) to have been due to the naval commanders refusing to take a quite different piece of advice from Alcibiades. He was living along the Hellespont at the time, and told the commanders that Aegospotamoi was a poor place from which to provision the crews. They ignored him, and the Spartan navy caught them out to lunch. Sparta's navy, however, was by this time weakening, and the Persians were beginning to cease to see the point of continuing to finance it. Had the Athenians won at Aegospotamoi, they might well have won the war; Barry Strauss, 'Aegospotamoi Reconsidered', *American Journal of Philology*, 104 (1983), pp. 24–35; Morris, 'The Athenian Empire', considers some of the possible consequences of their having done so. A. Andrewes, 'The Spartan Resurgence' in D. M. Lewis *et al.*, eds., *Cambridge Ancient History*, V, *The Fifth Century BC* (Cambridge: Cambridge University Press, 1992), pp. 496–8, stops short of that, but is a brief, balanced and perceptive reflection on why Athens lost.

[15] After the first Spartan invasion of Attica in 431 – in 446 the Spartans, reputedly bribed by Pericles, had not pressed their advantage – the Athenian assembly agreed to set aside 1,000 talents to defend the city if it were to be attacked also from the sea (2.24.1). Yet despite the evident financial strains of the Sicilian expedition (e.g. 7.28.4), this reserve was not to be drawn on until a further crisis in 412–11 (the restriction on its use having then been lifted) (8.15.1).

point: Athens was already extended, and did not have the land forces with which to hold Sicily. 'I have many ... reasons to hope for success', Pericles had told an assembly in the city in 432, urging the citizens to support his determination to go to war with Sparta, 'provided you agree not to extend your empire while the war is going on and not to add to our dangers in ways of your own making. The truth is, I fear our own mistakes more than I fear the plans of the enemy' (1.144.1). One does not need hindsight to see that Alcibiades' enthusiasm for expansion carried evident risks. Pericles had the more prudent case.

Thucydides' argument, the third of the three answers, has been one of the more discussed issues in his work. It is more difficult to assess. He insists – it is the third time in the first of the eight 'books' that he does so – that 'at last the power of the Athenians was clearly understood and their actions were affecting the Peloponnesian league. Then [the Spartans] could no longer endure the situation, and it appeared to them that they had to put all their energy into their attempt and destroy the might of the Athenians, if they could, by taking on the war' (1.118.2). Yet the Spartans would seem to have had fewer reasons to fear an Athenian attack in the years between 446 and 435 than they had had before. Athens had ceased to be aggressive on land, and the Spartans themselves had been able to determine the crucial terms of the thirty-year peace in 445. Their real fears were about themselves.[16] Spartan policy, Thucydides later remarks, had always been governed by the need to take precautions against revolts by its helot, serf class in Messenia (4.80.3). In 462 or 461, Athens, then still in its old alliance with Sparta against the Persians, had been invited to help put down just such a revolt, only to be sent away when it occurred to the Spartans that the Athenians might be tempted to foment political change in Sparta itself (1.102.3–4). (Athens was offended, and revoked the alliance.) The Spartans had also become nervous about their own power and standing in the league. Some of the smaller states in the Peloponnese had ambitions to extend their own dominions. Some, Elis, Mantinea and Sicyon, were also showing a worrying

---

[16] On these and Sparta's ambitions, see P. A. Brunt, 'Spartan Policy and Strategy in the Archidamian War' in *Studies in Greek History and Thought* (Oxford: Clarendon Press, 1993), pp. 84–111. The Spartan league has been described as a set of states which were committed to having the same friends and enemies but did not otherwise have continuous relations with each other, and should not therefore be described as 'allies'.

inclination to democracy; so was Megara. Argos was outside the league but potentially the most powerful state in the Peloponnese after Sparta itself and irremediably hostile, held in check only by a temporary truce. And in a contest between Corcyra (now Corfu) and Corinth over who should exercise power over Epidamnus after the eruption in 435 of a long civil war in that remote city (so remote that even Thucydides felt it necessary to explain where it was – it is now Durrës in Albania), the Corinthians were urging Sparta to attack the Athenians for supporting Corcyra and threatening to defect from the Peloponnesian league if it refused (1.71.4). The Spartans would have known that the Corinthians had nowhere to defect to; Argos, with a truce still to run with Sparta, was unavailable, and Athens was inconceivable. But Corinth had the largest navy in Greece after that of Athens, and its disaffection, more than that of any other member, could be a blow to the potential power of the league as well as to Sparta's honour and standing with other Greeks.

The fear that Thucydides detected of Sparta for Athens, in contrast to the fears that Sparta had about itself and its standing in its league, may not have been reasonable. But did it really pre-empt a more practical rationality, as Thucydides (and Stahl after him) suggest? If so, did it do so on each side? And if we accept that it did, what kind of explanation are we then offering for the war? We cannot say that considered judgement played no part. Athens, as I have said, had been careful not to be seen to be breaching the terms of the thirty-year peace and had deliberately not been expanding its empire in any way that might threaten Sparta or its allies. Sparta had its enduring worry about its helots and was not wholly confident of its league. In any event, the one could not expect to win on land, and the other could not expect to do so on the sea. Outright victory would seem to have been impossible for both. Neither appeared to have good reason to be at war with the other for anything more than the defence of what it already had, and what each already had did not seem to be being seriously threatened by the other.[17] If this is wrong, and there were acts that could be read as threats, then given that an outright victory for either side was difficult to envisage, would it not have been reasonable to try to contain them? Was there no attempt to do so? If there was, did reason fail? If there

---

[17] Morris, 'The Athenian Empire', considers the nature and likelihood of larger ambitions in Athens.

was not, why not? If there was indeed no attempt, or if any attempt there was did fail, then notwithstanding Thucydides' assessment of him – and his assessment of himself – was Pericles as responsible as those who led Sparta? To answer these questions, one has to consider the second of the three kinds of explanation that have been offered for the war, the question, for each side, of mistakes.

'The great moments of decision', observes de Ste Croix, and, one might add, the opportunities therefore for error, 'occupy a far greater proportion of space in the History of Thucydides than in any other historical work from antiquity'.[18] I consider four before the attack on Plataea by Thebes in the spring of 431, the moment that for Thucydides marks the 'real beginning' of the war, the moment after which the only communication between the powers was by herald (2.1), and later suggest a fifth, in 430. The first was the question presented to each power about whether to involve itself in the battle between Corcyra and Corinth over Epidamnus. In the eruption in that city in 435, the 'democratic' party had appealed to Corcyra for help;[19] Corcyra had founded Epidamnus, was itself a democracy, and was not a member of either of the leagues. But it refused, and the Epidamnians appealed to Corinth instead. The Corinthians were pleased to have a dispute with the Corcyreans, who had long resisted paying what the Corinthians regarded as the respect due to them for having themselves founded Corcyra. (The first recorded naval battle between Greek states had been between the Corinthians and the Corcyreans in about 664.) Corinth sent settlers and troops to Epidamnus, Corcyra responded by asking the Epidamnians to take back those who had fled to their island, the Epidamnians refused, and when they also resisted the Corcyreans' demand that all who did not want to be regarded as enemies should leave the city, Corcyra besieged it. The Corinthians responded by deciding to recruit new colonists and take them to Epidamnus in a fleet of ships of their own and from other states that were, like them, members of the Peloponnesian league. (Sparta, it seems, was not asked.) Hearing of these preparations, Corcyreans went to Corinth with envoys from Sparta and Sicyon, asked for the new colonists to be removed, and

---

[18] De Ste Croix, *The Origins of the Peloponnesian War*, p. 297; De Ste Croix's argument is that responsibility for the outbreak of hostilities lay firmly with Sparta.

[19] 'Party' here and elsewhere means merely 'faction', 'group' or 'side'. There were no political parties in the modern sense in Greece.

offered to submit all claims to arbitration by agreed Peloponnesian powers and to consult the oracle at Delphi. If Corinth would not agree, they said, they would seek powerful allies. The Corinthians replied that they would not go to arbitration unless the Corcyreans first withdrew from Epidamnus. The Corcyreans said that they would only do this if the Corinthians would themelves withdraw; otherwise, they said, arbitration would have to proceed with both forces in place. ('How familiar these diplomatic exchanges seem', commented Gomme wearily in the early 1940s.[20] How familiar indeed.) The Corinthians did not accept either proposal, declared war on Corcyra, and prepared to do battle at Epidamnus itself. They were defeated, and retreated. They spent the next two years, 434 and 433, building up their fleet. The Corcyreans were alarmed, and decided to appeal to Athens for help. The Corinthians went to Athens too. After due flattery and some flummery about justice, the Corcyreans explained that they were not prepared to be demeaned by the Corinthians, that it would be far better for the Athenians to have the Corcyrean navy, the third largest in Greece after Athens' own and Corinth's, on their side, and that the provisions of the thirty-year peace, which allowed for neutrals to join either side while the peace was in force, should not be ignored. 'As to the war', they said, 'in which we could be of service to you, any of you who thinks that it will not happen is deluded and fails to understand the situation: the Spartans are ready to go to war through their fear of you; while the Corinthians, who have influence with them and are hostile to you, are seeking to deal with us first in preparation for a direct attempt on you, their intention being to prevent us uniting with each other and making common cause against them; they mean to keep the advantage in one of two ways, either by damaging us or adding to their own strength.' The Corinthians disputed this, arguing that the treaty of 445 did not intend to allow a neutral power to join one side in order to injure a state on the other, that the Corcyreans had indeed insulted them, and that the Athenians would remember that they, the Corinthians, had not voted with Sparta at a congress in that city in 440 when Samos had asked for help against Athens.[21] 'The

---

[20] A. W. Gomme, *A Historical Commentary on Thucydides,* I, *Introduction and Commentary on Book 1* (Oxford: Clarendon Press, 1945), p. 163.

[21] A poor argument: in 441–40, Samos was a member of the Athenian league; in 433, Corcyra was a member of none.

right thing for you to do, surely, is to stand aside from both parties or, failing that, to take the opposite course of joining us against them.' 'You benefited from our vote and you should not now damage us with yours' (1.23–43).

The Athenians discussed the matter in two assemblies. In the first, Thucydides says that they heard the Corinthian case with some sympathy, but did not decide one way or the other. At the second,

they changed their minds in favour of making an alliance with the Corcyraeans; this would not be a full alliance, where they would recognise the same friends and enemies (for if the Corcyraeans required them to sail with them against Corinth they would be breaking the treaty with the Peloponnesians), but a defensive alliance[22] to protect each other's territory against attacks. For they thought that there would in any case be a war with the Peloponnesians and they did not want Corcyra, with a fleet of the size it had, to fall into Corinthian hands.

In practice, this meant sending a squadron of ten ships solely to prevent the Corinthians landing on Corcyra or any of its possessions and otherwise avoid engagement (1.44.1–2). The Corcyreans, however, were getting the worst of the battle that followed; despite their instructions, the commanders of the ten Athenian ships found themselves drawn in; and when the Corinthians saw twenty more vessels arriving in the dusk, they feared an even larger number and backed off. The Athenians tried to make themselves clear the next day. 'We are not starting a war, men of the Peloponnese, nor are we breaking the treaty, but we have come to help these Corcyreans here, who are our allies.' 'Thus Corcyra came through the war with Corinth', Thucydides explains, 'and the Athenian fleet withdrew from their territory. And for the Corinthians this constituted the first reason for the war with Athens. that despite their treaty the Athenians had joined in the sea battle on the side of Corcyra against them' (1.45–53, 55.2).

Sparta scarcely involved itself at all in this dispute. A Spartan envoy did go with the Corcyreans when they showed an inclination to try to negotiate with the Corinthians. Gomme and de Ste Croix read this

---

[22] Jeremy Mynott notes: *epimachia*, a rare technical term. The usual word for an alliance is *summachia* which I have here translated 'full alliance' just to make the contrast.

as Spartan 'support' against the possibly dangerous consequences of an angry Corinth; Brunt even as an 'attempted mediation'.[23] But there is no evidence that it was either; or if it was, that Sparta had the will to pursue it. One can see that the Spartans would not have wanted to antagonise Corinth. But they would have known that, in any larger war, the Corinthians could not stand alone and would be unlikely to go to the Athenian side. Their best interest would seem to have been not to support either. Thucydides reports that this was certainly what some Athenians believed for themselves in 433: the antagonists should be left to fight it out 'so that the Corinthians and other naval powers would be much weakened if the need arose and they had to go to war with them' (1.44.2). As it was, the Athenians settled, we know not how, on the device of the defensive alliance. Gomme recalls Plutarch's report of 'the story that Pericles had Lacedaemonius' – the revealingly named son of his former peace-making, Sparta-friendly adversary Cimon – 'appointed to this small and difficult command in spiteful memory of his old rival: ten ships made too small a squadron for success and might easily be led into disaster'. 'It is entirely characteristic of Thucydides', Gomme adds, 'that he ignores [this] and all similar scandal' surrounding Pericles. de Ste Croix, partial to Athens and insisting that we do not actually know just how influential Pericles himself was in these decisions, dismisses that as 'propaganda'.[24] But Gomme points out that the decision was in fact criticised at the time. The figures certainly suggest that Athens did not need the Corcyrean fleet; Athens' own would still be greatly superior. Even if the small squadron had not thought it necessary to engage against the Corinthians, the decision to make a defensive alliance had been provocative. Either Pericles, although plainly the 'first man of his time' in Athens by 432–31, was not decisive in a debate no more than eighteen months or so before; or he judged badly, and, if we believe Plutarch, also cynically. Athens would indeed have been wiser to leave the two states to themselves.

A second point of decision, which followed 'almost immediately' and in Thucydides' opinion also contributed to hostilities, certainly

[23] Gomme, *A Historical Commentary on Thucydides*, I, p. 162; de Ste Croix, *The Origins of the Peloponnesian War*, p. 69; Brunt, 'Spartan Policy and Strategy in the Archidamian War', p. 88.

[24] Gomme, *A Historical Commentary on Thucydides*, I, p. 178; de Ste Croix, *The Origins of the Peloponnesian War*, pp. 76–7.

suggests that Athens would have gained an advantage in so doing. For Corinth was now looking for revenge. The Athenians suspected as much and tried to pre-empt this by ordering the inhabitants of Potidaea on the isthmus of the peninsula of Pallene in Chalcidice in the north-west Aegean, originally a Corinthian colony but now an important 'tributary ally' of Athens, to raze a wall, deliver hostages, expel their Corinthian magistrates and receive no new ones (1.56.1–2). The politics was complicated. It was not only the Corinthians who had a grievance against the Athenians in the north. The king of Macedonia, Perdiccas, had one also. He had been an ally of Athens. But earlier in the 430s, the Athenians seem to have had doubts about his command, or his constancy – he was indeed to change sides nine times in the course of the war – and switched to supporting his brother and another rival against him. Perdiccas tried to enlist Sparta and Corinth against his ertswhile ally, and to encourage rebellion amongst Athenian subjects, including Potidaea, on his southern borders. Potidaea itself did not at first react to Athens' demands or to Perdiccas' incitement. It sent envoys to Athens to plead its case, and to Sparta to seek a promise of support if the Athenians did not relent. (Sparta, the Athenians may not have known, agreed to support it. Corinth later sent a force of 'volunteers', thereby hoping to avoid censure under the terms of the thirty-year peace.) Potidaea also paid its tribute in the spring of 432. But Athens had under-estimated its anger, and the danger. In the summer, Potidaea and several other Athenian subject cities in the area rebelled. Perdiccas backed them, and Athenian support for a putsch in Macedonia against him failed. Potidaea was to preoccupy Athens and drain it financially until it was starved down two years later.

At the start of this affair, one can assume, as I have said, that Pericles was the 'first man' in Athens; there is certainly nothing to suggest that these decisions were taken against his will. They were not, in hindsight, good decisions. The Potidaeans and others in the region were angrier than he had imagined, and Perdiccas stronger. This is not to say that Pericles' judgement was obviously at fault, and that he misled the assemblies. He did have reason to believe that the Corinthians would threaten this important edge of the empire, and his intelligence on Macedonia and its anxious king would perhaps have been poor. But he had not previously had good reason to make anything as provocative as a defensive alliance with Corcyra and

thereby anger the Corinthians in the first place. Realising his mistake
about the situation in the north, he quickly made an alliance with the
king of Thrace, to the east, in the summer of 431, and through this
effected a reconciliation – for a while – with Perdiccas (2.29). By then,
the Spartans had decided that Athens had indeed broken the treaty of
445, and that they were at war.

    This was the third moment of decision; more exactly, of a decision
that came in two successive moments in July and August 432. The
first was at a gathering of Sparta's allies. This had been urged by
the Corinthians, and although Thucydides says that it was delegates
from Aegina – an island to the south of Salamis, not a member
of the Peloponnesian league but with a long grievance against
Athens – who spoke most strongly, it is the Corinthians' speech
and one by Athenians who 'happened to be there on other business'
(1.72.1) that he reports.[25] The Corinthians, as had become usual,
were intemperate, aggressive and careless in their reasoning, the
Athenians annoyingly disdainful. Neither were likely to calm those
present. The Corinthians contrasted the restless ambition, vigour
and success of the Athenians with the cautious, conservative and,
if they were to go on as they had been doing, self-defeating disposition of the Spartans. It was on this occasion that they hinted that
if Sparta did not actively respond to the evident threat presented by
Athens, the 'rest of us' in the league might be 'encouraged in despair to seek out some other alliance' (1.71.4). The visiting Athenians
reminded the gathering of Athens' contribution to the defeat of the
Persians, and explained that the city had constructed the empire
that the Spartans had declined for reasons of continuing fear of the
Persians, honour in Greece, and its own 'interest'. 'There is nothing
remarkable or contrary to normal human behaviour in what we have
done, just because we accepted an empire when one was offered and
then declined to let it go, overcome by these strongest of all motives'
– the order now changed – 'honour, fear and self-interest'. They
also pointed out that they had not been 'the first to take this course,
[for] it has always been established practice for the weaker to be

---

[25] The question of who actually spoke for the collectivities, 'Corinthians',
'Athenians' and so on, is unresolved. There has also been a particular dispute
about the 'visiting' Athenians. Some argue that they are a dramatic fiction,
others accept them as a fact. The issue is not crucial here; I assume that they
were present and did speak along the lines that Thucydides reports.

ruled by the stronger' (1.76.2). Alluding to the Spartans' reputation for incompetent harshness in their dealings with other Greek states after the Persian war, they claimed that they treated their own subjects justly. And they warned that a war against them would be foolish and unnecessary. If there were good grounds for dispute, the treaty of 445 provided for arbitration.

The Spartans dismissed the delegates and agreed among themselves – quite quickly, the pace of Thucydides' narrative suggests – that 'the Athenians were open aggressors, and war must be declared at once'. The one of the two Spartan kings who was then present, Archidamus, told them that it would be wise for them to adopt their famed caution. They were not ready for the kind of war that would be needed to defeat the Athenians.

Send envoys to Athens to discuss Potidaea; and send envoys to discuss the wrongs our allies claim to have suffered, especially now that the Athenians are ready to submit to arbitration – since it is not lawful to initiate attacks in such a case, as if against a wrongdoer. At the same time prepare for war. These are the policies to put us in the strongest position and to scare our enemies the most. (1.85.2)

But the Spartan leadership was divided. Archidamus was contradicted in a rhetorical burst from one of the five elected ephors, who disregarded the arguments, put a silly one of his own – that the Athenians 'deserve a double dose of punishment for changing from good to bad' – declared that Sparta's honour was at stake, and insisted that 'we must hit back quickly and as hard as possible' (1.86.1, 3). Once again pressing his view of the deep cause of the war, Thucydides writes that 'the Spartans voted that the treaty had been broken and that they must go to war not so much because they were persuaded by the arguments of their allies as because they feared further increase in the power of the Athenians, seeing' – for the first time, one might ask, and accurately? – 'the greater part of Greece now under their control' (1.88).

A congress of the full Peloponnesian league was convened in August. Most of the members spoke, and against Athens. The Corinthians, shrewdly waiting until last, produced more bad arguments.

When the Spartans had heard everyone's opinion, they put the vote to all the allies present in order, both the large and the small states, and the majority voted to go to war. After this resolution, it was not possible for them in their state of unpreparedness to attack immediately, but it was decided what contributions were to be provided by each and that there was to be no delay. Time was nevertheless taken in preparing what they needed, not a year but somewhat less, before they invaded Attica and openly began the war. (1.125.2)

The fourth set of moments for decision came in this interlude. The Spartans used it to send 'embassies to Athens and made charges, in order to have as good a reason as possible for going to war if the Athenians paid no attention' (1.126.1). One supposes that those less keen on war hoped that the Athenians would pay attention. The attention that the Athenians did pay, however, was not to the Spartans' liking. The first embassy tried to revive an ancient curse on Pericles' maternal line, hoping that the Athenians would be moved to banish him. The Athenians merely responded by pointing to a curse that lay on the Spartans themselves. The second embassy appeared to be more serious. This 'told Athens to lift the siege of Potidaea and leave Aegina autonomous, and they especially and with unmistakable clarity told them that there would be no war if they revoked the decree against the Megarians, in which it was stated that the Megarians could not use the ports of the Athenian empire or the market of Attica'. To begin with, Thucydides continues, 'the Athenians neither yielded on the other matters nor revoked the decree, accusing the Megarians of extending cultivation into consecrated ground and unassigned land on their border, and of harbouring runaway slaves'. The third embassy simply announced that 'the Spartans wish there to be peace, and there would be if you leave the Greeks autonomous' (1.139.1–2).

The Athenians decided to discuss the Spartans' offers. Thucydides reports that many speakers came forward and gave their support to one side or the other, urging the necessity of war, or the revocation of the decree and the folly of allowing it to stand in the way of peace (1.139.4). Unfortunately, however, he only reports the speech of Pericles, who was adamant. There should be no concession. The Spartans had not offered arbitration, which the treaty of 445 required. Megara may seem a trifle, but if the Athenians were to concede on one thing, they would find themselves being asked to concede on others. His rhetoric rose. 'All claims from an equal urged upon a neighbour as commands, before any attempt at arbitration, be they great or be they small, have only one meaning, and that is slavery' (1.141.1). He emphasised Athens' political, financial and military advantages for war, and he said that 'we will grant the Megarians access to our markets and harbours, if the Spartans for their part stop expelling us and our allies as aliens (there is nothing in the treaty to prevent either of these moves)', and that 'we will let the cities have their independence, if they were independent when we made the treaty [in 445] and as soon as the Spartans grant the cities in their own alliance the right to be independent in a way that suits their own individual wishes rather than the Spartans' interests'; he explained that Athens would not make the first move but would resist any who did, reminded the citizens of the glory that could be theirs, and insisted on the importance of passing 'on our heritage intact to those who follow after' (1.140–4).

The Spartans were not in a diplomatically steady state; their internal divisions and inexperience precluded that. (Some nevertheless revealed their reputation for not taking words seriously. Plutarch says that when Pericles explained to a member of the second embassy that he could do nothing about the legal prohibition against repealing the decree against Megara, the Spartan asked why he did not simply turn the inscription in which it was recorded to the wall.) The attempt to revive a curse was foolish; the suggestion that Athens disband her empire equally so. But the question of Megara had force. Popular opinion in Athens believed so, Pericles plainly thought it necessary to consider it, and Aristophanes joked about it. (The decree caused the war, the harbouring of slaves caused the decree, the slaves belonged to Pericles' mistress, Aspasia, and, her origins being what they were, were whores; Aspasia ruled Pericles; so the Olympian stirred up the war.)[26] It is not known when the decree was imposed. Its sanctions, it appears, were purely economic. Brunt is inclined to believe that its grounds, as the Athenians claimed, may indeed have been religious;[27] others see that as an excuse. What is clear is that Pericles had been chastened by the loss of Megara in 446. He was to take what Thucydides describes as 'the largest army of Athenians

---

[26] Gomme, *A Historical Commentary on Thucydides*, I, p. 451. As Gomme observes, this concludes in a clever parody of the opening lines of Herodotus' *Histories*.

[27] P. A. Brunt, 'The Megarian Decree' in *Studies in Greek History and Thought* (Oxford: Clarendon Press, 1993), p. 14.

ever assembled', in 431, at the start of the Peloponnesian war itself, to invade it. (The Athenians were to repeat the attempt, Thucydides reports, twice a year for several years [4.66.1]. The Megaran port of Nisaea, on the Athenian side of the isthmus, was not to be captured until 424.) It is conceivable that if the second of the three Spartan embassies was more serious than the other two, and if it had agreed (assuming it had the discretion) or had managed to persuade Spartans at home (assuming it did not) to agree to compromise on Megara, then the war, for the moment at least, might have been averted. But either they were not serious or they took Pericles not to be. His combining what was at worst a harmlessly impertinent request to make exceptions for Athenians in the general Spartan policy of expelling foreigners in return for an agreement on Megara with as unrealistic a proposal for their league as they were making for Athens' own suggests that he was not. The Spartans said no more. In May 431, two months after Thebes' attack on Plataea, Archidamus marched, cautiously, into Attica.

These moments of decision, moments at which something else could perhaps have been decided, moments at which mistakes, if they were mistakes, could have been avoided, raise questions both about the divided and uncertain Spartans and about the Athenians, effectively directed or strongly influenced by Pericles. The first question about Pericles is whether, from where he stood at the moments in question, it would have been reasonable of him to decide to take a course other than he did, and at the very least thereby delay the outbreak of a war the course of which, he admitted, neither he nor anyone else could foresee. The second is whether, from where he stood at any moment in the years between 435 and 431, he would have wished to. To the first, one can answer that it would have been possible and sensible of him to have refused to support Corcyra or Corinth in their dispute over Epidamnus. Despite what both states said, Athens had no practical need for Corcyra's navy.[28] To have let Corinth weaken itself could only have been to Athens' strategic and economic advantage in the Adriatic and the northern Aegean and would have itself weakened the power, standing and morale of

---

[28] Corcyra's navy was plainly less skilled. Its ships were later to sail with the Athenian fleet on at least two expeditions, but, after civil war there in 427, played no further part in the war.

Sparta itself. The assembly had been uncertain. If it was Pericles himself who persuaded it to decide as it did, one can only suppose either that he thought that he would be seen to be favouring the Corinthians if he accepted their suggestion that Athens did not intervene, or that he could not resist the opportunity to make a fool of an internal enemy by sending Lacedaemonius as a commander of the small defensive force, or perhaps both. A matter either of honour or of petty vengeance had got in the way of his better judgement. One can also answer that even having decided to follow a course of action that could only annoy Corinth, Pericles' pre-emptive ulti- matum to Potidaea, in itself and in the light of the political circum- stances in the north-west, was rash. One is less confident of this only because Athens' intelligence on the situation in the region in general and on the divided and turbulent politics of Macedonia in particular appears to have been poor, perhaps irremediably so. To his credit, Pericles learnt quickly and was soon able to make an alli- ance in Thrace and through that, for a while again, with the anxious Perdiccas; it is next to impossible to judge whether, even had he had the thought a year earlier, this option would then have been open to him. One can be more confident however that from where he and Athens itself stood in the winter of 432–31, after the Spartan vote for war, Pericles did still have room to manoeuvre. It is true that Spartan diplomacy at that moment was clumsy and difficult to read. But Pericles would have known that the sanctions on Megara would not prevent the Spartans marching into Attica. He would not there- fore have lost anything strategically in conceding something on the decree, merely his pride or what he may have construed as Athens' honour; and if the Spartans' second embassy had turned out to be a bluff, he would with advantage have called it.[29] His view appears to have been that he did not need to. The Spartans had neither the idea nor the resources to do anything but march into Attica and hope to entice the Athenians to engage them and be defeated. If the Athenians stayed in the city and refused, they could only go back. The city itself was secure. Within three years, Pericles believed, the

[29] As I explain, it does not follow, *pace* de Ste Croix, *The Origins of the Peloponnesian War*, p. 258, that if one grants something to the Spartans, one is thereby accusing Pericles of 'deliberately provoking the war'. For different reasons, neither state was entirely in control of itself. Which ever is?

period for which he had funds for war, the Spartans would see that they must abandon their strategy and sue for peace. The two powers would then return to the position of 445 (1.141–3).

But 'where Pericles stood' at any moment is not just a strategic matter. One has also to ask the second question, of whether he wished to avoid war: more exactly, of what it would have been for him to wish to do so. Here, Thucydides' own argument returns. At the moment in 433 when the Athenians were considering how to respond to the cases that had been put to them by Corcyra and Corinth, they began, says Thucydides – vague about the details – to feel 'that there would in any case be a war with the Peloponnesians'. If Pericles did wish for war, did he in his mind set that wish against at least the possibility of not wishing for it? Or had he already brought himself and Athens to a position in which he could not not do so?

Pericles was 'first man' by 443. Learning from the defeats in the 450s and the paradoxical advantages of the peace of 445, he had in the course of the later 440s and 430s made Athens and its empire more secure and increasingly prosperous, and extended the citizens' involvement in the democracy; had connected this involvement in the minds of most citizens, including the large number who depended materially on the empire, with imperial power; and had thereby widened and strengthened the legitimacy of his personal authority in the city and the ways in which he was using it. By the middle of the 430s, he had succeeded in exciting the delight of almost all Athenians (only a few fastidious intellectuals demurred) in their activism, involvement and willingness to take risks: delighted them, that is to say, in their sense of the power and superiority that was theirs – the qualities that the Corinthians were to ascribe to them at Sparta in 432 and that Pericles was himself so vividly (if also tendentiously) to explain to them in the subsequently much admired funeral oration in the first winter of the war, in 431, qualities that it had previously been the prerogative of oligarchs and tyrants to display to each other in front of what was then a politically inert and often suffering populace. Athens was by this time a singular political creation, and it was his.[30]

---

[30] My formulation here, although not the conclusions that I draw from it, owes much to Kurt A. Raaflaub, 'Democracy, Power and Imperialism in Fifth-Century Athens' in J. Peter Euben, John R. Wallach and Josiah Ober, eds., *Athenian Political Thought and the Reconstruction of American Democracy* (Ithaca, NY: Cornell University Press, 1994), pp. 103–46. Raaflaub's otherwise

But the creation was a beast, and Pericles had to ride it. It is this that would seem most readily to explain what Thucydides insists on: that Athens' power seemed to be growing, and was frightening the Spartans. The actual threat from Athens had not increased. Pericles' achievement was as much theatrical as real, and in the democracy, he had created what was at once an enthusiastic audience and a vigorous chorus. If we read the Athenians who were in Sparta in 432 'on other business' to have been conveying what Pericles wished to have conveyed, he hoped also to use this to deter Sparta and its allies from challenging Athens. On this, indeed, these speakers were quite clear: war is the last resort, not the first, and the longer it lasts, 'the more likely is it to turn on matters of chance, which we are all equally unable to control and whose outcome is a matter of risk and uncertainty' (1.78.3). But Pericles had become his own political prisoner. To maintain the impression of the city's power to others and the impression of his own in Athens itself, he had consistently and repeatedly to affirm it. In so doing, he had to suppress his practical judgement – his better judgement, perhaps, for when the choice was upon him, his arguments turned largely on pride – about how he could manoeuvre (or not) in the moments of decision that in 433–30 would have allowed him to allay the fears of Sparta and its allies and avert or at least delay the confrontations that these fears caused. The parties in Sparta itself were divided between themselves and anxious on their own account, and they read his performance with different degrees of alarm and anger. Their predominant reading, however, was that Athens' threat was real. And this, as distinct from any actual desire for war, was what Pericles had wanted to convey. But the distinction was a fine one and difficult for the Spartans (and others) to discern. Their reading was understandable, if unfortunate, and it produced an outcome that neither side was sure it wanted.

There is no great mystery in the formidable set of qualities, personal and political, that good political judgement demands: a clear purpose and a practical view of what has to be done to realise it; an achievable idea of how to command the power and resources to succeed,

---

excellent review of 'Warfare and Athenian Society' (note 7 above) does not consider the changes of circumstance in Athens between 432 and 430 and the effect that these evidently had on the citizens' enthusiasm for war, suggesting (at 113) that 'a reaction to a policy of aggressive imperialism ... is visible only much later'.

including a sensitivity to the views and likely strength of those who might support one and those who might not; a sense of how and when to tell the truth, varnish it, lie, or be silent; confidence, courage, patience, and a good sense of timing; the capacity to imagine the next move but one and the choices that this can present; and what, all along, might go wrong. Thucydides and Pericles himself were probably right. Pericles possessed most of these qualities most of the time, and the gift also of knowing how, in the political settings of later fifth-century Athens, to deploy the combination best suited to the occasion. He lacked only two things. One was the discipline, in Athens itself and in Sparta, of politically and strategically coherent adversaries. He knew that things could go wrong. But he had not imagined that the dominant reasoning in Sparta would not be his own, and that the Spartans would be determined to pursue the war.[31] The other, at least at the end, was the will, or capacity, in Athens' own interests, to listen to the citizens.

For following the second Spartan invasion of Attica in the early summer of 430, Thucydides reports, 'the Athenians, since their land had now been ravaged for the second time and in addition the plague had afflicted them along with the war, had undergone a change in their attitude'; 'with their minds reduced to despair on every count, they railed against Pericles. Seeing them incensed at the situation and in every way acting as he had expected' – some had even sent an embassy to Sparta to talk about peace – 'he called an assembly ... wishing to encourage them and make them calmer by ridding their minds of anger' (2.59.3). Their private miseries, however, continued, and their anger remained. They fined Pericles and then, as 'a multitude', Thucydides says, 'is apt to behave, not much later elected him and entrusted all their affairs to him, since by now they were more inured to the pain that each felt over personal concerns and considered him the most valuable man for the needs of the whole city' (2.65.1–2). On this, they were wrong. In his last recorded speech, in 430, he

---

[31] Had Sparta been more focused, it is just conceivable that in this late fifth-century 'security dilemma' – each side defending its security and allaying its fears in ways that heightened the fears of the other – the two powers might have managed to restrain themselves in the way in which the United States and the Soviet Union just managed to do in the Cold War. The classic modern statement of the dilemma is John H. Herz, 'Idealist Internationalism and the Security Dilemma', *World Politics*, 2 (1949–50), pp. 157–80.

reminded the citizens that it was they who had previously voted for war; that it was they, not he, who had changed their minds; that he was still the very best leader they could have; and that Athens was ready for the conflict. At the end, however, in words that suggest he was trying not only not to hear popular opinion but also to conquer a terrible doubt about his own judgement, he abandoned the democracy, reason, and with them reality. He did not now need to sustain his authority, as he had earlier, by urging war. The citizens did not now want it, and he could safely have agreed terms of peace. He had no reason to persist, but did. Athens had been great, he reminded the assembly, and it could be great again. The empire was a tyranny and had been unjust to obtain. But it would be fatal now to let it go. It would in the end go down; all things do. But what mattered was that 'the brilliance of the moment survives as future glory in everlasting memory' (2.64). With that 'syntactical ball', as Macleod so exactly says, he tried 'to tear through the gates of oblivion'.[32] With it, he also lost all political reason. He revealed that he could not bring himself – his anguish perhaps revealed that he was aware that he could not bring himself – to do what he was urging the citizens not to do but what they now wanted him to do and what he himself knew made sense: to suspend the political theatre, make moves to stop the war that neither they nor the more realistic Spartans wanted, and thereby prevent his own political creation being diverted and conceivably defeated by what he himself had called the 'senselessness' of events (1.140.1). Pericles failed the people whose political will he had shaped and depended on and which, to the advantage of no one, he was now flouting. Unless one allows the reasonableness of pursuing future glory in valiant defeat, this was pure unreason. Pressing it with his usual rhetorical success, and strengthened by the citizens' renewed but now misplaced confidence in him, Pericles opened Athens to what he himself knew was the unreason of war.

The unreason of power is a not unfamiliar kind. What in any instance drives it is often less clear. What drove Pericles' unreason in 430 may be wholly opaque. It is certainly difficult to determine. He may have believed that the citizens had a real interest, temporarily diverted, in war, although that had not been his view between 445 and 433, and he knew the uncertainties in fighting one; by 430, he was more aware

---

[32] Macleod, 'Thucydides and Tragedy', p. 153.

of the difficulties in controlling the expense of doing so. He may have thought that his honour was at stake, although it was not; now that the citizens were saying that they did not want war, he would have suffered no shame in agreeing a peace. He may simply have been unwell; he did soon weaken, and was to die the following summer. Whatever the explanation, it is an interesting fact about assessments of political judgement, as well as about Thucydides, that in the case of Pericles, Thucydides gives good grounds on which to reject his own.

8 | *Accounting for human actions: individual agency and political judgement in Montaigne's* Essais

BIANCAMARIA FONTANA

An understanding of politics as it bears on human interests cannot hope to be a unified vision from a single point of view. For one thing, it must seek to do justice to the full heterogeneity of human points of view ... it must also try to register the implications for what the interests of human beings really are of the bewildering variety of human imaginings across cultures, across space, across time and across the lifetime of every individual.[1]

The view that human sentiments and human behaviour are characterised by their varied and ever-changing nature is one of the best-known features of Montaigne's work. From the pages of the *Essais* the human self emerges as infinitely diversified, as well as engaged in a process of constant transformation: on the stage of a world inhabited by a variegated palette of tribes and cultures, each human being is still unique, while personal identities – including the writer's own – are reshaped through time by particular, and ultimately incomparable, individual experiences. This belief in the instability of the human condition formed an essential part of Montaigne's sceptical approach: from the somewhat conventional discussion of classical historiographical topics in the earlier sections of the text, to the bolder analysis of contemporary political circumstances in Book III, the 'inconstancy' of human nature contributed to undermine any attempt to explain individual and collective action through fixed patterns and stable rules.[2]

[1] John Dunn, *The Cunning of Unreason: Making Sense of Politics* (London: HarperCollins, 2000), pp. 101–2.
[2] All references to the text of Montaigne's *Essais* use the English translation by Donald M. Frame: Michel de Montaigne, *The Complete Works: Essays, Travel Journal, Letters* (London: Everyman's Library, 2003). They are followed by the reference to the French text in the edition by Pierre Villey: Michel de Montaigne,

This suspension of judgement over the general principles supposedly ruling human agency was not merely a philosophical posture, a clever but essentially speculative attitude. On the contrary, Montaigne's acute sensibility for the predicament of individual human beings allowed him to develop a distinctive and utterly original understanding of the crisis experienced by contemporary European society; it guided him, away from the dominant doctrines of absolutism and reason of state, towards a vision of politics as a complex practical activity, one which must confront at every step the intricate motivations, confused hopes and particular needs of ordinary individuals.

I Diversity

Montaigne's perception of the extraordinary variety of human experiences derived from a range of different considerations, which focused both upon people's inborn physical and moral characteristics and upon the context of their lives.

On the whole, external factors dictating differences were more obvious and easier to recognise: one of the most salient features of the *Essais* was precisely the author's illustration of alien and exotic customs, highlighting the striking diversity of human cultures in various geographical settings across the world. Ranging from the primitive society of the cannibals (loosely inspired by contemporary descriptions of Brazil), to the elaborate structure of the Chinese empire (in the somewhat idealised picture offered by Jesuit sources), Montaigne's

Les essais: édition conforme au texte de l'exemplaire de Bordeaux (Paris: PUF, 1988), 3 vols. It should be kept in mind that the numbering of the essays is a modern convention and may vary from one edition to the other. On Montaigne's sceptical philosophy see: Richard H. Popkin, *The History of Scepticism, from Erasmus to Spinoza* (Berkeley: University of California Press, 1979); John Christian Laursen, *The Politics of Skepticism, in the Ancients: Montaigne, Hume and Kant* (Leiden, New York and Cologne: E. J. Brill, 1992); Frédéric Brahami, *Le scepticisme de Montaigne* (Paris: PUF, 1977); Frédéric Brahami, *Le travail du scepticisme: Montaigne, Bayle, Hume* (Paris: PUF, 2001); Sylvia Giocanti, *Penser l'irrésolution: Montaigne, Pascal, La Mothe Le Vayer* (Paris: Honoré Champion, 2001); Hubert Vincent, 'Scepticisme et conservatisme chez Montaigne, ou qu'est-ce qu'une philosophie sceptique?' in Pierre François Moreau, ed., *Le scepticisme au XVIème et XVIIème siècle*, II, *Le retour des philosophies antiques à l'âge classique* (Paris: Albin Michel, 1999–2001); Ann Hartle, *Michel de Montaigne, Accidental Philosopher* (Cambridge: Cambridge University Press, 2003).

account of human civilisation on earth showed how the most disparate and eccentric, and even perverse, practices were equally regarded, by those who espoused them, as 'natural' and necessarily superior to any other. This ethnographical evidence deprived the very notion of a shared 'natural law' of any real substance: men were in fact capable of creating totally different forms of society, often resting upon conflicting and incompatible norms; far from conforming to the common diktats of nature, they constantly altered and reshaped their environment to suit their own particular needs and to serve their own distinctive prejudices, thus experiencing life through the filter of very dissimilar perspectives.[3]

Another important set of differences were connected with time and historical change: civilisations developing in different ages were at least as remote from one another as foreign and unexplored nations; indeed, the impossibility of fully penetrating the mentality of past generations represented a major obstacle in the way of any objective historical interpretation. Here Montaigne (himself a voracious reader of modern, as well as of ancient, history) expressed his unease towards the historical culture of his own time, a culture that remained dominated by the examples of antiquity and the cult of the classical past, while being unable to comprehend, let alone to reproduce, its values.[4]

---

[3] On the variety of human customs see in particular Book I, essays 23: 'Of Custom, and Not Easily Changing an Accepted Law' and 31: 'Of Cannibals'; on Montaigne's anthropology see Bernard Mouralis, *Montaigne et le mythe du bon sauvage, de l'antiquité à Rousseau* (Paris: Bordas, 1989); Edwin M. Duval, 'Lessons for the New World: Design and Meaning in Montaigne's "Des cannibales" (I, 31) and "Des coches" (III, 6)' in Gérard Defaux, ed., *Montaigne: Essays in Reading*, special issue of *Yale French Studies*, 64 (1984); Frank Lestringant, *L'Huguenot et le sauvage: L'Amérique et la controverse coloniale en France au temps des guerres de religion (1555–1589)* (Geneva: Droz, 2004); Frank Lestringant, *Le cannibale: grandeur et décadence* (Paris: Perrin, 1994). Montaigne's main source on China was Juan Gonzales, *Historia de las cosas mas notables de la China* (Rome, 1585), French trans. by L. de la Porte (Paris, 1588).

[4] On the historical sources of Montaigne's work see Pierre Villey, *Les livres d'histoire moderne utilisés par Montaigne: contribution à l'étude des sources des 'Essais': suivi d'un appendice sur les traductions françaises d'histoires anciennes utilisées par Montaigne* (Paris: Hachette, 1908; repr. Geneva: Slatkin, 1972); see also Isabelle Konstantinovic, *Montaigne et Plutarque* (Geneva: Droz, 1989); Julian H. Franklin, *Jean Bodin and the Sixteenth Century Revolution in the Methodology of Law and History* (New York: Columbia University Press, 1963).

Thus most of the time the efforts engaged in revising and correcting the works of ancient historians proved a self-defeating exercise, since at least those writers (whatever their errors and exaggerations) understood what they were talking about, unlike their modern counterparts. In the essay 'Defence of Seneca and Plutarch' (II, 32) Montaigne defended Plutarch from the criticism addressed to him by Jean Bodin: Bodin, he commented, was a 'good author ... equipped with much more judgement than the mob of scribblers of this time'; and yet he was wrong when he accused Plutarch of 'ignorance', and of writing 'incredible and entirely fabulous things', on account of his descriptions of the harshness and severity of Spartan customs. 'We must not judge', he concluded, 'what is possible and what is not, according to what is credible and incredible to our sense ... and it is a great error, and yet one into which most men fall ... to balk at believing about others what they themselves could not do – or would not.'[5]

The same view, that it was difficult to share the experience of another age, made Montaigne suspicious about any broad assumptions concerning future historical developments and future generations. The climate of corruption and violence associated with the religious wars had given credit to the view that human civilisation on earth was approaching its terminal decline. Yet this inference, however plausible in the present circumstances, was cognitively unsound, since it rested upon the limited experience of one particular part of the world at a particular time; it was perfectly possible, for example, that while France suffered the effects of a civil war, other nations, yet unknown to Western observers, might be living happily in peace.[6] France itself may find, in the near future, unsuspected resources towards its recovery, as the conditions for the preservation of states were often very difficult to assess or to anticipate.[7]

If space and time were crucial factors in diversifying human experience, social inequalities, and the differences in education and lifestyle which derived from them, were at least as significant. The *Essais* presented France as a deeply divided society, in which people of high rank inhabited a world of privilege of their own, while the large majority of the labouring poor lived in conditions of extreme poverty

---

[5] Frame, pp. 662–5; Villey, II, pp. 722–5.
[6] Montaigne, 'Of Coaches' (III, 6); Frame, p. 841; Villey, III, p. 908.
[7] Montaigne, 'Of Vanity' (III, 9); Frame, pp. 890–2; Villey, III, pp. 959–61.

and deprivation, abandoned and marginalised by those institutions which were designed to protect them. The letters and petitions Montaigne addressed to King Henri III, when serving as Mayor of Bordeaux during the 1580s, provided a passionate account of this deplorable situation, and denounced the irresponsible neglect of the authorities.[8]

Quite apart from the question of social justice, this state of affairs resulted in the complete estrangement of different social groups from one another. For all his good will towards the common people, the writer was prepared to admit that the peasants who worked on his estates, or the vagrants begging at his door, lived lives so different from his own that they might have inhabited some exotic region of the earth: 'The Scythians and Indians', he observed, 'are in no respect more remote from my powers and ways.'[9] As a result of this extreme inequality of circumstances and condition, the poor represented an entirely separate culture, more like an alien tribe than the integrated part of a Christian community. Inevitably this absence of a common understanding and a common language between higher and lower orders transformed the exercise of governance into a form of sheer domination.

Human experience varied because of the diverse contexts of people's lives; it varied also because even the lives of individuals belonging to the same historical age, culture or social group could be so different from one another as to prove incomparable. Men's specific physical and mental traits led them to react differently to the circumstances and events of their lives. Montaigne insisted in particular on the importance of the physical make-up of individuals, since people's personalities were greatly influenced by their bodily responses and affections: thus the *Essais* discussed at length the implications of bodily strength

---

[8] See for example: 'To King Henry III: Letter of Remonstrance from the Mayor and Jurats of Bordeaux' (31 August 1583), English translation in Frame, pp. 1304–7; cf. 'Au Roy' in *Œuvres complètes de Montaigne*, ed. Maurice Rat (Paris: Gallimard, Bibliothèque de la Pléiade, 1962); for a version in modern French, see Montaigne, *Lettres*, ed. Claude Pinganaud (Paris: Arléa, 2004), pp. 63–70; the letter was jointly signed by Montaigne and by the other members of the Town Council. On Montaigne's role as mayor of Bordeaux see Alphonse Gruen, *La vie publique de Michel de Montaigne* (1855) (Geneva: Slatkin, 1970), and Donald M. Frame in his *Montaigne: A Biography* (New York: Harcourt Brace and World, 1965), ch. 4.

[9] Montaigne, 'Of Experience' (III, 13); Frame, p. 1011; Villey, III, p. 1082.

and weakness, the varieties of sexual experience, and the distinctive circumstances of persons suffering from chronic diseases, physical disabilities or mental troubles. Moreover physical conditions necessarily affected people's imagination, and imagination played a major role in shaping the emotions and judgement of individuals, proving often more powerful than any other material factor or objective constraint.

In the course of a man's life these inborn features, both physical and mental, would not remain unchanged: a variety of factors, such as family circumstances, education, accidental events, illnesses and bereavements, new experiences, and even the natural process of aging, contributed to modify people's nature, opening up an infinite variety of new possibilities. Men could also change through their own deliberate choice of imposing upon themselves a certain discipline, rather than seconding their own natural inclinations, or by following the example of others and submitting themselves to their influence. The masterful account offered in the *Essais* of the peculiarities and changing traits of the author's own personality was offered as an exemplary illustration of the fluid, malleable nature of the human self. The writer's case was exemplary, not because it mirrored necessarily other people's experiences, but precisely because, just like any other instance of human life, it was absolutely unique.[10]

At a more fundamental level this unique character of human beings rested upon the intimate relation which connected every conscience to God, a relation which was as exclusive as it was essentially inscrutable. In the text Montaigne did not explicitly address the questions of the immortality of the soul, of salvation and divine retribution: on these as on any other matters touching upon Christian dogmas the *Essais* were deliberately silent.[11] He did however stress one crucial implication

---

[10] Montaigne's use of autobiography is possibly the most widely studied aspect of his work and is the object of an immense critical literature; for an essential reference see Antoine Compagnon, *Nous, Michel de Montaigne* (Paris: Seuil, 1980); see also Craig B. Brush, *From the Perspective of the Self: Montaigne's Self-Portrait* (New York: Fordham University Press, 1994); Ian J. Winter, *Montaigne's Self-Portrait and Its Influence in France: 1580–1630* (Lexington, KY: French Forum, 1976).

[11] On Montaigne's attitude towards dogma and religious censorship see Malcolm Smith, *Montaigne and the Roman Censors* (Geneva: Droz, 1981). The question of Montaigne's religious beliefs remains very controversial; for an overview of contrasting interpretations on the subject see Maturin Dréano, *La pensée religieuse de Montaigne* (Paris: G. Beauchesne, 1936); Clément Sclafert, *L'âme*

of the very existence of an individual conscience: all human actions carried necessarily a personal moral responsibility. Even when a man played an apparently marginal role in collective actions or broad historical events, he remained individually accountable for what little he had done, and even for what he should have done, but had failed to do. In a striking passage of the essay 'Of Vanity' (III, 9) he stressed this point in relation to the corruption of the times, and to his own particular responsibility:

The corruption of the age is produced by the individual contribution of each one of us; some contribute treachery, others injustice, irreligion, tyranny, avarice, cruelty, in accordance with their greater power; the weaker ones bring stupidity, vanity, idleness, and I am one of them.[12]

Human beings were always actors in the world they inhabited; no historical process, political movement or collective experience could be fully understood, unless it was seen as the product of a multitude of individual motivations and individual choices, even when these choices consisted (as they often did) in the passive acceptance of the initiatives of others and of seemingly overwhelming forces.

II Opacity

The variety of circumstances and the unstable nature of the human self made men's experience infinitely diverse; accordingly, their motivations and responses rarely conformed to simple patterns, but were generally complex and opaque. The fact that men had a limited capacity for acting according to reason, and were generally ruled by their passions, their beliefs and their imagination, meant that accounting for the behaviour of any individual was always a problematic

---

religieuse de Montaigne, part II, *La morale chrétienne de Montaigne* (Paris: Nouvelles Editions Latines, 1951); Jacques de Feytaud, 'L'église catholique face aux *Essais*' in Jacques Lemaire, ed., *Montaigne et la révolution philosophique du XVIème siècle* (Brussels: Editions de l'Université de Bruxelles, 1992); Don Cameron Allen, *Doubt's Boundless Sea: Scepticism and Faith in the Renaissance* (Baltimore: Johns Hopkins University Press, 1964), pp. 75–110; Max Gauna, *The Dissident Montaigne* (New York: Peter Lang, 1989), pp. 73–154, 166–70. See also Henri Busson, *Le rationalisme dans la littérature française de la renaissance, 1533–1601* (Paris: Vrin, 1971).

[12] Frame, p. 877; Villey, III, p. 946.

exercise; indeed sometimes it was difficult to explain the conduct of the person whose circumstances and character one was supposed to know best, that is to say oneself. The writing of biography offered a good illustration of this difficulty: historians, who narrated and assessed the deeds of the great men of the past, were inclined to fill the gaps in their information, or to gloss over any apparent contradictions in the conduct of their subjects; they adjusted their narrative to some ideal notion of how famous kings or heroic leaders should behave, creating a coherent, smooth image, which did not in fact correspond to reality:

Those who make a practice of comparing human actions are never so perplexed as when they try to see them as a whole and in the same light; for they commonly contradict each other so strangely that it seems impossible that they have come from the same shop ... There is some justification for basing a judgement of a man on the most ordinary acts of his life; but in view of the natural instability of our conduct and opinions, it has often seemed to me that even good authors are wrong to insist on fashioning a consistent and solid fabric out of us.[13]

The difficulties associated with the explanation of human behaviour could hardly be expected to disappear, when it came to interpreting the actions of groups of people or of large crowds: indeed, the complexity of motivations would be simply multiplied and complicated even further by the influence that the persons taking part in some collective action exercised upon one another. Naturally Montaigne recognised the fact that men could act together, driven by some obvious shared impulse or interest, that in events such as a rebellion or civil conflict individual motivations would be assimilated into a broader collective movement. In the *Essais* such mass phenomena were often illustrated by physical metaphors: they were compared to the symptoms of a disease, such as bouts of fever or poisonous 'humours', which invaded the body of society and then retreated from it, once the 'infection' had passed; in other passages the moods of crowds were assimilated to currents or telluric movements, which run irresistibly, breaking down all obstacles to their passage. In one of the

---

[13] Montaigne, 'Of the Inconsistency of Our Actions' (II, 1); Frame, p. 290; Villey, II, p. 331.

few surviving letters Montaigne addressed to his patron, King Henry
of Navarre, written in January 1590, after the decisive victory of
Navarre's Protestant army at Arques, he resorted to the image of tidal
waves (*ondées*) to describe the flowing of popular support in favour
of the new sovereign.[14]

In his work *Alchemies of the Mind* (1999), Jon Elster describes
these uniform impulses, as they appear in the *Essais*, as 'mechanisms',
arguing that in Montaigne 'there is more generality than meets the
eye', that, for all their sceptical rhetoric, the *Essais* do in fact point
at some uniform trends in human actions and responses, even if
the trends do not lead to the actual formulation of general laws.[15]
Whatever the heuristic merits of the notion of 'mechanisms', and even
if Montaigne does occasionally resort to generalities, in his analysis
such collective human impulses remained cognitively inaccessible,
since it was impossible to determine their causes or to anticipate their
course. Popular opinion, and the moods of crowds, may seem to come
and go like the tide; but in practice observers would be unable to tell
beforehand if, and when, they would do so, with what speed and
intensity, in response to what particular impulse or provocation. If
men were quite capable of forgetting their differences and of joining forces in some collective action, their separate individual motivations would not vanish altogether; on the contrary, they were likely
to reassert themselves, once the first impulse which had brought them
together subsided. Their striving towards a common goal would then
be replaced by the original jumble of diverse and incoherent motivations which had led them to mobilise in the first place.

The best illustration of the cognitive difficulties associated with collective action can be found in Montaigne's observations about the religious wars. Before the wars began, French society had been traversed
by all manner of divisive conflicts: social, economic, institutional, territorial and so on; indeed, the intensity of these latent tensions was
such that it might easily have led at any time to open rebellion or violent confrontation. However, to the surprise of many contemporary

---

[14] 'Popular inclinations go in waves; if the leaning in your favour is once established, it will gather its own momentum and go all the way.' Montaigne to
   Henry of Navarre, 18 January 1589, Frame, p. 1333; French text in *Œuvres
   complètes*, ed. Rat, p. 1398; Montaigne, *Lettres*, p. 124.
[15] Cf. Jon Elster, *Alchemies of the Mind: Rationality and the Emotions*
   (Cambridge: Cambridge University Press, 1999), pp. 13–17.

observers and of the writer himself, the civil conflict finally exploded
not over one of these obvious objects of dispute – poverty, taxation, the
administration of justice, local interests – but over a set of dogmatic
controversies, that had little or no impact upon the circumstances of
people's lives, and that were in fact incomprehensible to the large majority of them. If one then considered why a large number of persons,
many of them of humble origins, were ready to suffer martyrdom for
the sake of obscure dogmatic notions, it became clear that their motivations were in fact very heterogeneous: the authority of social superiors,
family ties, local attachments, sentiments of personal loyalty, defiance
or self-dramatisation played a far greater role in dictating their choices
than any genuine understanding of religious doctrines.[16]

Montaigne's attention to the complexity of individual motivations
within the religious crisis sets his work apart from the mass of contemporary sources, which favoured broad ideological justifications and
simple psychological assumptions. In contrast the *Essais* presented an
intricate tableau in which opportunism, fear, greed, arrogance, stupidity, credulity and ingrained brutality, but also loyalty, devotion, religious zeal, generosity and idealism combined together in unexpected
ways, to form the explosive cocktail which brought French society to
the brink of self-destruction. In particular they showed how it was
practically impossible to disentangle men's interests from their beliefs:
it was beliefs that dictated men's actions, and these beliefs often bore
a very distant relation to their real needs and circumstances. By probing into the content of people's religious convictions, the contemporary controversy over dogma had brought to light a far more general
aspect of human psychology: the power and imperviousness of individual opinions and imagination.[17]

III   The cunning of unreason

The experience of the religious wars gave immediate substance to
the doubts Montaigne had gradually developed towards the modern

---

[16] See for example the essays 'That the Taste of Good and Evil Depends in Large
Part on the Opinion We Have of Them' (I, 14), and 'Of Custom, and not Easily
Changing an Accepted Law' (I, 23), *passim*.

[17] On Montaigne's response to the religious wars see Biancamaria Fontana,
Montaigne's Politics: Authority and Governance in the 'Essais' (Princeton:
Princeton University Press, 2008), chs. 3 and 4.

ambition of systematising historical knowledge, turning clusters of particular cases into general laws – an ambition exemplified by fashionable works such as Machiavelli's *Discorsi* or Jean Bodin's *Methodus*.[18] It was understandable (if regrettable) that, in an age of fear and uncertainty, people should turn to the deceitful arts of prophecy – supposedly set aside with the advent of Christianity – in the hope of discovering what the future had in store for them. This regression to ancient superstitions must be set against the failure of serious philosophical investigation to master the bewildering variety of human circumstances, and to derive firm conclusions from the vast range of examples and counterexamples offered by historical experience.[19] In the *Essais* the dissection of current systematic accounts of human agency had an obvious polemical target in the futile generalisations of philosophers, and in the redundant, self-referential production of historical, philological and legal taxonomies which formed the bulk of sixteenth-century literature.[20] Yet Montaigne's critique was not just directed at modern neo-scholasticism: it was also an attack against some prevailing ways of thinking about politics and of operating in the public domain. But how precisely should we understand his critique?

Commentators have generally assumed that his main targets were the promoters of social change; reformers and revolutionaries. Because, in all circumstances, it was impossible to predict human behaviour and to master the unintended consequences of human actions, it would be generally more prudent to rally to the status quo – however unsatisfactory – and to submit to the established authorities, rather than taking the risk of subverting social order. Change may in

---

[18] Niccolò Machiavelli, *Discorsi sopra la prima Deca di Tito Livio*, ed. Francesco Bausi (Rome and Salerno: Edizione Nazionale delle Opere di Niccolò Machiavelli, 2001), 2 vols. On Montaigne and Machiavelli see Géralde Nakam, *Les essais, miroir et procès de leur temps* (Paris: Nizet, 1984), pp. 245–50; Thomas Berns, *Violence de la loi à la renaissance: l'originaire du politique chez Machiavel et Montaigne* (Paris: Kimé, 2000); Jean Bodin, *La méthode de l'histoire*, trans. and ed. Pierre Mesnard (Paris: Les Belles Lettres, 1941); Marie-Dominique Couzinet, *Histoire et méthode à la renaissance: une lecture de la 'Methodus' de Jean Bodin* (Paris: Vrin, 1996), pp. 114–20.

[19] On the role of prophecy see the essay 'Of Prognostications' (I, 11).

[20] For an illustration of Montaigne's attitude towards learning and contemporary cultural fashion see the essays 'Of Pedantry' (I, 25), 'Of the Education of Children' (I, 26) and 'A Consideration upon Cicero' (I, 40).

fact generate new evils, without necessarily correcting the old ones; human societies would in any case have a natural tendency to relapse into old ways and practices. In other words, Montaigne's scepticism about the intelligibility of human agency supposedly resulted in a kind of conservative quietism, which privileged stability over improvement, and individual survival over public goals. Because in contemporary France the established authority was represented by the monarchy (in its equally absolutistic Valois and Bourbon variants), the same line of interpretation has led to the assumption that Montaigne must be an advocate – though possibly an unenthusiastic one – of royal absolutism.[21]

If some elements of this reading of the *Essais* are plausible, the resulting picture of Montaigne's critical intentions and of his own political views seems partial and misleading. As a sceptic Montaigne was indeed suspicious of political utopias, whether they led to pursuing abstract notions of the public good, or to designing ideal regimes, since 'all ... imaginary, artificial descriptions of a government [proved] ridiculous and unfit to put into practice'.[22] This mistrust had obvious affinities with traditional conservative arguments about the certain evils, and uncertain benefits, of change. A strong bias against the use of violence – which pervades the text of the *Essais* – reinforced the writer's reluctance to endorse any form of political action that might involve sacrificing human lives on a large scale.

In addition to these general considerations, there were specific aspects of contemporary rebellion that help to explain Montaigne's negative judgement: compared to other subversive doctrines, the ideology of religious dissent had the additional demerit, in his eyes, of ignoring the real sufferings and grievances of the French people, focusing instead upon something as unattainable by human agents

---

[21] On Montaigne's supposed conservatism see Frieda S. Brown, *Religious and Political Conservatism in the* Essais *of Montaigne* (Geneva: Droz, 1963); Nannerl O. Keohane, *Philosophy and the State in France: The Renaissance to the Enlightenment* (Princeton: Princeton University Press, 1980), pp. 98–116; Judith Shklar, *Ordinary Vices* (Cambridge, MA and London: The Belknap Press of Harvard University Press, 1984); Richard Tuck, *Philosophy and Government, 1572–1651* (Cambridge: Cambridge University Press, 1993), pp. 45 ff.; for a contrasting view on this point see David Lewis Schaefer, *The Political Philosophy of Montaigne* (Ithaca, NY and London: Cornell University Press, 1990), pp. 153–76.

[22] Montaigne, 'Of Vanity' (III, 9); Frame, p. 887; Villey, III, p. 957.

as the laws of God. The elitist character of the Huguenot leadership, held by a group of ambitious and opportunistic aristocrats, meant that the party of reformers was tainted with the same vices as its Catholic counterpart. Thus the strong disapproval of religious novelty expressed in the *Essais* was inseparable from the feeling that such novelty represented a diversion from the country's real social and political problems, and that it was imposed from above, by a ruthless oligarchy, over a vulnerable and uncomprehending population. Unsurprisingly, the changes brought about in this way would alter the surface and appearance of things, rather than their substance:

Those who in my time have tried to correct the world's morals by new ideas, reform the superficial vices; the essential ones they leave as they were, if they do not increase them; and increase is to be feared. People are likely to rest from all other well doing on the strength of these external, arbitrary reforms, which cost us less and bring greater acclaim; and thereby they satisfy at little expense the other natural, consubstantial and internal vices.[23]

Montaigne's preoccupation with the authoritarian and elitist use of political authority points at the main critical target of his reflection, a target represented by those fashionable doctrines – loosely connected with the tradition of reason of state – which understood politics as a means towards the control and manipulation of human beings. In the *Essais* (more particularly in Book III, that began with the programmatic chapter 'On the Useful and the Honest') he took apart one by one the presuppositions of this kind of approach to politics: the vision of the art of government as a superior form of rationality; the belief that the populace could be led as a passive, easily manipulated mass; the separation of substance and appearance in public conduct; the resort to calculation and deceit in the pursuit of particular strategic goals; the exploitation of other men's vices and credulity to one's advantage.

He did not deny that the dismal assumptions of such doctrines were frequently confirmed by experience: men were only too often led by their vices; people did generally prove credulous and easy to

---

[23] Montaigne, 'Of Repentance' (III, 2); Frame, p. 746; Villey, III, p. 811.

manipulate; the populace did respond in predictable ways to the solicitations of leaders and demagogues; princes – old and new – may strengthen their power by means of calculated deceit. So why was the whole project of manipulative politics essentially unconvincing? If the writer's critical intention emerges from the text with sufficient clarity, it is still difficult to distinguish in his intricate, and often elusive, discussion of this issue the objections which focus upon the efficacy of manipulation from those that address its moral consequences.

Montaigne endorsed the philosophical view that all human endeavours and expectations were exposed to overwhelming hazards (where 'hazard ' may also be interpreted as the inscrutable design of the Divinity): a view originally set forth by classical sceptic and stoic doctrines, and subsequently recast by the Christian tradition. This pessimistic view of man's control over his fate applied in the first instance to the running of individual lives, but extended necessarily to broader public enterprises. In this perspective there was nothing much men could do in the face of threats beyond the control of any human agent, such as natural accidents, disease or death, except being spiritually prepared for them. However, things were somewhat different when the risks they faced came from the actions of other human beings.

Those who advocated manipulation as a strategy assumed that the risks coming from other people could be mastered more effectively by deceiving, tricking or intimidating those others into serving one's own designs. In politics the natural object of this exercise is the populace, who lend itself to it because of its ignorance, volatility and wish to be comforted by rosy expectations:

I have in my time seen wonders in the undiscerning and prodigious ease with which peoples let their belief and hope be led and manipulated in whatever way has pleased and served their leaders, passing over a hundred mistakes one on top of the other, passing over phantasms and dreams. I am no longer amazed at those who are hoodwinked by the monkey tricks of Apollonius and Mahomet. Their sense and understanding are entirely smothered in their passions. Their discernment is left no other choice than the one that smiles upon them and comforts their cause.[24]

---

[24] Montaigne, 'Of Husbanding Your Will' (III, 10); Frame, p. 943; Villey, III, p. 1013.

However, the strategy of controlling risk by mastering other people's will was both morally and cognitively flawed. Manipulative relations were morally unacceptable, because the exercise of mastery (*maistrise*) violated the natural equality and liberty of all human beings, placing some people in a state of moral (if not material) subjection to others. Domination – like enslavement – went against the aims of a truly Christian, humane community, that must be based upon relations of cooperation and understanding, not upon force or deceit. In addition to being immoral, manipulative relations were also cognitively unsound, as manipulators assumed, wrongly, that they would be able to foresee with some accuracy the future consequences of their strategies. Thus manipulative relations were essentially unsafe: they were unsafe for the victims of manipulation, as they would be led to act in ignorance of the true goals and full consequences of their actions, possibly against their own interest; they were unsafe for the manipulators themselves, as by appealing to popular passions and credulity they set in motion powerful and unpredictable forces they could not hope to control.

In most cases the unintended consequences of all human initiatives were so intricate and difficult to predict that 'vain cunning devices' (a phrase which gives the title to essay 54 in Book I) did not necessarily prove more effective, in their final outcome, than actions undertaken by simple impulse. Possibly in some cases calculating strategies might work; but in a complex situation, involving many actors, with a long chain of causal relations, elaborate calculations may still miss their final target.[25] Similarly, the pursuit of a goal by foul means – such as deceit or betrayal – offered no guarantee of success, and might as easily fail as a line of conduct dictated by sincerity and loyalty. In other words: manipulation created the illusion of control, but this *hubris* of mastery had often a very tenuous relation to reality. The support that people gave to particular leaders or regimes was, in all circumstances, unstable and volatile; if this support was obtained through artifice and false pretences, the consequent erosion of public confidence would undermine the stability of the very power that the deceiving ruler was trying to secure.

[25] On the uncertainty of human calculations, see in particular the following chapters: I, 47 ('Of the Uncertainty of Our Judgement'); I, 54 ('Of Vain Subtleties'); II, 14 ('How Our Mind Hinders Itself'); II, 20 ('We Taste Nothing Pure').

IV   Trust

In contrast with the Machiavellian ideal of power secured by cunning, the *Essais* exalted the image of the vulnerable individual, who confronted danger and threats by appealing to the humanity of his opponents. The gesture of the man or woman of good will, who gained the confidence of enemies by some gesture of appeasement – disposing of weapons, refraining from revenge, pleading for mercy or simply talking to them – was a recurrent theme in the text, where it appeared in a variety of ancient and modern historical settings. With a single act of faith and generosity the individual actor could hope to turn the tide of those overwhelming forces that were threatening to crush him. Uncharacteristically, the writer could not resist the temptation of casting himself in this exemplary role, by recalling some episodes in his own life, where a show of confidence towards his potential aggressors had rescued him from grave dangers.

When he was mayor of Bordeaux, his decision to allow a military parade of troops suspected of plotting a coup had won him the enduring loyalty of those soldiers. Captured by a band of masked men while he was travelling through a forest (kidnappings for ransom were common during the religious wars), he had obtained his instant release by confronting his captors with a 'frank and open countenance'; a similarly open attitude had delivered him from another gang of marauding soldiers, who were trying to get into his castle. These autobiographical narratives were presented in confidential, semi-ironical fashion: if they betrayed a certain vanity on the part of the writer, they contributed to show that such acts of confidence did not require any heroic performance, but were simple, ordinary human responses, within the reach of anyone. The narrator knew perfectly well that, if those personal episodes had a happy ending, many similar gestures ended in disaster; but he maintained that relations of confidence were the only type of interaction appropriate to the dignity of human beings, and which could form the basis of human society.[26]

---

[26] For these autobiographical episodes see Montaigne, 'Various Outcomes of the Same Plan' (I, 24); Frame, pp. 115–16; Villey, I, pp. 130–1; 'That Our Desire Is Increased by Difficulties' (II, 15), *passim*, and 'Of Physiognomy' (III, 12); Frame, pp. 988–91; Villey, III, pp. 1060–2.

Communities and political regimes were held together and supported by trust.[27] Undoubtedly the erosion and destruction of this
trust did not necessarily result in the complete collapse of social order:
witness the case of contemporary France, which had survived a high
degree of corruption and decades of a ferocious civil war. Human
societies might continue to function even when nothing but habit and
inertia united their members, who went on sharing the same space,
like objects thrown together at random in a heap;[28] yet such a state
of affairs was essentially pathological and contradicted the very purpose of society, that of developing peaceful bonds of cooperation and
exchange amongst its members.

Those doctrines claiming that trust was superfluous to the survival
of political communities were right, to some extent, in their assessment of what was practically viable. However, they advocated a form
of association and a style of governance that ignored the elementary
needs of ordinary people (like the writer himself) by failing to offer
them the basic advantages of peace, security and freedom. In the
particular circumstances of contemporary France, it was difficult to
imagine how political authority and social order could be restored to
normality, without going through a process of reconstruction of public trust: re-establishing confidence was the first duty of whoever had
a legitimate claim to the crown, and of those responsible for public
institutions; but it was also the duty of each member of the community, whatever their position. Thus, in contrast with the official policy
of collective 'oblivion' (*oubliance*) that characterised the legal settlements of the civil war, the writer believed that only an open process
of reconciliation, the mutual acknowledgement of past wrongs and
sufferings, could recreate a sense of community and restore durable
peace.[29]

---

[27] On the issue of trust see John Dunn, *Interpreting Political Responsibility:
Essays, 1981–1989* (Cambridge: Polity Press, 1990); Diego Gambetta, ed.,
Trust: Making and Breaking Cooperative Relations (Oxford: Basil Blackwell,
1990); Bernard Williams, *Truth and Truthfulness* (Princeton: Princeton
University Press, 2002).

[28] Montaigne, 'Of Vanity' (III, 9); Frame, p. 887; Villey, III, p. 956.

[29] The formulation which appeared in the Edict of Nantes was: 'que la mémoire
de toutes choses passées d'une part et d'autre ... demeurera éteinte et assoupie,
comme de chose non advenue': *L'Edit de Nantes*, ed. Janine Garrison (Biarritz:
Atlantica, 1997), p. 29, article I. For the Edict, 'obliviousness' began at a
specific date, that of Henri IV's accession to the throne (March 1595).

V Setting the people free?

The claim that political regimes should be founded upon trust is a significant illustration of the importance that the 'common' perspective occupied in Montaigne's reflection: it was impossible, in practice, to establish real bonds of confidence between rulers and their subjects, without giving expression to the needs and expectations of ordinary people. The *Essais* were not conceived as a work of political or constitutional theory, and their author did not resort to the language of contract to describe the particular form of popular consensus which defined legitimate political regimes. What he did offer instead was a very articulated reflection of what it meant, for particular persons, to be part of a community and to submit to a given political authority. Montaigne was ready to admit that the mass of the people were generally inclined to trust their rulers, regardless of the fact that, most of the time, they had no valid reason for doing so. Indeed, experience showed that bad princes could often command as much loyalty as good ones, simply because people had very vague and unrealistic notions about the true character and actions of those who governed them; in monarchies, the aura which surrounded the figure of the sovereign, his physical and psychological isolation from the mass of the people, increased this distance between rulers and subjects.[30]

In this respect it is possible to recognise continuity between the analysis of royal power offered in the *Essais* and the arguments set forth, towards the middle of the century, in the famous *Discours de la servitude volontaire*. Generally attributed to Montaigne's friend Etienne de la Boétie – but believed by some scholars to be Montaigne's own work – the *Discours* denounced the blind subjection of millions of people to a single 'tyrant', supported by a small entourage of greedy and corrupt oligarchs, and hinted at popular rebellion as the only valid response to this state of affairs. The *Essais* implicitly accepted this judgement about the unjustified servitude of the large majority of the people to a small, predatory minority; unlike the *Discours*, however, they investigated in greater depth and called into question the reasons for this voluntary and unreflecting enslavement of the many to the few.[31]

---

[30] See in particular the essays 'Of the Inequality that Is Between Us' (I, 42) and 'Of the Disadvantage of Greatness' (III, 7).

[31] Etienne de la Boétie, *Discours de la servitude volontaire ou contr'un*, ed. Malcolm Smith and Michel Magnien (Geneva: Droz, 2001). On the question

One of the best-known arguments developed in the *Essais* was the importance of habit and tradition in stabilising social practices and political regimes. The natural attachment of the people to established norms and authorities, regardless of their intrinsic merits, explained to a large extent their passive acceptance of bad princes and oppressive regimes. The same attachment suggested that, whenever circumstances created a discontinuity in the established power (for example through conquest or revolution), each nation would tend to return to the form of government to which they were accustomed: the subjects of monarchies, freed from the power of one sovereign, would rush into slavery to another master, while the citizens of republics would never willingly submit to an autocratic regime.[32]

While the *Essais* presented the empire of custom as a constant feature of human societies, they also brought to light one particular cause of the passive acceptance of authority: the separation between public discourse on the one hand and popular expectations on the other: the alienation of the subjects from the pronouncements and intentions of rulers. Montaigne associated this alienation mainly with autocratic rule, in which there was no public debate and the people had no means of expressing themselves. Once again he found his inspiration in contemporary circumstances. The corruption of the French monarchy and of its institutions had, amongst its effects, the debasement of public language. The most striking aspect of this phenomenon was the lack of transparency of the letter of the law: traditional French laws were inaccessible to the people, because they were written in a dead language (Latin) that normal persons could not understand without the (paid) assistance of specialists; on the other hand, modern laws, especially royal decrees issued to deal with

---

of the attribution of the text see Paul Bonnefon, *Estienne de la Boétie: sa vie, ses ouvrages et ses relations avec Montaigne* (Bordeaux: P. Chollet, 1888, repr. Geneva: Slatkin, 1970); Arthur Armaingaud, *Montaigne pamphlétaire: l'énigme du contr'un* (Paris: Hachette, 1910); Anne-Marie Cocula, *Etienne de la Boétie* (Luçon: Sud Ouest, 1995); Simone Goyard Fabre, 'Introduction' to Etienne de la Boétie, *Discours de la servitude volontaire* (Paris: Flammarion, 1983); for a recent discussion see David Lewis Schaefer, ed., *Freedom over Servitude: Montaigne, La Boétie and 'On Voluntary Servitude'* (Westport, CT and London: Greenwood Press, 1998), ch.1, 'Montaigne and La Boétie'; this volume includes the English translation of the *Discours*.

[32] See Montaigne, 'Of Custom, and Not Easily Changing an Accepted Law' (I, 23), and for a later reformulation of the same themes, 'Of Experience' (III, 13).

religious dissent, used such an ambiguous and shifting terminology that they blurred all distinction between right and wrong, between permitted and forbidden actions.[33]

This corruption of the letter of the law was not merely a formal problem: it deceived and confused the people, depriving the nation of that access to justice which was her due, and undermined the credibility of royal authority. The only means of restoring this credibility was a radical change in the style of public discourse: laws should be formulated without ambiguity, in the language currently spoken by the French population, rather than in some obscure ancient jargon; political arguments should be honest and truthful, rather than manipulative, and should be intelligible to common people. Socrates, just like Christ himself, had proved that it was possible to address ordinary persons, about very important questions, so as to be understood by them. After all, society was sustained, and made practically possible, by the work of those humble individuals who performed common, useful tasks; promoting understanding and exchanges amongst human beings was the only alternative to a state of affairs where all tensions and conflicts were addressed through domination and violence:

Socrates makes his soul move with a natural and common motion. So says a peasant, so says a woman. His mouth is full of anything but carters, joiners, cobblers and masons. His are inductions and smiles drawn from the commonest and best-known actions of men; everyone understands him ... By these vulgar and natural motives, by these ordinary and common ideas, without excitement or fuss, he constructed not only the best regulated but the loftiest and most vigorous beliefs, actions and morals that ever were ... even the simplest can recognize in him their means and their strength.[34]

---

[33] On the particular issue of the obscurity of the language of the law see Biancamaria Fontana, 'The Rule of Law and the Problem of Legal Reform in Montaigne's *Essais*' in José Maria Maraval and Adam Przeworski, eds., *Democracy and the Rule of Law* (Cambridge: Cambridge University Press, 2003).

[34] Montaigne, 'Of Physiognomy' (III, 12); Frame, pp. 965–6; Villey, II, pp. 1052–3; on the figure of Socrates in the *Essais* see Joshua Scodel, 'The Affirmation of Paradox: A Reading of Montaigne's "De la phisionomie"' in Gérard Defaux, ed., *Montaigne: Essays in Reading*, special issue of *Yale French Studies*, 64 (1983), pp. 209–37. The most developed discussion of the topic of speech and dialogue in the *Essais* is in essay 8 of Book III, 'Of the Art of Discussion'; see also Antoine Compagnon, 'Montaigne ou la parole donnée'

More than four centuries after the publication of the *Essais*, it is quite difficult to know what to make of Montaigne's pleading for a less arrogant, less authoritarian language of morals and politics, and to explain his concern for what could be described as a democratisation of public discourse. Naturally, in the aftermath of the religious wars, restoring the credibility of institutions and promoting civil reconciliation were obvious priorities. It is unsurprising, for example, that a shrewd political operator like Henry of Navarre, when he finally arrived within reach of the French crown, should choose to address the *parlements* and the people in passionate, brotherly tones, adopting a novel rhetorical style that Germaine de Staël would still regard as exemplary in 1789.[35] Yet nobody – least of all Montaigne himself – really expected that the restoration of peace, and even the establishment of religious coexistence, might alter the way in which social and political power was distributed and exercised within the French state.

Moreover, the vices of arrogance and untruthfulness, the practice of talking down to the people, were not the exclusive prerogatives of monarchies and aristocratic regimes. Clearly a society characterised by rigid hierarchies and huge inequalities, such as the French one, could only exacerbate the rift between the people and its rulers. But Montaigne knew perfectly well that popular republics – the form of regime he himself regarded as most just and natural – were far from innocent of the practice of manipulation and deceit: witness the example of the ancient republican polities, where the art of rhetoric had transformed public speech into a dangerous instrument of power, rather than the means of genuine popular deliberation.[36]

in Frank Lestringant, ed., *Rhétorique de Montaigne* (Paris: Champion, 1985); Marc Fumaroli, *La diplomatie de l'esprit: de Montaigne à La Fontaine* (Paris: Herman, 2001); David Quint, *Montaigne and the Quality of Mercy: Ethical and Political Themes in the 'Essais'* (Princeton: Princeton University Press, 1991); Yves Delègue, *Montaigne et la mauvaise foi: l'écriture de la vérité* (Paris: Honoré Champion, 1998); Philip Knee, *La parole incertaine: Montaigne en dialogue* (Saint Nicolas, Quebec: Presses de l'Université de Laval, 2003).

[35] Cf. Germaine de Staël, *Considérations sur la Révolution française*, ed. Jacques Godechot (Paris: Tallandier, 2000), p. 74. See also Michel de Waele, 'Henri IV, politicien monarchomaque? Les contrats de fidélité entre le roi et les Français' in Jean-François Labourdette, Jean-Pierre Poussons and Marie-Catherine Vignal, eds., *Le Traité de Vervins* (Paris: Presses de l'Université de Paris-Sorbonne, 2000).

[36] Montaigne, 'Of the Vanity of Words' (I, 51); Frame, p. 269; Villey, I, p. 305; for the definition of democratic rule (*domination populaire*) as 'most natural and

So what did Montaigne have in mind when he offered the example of Socrates conversing with an audience of manual labourers? After all it seems unlikely that, like Majakowski in one of his boisterous militant moods, he might be advocating the instruction of cooks in the art of government.

The most common interpretation is that his aims were essentially moral and educational. Thus the *Essais* are often read within the context of a tradition of moralising works – broadly associated with the Counter-Reformation – which advocated the return of the French aristocracy to the basic Christian values of humility and charity. This restoration of upper-class morality implied major changes in current pedagogic practices: the new, more self-conscious style of education should aim at moderating the violent and essentially military disposition of the aristocracy, while at the same time curbing their social pride and strengthening their piety. In this perspective, the choice of conversing with the lower orders would combine the rejection of intellectual arrogance with a suitable display of evangelical simplicity. The social ideal associated with this moral project was summed up in the concept of 'honesty' (*honnêteté*): the honest man was identified with the independent gentleman, who lived in dignified retirement, away from the seductions and intrigues of the court, placing personal integrity and fidelity to Christian values before worldly success.[37]

This interpretation of the *Essais* as a moralising work is supported to some extent by the text. It is true that Montaigne showed a keen interest in pedagogical issues, and that he militated in favour of a more 'humane' approach to the education of children; he also believed, like Erasmus before him, that the re-education of European elites away from the military ideals of the feudal nobility

equitable', see Montaigne, 'Our Feelings Reach Out Beyond Us' (I, 3); Frame, p. 14; Villey, I, p. 20. On the role of rhetoric in ancient polities see Nicole Loraux, *L'invention d'Athènes* (Paris: Payot, 1993); Robert Morstein-Marx, *Mass Oratory and Political Power in the Late Roman Republic* (Cambridge: Cambridge University Press, 2004).

[37] On the concept of 'honnêteté' the classical reference is Maurice Magendie, *La politesse mondaine et les théories de l'honnêteté en France au XVIIème siècle* (1925) (Geneva: Slatkin reprints, 1993); see also Marc Fumaroli, *L'âge de l'éloquence* (1980) (Paris: Albin Michel, 1993); Emmanuel Bury, *Littérature et politesse: l'invention de l'honnête homme, 1580–1750* (Paris: PUF, 1996).

was the necessary precondition for restoring durable peace.[38] It is also true that Montaigne's repeated assertions of autonomy and self-sufficiency did point at an ideal of moral and intellectual independence, which was implicitly critical of feudal servility and blind partisan loyalties.

The problem with this moralising perspective is that it fails to capture, and account for, the most radical undertones of the *Essais*: the merciless dissection of social inequalities and the devastating portrayal of the 'unnatural' position of monarchs in the text are difficult to read as respectful admonitions addressed to people of rank. The pervasive sense of the extreme brutality of *Ancien Régime* society, so powerfully conveyed by the book, goes well beyond the conventional display of compassionate Christian sentiments. Even the gracious ideal of detachment from the grubby ways of politics is somewhat misleading, when set against Montaigne's active loyalty to his patrons and his protracted engagement to keep himself and his fellow-citizens as far as possible out of trouble by relentless diplomatic negotiations.[39]

VI Political judgement

The centrality of particular concerns and the insistence upon the position of common people in the *Essais* have often been read as a move away from public values and political engagement into the

---

[38] On Montaigne's views on educational practices see Hubert Vincent, *Education et scepticisme chez Montaigne, ou pédantisme et l'exercice du jugement* (Paris: L'Harmattan, 1997); Gabriel Compayré, *Montaigne et l'éducation du jugement* (Paris: P. Delaplane, [no date]); see also Pierre Villey, *L'influence de Montaigne sur les idées pédagogiques de Locke et de Rousseau* (Paris: Hachette, 1911); Max Gauna, *Montaigne and the Ethics of Compassion* (Lewiston, NY: The Mellen Press, 2000); on pacifism in the Erasmian tradition see J. D. Tracy, *The Politics of Erasmus: A Pacifist Intellectual and His Political Milieu* (Toronto: University of Toronto Press, 1978); Jean-Claude Margolin, ed., *Guerre et paix dans la pensée d'Erasme* (Paris: Aubier, 1973); Philip C. Dust, *Three Renaissance Pacifists: Essays in the Theories of Erasmus, More and Vives* (New York and Berne: Peter Lang, 1987).

[39] On Montaigne's position within a network of aristocratic patronage see George Hoffmann, *Montaigne's Career* (Oxford: Oxford University Press, 1998); on the writer's engagement in his role of mayor of Bordeaux, see his correspondence with the marshal de Matignon, the king's lieutenant in the Guyenne during the 1580s, published in *Œuvres complètes*, ed. Rat, English trans. in *The Complete Works*, ed. Frame.

private self; but it is perhaps more plausible, less contradictory, to see it as a search for a new basis upon which political understanding and practice may be founded. Naturally Montaigne's view of contemporary circumstances was far from optimistic, and his text gave frequent expression to feelings of disaffection and discouragement; but the same text made it very clear that retreating into a supposedly private sphere was no viable option, not at least while gangs of masked horsemen were camping at one's gate. The stoic posture of distancing oneself from the world may be philosophically admirable, but offered no real protection from the ravages that power might inflict upon helpless human beings.[40]

In this respect the scepticism of the *Essais* reveals its eminently practical vocation. By rejecting general schemes and abstract models of explanation, the writer indicated individual experience as the only possible – if imperfect – source of human knowledge. Humans seem thus condemned to a sort of epistemic solipsism, as each personal experience was unlike any other; however experiencing meant, in practice, relating to other human beings, and this might lead to the discovery of similarities of sentiment and favour the search for a common ground.[41]

Like other contemporary observers, Montaigne was looking for a way out of the self-destructing pattern generated by the religious conflict; unlike others, however, he did not focus primarily upon possible new forms of state power, but looked at novel ways of thinking about the relations between individual persons and authority. This new perspective placed individual needs and expectations at the centre of political reflection, as the starting point of any real understanding of human actions, and also as the true measure of the success of any form of rule.

In the writer's own vision this reversal of perspective went together with the passionate aspiration to a different type of society: one in which the bonds of feudal dependence might be replaced by those of

---

[40] On the ambiguities in the use of the concepts of private and public, see Raymond Geuss, *Public Goods, Private Goods* (Princeton: Princeton University Press, 2001).

[41] Montaigne seems to have regarded the pursuit of sociability both as natural to humans and as a kind of moral obligation. The essential reference on the role of experience is essay 13 in Book III, 'Of Experience', which concludes the work; see on this point Fontana, *Montaigne's Politics*, ch. 6.

cooperation and exchange, conquest and pillage abandoned in favour of commerce, the rules of the law substituted for those of personal favour, the 'middling rank' valued as the most desirable social condition. What makes his work instructive for contemporary political theory, however, is not the ghostly apparition of the values of modern liberty amongst the ruins of feudal and fanatical warfare, powerful and striking though this apparition still proves for the reader of the *Essais*. Montaigne's most significant legacy to us is not the defence of a rather hazy ideology of modernity, with which he is sometimes credited;[42] it is instead a new, extremely sophisticated, relentlessly critical way of thinking about individual beliefs and motivations, and about what they mean for those (whoever they may be) who aspire to ruling the people. If his insights about the poverty of our explanatory categories, the bewildering richness of human realities, the arrogance and fragility of power, have a broader philosophical significance, it is the questioning of the foundation of popular consensus that brings his work surprisingly close to the heart of modern debates about the nature of democratic regimes.

---

[42] See for example Tzvetan Todorov, *Le jardin imparfait: la pensée humaniste en France* (Paris: Grasset, 1998); Joseph Macé-Scarron, *Montaigne notre nouveau philosophe* (Paris: Plon, 2002).

9 | Nehru's judgement

SUNIL KHILNANI

I

On 15 August 1946, exactly one year before the partition of India and the creation of the independent states of India and Pakistan, Mohammed Ali Jinnah and Jawaharlal Nehru met in Bombay. They convened at Jinnah's Malabar Hill mansion, after many months of tortuous, three-cornered wrangling between the two men, their respective parties, the Muslim League and the Congress, and the British, concerning the future Indian state that would succeed British rule in the subcontinent. The arguments turned on how power should be distributed once the British had departed. Would it be concentrated in a unitary central state, its legitimacy based on the democracy of numbers; or would power be devolved or divided, in ways that recognised Indian Muslims as a nation entitled to their own political arrangements, and in a form that would ensure them – though numerically a minority – political parity with their Hindu compatriots? As they talked that evening on Malabar Hill, Nehru – as on past occasions – hoped to persuade Jinnah to participate in an interim government and in a proposed constituent assembly (whose task was to write a constitution for a united India), and to assure Jinnah that in this united independent Indian state that Nehru envisaged, the security and rights of all religious groups, including minorities, would be protected. Nehru also reiterated to Jinnah that the Congress proposed to nominate one Muslim amongst its designated cohort in the interim government – a move designed to affirm Congress's claim to represent all Indians, Muslims included. Jinnah, as before, objected, claiming that his party alone had the exclusive right to speak for India's Muslims – stipulating that there would have to be separate constituent assemblies for Muslim and Hindu majority provinces, which only subsequently might meet to discuss any all-India arrangements. The encounter between the two ended fruitlessly, both parties once again frustrated, with Jinnah insisting on separate and self-governing territories for the subcontinent's Muslims. Nehru later told the Viceroy, Wavell, that his impression was 'that Jinnah had gone rather further out than he had intended to' – by which Nehru presumably meant the demand for a separate state of Pakistan – and now 'was at a loss how to get out'.[1] It was in all probability the last meeting between the two at which they might still have found a way to avoid the division of British India. Their conversation over, the same evening Jinnah announced that 'There will be no more meetings between me and Pandit Nehru.'[2] The very next day, Hindu–Muslim killings began in Calcutta – the 'great Calcutta killings', after which the drift to a partition of British India became irreversible.

In Jinnah's and Nehru's encounters during 1946 and 1947, a range of understandings, beliefs, values, hopes and fears collided: differing evaluations of what politically was most important (for Jinnah, security for religious minorities; for Nehru, a common freedom for all Indians); differing understandings of India's past (one which viewed it as a story of civilisational confluence, as against one which saw it as two nations, defined by religion, each coming into their own and acquiring a state); differing views of the authority of the state and of how it served as a mechanism for encouraging prudential choices (one which saw its legitimacy as based on strong identification with and trust in leaders on the basis of shared religious allegiance, contrasted with one that saw its legitimacy as resting on constitutional forms and democratic numbers); differences over sequence (Jinnah insisted that the Hindu–Muslim issue be resolved before the British departed, while Nehru pressed for independence first, after which the religious question could be resolved); and differing assessments of the future effects of that division or unity on the subcontinent (Nehru worried that the presence of two or more states would diminish the security and increase the dependence of these states on outside powers). And all this was given form in the shape of two very different individual temperaments, with entirely contrasting political styles: each having to act under pressure of

[1] Archibald Wavell, Record of Interview with Jawaharlal Nehru, 17 August 1946, India Office Records, R/3/1/117, available in *Selected Works of Jawaharlal Nehru* (New Delhi: Jawaharlal Nehru Memorial Fund, 1982), XV, p. 294.
[2] *The Bombay Chronicle*, 16 August 1946, p. 1.

time, in circumstances of partial knowledge and high uncertainty, and with very large stakes to play for.

There are three remarks about political judgement worth making at the outset. Judgement in politics is not simply – perhaps never – about the application of general maxims to particular cases; it is not, as it is thought of in some conceptions of law, like legal judgement. Political judgements are only very unusually – if ever – made under optimal conditions, and, because they involve choices about future states about which the actors cannot know, it is a condition of political judgement that one can be massively wrong. Nor can political judgement be thought of as punctual, summative, once and for all – for, even when one is wrong, or half-right, in politics one has to go on, to the next political judgement, and the next after that: and to face the consequences. Political judgements can have long after-lives, and thus a conception of responsibility is intrinsic to them. Finally, political judgement seen from the inside is a very intimate thing – it brings to bear, musters and tries to focus the entire experience of a person's life. This can be damagingly distorting, but it is also what imparts energy and sometimes authority to political judgement.

For those leading a political life, political leaders, people who have some power over their fellows, who – as Max Weber put it – hold in their hands 'some vital strand of historical events', this sense of responsibility, the sense that one's best intentions may in fact cause great harm, is a necessary part of their self-conception. 'Three qualities', Weber wrote, 'are pre-eminently decisive for a politician: passion, a sense of responsibility, judgement [proportionality].'[3] 'Simply to feel passion', Weber went on, 'however genuinely, is not sufficient to make a politician unless, in the form of service to a "cause", responsibility for that cause becomes the decisive lodestar of all action.' But judgement, Weber stresses, 'is the decisive psychological quality of the politician'.[4] Weber's purpose, in his argument here, was to set out the nature of responsibility – personal responsibility – appropriate to the modern political leader, as distinct from the merely professional politician (the state official, unthinkingly carrying out the command

[3] Max Weber, 'The Profession and Vocation of Politics' in Peter Lassman and Ronald Speirs, eds., *Weber: Political Writings* (Cambridge: Cambridge University Press, 1994), p. 352. This translation renders 'Augenmass' as 'judgment'.
[4] *Ibid.*, p. 353.

from above) or the moral purist, for whom the fineness of intentions outweighed thought about consequences.

Jawaharlal Nehru – sometime lawyer and journalist, speechmaker and rhetorician, Congress Party official and leader, Prime Minister of independent India from 1947 to 1964, a man whose hand certainly touched the wheel of history – is a peculiarly apt candidate to view through the prism of political judgement. It is hard to think of any other sequence of individual human judgement – on politics, the economy, the social order, the value of India's past and its possible futures – that have mattered more for India's modern history, that have been so consequential. As a leading actor in determining the shape and content of the independent Indian state, and then as the first elected custodian of its powers, Nehru's political judgements and their effects still shape the contexts in which Indians must today decide for themselves. So much so, that much of India's recent politics can be seen as representing a range of evaluations on what Indians have taken to be Nehru's judgements.

But, to be in a position to pass judgement on his judgements, to make a retrospective, historical assessment, one needs first of all to understand the basis of his own political judgements: to see the circumstances in which he had to judge politically. Here, a vital part of the context is the individual himself – and how he saw and felt the world, what appeared to him of value and of danger in it: and what assessments followed from this.

John Dunn has long insisted that any account of politics, and of why it is the way it is, must give a central place to the individual political actor – and must try to grasp as well as to evaluate his or her always partial capacities to judge. Such a perspective is perhaps especially appropriate to a figure like Nehru. Nehru, like Mahatma Gandhi, was not merely a historical actor in a momentous period: both were also continuous self-examiners of their most intimate thoughts, motivations, hopes and fears. Nehru avoided the politician's wilful uninterest in moral and intellectual reflection on power and its uses; equally though, he could ill afford the solace of the intellectual, the retreat into abstract and often microscopically focused moral argumentation, the getting straight of imaginary dilemmas faced in chosen, ideal conditions. He was – with Gandhi – a powerful moral critic of power unjustly wielded. But unlike Gandhi, who never held any political office, Nehru himself acquired power in its most concentrated modern form – command of a state – and he was forced to confront the dilemmas of its exercise. He had to make choices about its use.

Nehru certainly was driven by 'passionate commitment', by the sense of a cause, and he was aware of the self-consuming aspects of this. Yet he also sought distance from the world of politics – wishing sometimes to remove himself altogether from it, trying always to keep a gap between his active and his reflective self. Weber defined judgement as 'the ability to maintain one's inner composure and calm while being receptive to realities, in other words distance from things and people'.[5] Nehru valued this capacity for detachment: he cultivated it, even as he was often frustrated at his inability to achieve it. I think it also yielded a distinctive political approach, a particular way of thinking about and using power. Even when he was in the thick of it, we sense with Nehru that something is held back, resisting total consummation by the cause. He valued the ability to step outside the workings of the political world, and his own working of it, in order to observe both that world and his own role in it.

Nehru's own position can be contrasted with three other political types: the first is a figure like Gandhi, one who aims for moral clarity (tortuously won in Gandhi's case), and for whom politics is a detour towards the achievement of this higher goal. Gandhi, through appeal to his 'inner voice', could invoke a moral authority which removed the need to make certain judgements (or, at least, such decisions need not appear to others as the exercise of judgement). Gandhi wished to integrate his private and public selves, and he enjoyed the tensions and satisfactions of either/or choices – the resistance to food, physical pain and pleasure, sex, as ways of securing political and public ends. Nehru admired what he saw as Gandhi's 'application of an ethical doctrine to large-scale public activity', but remained always baffled and sceptical of its sources, of Gandhi's inner voice – which he saw as a form, sometimes, of moral absolutism.[6] The second are the ideological politicians, men like Subhas Chandra Bose and the Indian Communists, who believed they had privileged access to theoretical conceptions that they sought to realise, were committed to historical schemes, and dismissed moral positions, for instance, as expressions

---

[5] *Ibid.*, p. 353.
[6] Jawaharlal Nehru, *The Discovery of India* (Calcutta: Signet Press, 1946), p. 13.

of class interest. Nehru rejected such relativism, with its disregard of 'certain basic urges which had greater permanence'.[7] Third were what might be called the 'pure' politicians, men like Jinnah and Vallabhbhai Patel: who set themselves definite political goals, who wielded impressive forensic skills and analytic powers, and who were extraordinarily effective in using political means to achieve their ends.

Nehru was uncomfortable with and troubled by such positions. Writing in the summer of 1937 to Sheila Grant Duff, then an aspiring journalist down from Oxford, he insisted,

> I am quite sure we must stick to the truth as we conceive it to be. The difficulty lies not there but in knowing where truth lies, what is a major truth, and what is a minor. Sometimes, inevitably, we have to choose between the two evils and we choose the lesser one; sometimes also we are apt to be wrapped up in minor truths to the exclusion of the major one. Those who think they have got hold of a fundamental truth – the men of religion or the convinced communists or the equally convinced Nazis – apply that standard to everything and have a sense of mental security which others lack. I am afraid I am not one of those dogmatic believers of doctrine.[8]

On the other hand, he could sense the attractions of the positions taken by his own Indian mentors, colleagues and opponents: and yet he could never quite fit into any of these niches – ethical certainty, theoretical absolutism, pragmatic efficacy. More often than not, he found himself moving across and away from them.

I first set out some remarks on how Nehru himself tried to make sense of his own motives and actions, how he thought about history and causality, and how he situated himself in the world of political action. I move then to a discussion of Partition, a central instance of Nehru having to choose and act in ways that involved assessments about his values and about future outcomes. The purpose here is not to clinch a new interpretation, but to explore Nehru's own processes of judgement. In conclusion, I shall suggest that the experience of events such as Partition and its aftermath gave Nehru an acute sense of the destructive potentials of politics: his circumspection in the use of political power, his refusal, at times, of stark choices, were

---

[7] *Ibid.*, p. 13.
[8] Nehru to Sheila Grant Duff, 10 June 1937, Sheila Grant Duff Papers, Bodleian Library, Oxford.

themselves a political judgement – about the need for self-restraint in the use of power, and most importantly, about not pressing one's political values, even those most cherished, too far, too strongly.

II

Between April and September 1944 Nehru was imprisoned in Ahmednagar jail, serving his ninth and final term of imprisonment. Here, his sole steady companion the moon waxing and waning over the hills of the western Deccan, he wrote the manuscript later published as the *Discovery of India* (1946). Its opening sentence spoke of imprisonment; its final word, a thousand longhand pages later, was 'freedom'. Yet, for a book written by a nationalist whose country was poised for its independence, it is strangely unhortatory in tone, less manifesto and more spiralling rumination, often repetitive and sometimes self-indulgent, one of whose motifs is the finitude of politics and human action, and the potentialities of politics to bring about undesired effects. Two key judgements of this work are worth recalling. First, an insistence on seeing India as a unity, a confluence of civilisations, which had resulted in something unique: a plurality of cultures, religions and ways of living which, on the whole and over the long run, had found ways of existing alongside one another that were relatively peaceable – a view opposed, for instance, by Jinnah. Second, a sense that while such aspects of the past had to be valued and continued, there was also much else about India's past that was stifling, and India must release itself from the grip of this, and embrace the modern world – an evaluation opposed, for instance, to Gandhi's.

For Nehru, 'a prisoner perforce inactive when a fierce activity consumes the world', the act of writing his manuscript was an effort to infuse his 'seemingly actionless' life with a sense of possibility and activity.[9] He disclaimed any pretence of objectivity or disinterestedness in his account of the past: rather, 'by bringing it in some relation to my present-day thoughts and activities' (he likened the process to psychoanalysis), he hoped both to reconcile himself to and to free himself from the past's tyranny and compulsions.[10] Nehru wondered about the conditioning and even determining effects of the past upon

---

[9] Nehru, *The Discovery of India*, p. 20.   [10] *Ibid.*, p. 19.

him, and was intrigued by arguments for determinism and free will. He entertained the possibility that the urge to free action, the refusal to accept that all may be predetermined, the very desire we have to exercise free will, might themselves in fact all be the product of previous conditioning and determination. And yet, even if that were true, we would still have to act, *as if* free to do so.

A sense of the interconnectedness between past, present and future, each conditioning our understanding of the other, and to each of which we owe responsibilities, runs through *The Discovery of India*. Actions and events were embedded in history, with continuing and recursive effects that could never fully be transparent. History was of interest to Nehru from this perspective: not because it might offer a repertoire of examples or analogies which could guide present action, but because it was in some sense still active in the present. 'We seek to understand a particular event by isolating it and looking at it by itself, as if it were the beginning and the end, the resultant of some cause immediately preceding it', Nehru wrote.

Yet it has no beginning and it is but a link in an unending chain, caused by all that has preceded it, and resulting from the wills, urges and desires of innumerable human beings coalescing and conflicting with each other, and producing something different from what any single individual intended to happen. Those wills, urges and desires are themselves largely conditioned by previous events and experiences, and the new event in its turn becomes another conditioning factor for the future.[11]

To believe that a single individual – or, one might add, a single decisive event like partition – could somehow shake free of what he called 'the chain of happening' was simply illusory: 'The man of destiny, the leader who influences the multitude, undoubtedly plays an important part in this process, and yet he himself is the product of past events and forces and his influence is conditioned by them.'[12]

Nehru's interleaving of past history and his own circumstances encouraged in him a tendency to try to see his own lived present as if from the viewpoint of the future: 'the present also sometimes receded into the distant past and assumed its immobile, statuesque appearance', he wrote, and 'In the midst of intensity of action itself, there

[11] *Ibid.*, p. 423.   [12] *Ibid.*, p. 423.

would suddenly come a feeling as if it was some past event and one was looking at it, as it were, in retrospect.'[13] This capacity for detachment and perspective was of value in guiding political judgement not least because it forced one to consider how one's current values as well as actions might look, seen from the perspective of the future. Nehru recognised how, to himself, his own 'ideals and objectives of yesterday' had, as one approached them, lost some of their lustre and 'shining beauty' – the very pursuit of the values one held, the political actions necessary to achieve them, inevitably brought about a 'coarsening and distortion of what had seemed so right'.[14]

Detachment came also from his view of personal identity, as well as from his life outside politics. Observing his life, he saw it as a parade of selves, strung together by the connecting thread of sheer physical continuity– a parade containing past selves to which his present self continued to have responsibilities (the very fact of this sequence meant that no one self had priority, cancelling out the others: to each one had a certain responsibility): 'Dead and past selves pile up behind us but the new self, itself a thing of the moment, ever changing, carries the impress of all these past selves upon it, past experiences and thoughts and trails, dreams and reveries, and the hard knocks of existence', he observed to his daughter, Indira: 'looking back, one sees this long and interminable succession of past selves, fading into each other, like ghosts of things that were and are no more'.[15]

Nehru's tendency to see his political life from other perspectives was encouraged also from the fact that he had a rich life outside and beyond politics – one lived certainly in the imagination and also, sporadically, in reality – involving friendship, love, an engagement with ideas and nature. He felt acutely the costs exacted by a political career on this other life. The availability to him of a fairly broad range

---

[13] *Ibid.*, p. 8.   [14] *Ibid.*, pp. 9, 10.

[15] Nehru to Indira Gandhi, 31 December 1943, available in Sonia Gandhi, ed., *Two Alone Together: Letters between Indira Gandhi and Jawaharlal Nehru 1940–1964* (London: Hodder and Stoughton, 1992), p. 325. Cf. also Nehru to Edwina Mountbatten, 2 July 1948: 'We talk and think of a continuing existence from birth to death because there is no definite break, and yet how many of our previous selves die and are reborn from year to year. Sometimes I read passages from my autobiography in order to capture the picture of that old self. I recognise him, feel friendly and intimate, and yet different and apart. Even the writing seems to have been done by some other person whom once I knew.'

of lived experience is an important fact about him, and shaped his political horizons. In his books, *Glimpses of World History* (1934), *An Autobiography* (1936) and *Discovery* (1946), he tried to convey something of how his personal experiences shaped him politically, but as he noted: 'About much of this one may not write. There is an intimacy about one's inner life, one's feelings and thoughts, which may not and cannot be conveyed to others. Yet the contacts, personal and impersonal, mean much; they affect the individual and mould and change his reactions to life, to his own country, to other nations.'[16]

III

The idea that Partition was the result of a single set of human interactions, or that any one person was responsible, is, of course, absurd. Yet, personal relations and particular temperaments did bulk large. Whatever else it may have been – the collision of two differing assessments of the effects of democracy on minorities, a clash over the place of religion in public life, or even a clash of civilisations – it was also a clash over political judgements, and Jinnah and Nehru were central to how that clash came to be defined.

Historians have construed the relationship between Nehru and Jinnah in various ways. Some see it in terms of a historical narrative, in which secularism and communalism are in conflict – with Nehru and Jinnah as individuals embodying these opposed positions, and playing out this larger battle.[17] Others have framed it within a subcontinental conflict between centralist urges and a countervailing demand for regional autonomy and devolved power.[18] Many, though, have seen it as a simple clash between temperaments, personality and character.[19] Indeed, Nehru has often been blamed for the drift to partition – at different moments, his tactlessness, impetuosity, intransigence have all been held responsible.[20]

---

[16] Nehru, *The Discovery of India*, p. 13.

[17] See, for instance, S. Gopal, *Jawaharlal Nehru: A Biography* (Delhi: Oxford University Press, 1975), I (1889–1947).

[18] Ayesha Jalal, *The Sole Spokesman: Jinnah, the Muslim League and the Demand for Pakistan* (Cambridge: Cambridge University Press, 1985).

[19] See, for instance, Stanley Wolpert, *Jinnah of Pakistan* (Delhi: Oxford University Press, 1984).

[20] Nehru has been much criticised by both contemporaries and historians, for example, for his part in provoking the withdrawal by Jinnah of his agreement

Nehru was preoccupied with the inner springs of action and commitment – his self-questioning became part of his sense of himself as a political actor. In a diary kept while in Ahmednagar jail, he noted:

I sit down and think and reason: What must we do? What must we not do? Yet I know well that any vital action springs from the depths of being. All the long past of the individual and even the race has prepared the background for that psychological moment of action ... Influencing, yes, partly determining, possibly even largely determining; and yet surely it is not all determination. There is some loophole somewhere. However that may be, I have little doubt that irrepressible urges have pushed me into action in the past. In putting this in Hindustani the other day I used the word 'Jazbat' [the word, written in Devanagari script by Nehru, is difficult to render in English: it might be translated as 'innate feelings' or 'emotions/instinct'] and yet as I said it, it sounded wholly insufficient and ineffective – there may be emotion in it but surely there is far more than the emotions of the moment.[21]

to proposals of the 1946 Cabinet Mission led by Stafford Cripps. Nehru, just elected Congress President, in July 1946 declared to the press that the Congress Party was not bound by any element of the Cabinet Mission plan, and that the proposed constituent assembly in fact possessed sovereign and unfettered powers, and was at liberty to decide freely: a statement which confirmed Jinnah in his mistrust of Nehru and which, some have argued, opened the way for Jinnah to withdraw from the Cabinet Mission plan and for the Muslim League to call for a 'Day of Action' – which then resulted in the 'Great Calcutta Killings' of August 1946. Among Nehru's own colleagues in the Congress Party, Maulana Azad wrote of Nehru as having caused 'immense harm to the national cause', and assigned to him 'a large part of the responsibility' that led to the killings; Maulana Abul Kalam Azad, *India Wins Freedom* (New Delhi: Orient Longman, 1988) p. 170. And Sardar Vallabhbhai Patel was angered by what he saw as Nehru's 'acts of emotional insanity ... Opposition sometimes drives him mad, as he is impatient', Patel to D. P. Mishra, 29 July 1946, in *Patel's Correspondence*, III (Ahmedabad: Navajivan Publishing House, 1972), (1945–50), pp. 153–4. See also Peter Clarke's biography of Cripps, which is critical of Nehru exemplifying the 'rigidity of the Congress mindset', and of his inflexibility and unwillingness to offer a quid pro quo to those who claimed to speak for India's Muslims; Clarke also reprimands Nehru for his 'unpredictable impetuosity', and for his 'famous temper'; Peter Clarke, *The Cripps Version: The Life of Sir Stafford Cripps* (London: Allen Lane, 2002), pp. 403, 447, 463.

[21] Prison Diary, 11 November 1943, in *Selected Works of Jawaharlal Nehru* (New Delhi: Jawaharlal Nehru Memorial Fund, 1980), XIII, pp. 281–2.

Nehru's private judgements about Jinnah, shaped by intensely personal and emotional factors and aversions, certainly intruded into all his dealings with Jinnah. The two men were in various respects similar: both from marginal social groups (Jinnah a Khoja Muslim, Nehru a Kashmiri Pandit), trained as lawyers, Anglicised, fastidious, vain, and once colleagues in the Congress Party until Jinnah's resignation from it in 1920. Yet their dislike for one another was personal, intense and palpable. In their letters to one another, Nehru tended to the expansive and condescending ('Your tone and language', Jinnah let Nehru know, 'again display the same arrogance and militant spirit as if the Congress is the sovereign power'), while Jinnah's default response took the form of stilted cod-legal mannerisms ('I reciprocate the sentiments expressed in the last but one paragraph of your letter at the end of it', 25 January 1938), though exasperation frequently broke through: 'You prefer talking at each other whereas I prefer talking to each other' (17 February 1938), Jinnah told Nehru; 'it is really difficult for me to make you understand the position any further' (12 April 1938).[22]

Already in 1929, Nehru was for his part writing 'I do not see exactly how Jinnah will fit in. I find there is not very much in common between him and me so far as our outlooks are concerned.'[23] When it came to Jinnah's demands, Nehru repeatedly claimed that he could not understand what Jinnah really wanted, that his demands were vague. Unable to allow that Jinnah might have substantive objections and arguments, Nehru stuck to the view that Jinnah was driven merely – and purely – by personal considerations:

Jinnah has a curious way of proceeding. I have watched with amazement his methods and public utterances during the last year or so. It almost seems that he has lost all idea of perspective and balance. To him Indian politics are just a background for individuals, notably himself. I do not think he has any conception of principles or the big issues at stake.[24]

[22] *Nehru–Jinnah Correspondence* (Allahabad: All-India Congress Committee, 1940), Jinnah to Nehru, 12 April 1938 (p. 76), 25 January 1938 (p. 38), 17 February 1938 (p. 45), 12 April 1938 (p. 77).
[23] Nehru to K. T. Shah, 12 July 1929, in *Selected Works of Jawaharlal Nehru* (New Delhi: Jawaharlal Nehru Memorial Fund, 1973), IV, p. 564.
[24] Nehru to Dewan Chaman Lal, 7 October 1937, in *Selected Works of Jawaharlal Nehru* (New Delhi: Jawaharlal Nehru Memorial Fund, 1976), VII, p. 184.

There were moments when Nehru could strike a conciliatory note, even admitting his own fallibility. He wrote to Jinnah in late 1939:

I entirely agree with you that it is a tragedy that [the Hindu–Muslim problem] has not so far been settled in a friendly way. I feel terribly distressed about it and ashamed of myself, in so far as I have not been able to contribute anything substantial towards its solution. I must confess to you that in this matter I have lost confidence in myself, though I am not usually given that way.[25]

But on the whole, Nehru was irked by his perception that Jinnah was judging and acting as a mere politician, when the stakes were higher than that.

Jinnah's famous speech at Lahore in March 1940 – which set out more forcefully than ever before what Jinnah had in mind, arguing that 'the problem of India is not of an inter-communal but manifestly of an international character', and which declared that 'Musalmans are a nation according to any definition of a nation, and they must have their homelands, their territory and their State' – moved Nehru to confrontation and rupture.[26] Jinnah had re-described and transformed what Nehru had taken to be an Indian, internal problem of communal relations into a confrontation between distinct nations. 'The whole [Hindu–Muslim] problem has taken a new complexion and there is no question of settlement or negotiation now', he now said. 'The knot that is before us is incapable of being untied by settlement; it needs cutting open. It needs a major operation. Without mincing words, I want to say that we will have nothing to do with this mad scheme … The League is not interested in the Indian nation but in something else, and hence there can be no common ground between the Congress and the League.'[27] Late in 1943, in his Ahmednagar jail diary, Nehru privately unleashed his disgust:

[25] Nehru to M. A. Jinnah, 18 October 1939, in Jawaharlal Nehru, *A Bunch of Old Letters* (New Delhi: Penguin Books, 2005), p. 279.

[26] M. A. Jinnah, 'Presidential Address' to the Muslim League (1940), Lahore, in Sharifuddin Pirzada, *Foundations of Pakistan* (Karachi: National Publishing House, 1970), II, pp. 327–9.

[27] Nehru, Speech at Allahabad, 13 April 1940, in *Selected Works of Jawaharlal Nehru* (New Delhi: Jawaharlal Nehru Memorial Fund, 1978), XI, p. 17.

Jinnah … offers an obvious example of an utter lack of the civilized mind. With all his cleverness and ability, he produces an impression on me of utter ignorance and lack of understanding and even the capacity to understand this world and its problems … Instinctively I think it is better to have Pakistan or almost anything if only to keep Jinnah far away and not allow his muddled and arrogant head from interfering continually in India's progress.[28]

A few months after he wrote those words, Nehru began work on the manuscript that would become *The Discovery of India*, and he struggled here to make sense of circumstances, to separate out his personal from his political judgements – even as he acknowledged the great difficulty of such demarcation. At several points in his book, Nehru set out thoughts about the possibility of partition, and the position of Jinnah and the Muslim League. Nehru could acknowledge that Indian Muslims, as a numerical minority (around a quarter of the subcontinent's population), feared for their position, especially after a British departure – but to him this appeared as an unreasonable fear. His inability to grasp the irreducibility of such fear, especially that of a minority faced with the prospect of having to live within a democratic regime, made it impossible for him to grasp the edge of Jinnah's argument (it was only in the aftermath of Partition that he recognised the depth of this fear, and acted to assuage it). Democracy, the clarion call of the Congress, was from Jinnah's point of view exactly the problem. He invoked a liberal argument: precisely because Muslims – as Muslims – did not have the numbers to win elections, they should have parity, the equivalent of a veto power (which separate electorates would go some way to giving them).

Nehru, though, asked India's religious minorities to trust that they would indeed be protected: in part, through the propensity to toleration, a trait of Indian history; in part, through the usual provisions of basic rights; and in part, through economic and social development steered by the state. The legacies of the past, the laws of the present, and future remedies would ensure equal status to religious minorities.[29] This led Nehru to reject separate electorates for different communities (whereby religious and caste communities could only vote

[28] Prison Diary, 28 December 1943, in *Selected Works of Jawaharlal Nehru*, XIII, pp. 323–4.
[29] See Nehru, *The Discovery of India*, pp. 331–44.

for candidates of their own kind), a practice introduced by the British and one which Jinnah saw as essential to perpetuate if Muslim interests were to be protected. For Nehru, this would lead to the majority group – in this case, Hindus – losing interest in the so-protected minority, with the result that 'there is little occasion for mutual consideration and adjustment which inevitably take place in a joint electorate when a candidate has to appeal to every group'.[30] Nehru was committed to the Madisonian point about largeness of scale being a good check upon the dominance of any single interest or extremist position. A large and inclusive democracy was a more prudent political choice than a smaller and more selective one. Recalling his experience of the 1937 elections, which involved a significantly expanded Indian electorate, he noted that 'election evils' like corruption and demagoguery

were most prevalent when the election was small; many of them vanished, or at any rate were not so obvious, when the electorate was a big one. It was possible for the biggest electorate to be swept off its feet on a false issue, or in the name of religion (as we saw later), but there were usually some balancing factors which helped to prevent the grosser evils. My experience in this matter confirmed my faith in the widest possible franchise.[31]

As Nehru saw it, India's division into two or more states would result in 'a pitiful caricature full of contradictions and insoluble problems'.[32] His arguments for a unitary state, and his resistance to its division or to the devolution of political powers through a federated structure, rested on three main considerations. It would permit better political coordination, necessary for economic development and for decision-making. Scale and diversity were themselves good as mechanisms for moderating extremes. And, perhaps most important, India's security and defence would be better ensured in an undivided subcontinent. To Nehru, for whom the problem of India's military defence had long been important, the invention and use of atomic weaponry at the end of the Second World War had transformed the circumstances in which states must find their security:

In the modern context of the world, with the vast and terrible potentialities of the new atomic bomb, all of us have to think in new terms and discard many old and cherished notions. In this modern world it is not a division

[30] *Ibid.*, p. 334.   [31] *Ibid.*, p. 44.   [32] *Ibid.*, p. 472.

of a country that one can think of, but of ever larger federations of nations. Or else there is no freedom or independence or progress or self-defence.[33]

Nehru's early and implicit judgement was that with the invention of atomic weaponry, and the fact that only some states might possess this, would come dependencies, with smaller states looking to larger ones for protection: precisely a situation he wished to avoid on the subcontinent. As he put it to Stafford Cripps, 'from the point of view of defence there can be no real Pakistan, that is an independent state. Even if separated it could not continue independent.'[34] Nehru could not, of course, anticipate the later history of the state of Pakistan, one in which it had to seek its defence and security in ways that would compromise the independence of its state – requiring it to strike alliances with other powers, and to devote, to a degree that was to distort its politics, its internal energies and efforts to its defence. And yet, there was some foresight in his scepticism.

Despite the developmental, political and strategic arguments against it, Nehru sensed now that something like partition might be unavoidable, for what he termed 'psychological reasons'. There is, towards the close of *The Discovery of India*, a passage of around ten pages which Nehru entitled 'India – Partition or Strong National State or Centre of Supra-National State?' Here he considered the future shape of India. It is an intriguing and puzzling bit of writing, bearing visibly the strains of Nehru's efforts to fathom the impulses, reasons and arguments that he sensed were beginning to change beliefs and opinions about what India might be – which, as he came to realise, were making partition more likely. Dwelling a little on these pages offers some insight into the processes of judging, as Nehru saw them.

Personal desires and emotions, Nehru acknowledged, crowded in the space for political judgement:

It is difficult to discover a just balance between one's hopes and fears or to prevent one's wishes colouring the thinking of one's mind. Our desires seek out supporting reasons and tend to ignore facts and arguments that

---

[33] Statement drafted by Nehru for Maulana Azad, 17 August 1945, in *Selected Works of Jawaharlal Nehru* (New Delhi: Jawaharlal Nehru Memorial Fund, 1981), XIV, p. 73; see also XV, p. 121: 'Those who want can play about with guns and revolvers. But the atom bomb will decide wars in the future.'

[34] Nehru to Stafford Cripps, 27 January 1946, in *Selected Works of Jawaharlal Nehru*, XIV, p. 143.

do not fit in with them. I try to reach that balance so that I may be able to judge correctly and find out the true basis for action, and yet I know how far I am from success and how I cannot get rid of the multitude of thoughts and feelings which have gone to build me up and to fence me in with their invisible bars.[35]

In trying to make sense of the diverging views now surfacing about India's future shape, Nehru intriguingly invoked the concept of *Karma*. Yet he used this as a historical concept, not as a religious one – relating it not to the idea of spiritual rebirth and destiny (or ethical recompense), but to the presence of causalities that extend across historical generations, linking past actions and future consequences, in ways that meant that no act or judgement was ever fully ended or closed:

The individual and the national group fashion their own destiny by their actions; these past actions lead to the present and what they do today forms the basis of their tomorrows. *Karma* they have called this in India, the law of cause and effect, the destiny which our past activities create for us ... That past *Karma* is a powerful factor in shaping the individual and the nation, and nationalism itself is a shadow of it with all its good and bad memories of the past.[36]

Yet what *Karma* in this historical sense proposed was not an 'invariable destiny', but one where the 'individual's will' did have 'some play'. It was subject, however, to distorting forces – the passions unleashed by war, or the 'shadow' of nationalism, for instance, which swayed and impaired judgements, especially of large numbers of human beings, resulting in 'ruthlessness and brutality, and a refusal even to try to understand the other's viewpoint'.[37] There is a sense of self-recognition, if not self-transformation, in Nehru's insight here.

To see the chain of historical happening in this way was to see that an act of partition, despite its air and promise of decisiveness, would not be a simple or final resolution of anything at all. Much worse than the damage to India's potential economic progress 'will be the inner psychological conflict between those who wish to reunite her and those who oppose this. New vested interests will be created which will resist change and progress, a new evil *Karma* will pursue

[35] Nehru, *The Discovery of India*, p. 463.   [36] *Ibid.*, p. 463.   [37] *Ibid.*, p. 463.

us into the future.'[38] Through the obscurities of his meaning here, it is clear that he did not see the idea of partition as a resolution, a closure of the question of religious cohabitation on the subcontinent. To see it as a resolution was to make a mistake in judging its consequences.

Yet no sooner had he expressed this than he seemed to accept the likelihood of a partition. As he put it, in reasoning gnarled but powerful: 'One wrong step leads to another; so it has been in the past and so may it be in the future. And yet wrong steps have to be taken sometimes lest some worse peril befall us; that is the great paradox of politics, and no man can say with surety whether the present wrongdoing is better and safer than the possibility of that imagined peril.'[39] Unity was to him personally desirable, and the collective benefits of this were also logically clear. 'But an enforced unity is a sham and a dangerous affair, full of explosive possibilities': it would be a political mistake. Invoking a notion of *Karma* did not erase individual responsibility. Although he had seemed initially to lay the blame at the door of the English, he now wrote: 'It [the splitting of India] is our fault of course, and we must suffer for our failings' – that is, all who lived on the subcontinent had to take responsibility for it, and find a way to live with the negative consequences.[40]

He echoed these views to Stafford Cripps, writing to Cripps before the latter arrived in India with his Cabinet Mission in the spring of 1946. While he sought to dissuade Cripps from ideas of a division of India, and offered arguments to this effect, he also acknowledged that

the problem is not one so much of logical analysis as of psychological appreciation ... Apart from the long past history of India and England, the past six years of war have had a powerful effect on shaping the Indian mind and new forces are at work, which I can understand but not easily fathom ... Perhaps I have a deeper understanding of Indian happenings than most people even in India, for I have made myself receptive to India's moods. And yet I sometimes feel I am rather out of date. To ignore these deeply significant changes in India is to misjudge everything. Any action based on this lack of judgement is likely to be wrong and to lead to unhappy results. It is not enough to wish well and to be conscious of one's own rectitude.[41]

[38] *Ibid.*, p. 465. [39] *Ibid.*, p. 465. [40] *Ibid.*, p. 465.
[41] Nehru to Stafford Cripps, 27 January 1946, in *Selected Works of Jawaharlal Nehru*, XIV, pp. 143–4.

Nehru had the intellectual arguments for why a partition was not in the interest of the subcontinent's inhabitants. Emotionally too he was resistant to the idea. Yet what is striking is that, between his own emotional resistance to the idea and his logical rejection of it, he felt himself at some level required to make the political judgement that it had to be accepted, given – as he put it – the emotional attachment of large numbers of people to the idea.

In *The Discovery of India*, in his words to Cripps, one senses Nehru working through to a political judgement which went against both his personal inclinations and his logical assessment. He was talking himself round to accepting the responsibility and burden of one kind of defeat: but his judgement might also be seen to salvage a certain gain, by being willing to sacrifice his emotions and logic, and refusing a political compromise which might have weakened India as a strong central state. The arguments for Partition, he believed, were bad; but the consequences of trying to prevent it – by, for example, agreeing to a federated India – were worse in his judgement. He had here to confront and acknowledge a sense of the bleak disappointments of politics – a domain governed by the paradox of having to do the less good to prevent the still worse.

IV

Nehru had been a central actor in the sequence of decisions that resulted in the Partition of India on 15 August 1947. After it actually happened, he felt himself transformed into a spectator. He observed, as he flew over the Punjab, the endless *kafilas*, columns of refugees moving across the plains; he saw the riots in Lahore, a city he knew so well from childhood visits there with his mother; and constantly he received reports of the killings, of the ghost trains from and to Pakistan. From the refugees in the camps, the questions were insistent, and haunting: ' "Why were we not evacuated before Partition?" "Why did you have the Partition without asking us?" "Where shall we go? How shall we start anew?" '[42]

'I feel peculiarly helpless', Nehru wrote to Louis Mountbatten, in a letter he confessed was 'totally unnecessary':

[42] Letter from Nehru's sister, Krishna Hutheesingh, to Louis Fischer, 20 March 1948, Louis Fischer Papers, Princeton.

In action one can always overcome this feeling whatever the result of action might be. But as I cannot take immediate action that can have any effect, the burden becomes heavy. I suppose I am not directly responsible for what is taking place in the Punjab. I do not quite know who is responsible. But in any event I cannot and do not wish to shed my responsibility for my people. If I cannot discharge the responsibility effectively, then I begin to doubt whether I have any business to be where I am. And even if I don't doubt it myself, other people certainly will.[43]

Indeed, of all those individuals whose actions and decisions at the level of high politics resulted in the division of India, it was Nehru who had to deal most seriously with its enduring effects. The British had withdrawn from the scene, Gandhi and Jinnah were dead more or less within a year of the event, and Patel died two years later, at the end of 1950. Nehru had to bestir himself out of any sense of helplessness. Through the violence and aftermath of partition, he came to recognise the depth of fear instilled in India's Muslims by the prospect of an independent, democratic India. In the years after 1947, he worked to assure Muslims of their place as full citizens of India. He refused, for instance, the proposal from Patel to purge Muslims from the higher government bureaucracy. Equally, he found abhorrent and dismissed the idea that religious minorities – Muslims in India, Hindus in Pakistan – might be treated as 'hostages' by each state, to ensure the good conduct of their neighbour (this was an idea entertained by both Jinnah and Patel). Full religious freedoms were established by the Constitution, which also enabled the law to recognise Indians as attached to religious communities: in matters of civil or customary law, citizens could choose to be governed either by the practices of their own religion, or by the state's civil law, a form of legal pluralism that was crucial in integrating Indian Muslims into the political order.

As Nehru saw it, there was something politically disastrous in making religious allegiance a source of identification in modern politics, in using it to build political support for control of a modern state: the effects of this choice would linger far beyond the specific moment of its making. It was, of course, a spectacularly effective political choice,

---

[43] Nehru to Louis Mountbatten, 27 August 1947, in *Selected Works of Jawaharlal Nehru* (New Delhi: Jawaharlal Nehru Memorial Fund, 1986), Second Series, IV, p. 26.

as Nehru, on hearing news of Jinnah's death, acknowledged with his customary condescension:

Jinnah did mould history in India, in the wrong way it is true, and let loose forces which have done so much evil ... How shall we judge him? I have been very angry with him often during these past years. But now there is no bitterness in my thought of him, only a great sadness for all that has been ... Outwardly he succeeded in his quest and gained his objective, but at what a cost and with what a difference from what he had imagined. What must he have thought of all this, did he feel sorry or regret for any past action? Probably not, for he wrapped himself in a cloak of hatred and every evil seems to flow from those whom he hated. Hatred is poor nourishment for any person.[44]

Yet, by seeking to explain Jinnah's actions through the charged category of hatred, Nehru shut out the possibility of any more careful analysis of his great rival's motives and intentions. In the end, there is an ineliminable opacity that hovers between Nehru and any understanding of his most decisive antagonist.

Yet Nehru never answered such questions for himself, about his own role – at least not with the degree of attention and intimacy that marked his earlier jail writings. In part of course, once in the prime ministerial office, he lacked the leisure to reflect at any length on what Partition meant – though even if he had had the opportunity, it was probably still too raw for him to try really to make sense of it. But one might discern its effects on him in other ways: for instance, in his understanding of political power. It showed him the destructive potentialities of politics, and therefore the need to use power with great circumspection. And it also shaped Nehru's growingly complex view of values and their pursuit.

In India's post-1947 politics, he judged against stark choices. He pursued sometimes diverging values, without lunging in one or other direction. He tended to proceed often by small steps, in a variety of directions: what looks like vacillation, compromise or conservatism can equally be seen as a judgement about how to act politically in circumstances where a range of important values existed – and where sharp moves towards or against one could have damaging long-range

---

[44] Nehru to Edwina Mountbatten, 12–13 September 1948.

effects. In Nehru we can see enacted a view about the complexities of value judgements.

Nehru's refusal of certain choices was itself an exercise of political choice. To adopt, for instance, during the Cold War, a position of 'non-alignment', to seek equidistance from the superpowers, was to risk having no friends at all. In this respect, Nehru shared Gandhi's ability to resist the call of those in possession of great power. The wielders of power saw in Nehru's aloofness nothing more than a Machiavellian, hypocritical pose. Although initially Nehru inclined towards the USA, and his personal and emotional ties lay with the West, he resented American insistence that India join the Western powers, and above all its claim to monopolise the voice of the free, democratic world.[45]

In November 1961, some days before Indian troops entered Goa (a decision to use force against another power, the Portuguese, which provoked widespread international criticism), Nehru was paid a visit by Sir Isaiah Berlin, in India for celebrations to mark Rabindranath Tagore's birth centenary (Berlin carried an introduction from Nehru's friend from the 1930s, Sheila Grant Duff). Berlin subsequently reported his impressions back to her:

Like Roosevelt, he has obviously betrayed his class in order to serve his people, and like Roosevelt again, he plays by ear. I think he is a man of genuine ideals, but I should say not many principles. Goa did not surprise me in the least ... he knows which side of the river he is fishing, and I think in a sense he is quite open, not to say cynical ... Mr N's charm seems to be enormous ... [But] if I were a politician, I should certainly not trust him as an ally beyond the point at which his interests operated.[46]

Berlin, apart from his personal fascination with men of power, was interested in the political issue of whether or not Nehru could

---

[45] See 'Nehru on the Tragic "Paradox of Our Age"', *New York Times Magazine*, 7 September 1958, and cf. Reinhold Niebuhr, *Nations and Empires* (London: Faber and Faber, 1960), pp. 295–6; Niebuhr, sympathising with Nehru's position, concluded: 'We may well be baffled by these strange historical developments and ask whether there is any genuinely "ultimate" judgement for historically conditioned man. Perhaps the only judgement is the negative one that despotism is always dangerous' (p. 296).

[46] Isaiah Berlin to Sheila Grant Duff, 16 January 1962, Isaiah Berlin Papers, Oxford.

be relied on as an ally of the West in its stand-off with the Soviet Union. Berlin produced an assessment of Nehru, based on his hour and half talk, which he passed on to the British High Commissioner in New Delhi, Paul Gore-Booth – and which was discussed at a 'seminar' at the Delhi High Commission.[47] From a political point of view, Berlin, like the British and American governments, wanted Nehru to choose – to join the Western camp. In his note, though, he tried to make sense of Nehru's refusal to do so, setting out what he saw as Nehru's view of world politics. (And later, Berlin explained to the historian of ideas Andrzej Walicki: 'The criticisms of him in both English and American papers miss the nature of his problems and the kind of solutions he brings to them. In short, I am for him and against his critics.')[48]

Politicians, as well as most intellectuals, have a professional weakness for clear and decisive choices of value and ideology. Yet in this respect Nehru was irritatingly unspectacular. He was not a figure of extremes, he did not usually exaggerate in one direction – in the manner that intellectuals often find so appealing. Commitment to a range of values requires judgement – in deciding when and how to pursue each of these; in deciding to go on when one has to abandon or weaken one in favour of another; and in recognising that, in pursuing several values simultaneously, one might have to face the likelihood that no single one might fully be achieved (the inverse of what Isaiah Berlin had famously described as the tragic choice of selecting one value over another, thereby shrinking the range of values in play). If one is simply committed to a single value – say, equality, or liberty, or a particular definition of the nation or the state – the dimension of judgement is less pressing; but commitment to both, or several, requires the constant exercise of judgement.

Nehru, in his private life, valued self-restraint and discretion (as he told his daughter, Indira: 'It was impossible for me to bare my heart before anybody', a reserve that he thought protected him against being swept away, as he put it, by sentiment).[49] As he saw it, it was an abundance – not an absence – of emotion that made self-restraint

[47] See Paul Gore-Booth to Sir Savile Garner, 19 February 1962, National Archives/PRO, DO 196/120.
[48] Isaiah Berlin to Andrzej Walicki, 13 March 1962, Isaiah Berlin Papers.
[49] Nehru to Indira Gandhi, 15 May 1941, in *Selected Works of Jawaharlal Nehru*, XI, p. 593.

necessary. There is, I think, a connection between this self-restraint and his judgements about the use of power in the public realm. In the twentieth century, the smell of power has been intoxicating, especially for those who, long excluded from it, came suddenly – often through hard struggle – to acquire it. So often rulers of new states have been overwhelmed by the thrill of having the levers of command in their hands; they have pulled too sharply, sending their societies careering into catastrophes of one kind or another. The last century has seen a frenetic effort at remaking societies – usually to some kind of recipe devised by the divine or human mind. One of Nehru's subtlest virtues, after independence in 1947, was his judgement about the uses of public power. If many twentieth-century minds have been reckless in allowing themselves to be seduced by power, Nehru was more heedful of its dangers.

PART IV

Democracy and modern political judgement

10 | *Democracy, equality and redistribution*

ADAM PRZEWORSKI

Introduction

Democratic citizens are not equal but only anonymous, indistinguishable by any traits they may possess.[1] Democracy only places a veil over distinctions that exist in society. Even the one sense in which equality can be said to characterise democracy – equality before the law – is derivative from anonymity: the law has to treat all citizens equally because they are indistinguishable.

This norm of anonymity was circumvented in most early representative systems by an elaborate intellectual construction that justified restrictions of suffrage. The argument held that the role of representatives is to promote the good of all, yet the intellectual capacity to recognise the common good and the moral qualities necessary to pursue it are not universal. These traits can be recognised by using some indicators, such as wealth, age and gender. Hence, relying on such indicators to restrict suffrage does not violate democratic norms. The logic of the argument is unimpeachable, but it is easy to suspect that it rationalised interests. This is the way it was perceived by those excluded, poor males and women, as they fought for political rights.

Yet even if political rights are universal, to ignore distinctions is not to obliterate them. Democracy was a political revolution, but not an economic one. Should we be surprised that democracy turned out to be compatible with economic inequality? From its inception, representative institutions were haunted by the spectre of the poor using their political rights to redistribute property. Should we be surprised that democracy did not undermine property, that the

---

[1] For comments, I am grateful to Pasquale Pasquino, the editors of this volume, and an anonymous reviewer.

democratic revolution was never completed by being extended to the economic realm?

These three themes are developed below.

I Aristocracy and democracy

How did 'democracy' reappear on the historical horizon and what did it mean to its proponents and opponents?

The emergence of modern democracy is the topic of a monumental treatise by Robert Palmer,[2] and no more than a brief summary is necessary. Palmer's main point is that democracy was not a revolution against an existing system but a reaction against the increasing power of aristocracy. It was aristocracy that undermined monarchy; democracy outflanked it following in its footsteps. Palmer argues as follows: (1) By the early eighteenth century, the aristocratic system of government was institutionalised in assemblies of various forms, the participation in which was reserved to legally qualified groups (constituted bodies) that always included hereditary nobility but in different places (countries, regions, principalities, cantons, city republics) also clergy, selected categories of burghers, and in Sweden even peasants. In all cases these bodies were politically dominated by hereditary nobility. (2) In the course of the century, these estate-based bodies increased their political influence. (3) At the same time, access to nobility, however it was defined in different places, became increasingly closed: nobility turned into aristocracy. (4) The resulting aristocratic system suffered from several tensions, of which one was between birth and competence. (5) Politically crucial conflict was due to the exclusion from privilege of those who possessed all the qualifications to participate – wealth, talent, bearing – except for birth.[3] (6) Democracy emerged as a demand for access to these bodies, not as a movement against monarchy.

[2] R. R. Palmer, *The Age of the Democratic Revolution,* I, *The Challenge* (Princeton: Princeton University Press, 1959); R. R. Palmer, *The Age of the Democratic Revolution,* II, *The Struggle* (Princeton: Princeton University Press, 1964).

[3] In Sieyès's words, 'the people were told whatever are your services, whatever your talents, you will go only until here; you will not overtake others'. Emmanuel Sieyès, *Qu'est-ce que le tiers état?* (1789) Roberto Zapperi (Geneva: Droz, 1970), p. 29.

Hence, by the end of the eighteenth century, democracy was a slogan directed against *legal recognition of inherited distinctions of social status*. Democrats were those who agitated against aristocrats or aristocracy. As John Dunn observes,

> democracy was a reaction, above all, not to monarchy, let alone tyranny, but to another relatively concrete social category, initially all too well entrenched, but no longer plausibly aligned with social, economic, or even political or military, functions – the nobility or aristocracy ... *Democrat* was a label in and for political combat; and what that combat was directed against was aristocrats, or at the very least aristocracy.[4]

Thus, in 1794 a young Englishman described himself as 'being of that odious class of men called democrats because he disapproved of hereditary distinctions and privileged orders of every species'.[5] 'Could any further proof be required of the republican complexion of this system', wrote James Madison in *The Federalist* 39, 'the most decisive might be found in its absolute prohibition of titles of nobility'.[6] In France, the Constituent Assembly decided that aristocratic privilege was in conflict with the very principle of popular sovereignty.[7] The Batavian (Dutch) Republic established in 1796 required voters to swear an oath to the belief that all hereditary offices and dignities were illegal.[8] In Chile, General O'Higgins, the first Director of the State, abolished in 1818 all outward and visible signs of aristocracy.[9]

Here is a puzzle. While democrats fought against aristocracy, either as a system of government (the original meaning of the word) or as a legal status (nobility), this struggle did not have to result in abolishing other distinctions. One distinction could have been replaced

---

[4] John Dunn, 'Democracy before the Age of the Democratic Revolution' (2003), Paper delivered at Columbia University, p. 10. For a detailed account of the reappearance of 'democracy' in the modern era, see John Dunn, *Democracy: A History* (New York: Atlantic Monthly Press, 2005).

[5] Palmer, *The Age of the Democratic Revolution*, II, p. 10.

[6] James Madison, *The Federalist Papers by Alexander Hamilton, James Madison and John Jay* (1788), ed. Gary Wills (New York: Bantam Books, 1982).

[7] Biancamaria Fontana, 'Democracy and the French Revolution' in John Dunn, ed., *'Democracy: The Unfinished Journey, 508 BC to AD 1993* (Oxford: Oxford University Press, 1993), pp. 107–24, p. 119.

[8] Palmer, *The Age of the Democratic Revolution*, II, p. 195.

[9] Simon Collier and William F. Sater, *A History of Chile, 1808–1994* (Cambridge: Cambridge University Press, 1996), p. 42.

by another. The flagrant case is the Polish Constitution of 3 May 1791, which was directed against aristocrats defined as large land-owners, *magnates*, under the slogan of equality for the gentry at large (*szlachta*, which constituted about 10 per cent of the population),[10] while preserving a legal distinction of the latter. More generally, social traits that could serve as the basis for legal distinctions were many: property owners and labourers, burghers and peasants, inhab-itants of different localities,[11] clergy and army,[12] whites and blacks. Yet democrats turned against other distinctions. 'All the privileges', Sieyès declared, 'are thus by the nature of things unjust, despicable and contradictory to the supreme goal of all political society.'[13] From aristocracy, the enemy became any kind of *particularity*.[14] Thus, in far away Brazil, the four mulattoes who were hanged and quar-tered after the failure of the *Citade da Bahia Republicana* in 1798 were accused of 'desiring the imaginary advantages of a Democratic Republic in which all should be equal … without difference of color or condition'.[15] The French Revolution emancipated Protestants and Jews and freed slaves, not only Catholic peasants.

Pierre Rosanvallon claims that 'The imperative of equality, required to make everyone a subject of law and a full citizen, implies in effect considering men stripped of their particularistic determi-nants. All their differences and all their distinctions should be placed at a distance.'[16] Yet where did the imperative of equality come from? Thinking in the rational choice terms of modern political science, one would suspect that democrats instrumentally turned against other

---

[10] The slogan was *Szlachcic na zagrodzie równy wojewodzie*, loosely translated as 'A gentry man in a cottage equals a lord.'

[11] Palmer, *The Age of the Democratic Revolution*, II, emphasises that while the French tried to eradicate all sub-national differences, Americans recog-nised them. Division of France into departments was intended according to Rosanvallon to create a purely functional division, which would not refer to any social, political or cultural reality. Hence, democrats were centralisers in France; decentralisers in the USA. Pierre Rosanvallon, *Le modèle politique français: la société civile contre le jacobinisme de 1789 à nos jours* (Paris: Seuil, 2004), p. 35.

[12] They did enjoy special status, *fueros*, in the Cadiz Constitution of 1812 and several Latin American constitutions afterwards.

[13] Sieyès, *Qu'est-ce que le tiers état?*, p. 3.

[14] Rosanvallon, *Le modèle politique français*, p. 37 and throughout.

[15] Palmer, *The Age of the Democratic Revolution*, II, p. 513.

[16] Rosanvallon, *Le modèle politique français*, p. 121.

social distinctions just to mobilise the masses against aristocracy: to gain support against aristocracy. Herman Finer, for example, accuses Montesquieu of 'deliberately juxtaposing the Citizen to all the powers that be, either the King or the aristocracy: it was a convenient, a striking and useful antithesis; nothing could be better calculated to win the support of every man'.[17] There are facts that support this hypothesis: Tadeusz Kościuszko in Poland made vague promises to peasants to induce them to join the anti-Russian insurrection in 1794; the members of the French *Convention* flagrantly played up to the gallery filled by the ordinary people of Paris; Simón Bolívar made interracial appeals to recruit for the war against Spain. Yet it is also easy to believe that democrats truly believed that all men are equal, as the Declaration of Independence declared, or that men are born equal, as the Declaration of the Rights of Man would have it. The idea of innate equality certainly preceded the actual political conflicts. It could be found already in Locke's *Second Treatise* as the principle that '*equal Right* that every Man hath, *to his Natural Freedom*, without being subjected to the Will or Authority of any other Man'.[18] We do not have a theory of action in which people are moved by logic, in which they do things because they cannot tolerate logical contradictions. Yet if one is willing to accept that people can be moved by ideas, democrats would have turned against other distinctions by the sheer logic of their ideology: aristocrats are not distinct because all men are born equal; because all men are born equal, they cannot be treated differently. Abolishing other distinctions would then be a logical outcome of the struggle against aristocracy.

The fact is that democrats turned against all distinctions. The only attribute of democratic subjects is that they have none as such. The democratic citizen is simply without qualities.[19] Not equal, not

---

[17] Herman Finer, *The Theory and Practice of Modern Government* (New York: Dial Press, 1934), p. 85.

[18] John Locke, *Two Treatises of Government* (1689/90), ed. Peter Laslett (Cambridge: Cambridge University Press, 1988).

[19] I took this allusion to Robert Musil from Pasquale Pasquino, *Sieyès et l'invention de la constitution en France* (Paris: Editions Odile Jacob, 1998), pp. 149–50. Elsewhere, Pasquino claims that this conception was introduced by Hobbes in the context of religious distinctions: 'In the face of this type of conflict [religious], political order to Hobbes is founded on an *overlapping consensus* and is based on an anatomy of the city as a *society without qualities*.' Pasquale Pasquino, 'Political Theory, Order, and Threat' in Ian Shapiro

homogeneous, just anonymous.[20] Even the one sense in which equality does apply as a democratic norm, namely, before the law, is just a consequence of the principle that democratic citizens cannot be distinguished in any way. As Rousseau said, 'the sovereign [the people united] knows only the body of the nation and does not distinguish any of those who compose it'.[21] Since citizens are indistinguishable, there is nothing by which law could possibly distinguish them. The democratic citizen is simply an individual outside society. One can say an aristocrat, a wealthy person and male, but not an aristocratic citizen, a wealthy citizen, or a male citizen. As Sieyès put it, 'On doit concevoir les nations sur terre comme des individues hors de lien social.'[22]

II Democracy and equality

In spite of its egalitarian pedigree, I am about to argue, there is no sense in which equality could or does characterise democracy. 'One should not let oneself be trapped by words', Pasquino warns, 'the "society without qualities" is not a society of equals; it is simply a society in which privileges do not have a juridical-institutional status or recognition'.[23] In a scathing critique of 'bourgeois rights', Marx characterised this duality as follows:

The state abolishes, in its own way, distinctions of birth, social rank, education, occupation, when it declares that birth, social rank, education, occupation, are non-political distinctions, when it proclaims, without regard to these distinctions, that every member of the nation is an *equal* participant in national sovereignty ... Nevertheless the state allows private property, education, occupation to *act* in *their* way – i.e., as private

and Russell Hardin, eds., *Political Order*, Nomos XXXVIII (New York: New York University Press, 1996), pp. 19–41, p. 31.

[20] While anonymity is a more recent term, it may best capture the intent. A decision rule satisfies anonymity if the social choice remains the same when any two voters' preferences are interchanged. In other words, it matters not who the citizen is. See Kenneth O. May, 'A Set of Independent Necessary and Sufficient Conditions for Simple Majority Decision', *Econometrica* (1952), pp. 680–4.

[21] Jean-Jacques Rousseau, *Du contrat social* (1762), ed. Robert Derathé (Paris: Gallimard, 1964), p. 129.

[22] Sieyès, *Qu'est-ce que le tiers état?*, p. 183.   [23] Pasquino, *Sieyès*, pp. 149–50.

property, as education, as occupation, and to exert the influence of their *special* nature.[24]

Why then is political emancipation not a form of *human* emancipation, as Marx would have put it? Specifically, in what ways is the veil over distinctions compatible with various kinds of inequality?

Consider the different meanings in which equality appeared in democratic ideology. Why are or would be people equal? They could be because God or nature made them so, because society makes them so, or because the law makes them so. Equality can be innate or generated by spontaneous social transformations, but it can also be instituted by law or by the use of laws. Democratic equality may thus be a reflection of equality pre-existing elsewhere or it may be imposed by laws.

To return to the Declarations one last time, the point of departure of democrats was innate equality of human beings. Democratic equality is but a reflection of a pre-existing, natural, equality. Yet the implications of a pre-existing equality are indeterminate. As Schmitt observed, 'From the fact that all men are men it is not possible to deduce anything specific either about morality or about religion or about politics or about economics.'[25] Even if people were born equal, they may distinguish themselves by their merits and their merits may be recognised by others. More, to maintain order, some people must at each moment exercise authority over others. As Kelsen put it, 'From the idea that we are all equal, ideally equal, one can deduce that no one should command another. But experience teaches that if we want to remain equal in reality, it is necessary on the contrary that we let ourselves be commanded.'[26]

Moreover, even if all human beings are born only as such, society generates differences among them. Indeed, if their parents are unequal, they become unequal at the moment they are born. To make them equal again, recourse to laws is necessary. Montesquieu would thus observe that 'In the state of nature, men are born equal but they

---

[24] Karl Marx, *On the Jewish Question* (1844), http://csf.colorado.edu/psn/marx/Archive/1844-JQ.

[25] Carl Schmitt, *Théorie de la constitution*, trans. from the German by Lilyane Deroche (Paris: Presses Universitaires de France, 1993), p. 364.

[26] Hans Kelsen, *La démocratie: sa nature – sa valeur* (1929) (Paris: Economica, 1988), p. 17.

do not know how to remain so. Society makes them lose equality and they do not return to be equal other than by laws.'[27]

Yet must society make people unequal? Rosanvallon documents that when the term 'democracy' came into widespread usage in France after 1814, it connoted modern egalitarian *society*, not the political regimes associated with the classical Greek or Roman republics, what Tocqueville would refer to as equality of conditions. The tendency towards social equality was inevitable.[28] Taking a theme of Marquis d'Argenson, Tocqueville observed that 'The gradual development of equality of conditions ... is universal, it is durable, it escapes human intervention every day; every event, like every man, furthers its development.'[29] J. S. Mill noted the same in 1859: 'There is confessedly a strong tendency in the modern world towards a democratic constitution of society, accompanied or not by popular political institutions.'[30] Note that while Tocqueville saw political equality in the United States as a natural consequence of the equality of conditions, for Mill the fact of social equality did not have unique political consequences.

Whether modern societies must become more equal is a complex question. What matters here is that not everyone was willing to rely on the spontaneous evolution of society to generate political equality. Robespierre thought that 'Equality of wealth is a chimera.'[31] Madison (*Federalist* 10) listed all kinds of social differences and gradations, assuming they were there to stay. Most democrats believed, against Tocqueville, that citizenship creates equality, rather than that equals become citizens. Pasquino summarises this belief: 'Citizens are not simply equal before the law, in the sense in which the law does not

---

[27] Charles-Louis Montesquieu, *De l'esprit des lois* (1748), ed. Laurent Versini (Paris: Gallimard, 1995), p. 261.

[28] Pierre Rosanvallon, 'The History of the Word "Democracy" in France', *Journal of Democracy*, 5:4 (1995), 140–54, p. 149.

[29] Alexis de Tocqueville, *De la démocratie en Amérique* (1835) (Paris: Gallimard, 1961), I, p. 41. In a beautiful pastiche about a visit by Tocqueville to Mexico, Aguilar Rivera imagines how he would have reacted to an extremely inegalitarian New World society. José Antonio Aguilar Rivera, *Cartas Mexicanas de Alexis de Tocqueville* (Mexico City: Caly Arena, 1999).

[30] John Stuart Mill, *On Liberty*, Stefan Colini, ed., *On Liberty and Other Writings* (Cambridge: Cambridge University Press, 1989).

[31] Palmer, *The Age of the Democratic Revolution*, II, p. 109.

recognize either special rights or privileges, but they become equal by the grace of law and by law itself.'[32]

Democrats adhered to what Beitz calls a simple conception of political equality, namely, the requirement that democratic institutions should provide citizens with equal procedural opportunities to influence political decisions (or, more briefly, with *equal power over outcomes*).[33] Criticizing this notion, he points out that equality of the abstract leverage that procedures provide to each participant does not imply equality of the actual influence over the outcomes: the latter depends also on the distribution of the preferences and of the enabling resources. This disjunction between formal and effective political equality was a central concern in the United States and continues to be debated today. The social palliative to this divergence between formal and real influence is pluralism. The political answer, at least for Madison, was large districts.

As Mill would remark several decades later, without decent wages and universal reading, no government of public opinion is possible. Education was one instrument that would equip people to exercise their citizenship rights. Several early constitutions (of the Italian republics between 1796 and 1799, the Cádiz Constitutions of 1812) established systems of universal and free, although not compulsory, education. In the meantime, most solved the problem by restricting political rights to those who were in condition to exercise them. Yet when suffrage became universal and democracy found roots in poorer countries, the problem reappeared with a vengeance: masses of people acquired equal procedural opportunities without enjoying the conditions necessary to exploit them. Citizenship without the conditions to exercise it is a monster that haunts contemporary democracies. The absence of the effective capacity to exercise formal political rights remains at the heart of criticisms of the really existing democracy. To return to Marx, can people be politically equal if they are socially unequal?

---

[32] Pasquino, *Sieyès*, 109. According to Russell L. Hanson, 'Democracy' in Terence Ball, James Farr and Russell L. Hanson, eds., *Political Innovation and Conceptual Change* (Cambridge University Press, 1989), p. 71, this was the meaning of the Greek term *isonomia*, which referred both to equality before the law and, in a more directly political sense, to equality through law.

[33] Charles R. Beitz, *Political Equality* (Princeton: Princeton University Press, 1989), p. 4.

But political equality is vulnerable not just to social inequality but also to specifically political distinctions. Democracy, according to Schmitt, is 'the identity of the dominating and the dominated, of the government and the governed, of he who commands and he who obeys'.[34] But the issue is whether the very faculty of governing does not create a distinction, a political class. 'Political aristocracy' was seen to be as much of a danger as social aristocracy. The Anti-Federalists feared that if the rulers were other than the ruled, 'Corruption and tyranny would be rampant as they have always been when those who exercised power felt little connection with the people. This would be true, moreover, for elected representatives, as well as for kings and nobles and bishops.'[35] Hence, democrats were preoccupied with duration of terms, as short as six months in New Jersey at one time, term limits, restrictions on representatives determining their own salaries, and censuring procedures.

Yet these are palliatives. The distinction between the representatives and the represented is inherent in the representative system: parliaments seat representatives, not the people. And the very method of choosing representatives through elections, rather than by lot, is based on the belief that all people are not equally qualified to rule. Elections, Manin argues, are based on the assumption that the qualities necessary to govern are not universally shared and that people want to be governed by their betters.[36] These qualities need not be associated with distinctions of birth, so that elections are not 'aristocratic' in the eighteenth-century sense. But elections are a method for selecting one's betters and, as Manin amply documents, they are and were seen as a way of recognising a natural aristocracy of talent, reason, or whatever else voters would see as the index of the ability to govern.

Moreover, to be represented people must be organised, and organisation demands a permanent apparatus, a salaried bureaucracy, a propaganda machine. Hence, Roberto Michels bemoaned, some militants become parliamentarians, party bureaucrats, newspaper editors, managers of the party's insurance companies, directors of the

---

[34] Schmitt, *Théorie de la constitution*, p. 372.
[35] Cited in Ralph Ketcham, ed., *The Anti-Federalist Papers and the Constitutional Convention Debates* (New York: Mentor Books, 1989), p. 18.
[36] Bernard Manin, *The Principles of Representative Government* (Cambridge: Cambridge University Press, 1997).

party's funeral parlours, and even *Parteibudiger* – party bar-keepers.[37] As a disillusioned French communist would write many years later, 'The working class is lost in administering its imaginary bastions. Comrades disguised as notables occupy themselves with municipal garbage dumps and school cafeterias. Or are these notables disguised as comrades? I no longer know.'[38]

To summarise, the idea that political equality reflects some pre-existing state, either of nature or of society, is untenable on both logical and empirical grounds. Logically, equality pre-existing in other realms does not imply political equality. Empirically, even if all human beings were born equal, they become unequal in society, and even if societies experienced an inevitable tendency towards equality, the existing inequalities were and are sufficient to call for political remedies. In turn, political equality instituted by law is effectively undermined by social inequality. Political equality is equality in the eyes of a third party, the state, but not in the direct relation between any two persons. In no meaning then is equality the correct way to characterise democracy. If the founders used the languages of equality, it was to justify something else, better described as anonymity, generality,[39] or oblivion to social distinctions.

III Do suffrage restrictions violate democratic ideology?

Yet there is one fact that appears to undermine anonymity: restrictions of suffrage. Indeed, the French Declaration qualified its recognition of equality in the sentence that immediately followed: 'Men are born equal and remain free and equal in rights. Social distinctions may be founded only upon the general good.' While some early constitutions made male suffrage nearly universal, during most of the nineteenth century the right to vote and the right to be elected was confined to

---

[37] Roberto Michels, *Political Parties: A Sociological Study of the Oligarchical Tendencies of Modern Democracies* (New York: Collier Books, 1962), p. 270.

[38] Guy Konopnicki, *Vive le centenaire du P.C.F.* (Paris: CERF, 1979), p. 53.

[39] I am persuaded by Rosanvallon's insistence that the enemy of democrats was particularity of any kind, but I do not find the antonym he invokes, generality ('A l'esprit particulier ils opposent donc l'esprit de généralité', p. 37), enlightening. Generality entails the idea that there are some attributes to be generalised, while anti-particularity is just a veil over all attributes.

adult men who owned property, earned some amount of income or paid some amount of taxes.

The prevalence of *suffrage censitaire* may appear to contradict the norm of suppressing all distinctions in society and to be incompatible with the principle of political equality. Yet, even if the arguments were convoluted, franchise restrictions were not portrayed as such by their proponents.

Consider first the justification by Montesquieu, who starts from the principle that 'All inequality under democracy should be derived from the nature of democracy and from the very principle of democracy.'[40] His example is that people who must continually work to live are not prepared for public office or would neglect their functions. As barristers of Paris put it on the eve of the Revolution, 'Whatever respect one might wish to show for the rights of humanity in general, there is no denying the existence of a class of men who, by virtue of their education and the type of work to which their poverty had condemned them, is ... incapable at the moment of participating fully in public affairs.'[41] In such cases, Montesquieu goes on, 'equality among citizens can be lifted in a democracy for the good of democracy. But it is only apparent equality that is lifted.'

The generic argument, to be found in slightly different versions, is as follows: (1) Representation is acting in the best interest of all. (2) To determine the best interest of all one needs reason. (3) Reason has sociological determinants: not having to work for a living (disinterest), or not being employed or otherwise dependent on others (independence). As a Chilean statesman put it in 1865, to exercise political rights it is necessary to have 'the intelligence to recognise the truth and the good, the will to want it, and the freedom to execute it'.[42] In turn, the claim that only apparent equality is being violated was built in three steps: (1) Acting in the best common interest considers everyone equally, so that everyone is equally represented. (2) The only quality that is being distinguished is the capacity to recognise the common good. (3) No one is barred from acquiring this quality, so that suffrage is potentially open to all.

---

[40] Montesquieu, *De l'esprit des lois*, p. 155.

[41] Cited in Malcolm Crook, *Elections in the French Revolution* (Cambridge: Cambridge University Press, 1996), p. 13.

[42] A speech by Senador Abdón Cifuentes, cited in Erika Maza Valenzuela, 'Catolicismo, anticlericalismo y la extensión del sufragio a la mujer en Chile', *Estudios Politicos*, 58 (1995), pp. 137–97, p. 153.

The last two points are crucial. Legal distinctions of social status are valid only as indicators of the ability to govern and there are no barriers of any kind to prevent people from acquiring this ability and being relevantly indicated.

The Polish Constitution of 3 May 1791 illuminates the distinction between the democratic *régime censitaire* and the non-democratic regime of legal distinctions. The Constitution asserts in Paragraph VI that deputies to the local parliaments should be considered as '*representatives of the entire nation*' (italics in the original). Yet to become a deputy to the local parliaments (*sejmiki*, which in turn elect deputies to the national legislature, the *sejm*) one had to be a member of a legally defined group, the gentry (*szlachta*). In turn, only members of the hereditary gentry could own land entitling to political rights.[43] Hence, this was not a *régime censitaire* in the sense defined above: (1) it barred access to politics to everyone who was not a member of a legally recognised group, the landed gentry, and (2) it barred access to the landed gentry.

In fact, the Polish justification for privileging gentry was not reason but 'Respect for the memory of our forefathers as founders of free government'. (Article II). Simón Bolívar used the same principle in 1819 when he offered positions of hereditary senators 'to the liberators of Venezuela ... to whom the Republic owes its existence'.[44] His celebrated speech, known as the *Discurso de Angostura*, merits attention because its combination of appeals to reason with an acceptance of inequality became the hallmark of anti-democratic postures in Spanish America. Bolívar observed that most people do not know their true interests and went on to argue that 'Everything cannot be left to the adventure of elections: the People errs easily.' His solution was the institution of a hereditary Senate: future Senators 'would learn the arts, sciences, and letters which adorn the spirit of a public man; from infancy would know to what Providence destined them'.

---

[43] While according to the law on towns of 18 April 1791 burghers in all cities were to enjoy all the protections of the gentry (most importantly habeas corpus, which dated in Poland to 1433), could occupy public positions (except for bishops), and could own and buy land adjacent to cities, they could not participate in the local parliaments. Jerzy Kowecki, *Konstytucja 3 Maja 1791* (Warsaw: Państwowe Wydawnictwo Naukowe, 1991).

[44] Simón Bolívar, *Escritos politicos*, ed. Graciela Soriano (Madrid: Alianza Editorial, 1969), p. 109.

And he had the gumption to claim that 'The creation of a hereditary Senate would in no way violate political equality.'[45]

Restrictions of political rights based on religion were also couched in a universalistic language, but the appeal was not to reason but to common values. From Rousseau and Kant to J. S. Mill, everyone believed that a polity could function only if it is based on common interests, norms or values. In Latin America (indeed, also in the Spanish Constitution of 1812), the cement holding societies together was to be Catholicism: of the 103 Latin American constitutions studied by Loveman,[46] 83 proclaimed Catholicism as the official religion and 55 prohibited worship of other religions. While many arguments for restricting political rights to Catholics were openly directed against the principle of popular sovereignty – it is not for people to change what God willed – quite a few were pragmatic. For example, the Mexican thinker Lucas Alamán maintained in 1853 that 'Catholic religion deserves support by the state, even if we do not consider it as divine, because it constitutes the only common tie that connects all Mexicans, when all others are broken.'[47]

Restrictions on female suffrage present the most difficult issue. While early proponents of female suffrage observed that reason is not distributed along gender lines – after all, some rulers had been queens[48] – the main argument against giving the right to vote to women was that, like children, they were not independent, had no will of their own. Women were already represented by the males in their households and their interests were to be represented through a tutelary, rather than an electoral, connection. Thus the justifying criterion was dependence, not sex. Indeed, when a study in England in the 1880s discovered that almost one half of adult women lived in households in which there was no adult male, this justification collapsed, and only pure prejudice retarded extending suffrage to women.

---

[45] I put it this way because Bolívar's motives were suspect: he was trying to soften up the future senators towards granting him a hereditary presidency.

[46] Brian Loveman, *The Constitution of Tyranny: Regimes of Exception in Spanish America* (Pittsburgh: Pittsburgh University Press, 1993), p. 371.

[47] Cited by Roberto Gargarella, *Los fundamentos legales de la desigualdad: el constitucionalismo en América (1776–1860)* (Madrid: Siglo XXI, 2005), p. 93, who provides other examples.

[48] Sieyès according to Pasquino, *Sieyès*, 71.

Yet why were women not independent in the same way as some men were? If women could not own property, they were legally barred from qualifying for suffrage, so this would violate the democratic ideology. But where they could and did own property in their own name, why would property ownership not be a sufficient indicator? Condorcet, who defended property qualifications, thought it should be: 'The reason for which it is believed that they [women] should be excluded from public function, reasons that albeit are easy to destroy, cannot be a motive for depriving them of a right which would be so simple to exercise [voting], and which men have not because of their sex, but because of their quality of being reasonable and sensible, which they have in common with women.'[49] And Chilean suffragettes claimed that 'Wives and mothers, widows and daughters, we all have time and money to devote to the happiness of Chile.'[50]

Since this is an issue about which it is easy to fall into anachronisms, let me process it through an example. Suppose that it is in the best interest of each and all people to evacuate a coastal town if a hurricane is impending and not to evacuate it if the danger is remote. A correct decision is good for everyone: all men, women and children. The correct decision can be reached only by people who can interpret weather forecasts. This excludes children, so that the decision should be made by parents in the best interest of children. I suspect that – with some quibbles about where to draw the age line – most people today would accept this reasoning: all contemporary democratic constitutions do. But why should only men participate in making this decision? If the reason is that women are barred from taking meteorology courses in school, then we are back to 1791 Poland. But suppose they do take such courses. Now the argument must be that even if they had the same capacity to exercise reason, women would always follow the views of their male protectors, independently of their own opinions. This is then another sociological assumption, in addition to those that tied reason to property, income or education.[51]

---

[49] Condorcet, *Sur les élections et autres textes* (1785), texts selected and reviewed by Olivier de Bernon (Paris: Fayard, 1986), p. 293.

[50] An article in *El Eco*, 3 August 1865, cited in Maza Valenzuela, 'Catolicismo, anticlericalismo y la extensión del sufragio', p. 156.

[51] The assumption that women are not capable of exercising political rights was sometimes so self-evident – Kant refers to it as natural – that the 1776 Constitution of New Jersey, through an error in wording, admitted as voters

Now, Schumpeter argued that if any distinction is accepted, then the principle of making such distinctions must be as well: 'The salient point is that, given appropriate views on those and similar subjects, disqualifications on grounds of economic status, religion and sex will enter into the same class with disqualifications which all of us consider compatible with democracy.'[52] Yet each distinction is based on a specific assumption – for example, that twelve-year-olds are not prepared to vote – tying it to the capacity to exercise reason. Obviously, today we would and do reject most such assumptions, although not those based on age or legally certified sanity. Moreover, as we will see below, some such assumptions were driven by only thinly veiled self-interest. But if these assumptions are accepted, then restrictions of suffrage do not violate the principles of democracy.

To put it abstractly, theories of representation differed in whether they took as the input the actual or ideal preferences, the latter being restricted by some normative requirements, such as that they be other-regarding, consider common good, etc.[53] As Montesquieu would say, 'political liberty does not consist of doing what one wants ... liberty cannot be other but to be able to do what one *ought to* want

---

all inhabitants who held a certain amount of property. Many women did vote until 1807, when male was explicitly added as a qualification. A similar situation ensued in Chile, where the electoral law of 1874 failed to mention sex as a qualification for citizenship. Only when some women took this opportunity to register to vote did the Congress pass in 1884 a law explicitly excluding females. This was clearly an omission: as one Senator admitted, 'it did not occur to anyone to concede such rights' ('a nadie se le ha ocurrido concederle tales derechos'). Again the same occurred in France, where Mme Barbarousse claimed the right to vote, pointing out that *tout français* had this right according to the constitution, and it took a court ruling in 1885 to decide that *français* did not include *française* women.Immanuel Kant, 'The Principles of Political Right' (1793) in *Kant's Principles of Politics*, ed. and trans. William Hastie (Edinburgh: T. & T. Clark, 1891), p. 18. Maza Valenzuela, 'Catolicismo, anticlericalismo y la extensión del sufragio'; Trevor Lloyd, *Suffragettes International* (London: American Heritage Press, 1971), p. 14.

52 Joseph A. Schumpeter, *Capitalism, Socialism, and Democracy* (New York: Harper and Brothers, 1942), p. 244.

53 For a recent discussion of this distinction, see John Ferejohn, 'Must Preferences Be Respected in a Democracy?' in David Coop, Jean Hampton and John E. Roemer, eds., *The Idea of Democracy* (Cambridge: Cambridge University Press, 1995), pp. 231–44, as well as Cass Sunstein, 'Democracy and Shifting Preferences' in the same volume, pp. 196–230.

and not to be obliged to do what one *ought not to* want'.[54] Obviously, this distinction disappears if people naturally hold such ideal preferences. If they do not, the burden is placed on institutions, either to promote such preferences by educating citizens – a common theme from Montesquieu to Mill – or to treat such preferences in some privileged manner, by restricting suffrage or weighting votes. As Beitz observes,[55] the latter solution – defended by Mill[56] – is not unfair if those without such ideal preferences or without the conditions to develop such preferences are willing to accept it. Moreover, while inegalitarian, such a system can be justified in universalistic terms if everyone can acquire such preferences or the conditions to acquire them.

Yet whatever one thinks of this logic, the final outcome was that birth was replaced by wealth, aristocracy by oligarchy. Still only a select few were to rule in the best interest of all. The society was to be divided into 'the rich, the few, the rulers and the poor, the many, the ruled': which a Connecticut representative, Samuel Dana, thought was quite proper.[57] The drafter of the French Constitution of 1795, Boissy d'Anglas, declared that 'We must be ruled by the best … a country governed by property-owners is within the social order, that which is dominated by non-property owners is in a state of nature.'[58] The consensus in mid-nineteenth-century Colombia was that 'We want enlightened democracy, a democracy in which intelligence and property direct the destinies of the people; we do not want a barbarian democracy in which proletarianism and ignorance drown the seeds of happiness and bring the society to confusion and disorder.'[59] The right to make laws belongs to the most intelligent, to the aristocracy of knowledge, created by nature, a Peruvian constitutionalist, Bartolomé Herrera, declared in 1846; the Peruvian theorist José María

---

[54] Montesquieu, *De l'esprit des lois*, p. 325; italics supplied.

[55] Beitz, *Political Equality*, p. 35.

[56] John Stuart Mill, *Considerations on Representative Government* (London: Parker, Son and Bourn, 1861).

[57] Cited in Susan Dunn, *Jefferson's Second Revolution: The Election Crisis of 1800 and the Triumph of Republicanism* (Boston: Houghton Mifflin, 2004), p. 23.

[58] Cited in Crook, *Elections in the French Revolution*, p. 46.

[59] Francisco Gutiérrez Sanin, 'La literatura plebeya y el debate alrededor de la propriedad (Nueva Granada, 1849-1854)' in Hilda Sabato, ed., *Ciudadanía política y formación de las naciones: perspectivas históricas de América Latina* (Mexico City: El Colegio de Mexico, 2003), pp. 181–201, p. 185.

Pando maintained that a 'perpetual aristocracy ... is an imperative necessity'; the Chilean Andrés Bello wanted rulers to constitute a body of wise men (*un cuerpo de sabios*); while the Spanish conservative thinker Donoso Cortés juxtaposed the sovereignty of the wise to sovereignty of the people.[60] Still by 1867, Walter Bagehot would warn that

> It must be remembered that a political combination of the lower classes, as such and for their own objects, is an evil of the first magnitude; that a permanent combination of them would make them (now that many of them have the suffrage) supreme in the country; and that their supremacy, in the state they now are, means the supremacy of ignorance over instruction and of numbers over knowledge.[61]

It was perhaps not a full circle but a circle it was. And it left a legacy that gave rise to conflicts that in many countries lasted over a hundred years. These new distinctions were soon perceived as evidence that democracy did not fulfil its own ideals. Neither the poor nor women thought that their best interests were being represented by propertied men. They would struggle for suffrage, and suffrage was a dangerous weapon.

IV   Democracy and property

In a society that is unequal, political equality, if it is effective, opens the possibility that the majority would by law equalise property or the benefits of its use. This is a central theme in the history of democracy, as alive and controversial today as it was at the inception of representative government. Since, as distinct from liberty or happiness, property, the kind of property that can be used to generate incomes, always was and continues to be held by a minority, the right to protect property would have to hurl itself against the interest of majorities. Hence, a tension between democracy and property was predictable, and it was predicted.

---

[60] Gargarella, *Los fundamentos legales de la desigualdad*, p. 120.
[61] Walter Bagehot, *The English Constitution* (1867) (Ithaca, NY: Cornell University Press, 1963).

To sketch the history of this tension, one must begin with the Levellers, who are identified by Wootton as the first democrats who think in terms, not of participatory self-government within a city-state, but of representative government within a nation-state.[62] While they persistently and vehemently denied it, Levellers were feared by their opponents as wanting to make everyone equal by redistributing land:[63] in Harrington's words, 'By leveling, they who use the word seem to understand: when a people rising invades the lands and estates of the richer sort, and divides them equally among themselves.'[64] Some among them – those calling themselves True Levellers or Diggers – did set a commune on common land.

The demand for economic equality appeared during the French Revolution in Babeuf's *Plebeian Manifesto* of 1795. Until then, while the revolutionary government confiscated the lands of the Church and of the emigrant nobility, those were not redistributed to peasants but sold to rich commoners.[65] Babeuf did not want to equalise property, but to abolish it: 'We do not propose to divide up property, since no equal division would ever last. We propose to abolish private property altogether.' Claiming that stomachs are equal, Babeuf wanted every man to place his product in a common pool and receive from it an equal share. Hence, no one could take advantage of greater wealth or ability. He motivated his communist programme by a moral principle, *le bonheur commun*, which must lead to the *communauté*, comfort for all, education for all, equality, liberty and happiness for all.[66]

The demand for economic equality by the Babeuvists was derived from moral principles. Babeuf claimed that both legal and economic equality were only the natural outcome of the Enlightenment and both within the spirit of the French Revolution. Why should the fact

[62] David Wootton, 'The Levellers' in John Dunn, ed., *Democracy: The Unfinished Journey, 508 BC to AD 1993* (Oxford: Oxford University Press, 1993), pp. 71–90, p. 71.
[63] Demands for a redistribution of land were made intermittently in Latin America, most notably in Mexico by Hidalgo and Morelos in 1810 and by Artigas in Uruguay (then Banda Oriental) in 1813.
[64] James Harrington, *The Political Works of James Harrington*, ed. J. G. A. Pocock (Cambridge: Cambridge University Press, 1977), p. 460.
[65] Fontana, 'Democracy and the French Revolution', p. 122.
[66] All citations are from Palmer, *The Age of the Democratic Revolution*, II, pp. 240–1.

or the postulate that all men are born equal justify political but not economic equality? Why should reasons be treated as equal but stomachs not? If logic does not dictate this distinction, one can suspect that only interests do. Even if the ultimate value is to be free from domination by another, 'the right to *Natural Freedom*, without being subjected to the Will or Authority of any other Man', does not economic compulsion to sell one's services to another bind as much as the political subjugation to the command of another? Rousseau, at least, thought that 'no Citizen should be so opulent as to be able to buy another, and none so poor as to be constrained to sell himself'.[67]

But one can also think not on moral but on purely logical grounds that democracy, via legal equality, must lead to economic equality. Indeed, at some moment, legal and economic equality became connected by a *syllogism*: universal suffrage, combined with majority rule, grants political power to the majority. And since the majority is always poor,[68] it will confiscate the riches. The syllogism was perhaps first enunciated by Henry Ireton in the franchise debate at Putney in 1647: 'It [universal male suffrage] may come to destroy property thus. You may have such men chosen, or at least the major part of them, as have no local or permanent interest. Why may not these men vote against all property?'[69] It was echoed by a French conservative polemicist, J. Mallet du Pan, who insisted in 1796 that legal equality must lead to equality of wealth: 'Do you wish a republic of equals amid the inequalities which the public services, inheritances, marriage, industry and commerce have introduced into society? You will have to overthrow property.'[70]

[67] Rousseau, *Du contrat social*, p. 154.
[68] It is standard to emphasise the ambiguity of the concept of *demos* in democracy. As Hanson observes, we commonly translate *demokratia* as 'rule by the people', without making distinctions among 'the people', whereas *demos* originally referred also and quite specifically to 'common people' with little or no economic independence. Yet if common people constitute a numerical majority of the people and if decisions are made by majority rule, this distinction loses its edge. Russell L. Hanson, 'Democracy' in Terence Ball, James Farr and Russell L. Hanson, eds., *Political Innovation and Conceptual Change* (Cambridge: Cambridge University Press, 1989), pp. 68–89, p. 71.
[69] Cited by Andrew Sharp, *The English Levellers* (Cambridge: Cambridge University Press, 1998), pp. 113–14.
[70] Cited by Palmer, *The Age of the Democratic Revolution*, II, p. 230. Hamilton formulated something like this syllogism in his Plan for the National Government (cited in Ketcham, ed., *The Anti-Federalist Papers*, p. 75),

Note that, contrary to frequent misquoting, of which I am guilty as well, Madison (*Federalist* 10) thought that this consequence applied to direct but not to representative democracies.[71] Having identified a 'pure Democracy' as a system of direct rule, Madison continues that '*such* Democracies have ever been spectacles of turbulence and contention; have ever been found incompatible with personal security or the rights of property; and have in general been as short in their lives as they have been violent in their deaths' (italics supplied). Yet 'A Republic, by which I mean a Government in which the scheme of representation takes place, opens a different prospect and promises the cure for which we are seeking.' Still, he seems to have been less sanguine some decades later: 'the danger to the holders of property can not be disguised, if they are undefended against a majority without property. Bodies of men are not less swayed by interest than individuals … Hence, the liability of the rights of property.'[72]

Once coined, this syllogism has dominated the fears and the hopes attached to democracy ever since. Conservatives agreed with socialists[73] that democracy, specifically universal suffrage, must undermine property. The self-serving nature of the convoluted arguments for restricting suffrage to the propertied became apparent. The Scottish philosopher James Mackintosh predicted in 1818 that if the 'laborious classes' gain franchise, 'a permanent animosity between opinion and property must be the consequence'.[74] David Ricardo was prepared to extend suffrage only 'to that part of them which cannot be supposed

---

delivered at the Convention on June 18: 'In every community where industry is encouraged, there will be a division of it into the few and the many. Hence separate interests will arise. There will be debtors and creditors, etc. Give all power to the many, they will oppress the few.' Yet he thought, like Madison, that this effect can be prevented.

[71] The misquoting consists of skipping the 'such' in the citation below. See, for example, Russell L. Hanson, *The Democratic Imagination in America* (Princeton: Princeton University Press, 1985), p. 57, or Adam Przeworski and Fernando Limongi, 'Political Regimes and Economic Growth', *Journal of Economic Perspectives* 7 (1993), pp. 51–69.

[72] Note written at some time between 1821 and 1829, in Ketcham, ed., *The Anti-Federalist Papers*, p. 152.

[73] According to Rosanvallon, *Le modèle*, this particular word appeared in France in 1834.

[74] Cited in Stefan Collini, Donald Winch and John Burrow, *That Noble Science of Politics* (Cambridge: Cambridge University Press, 1983), p. 98.

to have an interest in overturning the right to property'.[75] Thomas Macaulay in the 1842 speech on the Chartists pictured the danger presented by universal suffrage in the following terms:

The essence of the Charter is universal suffrage. If you withhold that, it matters not very much what else you grant. If you grant that, it matters not at all what else you withhold. If you grant that, the country is lost ... My firm conviction is that, in our country, universal suffrage is incompatible, not only with this or that form of government, and with everything for the sake of which government exists; that it is incompatible with property and that it is consequently incompatible with civilization.[76]

Eight years later, from the other extreme of the political spectrum, Karl Marx expressed the same conviction that private property and universal suffrage are incompatible:

The classes whose social slavery the constitution is to perpetuate, proletariat, peasantry, petty bourgeoisie, it puts in possession of political power through universal suffrage. And from the class whose old social power it sanctions, the bourgeoisie, it withdraws the political guarantees of this power. It forces the political rule of the bourgeoisie into democratic conditions, which at every moment jeopardize the very foundations of bourgeois society. From the one group it demands that they should not go forward from political to social emancipation; from the other that they should not go back from social to political restoration.[77]

According to Marx, democracy inevitably 'unchains the class struggle': the poor use democracy to expropriate the rich; the rich are threatened and subvert democracy, by 'abdicating' political power to the permanently organised armed forces. The combination of democracy and capitalism is thus an inherently unstable form of organisation of society, 'only the political form of revolution of bourgeois society and not its conservative form of life',[78] 'only a spasmodic,

---

[75] In *ibid.*, p. 107.
[76] Thomas B. Macaulay, *Complete Writings* (Boston and New York: Houghton Mifflin, 1900), XVII, p. 263.
[77] Karl Marx, *Class Struggles in France, 1848 to 1850* (1851) (Moscow: Progress Publishers, 1952), p. 62.
[78] Karl Marx, *The Eighteenth Brumaire of Louis Bonaparte* (1852) (Moscow: Progress Publishers, 1934), p. 18.

exceptional state of things ... impossible as the normal form of society'.[79]

The 'fundamental contradiction of the Republican constitution' identified by Marx would not materialise either if property ownership would expand spontaneously or if the dispossessed for some reasons abstained from using their political rights to confiscate property.[80] On the other hand, Maier notes,

if the observer feared that social leveling would continue toward proletarianization, then the advance of democracy must appear an alarming trend. For this would suggest ... that all democracy must in effect tend towards social democracy. That is, the advent of popular government and expanded electorate would ineluctably lead to programmes for further social equalization and redistribution of wealth.[81]

Indeed, the idea that democracy in the political realm must logically lead to social and economic equality became the cornerstone of Social Democracy. For Jean Jaurès, 'The triumph of socialism will not be a break with the French Revolution but the fulfillment of the French Revolution in new economic conditions.'[82] Eduard Bernstein saw in socialism 'simply democracy brought to its logical conclusion'.[83] As Beitz observed, historically a main goal of democratic movements has been to seek redress in the political sphere for the effects of inequalities in the economy and society.[84]

Socialists entered into elections with ultimate goals. The Hague Congress of the First International proclaimed, 'the organisation of the proletariat into a political party is necessary to insure the victory of social revolution and its ultimate goal – the abolition of classes'. The first Swedish socialist programme specified that 'Social Democracy

---

[79] Karl Marx, *Writings on the Paris Commune*, ed. H. Draper (New York: International Publishers, 1971), p. 198.

[80] James Mill, for example, challenged the opponents 'to produce an instance, so much as one instance, from the first page of history to the last, of the people of any country showing hostility to the general laws of property, or manifesting a desire for its subversion' (cited in Collini *et al.*, *That Noble Science*, p. 104).

[81] Charles Maier, *Recasting Bourgeois Europe* (Princeton: Princeton University Press, 1975), p. 127.

[82] Jean Jaurès, *L'esprit de socialisme* (Paris: Denoel, 1971), p. 71.

[83] Eduard Bernstein, *Evolutionary Socialism* (New York: Schocken, 1961).

[84] Beitz, *Political Equality*, p. xvi.

differs from other parties in that it aspires to completely transform the economic organisation of the bourgeois society and bring about the social liberation of the working class.'[85] Even the most reformist among socialists, Alexandre Millerand, admonished that 'whoever does not admit the necessary and progressive replacement of capitalist property by social property is not a socialist'.[86] Yet on the road to these ultimate goals, socialists saw numerous measures that would reduce social and economic inequalities. The Parti Socialiste Français, led by Jean Jaurès, proclaimed at its Tours Congress of 1902, 'The Socialist Party, rejecting the policy of all or nothing, has a program of reforms whose realization it pursues forthwith', and listed fifty-four specific measures.[87] Swedish Social Democrats in 1897 demanded direct taxation, development of state and municipal productive activities, public credit, and legislation concerning work conditions and old age, sickness and accident insurance, as well as purely political rights.[88]

The question that haunted social democrats was whether, as Hjalmar Branting posed it in 1886, 'the upper class [would] respect popular will *even if it demanded the abolition of its privileges*'.[89] Were there limits to popular sovereignty, as exercised by electoral majorities? Would revolution not be necessary, as August Bebel feared in 1905, 'as a purely defensive measure, designed to safeguard the exercise of power legitimately acquired through the ballot'?[90]

Yet there is a prior question they did not consider. Can any political arrangement generate economic equality? Can equality be established by laws, even if the upper class would concede the abolition of its privileges? Or is some extent of economic inequality inevitable even if *everyone* would want to abolish it? Did egalitarian democrats fail or did they accomplish all that was within the reach?

[85] Herbert Tingsten, *The Swedish Social Democrats* (Totowa, NJ: Bedminster Press, 1973), pp. 118–19.
[86] Cited in R. C. K. Ensor, *Modern Socialism as Set Forth by the Socialists in Their Speeches, Writings, and Programmes* (New York: Charles Scribner's Sons, 1908), p. 51.
[87] *Ibid.*, pp. 345ff.   [88] Tingsten, *The Swedish Social Democrats*, pp. 119–20.
[89] Cited in *ibid.*, p. 361.
[90] Cited in Carl E. Schorske, *German Social Democracy 1905–1917: The Development of the Great Schism* (New York: Harper and Row, 1955), p. 43.

V By what should we be surprised?

According to Dunn, democracy surprisingly turned from a revolutionary project into a conservative one:

Where the political force of the idea of democracy came from in this new epoch was its combination of formal social equality with a practical order founded on the protection and reproduction of an increasingly dynamic system of economic inequality ... No one at all in 1750 either did or could have seen democracy as a natural name or an apt institutional form for the effective protection of productive wealth. But today we know better. In the teeth of ex ante perceived probability, that is exactly what representative democracy has in the long run proved.[91]

Should we share his surprise?

My argument has been that the sin was original. While, as Dunn emphasises, in the second part of the eighteenth century democracy was a revolutionary idea, the revolution it offered was strictly political.[92] Morally based arguments for redistribution or abolishment of property were marginal and ephemeral. In my reading, in its inception democracy was a project simply blind to economic inequality, regardless of how revolutionary it may have been politically. Moreover, by restricting suffrage, democracies replaced aristocracy by oligarchy.

Hence, I do not think that the surprise can be dated to 1750. In turn, viewed from the perspective of 1850, the coexistence of democracy with unequal distribution of property is hard to fathom. The syllogism according to which the poor would use their majority status to expropriate the rich was after all almost universally accepted. And it still makes logical sense today. Just consider the favourite toy of political economists, the median voter model:[93] each individual is characterised by an endowment of labour or capital and all individuals can be ranked from the poorest to the richest. Individuals vote on the rate of tax to be imposed on incomes generated by supplying these endowments to production. The revenues generated by this tax are either equally distributed to all individuals or spent to provide

---

[91] Dunn, 'Democracy before the Age of the Democratic Revolution', p. 22.
[92] Dunn, *Democracy: A History*.
[93] Allan G. Meltzer and Scott F. Richards, 'A Rational Theory of the Size of Government', *Journal of Political Economy*, 89 (1981), pp. 914–27.

equally valued public goods, so that the tax rate uniquely determines the extent of redistribution. Once the tax rate is decided, individuals maximise utility by deciding in a decentralised way how much of their endowments to supply. The median voter theorem asserts that there exists unique majority-rule equilibrium, that this equilibrium is the choice of the voter with the median preference, and that the voter with the median preference is the one with median income. And when the distribution of incomes is right-skewed, that is, if the median income is lower than the mean, as it is in all countries for which data exist, majority rule equilibrium is associated with a high degree of equality of post-fisc (tax and transfer) incomes, tempered only by the deadweight losses of redistribution.

Moreover, the demand for social and economic equality persists. While elites see democracy in institutional terms, mass publics, at least in Eastern Europe and Latin America, conceive of it in terms of 'social and economic equality'. In Chile, 59 per cent of respondents expected that democracy would attenuate social inequalities,[94] while in Eastern Europe the proportion associating democracy with social equality ranged from 61 per cent in Czechoslovakia to 88 per cent in Bulgaria.[95] People do expect that democracy should breed social and economic equality. Hence, the coexistence of democracy and inequality continues to be tense.

Yet income distributions appear to be amazingly stable over time. The strongest evidence, albeit for a relatively short period, comes from Li, Squire and Zou, who report that about 90 per cent of total variance in the Gini coefficients is explained by the variation across countries, while few countries show any time trends.[96] Longer time-series show that while income distribution became somewhat more equal in some democratic countries, redistribution was quite limited. These assertions are not contradictory: the main reason for equalisation was that wars and major economic crises destroyed

[94] Antonio Alaminos, 'Chile: transición politica y sociedad' (Madrid: Centro de Investigaciones Sociologicas, 1991).

[95] László Bruszt and János Simon, 'Political Culture, Political and Economical Orientations in Central and Eastern Europe during the Transition to Democracy', manuscript copy (Budapest: Erasmus Foundation for Democracy, 1991).

[96] Hongyi Li, Lyn Squire and Heng-fu Zou, 'Explaining International and Intertemporal Variations in Income Inequality', *Economic Journal*, 108 (1997), pp. 1–18.

large fortunes and they could not be accumulated again because of progressive income tax. Earned incomes show almost no variation during the twentieth century.[97] It appears that there are no countries that equalised market incomes without some kind of cataclysm. The cataclysms come in two kinds: (1) destruction of large property as a result of foreign occupation (Japanese in Korea, Soviet in Eastern Europe), revolution (Soviet Union) or war, or (2) massive emigration of the poor (Norway, Sweden).

Since the issue is burning, explanations abound. Most assert that for a variety of reasons those without property, even if they constitute a vast majority in all known societies, either do not want to or cannot use their political rights to equalise property, incomes, or even opportunities. For reasons of space, I can only list the explanations of why the poor would not want to redistribute: (1) false consciousness due to a lack of understanding of the distinction between productive and non-productive property; (2) ideological domination due to the ownership of the media by the propertied; (3) difficulty of the poor to coordinate when they have some non-economic heterogeneous tastes, such as religion or race; (4) expectations that the poor would become rich; (5) the fact that taxes are palpable, while public spending is amorphous. I am not taken by the idea that in general the poor would not want to lead better lives at the expense of the rich, but several arguments to the effect that political rights are ineffective against private property make eminent sense. Wealth holders enjoy disproportionate political influence, which they use to defend themselves successfully from redistribution.[98] Nominally equal political rights do not seem to be enough to bar the privileged access of the rich to politics. Put differently, being oblivious to economic

[97] For long-term dynamics of income distribution, see T. B. Atkinson and Thomas Piketty, *Top Incomes over the Twentieth Century: A Contrast between European and English-Speaking Countries* (New York: Oxford University Press, 2007).

[98] For a model in which the influence of the rich increases with income inequality, see Roland Bénabou, 'Unequal Societies: Income Distribution and the Social Contract', *American Economic Review*, 90 (2000), pp. 96–129. For mechanisms through which the rich buy political influence, see Gene M. Grossman and Elhanan Helpman, *Special Interest Politics* (Cambridge, MA: MIT Press, 2001); Michael J. Graetz and Ian Shapiro, *Death by a Thousand Cuts: The Fight over Taxing Inherited Wealth* (Princeton: Princeton University Press, 2005), tell one story in tantalising detail.

differences is not sufficient to protect politics from the influence of money.

Yet this entire way of thinking confronts an awkward fact that many governments were elected with the support of the poor, wanted to equalise incomes, and tried to do so. Hence, to the extent to which they failed, it must have been for reasons other than not wanting or not trying. Here are some possible reasons.

(1) Redistributing productive property or even incomes is costly to the poor. Confronting the perspective of losing their property or not being able to enjoy its fruits, property owners save and invest less, thus reducing future wealth and future income of everyone. As Machiavelli observed, 'everybody is eager to acquire such things and to obtain property, provided that he be convinced that he will enjoy it when it has been acquired'.[99] Prospects of redistribution reduce investment. This structural dependence on capital imposes a limit on redistribution even on those governments that want to equalise incomes.[100] Hence, while some democratic governments do correct distributions of income generated by the unequal ownership of assets, equalising assets ends up being a cataclysmic event, occurring only under exceptional circumstances.

(2) What are the assets that can be equalised in modern societies? Note that when the idea of equal property first appeared productive assets meant land. Land is relatively easy to redistribute. It is enough to take it from some and give it to others. Hence, agrarian reforms were frequent in the history of the world: there were at least 175 land reforms entailing redistribution between 1946 and 2000 alone. But today the distribution of land plays a relatively minor role in generating income inequality. In turn, other assets resist such a simple operation. Communists redistributed industrial capital by putting it into the hands of the state and announcing that the uninvested profits would be equally distributed to households. This solution engendered several

---

[99] Machiavelli, *Discourses on Livy*, II.2 cited after Steven Holmes, 'Lineages of the Rule of Law' in José María Maravall and Adam Przeworski, eds., *Democracy and the Rule of Law* (New York: Cambridge University Press, 2003), pp. 19–61.

[100] Adam Przeworski and Michael Wallerstein, 'Structural Dependence of the State on Capital', *American Political Science Review*, 82 (1988), 11–29.

negative consequences that need not be discussed. Alternatively, one could redistribute titles to property in the form of shares. But this form of redistribution has problems of its own.[101] Finally, one could, and many countries did, equalise human capital by investing in education. But people exposed to the same educational system acquire very different income earning capacities as a function of their social and economic background. Moreover, since people are born with different talents and since the use of these talents is socially beneficial, we would want to educate talented people more. In sum, redistributing productive assets seems to be difficult for purely technological, not just political or economic, reasons.

(3) Asking 'How laws establish equality in a democracy' – the title of Chapter 5 of Book 5 – Montesquieu takes as the point of departure equality of land. Then he goes on,

If, when the legislator makes such a division, he does not give laws to maintain it, he only makes a passing constitution; inequality will enter from the side the laws do not defend, and the republic will be lost. Therefore, although real equality would be the soul of the state, it is so difficult to establish that an extreme rigor in this respect is not always convenient. It is sufficient [he continues], to reduce differences to some point, after which, it is for particular laws to equalize, to put it this way, the inequalities, by the charges they impose on the rich and the relief they accord to the poor.[102]

Remember that Babeuf believed that redistribution of property would not solve the problem of inequality, 'since no equal division would ever last'. Suppose productive assets had been equalised. But individuals have different and unobservable abilities to transform productive assets into incomes. Moreover, they are subject to vicissitudes of luck. Assume that particular individuals (or projects they undertake) are subject to slightly different rates of return: some lose at the rate of -0.02 and some gain at the rate of 0.02. After twenty-five years,

---

[101] One is that, as the Czech experience shows, they could be and probably would be quickly reconcentrated. People who hold better shares would purchase from those with worse ones. Another problem is that dispersion of ownership lowers the incentives of shareholders to monitor the managers. While some solutions to this problem have been proposed, they do not seem to be very effective.

[102] Montesquieu, *De l'esprit des lois*, pp. 151–5.

the individual who generates a 2 per cent return will be 2.7 times wealthier than the individual who loses 2 per cent per year, and after fifty years (say from the age of eighteen to sixty-eight) this multiple will be 7.4. Hence, even if productive assets were to be equalised, inequality would creep back in.[103]

VI   Judging democracy

Analysing the Thatcher era, Dunn observes

the state at this point is more plausibly seen as a structure through which the minimally participant citizen body (those prepared to take the trouble to vote) select from the meagre options presented to them those they hope will best serve their several interests. In that selection, the meagreness of the range of options is always important and sometimes absolutely decisive.[104]

The issue is to what extent these choices are tightly circumscribed because the logic of electoral competition pushes political parties to offer and pursue similar policies and to what extent there is just little else they could do. The question is important because it affects our political judgement of democracy.[105] Suppose that economic inequality could be diminished below the levels prevailing in developed democracies without reducing future incomes and that it is not being diminished only because of the institutional features of democracy, however one thinks about them. Obviously, judging this trade-off would depend on other values we would have to give up by opting for equality. But there is no such trade-off.

Some degree of economic inequality is just inevitable. Democracy is impotent against it, but so is every other conceivable political

---

[103] The classical statement of this argument is by Vilfredo Pareto, *Cours d'économie politique* (Lausanne: F. Rouge, 1897), II, investigated recently by Dilip Mookherjee and Debraj Ray, 'Persistent Inequality', *Review of Economic Studies*, 70 (2003), pp. 369–93, as well as Jess Benhabib and Alberto Bisin, 'The Distribution of Wealth: Intergenerational Transmission and Redistributive Policies', working paper, Department of Economics, New York University.

[104] John Dunn, *The Cunning of Unreason: Making Sense of Politics* (London: HarperCollins, 2000), p. 147.

[105] On political judgement, see *ibid.* and the Introduction to this volume.

arrangement. Think of Brazil: during the past two centuries it was
a royal colony, an independent monarchy, an oligarchical republic, a
populist military dictatorship, democracy with a weak presidency, a
right-wing military dictatorship, and democracy with a strong presidency. Yet, to the best of our knowledge, income distribution did not
budge. Even the communists, who were out to *uravnit* everything,
and who did equalise assets in the form of public ownership, had to
tolerate the inequality arising from different talents and motivations.
Indeed, it turns out that the average household/individual income
inequality is almost exactly the same in democracies and in non-democracies at each level of per capita income.[106]

The quest for equality in the economic and social realm has been
perpetual in democracies. The original blinkers that modern representative institutions placed on economic and social standing of citizens could not effectively cover the glaring inequality of their life
conditions. At least since Babeuf, not to speak of Marx, limiting
equality to the political realm always seemed 'illogical'. Moreover, if
the right always feared that effective political equality would threaten
property, the left knew that equality limited to the political realm
cannot be sustained in the face of economic and social inequalities.
'Extending democracy from the political to the social realm' was a
call not just for social justice but for making democracy effective in
the political realm itself. But this quest may have its limits and the
knowledge of these limits is essential to judge democracy.

This is not to say that all democracies are the same. I am not arguing in support of Pareto's 'law', according to which income distribution remains the same whatever the institutional framework and in
spite of progressive taxation. Among contemporary democracies, the
ratio incomes of the top to the bottom quintile, which is perhaps the
most intuitive measure of inequality, range from about 33 in Brazil
to less than 6 in Finland, Belgium, Spain and South Korea. Hence,
we can compare and judge the choices parties offer to voters, as well
as policies of particular governments. Moreover, since conflicts over
distribution of opportunities, employment and consumption are the
bread and butter of democratic politics, we must be vigilant. But

---

[106] This is true at least in the data set collected by Klaus Deininger and Lyn Squire,
'A New Data Set Measuring Income Inequality', *World Bank Economic
Review*, 10 (1996), pp. 565–91, which covers the post-1960 period.

even the best governments operate under limits not of their making. The ratio of 6 is still very large: it means that in a country with per capita income of $15,000 (about average for these countries in 2002, counted in 1995 PPP dollars), a member of the top quintile would have an income of $27,000, while a member of the bottom quintile $4,500. Most survey respondents in Spain and South Korea see such inequality as excessive. Yet perhaps this is just the extent to which any political system can equalise assets or incomes.

My point, thus, is that perhaps Dunn, and all of us, put too much burden on democracy.

11 | *Democracy and terrorism*

RICHARD TUCK

John Dunn's principal account of political judgement, *The Cunning of Unreason*, ends with an eloquent plea that we should feel more sympathy than modern intellectuals have been wont to do with the great structures within which we now lead our lives – that is, with a form of capitalism in our economic life, and with its associate, what Dunn calls the 'modern democratic republic', in our political life. These are the creations of political judgement, in his sense of the term: that is, they have come into being not through any systematic or 'scientific' theory of human goals, but through a much more complex and endlessly contestable process in which political agents are more important than political theorists, and in which the choices made in constrained and often tragic circumstances by real people in the end create the conditions in which we can live reasonably well and reasonably safely. As Dunn said in the last paragraph of the book,

We shall just have to see if this state form can muster the practical wisdom to rescue the world as a viable habitat for such vast numbers of humans in the centuries to come. We shall just have to see if it can continue to protect itself, co-operatively where possible but also in the end coercively when necessary, against the enemies which History will continue to send it. We owe it no veneration and we cannot reasonably expect to enjoy its ministrations over time. But we do owe it loyalty, and perhaps also some of our limited stock of patience. Human beings have done many more fetching and elegant things than invent and routinize the modern democratic republic. But, in face of their endlessly importunate, ludicrously indiscreet, inherently chaotic and always potentially murderous onrush of needs and longings, they have, even now, done very few things as solidly to their advantage.[1]

[1] John Dunn, *The Cunning of Unreason: Making Sense of Politics* (London: HarperCollins, 2000), p. 363.

It is this success that is (in Dunn's eyes) the great vindication of political judgement, and the great reproof to the fantasists – including on his account many sober political scientists who in fact live in a kind of romance of scientific realism – who throughout modern history have sought to push our politics into some kind of utopian form.

The modern democratic republic, he has argued in many places, acquired its first clear-headed defenders under the pressure of the French Revolution. In his fullest discussion of this process, in *Setting the People Free*, he characterised modern democracy by reviving a distinction employed by the French Revolutionary democrat and conspirator Filippo Michele Buonarotti, between the 'order of equality' and the 'order of egoism'.[2] The 'order of equality' was what Buonarotti, Babeuf and the other conspirators of 1796–7 wanted when they demanded the overthrow of the constitutional and representative structure of the Directory – that is, a fully participatory democracy in which all citizens meet on terms of economic and social equality and collectively decide the moral and political shape of their lives. Benjamin Constant would later call this the regime of 'ancient liberty'. The 'order of egoism', on the other hand, was essentially Constant's 'modern liberty', in which the business of a competitive commercial society filled up most of the space in a citizen's life, leaving participation in occasional elections and intermittent incursions into the activity of his representatives as the only genuinely political actions open to him. For Dunn, the order of egoism is – by and large – coextensive with the modern world, and more than any other writer today he has proclaimed the power and centrality of this fact, and the absurdity of pretending that it is not really so, and that modern governments can somehow borrow the lustre of the ancient or Revolutionary politics which it has been their prime task to suppress.

But the shape of our politics may not be entirely in our own hands. At the heart of the 'order of egoism' is representation and delegation, and nowhere is that more important than in military matters. The modern state, as Dunn stresses in *The Cunning of Unreason*, is in part a creation of standing armies, and though the great wars of the twentieth century did recreate the citizen armies of the Revolution,

---

[2] John Dunn, *Setting the People Free: The Story of Democracy* (London: Atlantic Books, 2005), pp. 124 ff.

the settled conditions of modern democratic capitalism require a sharp distinction between the soldier and the civilian: we buy the services of our soldiers just as (Constant believed) we buy the services of our politicians, in the sense that they both perform vital political tasks on our behalf and are ultimately accountable to us, but both allow us to devote much of our lives to other activities, notably economic self-advancement. But what happens if our enemies refuse to accept this distinction and insist on treating us all as soldiers? Once, this might have been an empty question; but the citizens of modern Western democracies have been forced to think about the actual character of their democracies, and how far they are fully distinguishable from the democracies or republics of the past, by an unexpected agent – an agent, moreover, which bids fair to form the actual politics of the world in the twenty-first century, as well as its self-understanding.

On 6 October 2002 a letter appeared under the name of Osama bin Laden and addressed to the people of the United States. It attempted to justify the terrorist attacks of September 11, 2001 (and other attacks purportedly carried out by groups to whom bin Laden was at least sympathetic, even if he was not their actual organiser), and it contained a variety of arguments, many of them quite sophisticated and clearly composed by someone who was reasonably well educated in standard Western political thought. Whether this in itself excludes bin Laden as the author, I do not know, and I do not think it matters very much; the arguments represent the most extended attempt to fashion from within the discourse of modern democratic thought a justification for acts which seemed to many people at the time to be as far outside the terms of such a discourse as it is possible to be, and in the process they put in an especially acute form the question of how far the judgement about modern politics which Dunn praises is in fact sustainable. The passage in which this question is raised is as follows, in which 'bin Laden' defends the use of terrorist attacks on innocent civilians, such as the occupants of the World Trade Center on that morning in 2001. Having argued that resistance against US policies, notably in Palestine, is justified, 'bin Laden' continued:

You may then dispute that all of the above does not justify aggression against civilians, for crimes they did not commit and offenses in which they did not partake.

This argument contradicts your continuous repetition that America is the land of freedom, and freedom's leaders in this world. If this is so, the American people are the ones who choose their government by way of their own free will; a choice which stems from their agreement to its policies. Thus the American people have chosen, consented to, and affirmed their support for Israel's oppression of the Palestinians ... The American people are the ones who pay the taxes which fund the planes that bomb us in Afghanistan ... the American army is part of the American people ... God, the Almighty, legislated the permission and the option to avenge this oppression. Thus, if we are attacked, then we have the right to strike back. If people destroy our villages and towns, then we have the right to do the same in return. If people steal our wealth, then we have the right to destroy their economy. And whoever kills our civilians, then we have the right to kill theirs.[3]

In a sense, 'bin Laden's' thought is the most obvious one to have about democratic politics: if we are all responsible for our state's actions, do we not share complicity in what its opponents might think of as the state's guilt? If the designated armed forces of the state can legitimately be attacked, why cannot the other members of the state? Medieval kings, it is sometimes alleged, would nominate champions who would fight on their behalf, with the duel between the two warriors determining the outcome of the war (though I am not sure that any such thing ever actually occurred outside the pages of courtly romance). Is the role of the armed forces in a democracy like this, with the democratic sovereign handing over both risk and responsibility to its champions? And if this were the case, would it be a morally justifiable stance for the sovereign to take up? After all, according to both Rousseau and Kant, the special character of democratic war-making is precisely that the citizens see that their decisions implicate all of them personally in the war, and do not behave like *ancien régime* monarchs casually sending their armies into battle for personal aggrandisement. But under the 'order of egoism', citizens might well suppose that they have handed responsibility for making war to a separate military organisation, just as they have handed responsibility for their politics to a separate set of political institutions, and that it is somehow unfair or immoral for them then to be held personally responsible for the activities of their armed forces or their government. 'Bin Laden's'

[3] *Messages to the World: The Statements of Osama bin Laden*, ed. Bruce Laurence, trans. James Howarth (London: Verso, 2005), pp. 164–5.

words, and terrorist attacks on civilians, come like a challenge from an earlier and less sophisticated – or adulterated – view of what democracy is; indeed, it may be the case that only someone who has spent his life in Saudi Arabia, Yemen and Afghanistan is nowadays in a position fully to appreciate the historical and conceptual peculiarities of democratic politics. But the actual responses of Western democracies to this challenge have revealed in a stark form some of the problems and inconsistencies in the conventional modern view; for the 'order of egoism' has never wholly driven out the older view that all citizens are indeed fully involved in the actions of their states.

Broadly speaking, the claims in 'bin Laden's' letter fall into three groups. The least interesting from our point of view is the most extensive group, devoted to the simple insistence that Islam is true and that all the world must convert; more important are the other two, one of which marshals relatively familiar arguments in defence of violence on behalf of national self-determination, and the other defends the use of violence in such a cause against the civilian citizens of the enemy. Before going on to consider these latter arguments, with which I am of course chiefly concerned, I want to consider the general question of armed struggles for national independence, since some of the principal questions about the distinction between civilian and military personnel have arisen in this context. In warfare between ordinary states it is in principle possible to distinguish between military and civilian personnel, though as we shall see the distinction even there quickly breaks down; but in armed struggles for national independence there can rarely be an easy distinction between a civilian and a military force, since by definition the rebels do not constitute an organised state with the standard accoutrement of an army. A widespread recognition that struggles of this kind are often legitimate has led most theorists to accept that at least some kinds of military action by civilians must be regarded as defensible.

It is true that in the international debates of the late nineteenth century, the formative period of the modern jurisprudence of war, both Germany and the United States argued that armed resistance by civilian populations to an invader could not be regarded as legitimate. The regulations issued to the Union armies in 1863 (the so-called 'Lieber Code') said:

Men or squads of men who commit hostilities … without commission, without being part or portion of the organized hostile army, and without sharing continuously in the war, but who do so with intermitting returns to their homes and avocation, or with the occasional assumption of the semblance of peaceful pursuits, divesting themselves of the character or appearance of soldiers – such men or squads of men are not public enemies, and therefore, if captured, are not entitled to the privilege of prisoners of war, but shall be treated summarily as highway robbers or pirates.[4]

Similarly, the Prussian forces in the Franco-Prussian War notoriously refused to recognise the *franc-tireurs* as legitimate soldiers. But this position was never unquestioned. As many contemporaries understood, the interests of the smaller states of Europe lay in asserting the right of popular and unorganised resistance to invasion, and their views (interestingly) were on the whole backed by the British against the other great powers. The Hague Convention of 1899 allowed as a compromise 'the population of a territory not under occupation ... spontaneously [to] take up arms to resist the invading troops without having had time to organise themselves', though in the Convention of 1907 (in the Regulations which still essentially govern the conduct of war) on the prompting of the German delegate it was added that they must 'carry arms openly'.[5] The British delegate at the conference of 1899 had tried to get a more extensive right of popular resistance written into the Regulations, but had failed.[6] The British had of course relied on guerilla fighters in the Peninsular War, and they were in general keen to keep the laws of war as permissive as possible, while the Germans continually sought to narrow the domain of legitimate warfare.

The experiences of the Second World War, when the German troops in occupied France took what in their eyes were traditional measures against the Resistance, changed for ever the moral attitudes

---

[4] Francis Lieber, *Instructions for the Government of Armies of the United States, in the Field: Revised by a Board of Officers* (New York: Van Nostrand, 1863), Regulation 82, pp. 21–2.

[5] A. Pearce Higgins, ed., *The Hague Peace Conferences* (Cambridge: Cambridge University Press, 1909), pp. 221, 261.

[6] *The Proceedings of the Hague Peace Conferences: Translation of the Official Texts. The Conference of 1899*, ed. James Brown Scott (New York: Oxford University Press, 1920), p. 550. For the opposition of the German delegate, see p. 552. The outcome was the well-known (among international lawyers) 'Martens compromise', which avoided committing the Conference to a final decision on the matter.

of modern populations; the formal jurisprudence of war tried to catch up at the Geneva Conference on Humanitarian Law in 1977, when paragraph 3 of Article 44 accepted that a guerilla fighter in occupied territories and 'in wars of national liberation' should be treated as a combatant if he 'carries his arms openly during each military engagement and during such time as he is visible to the adversary while he is engaged in a military deployment'. On this occasion, it was the Federal Republic of Germany which engineered this formula, as a compromise between many post-colonial nations who wanted their struggles to be recognised as legitimate wars, and the great powers who as always wanted to minimise the role of civilians in war. Germany was clearly motivated in large part by its sense that German policy in the Second World War had destroyed the old confidence in the distinction between combatant and non-combatant.[7] The requirement that the civilian carries his arms openly was intended to preserve something of the old notion that combatants should be clearly distinguishable from a civilian population, but it has of course proved virtually impossible in practice to distinguish clearly between cases where guerillas conceal their arms, cases where they reveal them a moment before an engagement begins, and cases where they carry them openly for some time before encountering an enemy. The fact that the 1977 Article specifically mentions 'wars of national liberation' also corresponds to the intuitions many modern liberals have (unlike, of course, most of the delegates to the nineteenth-century conferences) that warfare is legitimate if it is intended to defeat an imperial power which will not allow its subjects democratic rights, including the right to declare independence, even if the imperial power has been in place for many generations and has governed in a reasonably liberal fashion (French Indo-China, for example, and conceivably nineteenth- and early twentieth-century Ireland). It should be said that although the Geneva protocols of 1977 represented the views of the principal jurists of war, and may also represent a reasonable version of modern liberal opinion, they did not become part of the general jurisprudence of nations, as the USA refused to ratify them. Much of the juridical tangle in which the US government has found itself with

---

[7] See D. Fleck, ed., *The Handbook of Humanitarian Law in Armed Conflicts* (Oxford: Oxford University Press, 1995), p. 77.

regard to the prisoners at Guantánamo Bay is the direct result of this refusal to follow the rest of the world in 1977.

A special case within the category of national liberation is where the warfare is between two groups both of which think of themselves as living in the same territory and as being historically closely connected to one another. Here we may often have much less confidence about the legitimacy of violence. The ANC, for example, did not attack an imperial power, based in another territory, but another group with what one might term settlement claims on the same land, and though most Western liberals probably supported the ANC's activities, many had reservations. It is worth observing that settler rebellions and settler struggles are peculiarly resistant to theoretical analysis and – no doubt as a result – practical mediation; many settler populations have felt for generations that they were never going to be safe from attacks from the 'native' population, and that in the end only a clear domination of the indigenous groups would protect them. The North of Ireland is the most familiar case to us, but the *pieds noirs* of Algeria, the National Party in South Africa in 1948, and – I would say – the English colonists in the Thirteen Colonies in 1776, are equally striking examples, and (like Ulster in 1912) share the frequent characteristic of these situations that the settlers feel they have either to capture or, if that fails, to repudiate their own metropolitan government before they can be really secure in their territory. Palestine is obviously a contemporary example of this process. It is very hard indeed to have a clear-cut theory about these cases; but it is ridiculous to say that groups which think of themselves as having a long history of mutual conflict and betrayal should simply by an effort of will begin to trust one another and behave as if they were the fellow-citizens of a reasonably peaceful democracy. We need grounds to trust one another, and long historical experience of betrayal is – however unfortunately – grounds for mistrust. The very process of peace-making, particularly where outsiders are involved, with all its necessary secretiveness and bargaining, can itself reawaken old fears of duplicity, as it may have done in both Ireland and Palestine. There is also something about settlement as such that raises intransigent moral issues: on the one hand, the settled territory has often been acquired in illegitimate or morally dubious ways, but on the other hand the settlers put an enormous amount of work and creativity into fashioning their land, and come to believe (and not simply from reading Locke) that their labour clearly entitles them to the ownership of the territory.

In practice in these situations, many modern liberals get by with a vague reliance on the United Nations – if the UN determines that a particular struggle is legitimate, then that will distinguish between the various intractable cases. To some extent, that is reasonable, but it would be hard to put very great weight on it as a major moral principle. The UN is (reasonably enough) swayed by all sorts of considerations, and it may well not seem to the people concerned with a particular struggle that it adequately dealt with their case; moreover – and this is the most troubling aspect of the UN's deliberations – it almost inevitably comes to discuss an independence struggle only when violence has already been committed. A peaceful and responsible movement will get less international attention than a violent one. It is possible to imagine a world where this is not the case, but it is not the world we currently inhabit, and as long as it is not, it will be hard to say with confidence that armed struggles of this kind are clearly legitimate or illegitimate.

The idea that a civilian population may legitimately take up arms in the cause of some political goal has thus met with a considerable degree of assent, even in the official jurisprudence of war, and to that extent 'bin Laden's' claim that violence is justified in the interests of the Palestinians cannot be regarded as ridiculous, though it may of course not be *true*; just as it cannot be ridiculous to say that the Israelis are entitled to use violence to protect their settlements, though that also may not be true. The startling claim in 'bin Laden's' letter is not that violence may be exercised *by* civilians, but that it may be exercised *on* civilians, in the form of terrorism. Most modern Western liberals express sympathy with almost any struggle for self-determination, while very clearly ruling out terrorist attacks on civilians as morally unacceptable. If this renders the struggle ineffective, as in many cases it will (for modern armed forces are hard things for guerilla fighters to defeat), then – I take the reasonable liberal response to be – so much the worse for the struggle.

However, the question of the status of civilian non-combatants in a legitimate war is, historically, much more contentious than many modern commentators imagine.[8] It was assumed by most ancient

---

[8] The only modern discussion of this history is by Karma Nabulsi in her *Traditions of War: Occupation, Resistance, and the Law* (Oxford: Oxford University

writers on war (even including Augustine) that an entire population might be at risk in a legitimate war, and what are by modern standards astonishing atrocities were regularly visited upon civilian populations by the armies of states such as Athens and Rome. (It is, incidentally, worth considering in this context that in some ways Islam is a more straightforward inheritor of some of the beliefs and practices of the Roman world than is the modern West, despite the West's self-image.) It seems to have been a distinctively medieval Christian idea that a distinction might be drawn between combatants and non-combatants: Gratian incorporated into his *Decretum* a canon of Pope Nicholas II (1059) expressly exempting pilgrims, clerics, monks, women and 'the unarmed poor' (*inermes pauperes*) from the list of legitimate targets of violence in a just war,[9] and throughout the Middle Ages it was canonists and not civil lawyers who emphasised the distinction. Scholastic theologians, as one might have expected, endorsed the canonists' view; thus the most influential scholastic writer on the law of war, the sixteenth-century Spanish theologian Francisco de Vitoria, argued that

Even in wars against the Turks we may not kill children, who are obviously innocent, nor women, who are to be presumed innocent at least as far as the war is concerned (unless, that is, it can be proved of a particular woman that she was implicated in guilt). In wars against fellow-Christians, the same holds true of harmless farming folk, and other peaceful civilians (*gens togata*), who are all to be presumed innocent unless there is evidence to the contrary; and also travellers and visitors.[10]

This idea went along with a general unhappiness among the theologians about many features of ancient warfare, including such things as pre-emptive or preventative strikes against an enemy.

Press, 1999). As will be clear later, I have a different view of the relationship between the 'Grotian' and 'Republican' traditions which she describes, though I share her view of writers such as Rousseau.

[9] *Decretum,* II causa xxiv qu. iii c. xxv, *Corpus iuris canonici*, 2nd edn (Graz: Akademische Druck- u. Verlagsanstalt, 1959), I, p. 997. The Lateran Council of 1179 under Alexander III added 'mercatores, rustici, euntes et redeuntes, et in agricultura existentes, et animalia, quibus arant et quae semina portant ad agrum' to the list (*Decretales*, I tit. xxxiv *De treuga et pace*, c. ii, *Corpus iuris canonici*, II, p. 203).

[10] Francisco de Vitoria, *Political Writings*, ed. Anthony Pagden and Jeremy Lawrance (Cambridge: Cambridge University Press, 1991), p. 315.

But (as I argued in *The Rights of War and Peace*)[11] humanist writers from the fifteenth century onwards were prepared to reinstate Roman ideas about warfare, including not just a defence of pre-emption, but also a sense that wars were conducted between entire communities, in which the distinction of combatant and non-combatant did not make much sense. The best example of this is the *De jure belli* of Alberico Gentili, Professor of Civil Law at Oxford in the late sixteenth century and an influential theorist about the Elizabethan wars with Spain. Gentili famously believed that the mere power of a rival state gave sufficient reason to attack it:

it is better to provide that men should not acquire too great power, than to be obliged to seek a remedy later, when they have already become too powerful … Is not this even to-day our problem, that one man may not have supreme power and that all Europe may not submit to the domination of a single man? Unless there is something which can resist Spain, Europe will surely fall.[12]

But he also argued that all the residents of a state were vulnerable to attack.

Those who become members of some corporate body surely wish to be considered a part of that body. So it is, too, in war, since war is not one of the things to which the state is unaccustomed. In a matter of universal right it will not be possible to say that one had in mind one point and not another. Is it not their duty to defend the state (*civitas*)? Therefore they are obliged to endure the opposition of others who attack the state.[13]

He concluded from this that the traditional exemption from hostilities granted for example to merchants was unfounded, and though he was to some extent willing to consider an exemption for husbandmen (on the grounds that food had to be grown), he was also willing to sanction the destruction of crops as part of a military campaign. Even

[11] Richard Tuck, *The Rights of War and Peace: Political Thought and the International Order from Grotius to Kant* (Oxford: Oxford University Press, 1999).
[12] *De iure belli libri tres*, trans. John C. Rolfe (Oxford: Oxford University Press, 1933), II, p. 65.
[13] *Ibid.*, p. 264.

more strikingly, and completely unlike both earlier and most later writers, he defended the destruction of cultural monuments such as temples and art galleries, at least if one's own had been attacked.[14] He was also prepared to take a wide view of what constituted military activity on the part of one's opponents, defending (for example) the forcible English seizure of neutral shipping in the war with Spain on the grounds that '*Et in exercitu hostium est, qui exercitui hostium necessaria ad bellum administrat*'[15] – which in a modern context (and perhaps also in a Renaissance one) makes every productive member of a state in effect a member of its army, as the belligerents in the Second World War came to believe. The only clear exemptions Gentili granted were to children, and to women who had not disgraced their sex by taking part in military activities.[16] The key thought is contained in his remark, 'Those who become members of some corporate body surely wish to be considered a part of that body': given that humanist writers in general assumed that states are bodies of citizens, even if they are governed by princes, they were naturally led to suppose that all the members of the state were to be treated potentially as combatants. Though 'bin Laden's' jibe is directed at modern democracies, it is equally applicable to Renaissance 'republics', and indeed to the republican governments advocated by Rousseau or Kant.

Even Hugo Grotius, although he was praised in the late nineteenth century as the founder of the modern jurisprudence of war (and his portrait put at the entrance to the Peace Palace constructed in the Hague following the 1907 conference), was closer in many respects to the humanists than to the scholastics, and the *De iure belli ac pacis* of 1625 contained a notable (though qualified) defence of warfare against civilian populations. Grotius distinguished between what armies were *entitled* to do, as a matter of *rights*, and what 'humanity' might require of us. As far as strict right went,

that Licence which a just War gives to an Enemy to hurt another … is of large Extent, for it reaches not only those who are actually in Arms, and the Subjects of the Prince engaged in War, but also all those who reside within his Territories; as may appear from that form in *Livy, Let him, and all that live within his Country, be our Enemies*. And no wonder, since we

---

[14] *Ibid.*, pp. 270–7 (II chapter 23).
[15] *Ibid.*, p. 267 (original text Vol. I, p. 438).   [16] *Ibid.*, p. 253.

may apprehend Damage from them, which in a general and uninterrupted War is enough to justify the Right here spoken of. (III.4.5 – 6)

Such as are really Subjects of the Enemy, that is, from a permanent Cause, if we respect only their Persons, may in all Places be assaulted; because when War is proclaimed against a Nation, it is at the same Time proclaimed against all of that Nation ... They may then lawfully be killed in their own Country, in the Enemies Country, in a Country that belongs to no Body, or on the Sea. (III.4.8)

How far this Licence extends itself, will hence appear, that the Slaughter of Infants and Women is allowed, and included by the Right of War ... Neither were Prisoners exempted from this Licence. (III.4.9–10)

To kill an Enemy any where is allowed, both by the Law of Nature and of Nations ... neither is it of any Concern, how many or how few they be who kill or are killed. (III.4.18.2)

Not only they who surrender themselves, or submit by Promise to Slavery, are reputed Slaves; but all Persons whatsoever taken in a solemn War, as soon as they shall be brought into a Place whereof the enemy is Master ... Neither is there any previous Crime required, for here every one's Condition is alike, even of those who have unhappily been found among the Enemies, upon the sudden breaking out of the War. (III.7.1)

Given that Grotius was committed to the idea that all the members of a state formed (as he put it) the 'common subject' of sovereignty, with the rulers being the 'proper' subject (just as, he said, the body is the 'common' subject of sight, and the eye is the 'proper') (I.3.7), it is not surprising that he should suppose that any legitimate war might be directed indiscriminately at all the inhabitants – this is precisely the thought from which, as I have said, any 'republican' or modern democrat might start.[17]

It should be said that after putting forward these extremely far-reaching claims, Grotius promptly retracted them, at least in part. 'I must now reflect, and take away from those that make War almost all the Rights, which I may seem to have granted them', he wrote at the beginning of III.10. Humanity and (in one sense) Justice requires us to 'abstain from such Things' as we may claim a strict right to; as

[17] All quotations from the 1738 translation of Jean Barbeyrac's edition of the *De iure belli ac pacis*, reprinted as *The Rights of War and Peace*, ed. Richard Tuck (Indianapolis: Liberty Press, 2005).

Seneca said, '*How small a Matter is it, to be a good Man, only so far as the Laws require? How much larger is the Rule of Duty than of Right?*' If we think about the claims of humanity, he argued, women, children and 'men, whose Manner of Life is wholly averse to Arms' should be spared, including monks, husbandmen and merchants, while prisoners should not be enslaved. The distinction between Right and Humanity was broadly the distinction between perfect and imperfect obligation, or what Kant would later term the 'Doctrine of Right' and the 'Doctrine of Virtue' – that is, only if one's rights are violated can one claim to be *wronged* or *injured*, and only in these circumstances can the wronged party claim the right to use violence upon the injurer. Imperfect obligations are genuine obligations, and we are under a duty to follow them; but no action can be taken against people or states who fail to do so. They cannot, for example, be punished by third parties for failing in duties of humanity, though they may (said Grotius) legitimately be punished for failing to respect another's rights. (See notably II.21.16.)

Grotius' discussion of the rights of war was thus highly ambiguous, as he himself admitted, and it could easily be argued by his successors (notably of course both Selden and Hobbes) that only the strict rights of war were of full moral significance, both because only they led to a proper jurisprudence of war, and because the claims of humanity were contentious and varied over time and place. On the other hand, it should be remembered that Hobbes always argued that 'cruelty' – violence which the perpetrator did not believe to have a pragmatic point to it – was in all circumstances against the law of nature, and to that extent he introduced into the domain of rights a consideration of what would later be regarded as (part of) the principle of proportionality. Samuel Pufendorf too acknowledged that natural justice might allow the killing of women and husbandmen, though he also urged that humanity would forbid the exercise of such a right.[18] Grotius' discussion indeed left the status of the principles of humanity very unclear, since he occasionally wrote as if they were principles which arose from the mutual arrangements of civilised nations; thus the pure rights of war survived 'if we should have to do with a State

---

[18] *Elementorum jurisprudentiae universalis libri duo* (Oxford: Oxford University Press, 1931), II, p. 256; *De jure naturae et gentium*, trans. as *The Law of Nature and Nations* (London, 1749), VIII.6.7.

so barbarous, as to think it lawful without any manner of Reason, or Denunciation of War, to treat in a hostile Manner the Persons and Goods of all Strangers' (III.9.19). They would thus have been closer to Kant's principles of 'international right', rather than to Kant's 'cosmopolitan right', which (as I argued in *The Rights of War and Peace*) was in fact extremely minimal in character.

In both Grotius and Hobbes (as Rousseau later realised) we thus find a clear-eyed acceptance of the possible moral consequences of equal participation by all men in the citizenship of their states, and a willingness to recognise that no easy distinction could be drawn between combatants and non-combatants. Many of their opponents in the eighteenth century scrambled to avoid these consequences, in the process – as Rousseau also realised – backing away from the democratic implications of the theories (and it may even be that one of the fears of the *ancien régime* writers was precisely that democracies would disregard the constraints under which the civilised monarchs of Europe made war). Vattel was the perfect example of this process, and exactly the sort of complacent writer whom Rousseau detested; in his *Le droit des gens* of 1757 (two years after he had published a very critical review of Rousseau's Second Discourse), Vattel observed smugly that:

In former times, when a Nation went to war, and especially when it was attacked, every man able to carry arms became a soldier ... At the present day war is carried on by regular armies; the people, the peasantry, the towns-folk, take no part in it, and as a rule have nothing to fear from the sword of the enemy. Provided the inhabitants submit to him who is master of the country, and pay the contributions demanded, and refrain from acts of hostility, they live in safety as if they were on friendly terms with the enemy ... Such treatment is highly commendable and well worthy of Nations which boast of civilisation.[19]

Even the Seven Years War (in which Vattel acted as an adviser to Frederick) was not really fought in this way; but of course the French Revolutionary wars, like the Second World War, utterly destroyed these confident illusions, and reduced Vattel in retrospect to merely

[19] *Le droit des gens; ou, principes de la loi naturelle appliqués à la conduite et aux affaires des nations et des souverains*, ed. Albert de Lapradelle (Washington, DC: Carnegie Institution, 1916), III, p. 283 (III.147).

the 'sorry comforter' of Kant's famous stricture. Like Rousseau, Kant had no illusions about the character of modern war, nor about the intractable moral problems posed by the responsibility of all citizens for the doings of their state, and nowhere did he distinguish between combatant and non-combatant along the traditional lines.

Although nineteenth-century diplomats worked hard to reinstate something like the Vattelian view after the trauma of the Revolutionary Wars, the reality of modern war (particularly, as we have seen, the American Civil War and the Franco-Prussian War) continually pushed them back towards the position taken up by Gentili, Grotius or even Hobbes. While representation and a professional army might seem to be the appropriate institutions for the post-Revolutionary states, both an armed citizenry and citizen populations as the target of military activity constantly re-emerged in the actual political struggles of the nineteenth century, and even more so in those of the twentieth century. In 1940, the demoralisation of the German civilian population presented itself as a necessary objective for the British; as Churchill said in a memorandum that year, if Hitler were 'to be repulsed here or not try invasion, he will recoil eastward, and we have nothing to stop him. But there is one thing that will bring him back and bring him down, and that is an absolutely devastating, exterminating attack by very heavy bombers from this country upon the Nazi homeland.'[20] By the end of the twentieth century the conjunction of democracy and total war which Hobbes and Rousseau had foreseen was everywhere apparent, and with the entry of women into full citizenship the longest-lasting and most powerful exemption for civilians from armed attack vanished. So when 'bin Laden' points this out, there is little point in our merely reiterating, as if it was a clear moral truth, that civilians can never be the objects of violence even in a legitimate war.

How instead should we now think about this question? The most important point to make is that the limits on military action which were suggested by those early thinkers whom I have treated as republicans or democrats, notably Hobbes and Rousseau and (in this context) Grotius, still seem to be the plausible ones. Hobbes put it neatly when he condemned *cruelty* or *revenge* which does not seek some

[20] Quoted in Martin Gilbert, *Second World War* (London: Fontana/Collins, 1990), p. 108.

future good.[21] It is reasonable to say that we should use the minimum violence necessary to achieve our ends, and that this is true whether we are attacking another army or a city with many civilian inhabitants. It will often be the case in modern warfare that attacking civilians is unnecessary, since they are by definition not armed and therefore pose no immediate threat; but it will also quite often be the case that it will be necessary to attack the factories and railways which supply the enemy armies, and even the homes of the workers in those factories. No particular category of people seems now to be automatically immune from attack, but the level of slaughter of all citizens, armed and unarmed, should be carefully restricted. The United States and Britain have given mixed messages about this in recent years; sophisticated targeting of missiles has replaced the fearsome aerial bombardments of the Second World War or Vietnam, but the retreating Iraqi army in the first Gulf War seems to have been slaughtered with almost Roman savagery, as if governments take very seriously their responsibilities towards enemy civilians, but feel they have no responsibilities towards enemy combatants. It is of course true that they did not believe that Iraq and Afghanistan were democracies, and therefore presumably did not take their civilians to be complicit in the acts of their government; but, by the same token, forcibly drafted soldiers (as they were in Iraq) are not complicit either. Strictly speaking, in a dictatorship most soldiers and most civilians can be thought of as prisoners to be freed with minimal collateral damage (if it is indeed the case that there genuinely are dictatorships of the kind which some American politicians imagine, in which a single person somehow rules an entire people by fear). Unfortunately, the requirement of minimal force, when applied to civilians fighting against modern states, does not necessarily rule out terrorist attacks, since they may achieve their object with much less slaughter than would be necessary to defeat a modern army. Rousseau, again, observed something important when he remarked that one might defeat a state without killing many of its inhabitants if one sufficiently demoralised its citizens.

What is it then to make war on a sovereign? It is to attack public convention and everything that results from it, for the essence of the state consists

---

[21] See e.g. *De cive*, III.11.

only in that. If the social pact could be broken apart in one blow, at that instant there would no longer be war; and by this one blow the state would be killed without a single man having died.[22]

It is sometimes very reasonably said that terrorism of the kind defended by 'bin Laden' differs from the killing of civilians in conventional war (even, perhaps, in the Second World War) in that civilian deaths in conventional wars are an unintended and undesirable side effect of attacks on military targets, whereas in modern terrorism civilian deaths are the intentional outcome of the attack, and that this constitutes a profound moral difference between the two activities. There is some truth in this, but we should make a distinction between situations where civilians are killed by combatants who could, if they chose to do so, attack military targets instead, and situations where military targets are impossible to attack. Much of the terrorism practised by the Nazis in the Second World War fell into the former category, with no obvious military point to it (and indeed it often actually undermined the Nazis' military objectives), and it would therefore be clearly condemnable on the principle of minimal harm to others. But this is not obviously true of much of the terrorism which is experienced by modern democratic societies, for only another highly developed state now has the ability to attack these societies' military forces, and a non-state group which believes that it has the right to attack one of these societies might therefore believe that it has the right to attack the society's civilian population without abandoning the principle of minimal harm. I should emphasise again that this presupposes that the cause for which the group is fighting is itself justifiable, and that the group is justified in taking it up; these questions seem to me to be the central ones in thinking about terrorism, as they should be in thinking about violence of all kinds. We often forget that the second of these questions is as important as the first, though it was a standard element in the traditional jurisprudence of war: thus even if one were to believe (for example) that Palestinian self-determination justified violence, one might also believe that only a group properly commissioned in some

[22] From his fragment 'L' état de guerre', Appendix A in Grace Roosevelt, *Reading Rousseau in the Nuclear Age* (Philadelphia: Temple University Press, 1990). This passage is on p. 197.

way by a Palestinian authority was entitled to use violence, and not a self-appointed set of fanatics.

So it may not be as easy as Dunn thinks to follow our own political judgement and reject older ideas of democracy: we may all be held responsible by our enemies for the actions of our governments to a degree which goes far beyond the intermittent checking up on governmental activity which is appropriate to the order of egoism. The citizen armies of the twentieth century will presumably never reappear in their original form, since an unskilled mass labour force is no more wanted in military affairs than in any other contemporary industries. But the appearance of terrorism aimed indiscriminately at the citizens of Western democracies has in a sense recreated them, in that it has made all citizens combatants of a kind, and has reminded us that the order of egoism may only be achievable in a relatively benign international setting. It may also have changed our understanding of one of the most famous political science shibboleths of the moment, the idea of the so-called 'democratic peace'. Some political scientists believe that the only true proposition which has ever been discovered in their subject is that democracies do not make war on one another; this is usually explained nowadays as being something to do either with shared values, or with a justifiable fear of the lengths to which democracies will go once they have committed themselves to a fight.[23] The originators of the idea, Rousseau and Kant, believed (as I said earlier) that citizens of democracies will go to war very cautiously because they know that their own lives are at stake, and that democracies would evince this caution even when considering war against non-democratic states. Modern political scientists have observed that this does not in fact seem to be the case, since democracies are not at all unwilling to fight against non-democracies; but of course, late twentieth-century democracies by and large came to acquire extremely socially segregated professional armies, which they did indeed employ as if they were the medieval champions I mentioned earlier, and the citizens of modern democracies during the past sixty years did not until now actually face personal danger in their wars. The reasoning of Rousseau or Kant has not been put to the test

[23] E.g. Bruce Bueno de Mesquita, James Morrow, Randolph Siverson and Alastair Smith, 'An Institutional Explanation of the Democratic Peace', *American Political Science Review*, 93:4 (1999), pp. 791–807.

except in the great wars of the Revolution and the twentieth century. But the changed character of modern war, in which it is potentially once again something whose effects we may all feel, has reopened the question of whether after all Rousseau and Kant may have been right, and the modern interpretation of 'democratic peace' too limited; under the conditions of current international affairs it may indeed be the case – for good or ill – that citizens of democracies will pull their governments back from war out of fear of the war being brought to them.

Bibliography of the works of John Dunn

I Books

The Political Thought of John Locke (Cambridge: Cambridge University Press, 1969. Italian translation (Bologna: Il Mulino, 1992); French translation (Paris: Presses Universitaires de France, 1991).

Modern Revolutions: An Introduction to the Analysis of a Political Phenomenon (Cambridge: Cambridge University Press, 1972). 2nd edn (with new Introduction), 1989. German translation (Stuttgart: Verlag Reclam, 1974); Japanese translation (Tokyo: Chuo University Press, 1978).

(with A. F. Robertson) *Dependence and Opportunity: Political Change in Ahafo* (Cambridge: Cambridge University Press, 1973).

(editor and contributor) *West African States: Failure and Promise. A Study in Comparative Politics* (Cambridge: Cambridge University Press, 1978), pp. 1–21, 211–16.

Western Political Theory in the Face of the Future (Cambridge: Cambridge University Press, 1979). First Spanish translation (Mexico City: Fondo de Cultura Economica, 1981); Japanese translation (Tokyo: Misuzu Shobo, 1983); Italian translation (Milan: Feltrinelli, 1983). 2nd edn, with new Conclusion (Cambridge: Cambridge University Press, 1993). Chinese translation, arranged with Jilan People's Publishing House (Beijing, 2005); Spanish translation: *Agonia del Pensamiento Politico Occidental* (Cambridge: Cambridge University Press, 1996).

Political Obligation in Its Historical Context: Essays in Political Theory (Cambridge: Cambridge University Press, 1980).

Locke (Oxford: Oxford University Press, 1984). Reissued with new material as *Locke: A Very Short Introduction* (Oxford: Oxford University Press, 2003). Japanese translation (Tokyo: Iwanami Shoten, 1987); Chinese translation (Taiwan: Linking Publishing Company, 1991); Hungarian translation (Budapest: Atlantis, 1992); Indonesian translation (Jakarta: PT Pustaka Utamo Grafiti, 1994); translation arranged into Korean (Seoul: Sigongsa, 2000); Greek translation (Patras: Patras University Press, 2002); Portuguese translation (Sao Paolo: Edições Loyola, 2003). *Locke: A Very Short Introduction*, translation arranged into Albanian (Tirana: Ideart, 2006); translation arranged into Turkish (Ankara: Dost, 2006); translation arranged into Greek (Athens: Ellinika Grammata/To Vima, 2008); translation arranged into Romanian (Bucharest: Editura, 2008).

The Politics of Socialism: An Essay in Political Theory (Cambridge: Cambridge University Press, 1984).

Rethinking Modern Political Theory: Essays, 1979–83 (Cambridge: Cambridge University Press, 1985).

(editor and contributor) *The Economic Limits to Modern Politics* (Cambridge: Cambridge University Press, 1990), pp. 1–40, 195–219. Korean translation (Seoul: Young Joe Park, 1992).

(editor and contributor, with Donal Cruise O'Brien and Richard Rathbone) *Contemporary West African States* (Cambridge: Cambridge University Press, 1989), pp. 181–92.

Interpreting Political Responsibility: Essays 1981–1989 (Cambridge: Polity Press and Princeton: Princeton University Press, 1990). Chapter 5, 'La libertad como valor politico sustantivo', printed in Spanish translation in Luis Castro Leiva, ed., *El liberalismo como problema* (Caracas: Monte Avila Editores, 1992), pp. 41–67.

Storia delle dottrine politiche (Milan: Jaca Book, 1992). French translation (Paris: Editions Mentha, 1992). Repr. in *Politica, Enciclopedia d'Orientamento* (Milan: Jaca Book, 1994). Hungarian translation in Ferenc Horcher, ed., *The Cambridge View of Early Modern Political Thought* (Budapest: Tanulmany Kiado, 1996), pp. 263–85.

(editor and contributor) *Democracy: The Unfinished Journey, 508 BC to AD 1993* (Oxford: Oxford University Press, 1993), pp. v–vii, 239–66. Spanish translation (Barcelona: Tusquets Editores, 1995). Conclusion repr. in French translation as 'Démocratie: état des lieux', *La Pensée Politique*, 1 (1993), pp. 76–97. Italian translation (Venice: Marsilio Editori, 1995); Greek translation (Athens: Institut du Livre, 1997); Hungarian translation (Budapest: Akademiai Kiado, 1995); Chinese translation (Beijing: Jilan's People's Publishing House, 2001).

(editor and contributor) *Contemporary Crisis of the Nation State?* Special issue of *Political Studies* 1994. Published as paperback book (Oxford: Blackwell, 1995).

The History of Political Theory and Other Essays (Cambridge: Cambridge University Press, 1996).

(ed. with Ian Harris) *Great Political Thinkers* (Cheltenham: Edward Elgar, 1997), 21 vols.

The Cunning of Unreason: Making Sense of Politics (London: HarperCollins and New York: Basic Books, 2000).

Pensare la Politica (Rome: Di Renzo Editore, 2002).

Setting the People Free: The Story of Democracy (London: Atlantic Books, 2005). Italian translation, *Il mito degli uguali: la lunga storia della democrazia* (Milan: Egea, 2006); translations arranged into Chinese (Shanghai: Sinhui Culture and Press Ltd; Taipei: Shanghai and Linking Publishing Company); translation arranged into Arabic (Riyadh: Arabic Obeikan Books); translation arranged into Korean (Seoul: Humanitas Publishing Company).

II Articles and chapters in books

'Consent in the Political Theory of John Locke', *Historical Journal*, 10:2 (1967), pp. 153–82. Repr. in G. Schochet, ed., *Life, Liberty and Property: Essays on Locke's Political Ideas* (Belmont, CA: Wadsworth Publishing Company, 1971); and in Richard Ashcraft, ed., *John Locke: Critical Assessments* (London: Routledge, 1991), III, pp. 524–66.

'Justice and the Interpretation of Locke's Political Theory', *Political Studies*, 16:1 (1968), pp. 68–87. Repr. in Richard Ashcraft, ed., *John Locke: Critical Assessments* (London: Routledge, 1991), III, pp. 43–63; and in Patrick Dunleavy and Paul Kelly, eds., *British Political Science: Fifty Years of Political Studies* (Oxford: Blackwell, 2000), pp. 25–32.

'The Identity of the History of Ideas', *Philosophy*, 43 (April 1968), pp. 85–104. Repr. in P. Laslett, W. Runciman and Q. Skinner, eds., *Philosophy, Politics and Society* fourth series (Oxford: Blackwell, 1972). Italian translation: *Filosofia Politica* (Bologna), 2, 1988); Spanish translation in Ambrosio Velasco Gomez, ed., *Resorgimento de la teoria politica en el siglo xx: filosofia, historia y tradición* (Mexico City: National Autonomous University of Mexico 1999), pp. 195–220.

'The Politics of Locke in England and America in the Eighteenth Century' in J. W. Yolton, ed., *John Locke: Problems and Perspectives* (Cambridge: Cambridge University Press, 1969), pp. 45–80.

'Politics in Asunafo' in Dennis Austin and Robin Luckham, eds., *Politicians and Soldiers in Ghana 1966–1972* (London: Frank Cass, 1975), pp. 164–213.

'The Eligible and the Elect: Arminian Thoughts on the Social Predestination of Ahafo Leaders' in W. H. Morris-Jones, ed., *The Making of Politicians: Studies from Africa and Asia* (London: Athlone Press, 1976), pp. 49–65.

'The Success and Failure of Modern Revolutions' in S. Bialer and S. Sluzar, eds., *Radicalism in the Contemporary Age*, III, Studies of the Research Institute on International Change, Columbia University (Boulder, CO: Westview Press, 1977), pp. 82–114, 305–18.

'Practising History and Social Science on "Realist" Assumptions' in C.
    Hookway and P. Pettit, eds., *Action and Interpretation: Studies in the
    Philosophy of the Social Sciences* (Cambridge: Cambridge University
    Press, 1978), pp. 145–75. German translation (Berlin: W. de Gruyter,
    1982).
'Individuality and Clientage in the Formation of Locke's Social Imagination'
    in Reinhard Brandt, ed., *John Locke: Symposium Wolfenbüttel 1979*
    (Berlin and New York: W. de Gruyter, 1981), pp. 43–73.
'Understanding Revolutions', *Ethics*, 92:2 (January 1982), pp. 299–315.
    Korean translation in Lee Shinhaeng, ed., *A New Trend in Political
    Change* (Seoul: Hyungsung Press, 1992), pp. 71–102.
'Country Risk: Social and Cultural Aspects' in Richard J. Herring, ed.,
    Managing International Risk, Wharton School Centennial Conference
    Papers (Cambridge: Cambridge University Press, 1983), pp. 138–67.
'From Applied Theology to Social Analysis: The Break between John Locke
    and the Scottish Enlightenment' in Istvan Hont and Michael Ignatieff,
    eds., *Wealth and Virtue: The Shaping of Political Economy in the
    Scottish Enlightenment* (Cambridge: Cambridge University Press,
    1983), pp. 119–35. Japanese translation (1990); chapter reprinted in
    Hungarian translation in Ferenc Horcher, ed., *The Cambridge View
    of Early Modern Political Thought* (Budapest: Tanulmany Kiado,
    1996), pp. 193–208.
'Social Theory, Social Understanding and Political Action' in A. C. Lloyd,
    ed., *Social Theory and Political Practice*, Wolfson Lectures 1981
    (Oxford: Oxford University Press, 1983), pp. 109–35.
'The Concept of Trust in the Political Theory of John Locke' in Richard
    Rorty, J. B. Schneewind and Quentin Skinner, eds., *Philosophy
    in History* (Cambridge: Cambridge University Press, 1984), pp.
    279–301.
'The Future of Political Philosophy in the West', *Shiso* (Tokyo) (November
    1984), pp. 24–49 (in Japanese translation).
'Totalitarian Democracy and the Legacy of Modern Revolutions:
    Explanation or Indictment?', in *Totalitarian Democracy and After*,
    Israel Academy of Arts and Sciences (Jerusalem: Magnes Press, 1984),
    pp. 37–55; 2nd edn, ed. Michael Burleigh (London: Frank Cass,
    2001).
'Defining a Defensible Socialism for Britain Today' in Peter Nolan and
    Suzanne Paine, eds., *Rethinking Socialist Economics* (Cambridge:
    Polity Press, 1986), pp. 35–52.
'The Politics of Representation and Good Government in Postcolonial
    Africa' in Patrick Chabal, ed., *The Politics of Domination in Modern*

Africa (Cambridge: Cambridge University Press, 1986), pp. 158–74, 200–5.

'Unger's *Politics* and the Appraisal of Political Possibility', *Northwestern University Law Review*, 81:4 (Summer 1987), pp. 732–50. Repr. in Robin W. Lovin and Michael J. Perry, eds., *Critique and Construction: A Symposium on Roberto Unger's Politics* (Cambridge: Cambridge University Press, 1990), pp. 71–89.

'Revolution' in Terence Ball, James Farr and Russell Hanson, eds., *Political Innovation and Conceptual Change* (Cambridge: Cambridge University Press, 1988), pp. 333–51.

'Rights and Political Conflict' in Larry Gostin, ed., *Civil Liberties in Conflict* (London: Tavistock, 1988), pp. 21–38.

'Trust and Political Agency' in Diego Gambetta, ed., *Trust: Making and Breaking Cooperative Relations* (Oxford: Basil Blackwell, 1988), pp. 73–93. Italian translation (Turin: Einaudi, 1990).

'"Bright enough for all our purposes": John Locke's Conception of a Civilised Society', *Notes and Records of the Royal Society*, 43 (1989), pp. 133–53. Repr. in John R. Milton, ed., *Locke's Moral, Political and Legal Philosophy* (Aldershot: Ashgate Press, 1999), pp. 315–35.

'Responsibility without Power: States and the Incoherence of the Modern Conception of the Political Good' (in Italian), *Teoria Politica* (Turin), 6:1 (1990), pp. 3–25.

'Freedom of Conscience: Freedom of Thought, Freedom of Speech, Freedom of Worship?' in O. P. Grell, Jonathan Israel and Nicholas Tyacke, eds., *From Persecution to Toleration* (Oxford: Clarendon Press, 1991), pp. 171–93. German translation as 'Lockes Konzeption von Toleranz' in Martyn P. Thompson, ed., *Locke und Kant* (Berlin: Duncker and Humblot, 1991), pp. 16–39; Italian translation as 'Le Tre Libertà: il principe della tolleranza come libertà di parolà, di pensiero o di culto', *Prometeo* (December 1991), pp. 6–17; French translation as 'L'exigence de liberté de conscience: liberté de parole, liberté de pensée, liberté de culte', *Philosophie*, 37 (1993), pp. 64–88. Partially repr. in Paul E. Sigmund, ed., *The Selected Political Writings of John Locke: A Norton Critical Edition* (New York: W. W. Norton and Co., 2005), pp. 366–9.

'Political Obligation' in David Held, ed., *Political Theory Today* (Cambridge: Polity Press, 1991), pp. 23–47. Estonian translation forthcoming in Juri Lipping, ed. *Contemporary Political Philosophy* (Tartu: EYS Veljesto Press).

'Property, Justice and Common Good after Socialism' in J. A. Hall and I. C. Jarvie, eds., *The Transition to Modernity: Essays in Honour of Ernest Gellner* (Cambridge: Cambridge University Press, 1992), pp. 281–96.

'Social Contract', *Enciclopedia delle scienze sociali* (Rome: Istituto dell'Enciclopedia Italiana, 1992) (in Italian translation), II, pp. 404–17.

'Specifying and Understanding Racism' (in Italian translation: 'Determinare e capire il razzismo') in Girolamo Imbruglia, ed., *Il razzismo, e le sue storie* (Naples: Edizione Scientifiche Italiane, 1992), pp. 13–28; English edition, 'Paradoxes of racism', *Government and Opposition*, 28:4 (Autumn 1993), pp. 512–25.

'Democracy: The Politics of Making, Defending and Exemplifying Community: Europe 1992' in Takashi Kato, ed., *The Future of Democracy in Asia* (Tokyo: Tokyo University Press, 1993) (in Japanese translation); in Spanish translation in *Revista Internacional de Filosofia Politica*, 1 (April 1993), pp. 21–39.

'Political Science, Political Theory and Policy-Making in an Interdependent World', *Government and Opposition*, 28:2 (Spring 1993), pp. 242–60.

'The Heritage and Future of the European Left', *Economy and Society* (November 1993), pp. 516–24. Swedish translation in *Smedgan*, 4 (October 1993), pp. 18–23. Repr. in R. Vialeed, *What is Left?* (Turin: La Rosa Editrice, 1998), pp. 25–38.

'Conclusion' in Tony Saich and Hans van de Ven, eds., *Essays on the Chinese Communist Revolution* (White Plains, NY: M. E. Sharpe, 1994), pp. 388–99.

'The Dilemma of Humanitarian Intervention: The Executive Power of the Law of Nature after God', *Government and Opposition*, 29:2 (Spring 1994), pp. 248–61. Italian translation, *Ragion Pratica*, 2 (1994), pp. 200–14.

'The Identity of the Bourgeois Liberal Republic' in Biancamaria Fontana, ed., *The Invention of the Modern Republic* (Cambridge: Cambridge University Press, 1994), pp. 206–25.

'The Nation State and Human Community: Obligation, Life Chances and the Boundaries of Society' (Italian translation: Milan: Edizioni Anabasi, 1994).

'How Democracies Succeed' in Sung Chul Yang, ed., *Democracy and Communism: Theory, Reality and the Future* (Seoul: Korean Association of International Studies, 1995), pp. 41–66. Repr. in *Economy and Society*, 25 (1996), pp. 511–28.

'Asian Culture and Democratic Potential: A Western View' in Jong Yil Ra, ed., *Democratization and Regional Cooperation in Asia* (Seoul: Kim Dae-Jung Peace Foundation, 1996), pp. 83–111.

'Hope over Fear: Judith Shklar as Liberal Educator' in Bernard Yack, ed., *Liberalism without Illusions* (Chicago: University of Chicago Press, 1996), pp. 45–54.

'The Construction of the Principle of Toleration and Its Implications for Contemporary States' in Young Seek Choue and Jae Shik Sohn, eds., *Tolerance, Restoration of Morality and Humanity*, Institute of International Peace Studies (Seoul: Kyung Hee University, 1996), pp. 299–324.

'The Contemporary Political Significance of John Locke's Conception of Civil Society', *Iyyun* (*Jerusalem Philosophical Quarterly*), 45 (July 1996), pp. 103–24. Repr. in Sudipta Kaviraj and Sunil Khilnani, eds., *Civil Society: History and Possibilities* (Cambridge: Cambridge University Press, 2001), pp. 39–57.

'The Transcultural Significance of Athenian Democracy' in Michel Sakellariou, ed., *Démocratie athénienne et culture* (Athens: Academy of Athens, 1996), pp. 97–108.

'Does Separatism Threaten the State System?' and 'Conclusion' in Trude Andresen, Beate Bull *et al.*, eds., *Separatism* (Bergen: Ch. Michelson Institute, 1997), pp. 130–45, 167–72.

'Situating Democratic Accountability' in Adam Przeworski, Susan C. Stokes and Bernard Manin, eds., *Democracy, Accountability and Representation* (Cambridge: Cambridge University Press, 1999), pp. 329–44. Italian translation, 'Responsibilità politica e democrazia', *Ragion Pratica*, 7 (1997), pp. 183–93.

'Democracy, Globalization and Human Interests', *Il Politico*, 63:3 (1998), pp. 353–74.

'Democracy and Development' in Ian Shapiro and Casimir Hacker-Cordon, eds., *Democracy's Value* (Cambridge: Cambridge University Press, 1999), pp. 132–40.

'How Politics Limits Markets: Power, Legitimacy, Choice' in Samuel Bowles, Maurizio Franzini and Ugo Pagano, eds., *The Politics and Economics of Power* (London: Routledge, 1999), pp. 85–100.

'Politics and the Well-Being of Future Generations' in Tae-Chang Kim and Ross Harrison, eds., *The Self and Future Generations: An Intercultural Conversation* (Cambridge: White Horse Press, 1999), pp. 70–81.

'The Debate on Big Government: The View from Western Europe' in Arthur A. Melzer, Jerry Weinberger and M. Richard Zinman, eds., *Politics at the Turn of the Century* (Rowman and Littlefield, 2001), pp. 192–208.

'Japan's Road to Political Paralysis: A Democratic Hope Mislaid', Third Maruyama Memorial Lecture, *Center of Japanese Studies, University of California, Berkeley, Occasional Papers*, 2 (2002). Japanese translation, 'Two Lectures by John Dunn', *Shiso*, 938 (June 2002), pp. 4–26.

'Subject to the Sphinx: Capitalist Democracy as Solution and Enigma', *C. J. S., Berkeley, Occasional Papers* 2 (2002). Chinese translation: 'Why Has Democracy Won? Two Lectures by John Dunn', *Societas* (Taipei), 1 (June 2002), pp. 151–75.

'The Emergence into Politics of Global Environmental Change' in Ted Munn, ed., *Encyclopaedia of Global Environmental Change* (London: John Wiley, 2002), V, pp. 124–36.

'Autonomy's Sources and the Impact of Globalisation' in Ludvig Beckman and Emil Uddhammar, eds., *Virtues of Independence and Dependence on Virtue* (Princeton, NJ: Transaction Press, 2003), pp. 47–61.

'Measuring Locke's Shadow' in Ian Shapiro, ed., *Locke's Letter on Toleration and Two Treatises of Government* (New Haven, CT: Yale University Press, 2003), pp. 257–83.

'The Aftermath of Communism and the Vicissitudes of Public Trust' in Ivana Markova, ed., *Trust and Post-Communist Transition*, *Proceedings of the British Academy*, 123 (2004), pp. 195–209.

'What History Can Show: Jeremy Waldron's Reading of Locke's Christian Politics', *Review of Politics*, 67:3 (2005), pp. 433–50.

'Tracing the Cunning of Unreason', Chinese translation, *Reflexion*, 2 (June 2006), pp. 53–71 (Taipei: Linking Books).

'Capitalist Democracy: Elective Affinity or Beguiling Illusion?', *Daedalus*, 136:3 (2007), pp. 5–13.

'Civilizational Conflict and the Political Sources of the New World Disorder', Japanese translation, *Seiji-Kenkyu*, 54 (March 2007), pp. 1–21 (Fukuoka: Kyushu University).

'Understanding Revolution' in John Foran, David Lane and Andreja Zivkovic, eds., *Revolution in the Making of the Modern World: Social Identities, Globalization and Modernity* (London: Routledge, 2007), pp. 17–26.

'Organizing, Focusing and Impeding Power: Gauging the Plasticity and Utility of a Classic Formula' in Sandrine Baume and Biancamaria Fontana, eds., *Les usages de la séparation des pouvoirs* (Paris: Michel Haudiard, 2008).

'UnManifest Destiny', in Ian Shapiro, James Madison, Alexander Hamilton and John Jay, eds. *The Federalist* (New Haven, CT: Yale University Press, 2009), pp. 483–501.

'Beyond Freedom and Equality' in Yersu Kim, ed., *Transformative Challenges: Modern Civilization and Beyond* (Seoul: Kyunhee University, forthcoming).

'The Significance of Hobbes's Conception of Power' in Johan Tralau, ed., *Hobbes and Schmitt: Critical Review of International Social and Political Philosophy* (London: Routledge, forthcoming).

III   Short articles

'Authorship of Gregory's Critique of Hume', *Journal of the History of Ideas*, 25:1 (1964), pp. 128–9.

'The Dream of Revolution' in David Martin, ed., *Anarchy and Culture* (New York: Columbia University Press and Routledge, 1969), pp. 148–54. (Repr. from *The Listener*.)

'Hannah Arendt on Revolution' in E. Homberger *et al.*, eds., *The Cambridge Mind* (London: Jonathan Cape, 1970), pp. 158–62. (Repr. from *The Cambridge Review*.)

'Order and the State', *Survival* (Institute for Strategic Studies), 12:12 (December 1970), pp. 419–22. (Repr. from *The Listener*.)

'But How Will They Eat?', review article on M. Owusu, *Uses and Abuses of Political Power, Transactions of the Historical Society of Ghana*, 13:1 (June 1972), pp. 113–24.

'Democracy Unretrieved: or the Political Theory of Professor Macpherson', *British Journal of Political Science*, 4:4 (October 1974), pp. 489–99.

'Fascists and Marxists', review article on A. James Gregor, *The Fascist Persuasion in Radical Politics, Government and Opposition*, 10:1 (Winter 1975), pp. 117–21.

Review Article on Robert Nozick, *Anarchy, State and Utopia, Ratio*, 19:1 (June 1977), pp. 88–95.

'Revolutions as Class Struggle', review article on E. Trimberger, *Revolution from Above, Government and Opposition*, 14:3 (Summer 1979), pp. 398–403.

'Identity, Modernity and the Claim To Know Better', *Dialectics and Humanism* (Warsaw), 4 (1983), pp. 165–79.

'John Locke: The Politics of Trust' in Brian Redhead, ed., *Political Thought from Plato to Nato* (London: Ariel Books, BBC, 1984), pp. 108–19. German translation (Bonn: Bonn Aktuell, 1987); American edition (Chicago: Dorsey Press, 1988); Portuguese translation (Rio de Janeiro: Imago Editora, 1987); Korean translation (Seoul, 1993).

'Libertà vo' perdendo: i rischi delle democrazie capitalistiche', *Panorama* (Milan), 20 (1984), pp. 180–5.

Review article on John Walton, *Reluctant Rebels: Comparative Studies of Revolution and Underdevelopment, Government and Opposition*, 19:4 (Autumn 1984), pp. 532–5.

'La politica del socialismo', *Transizione* (Bologna), 4 (1985), pp. 75–84.

'Identity, Modernity and the Claim To Know Better II: Postcolonial Tragedy from a Cosmopolitan Point of View', *Comparative Civilizations Review*, 17 (1987), pp. 1–20.

'La comunidad politica moderno como ficción y como destino' in Luis Castro Leiva, ed., *Usos y abusos de la historia en la teoria y en la practica politica* (Caracas: Serie Seminarios – Colección IDEA, 1988), pp. 45–71.

'A Nationalist World after Socialism', *Gaiko Forum* (Tokyo: in Japanese), 23 (August 1990), pp. 41–8.

'Review Article: A New Book by Albert Hirschman', *Government and Opposition*, 26:4 (Autumn 1991), pp. 520–5.

'The Future of Democracy in Asia', *Journal of Asian and Pacific Studies* (Seikei University), 9 (1992), pp. 29–34. Repr. in Subhrata Mukherjee and Sushila Ramaswamy, eds., *Political Science Annual* (New Delhi: Deep and Deep, 1993), pp. 147–53.

Foreword to English translation of Jean-François Bayart, *The State in Africa* (London: Longman, 1993).

'Trust' in Robert Goodin and Philip Pettit, eds., *A Companion to Contemporary Political Philosophy* (Oxford: Basil Blackwell, 1993), pp. 638–44.

'Political and Economic Obstacles to Rapid Collective Change', *Philosophy and the History of Science* (Taipei), 3 (April 1994), pp. 1–10; repr. in *Dialogue and Universalism* (Warsaw), 5 (1995), pp. 11–17.

(with Dr Kim Dae-Jung) 'The Future of the Twenty-First Century Depends on Asian Democracy', *Shindonga*, 414 (March 1994), pp. 42–54 (in Korean).

'The Postcolonial State in West Africa' in John Middleton, ed., *The Encyclopaedia of Subsaharan Africa* (New York: Simon and Schuster, 1998), III, pp. 465–9.

'The Record and Future of the Kim Dae-Jung Government' in *Achievements and Challenges of the Administration of President Kim Dae-Jung* (Seoul: Korean Overseas Culture and Information Service, 1999), pp. 191–4.

Preface to Paul Magnette, *La citoyenneté: une histoire de l'idée de participation civique* (Brussels: Bruylant, 2001), pp. v–vii.

'For *Societas*' (in English and Chinese), *Societas* (Taipei), 1 (June 2002), pp. iii–ix.

'Korea and the Prospects for Building Peace and Prosperity in East Asia in the Wake of the Long Cold War' in Jang Chip Choi, ed., *Post-Cold War and Peace: Experiences, Conditions and Choices* (Seoul: University of

Seoul Asiatic Research Center, 2003), pp. 177–93. Korean translation, *Journal of Asiatic Studies*, 45 (2002), pp. 79–95.

'Democracy as a European Inheritance' in Evangelos Chrysos, Paschalis Kitromilides and Constantine Svolopoulos, eds., *The Idea of European Community in History* (Athens: National and Capodistrian University of Athens, 2003), I, pp. 33–41.

'Revolutionary Movements in Comparative Perspective', *Archives Européennes de Sociologie*, 44:2 (2003), pp. 279–83.

(with Sir Tony Wrigley) 'Peter Ruffell Laslett, 1915–2001', *Proceedings of the British Academy, Biographical Memoirs of Fellows*, 4 (2005), pp. 109–29.

'The Future of Democracy in the Era of Globalization', in Inwon Choue, ed., *Dialogues for the 21st Century* (Seoul: Acanet, 2006), pp. 95–114.

Index